SIX THOUSAND YEARS OF BREAD

ITS HOLY AND UNHOLY HISTORY

Translated by Richard and Clara Winston

Forewords by Peter Reinhart and Lynn Alley

H. E. JACOB

Skyhorse Publishing

Seventieth Anniversary Edition 2014

Foreword copyright © 2007 by Peter Reinhart

First published 1944

All inquiries should be addressed to Skyhorse Publishing, 307 West 36th Street, 11th Floor, New York, NY 10018.

Skyhorse Publishing books may be purchased in bulk at special discounts for sales promotion, corporate gifts, fund-raising, or educational purposes. Special editions can also be created to specifications. For details, contact the Special Sales Department, Skyhorse Publishing, 307 West 36th Street, 11th Floor, New York, NY 10018 or info@skyhorsepublishing.com.

Skyhorse® and Skyhorse Publishing® are registered trademarks of Skyhorse Publishing, Inc.®, a Delaware corporation.

Visit our website at www.skyhorsepublishing.com.

10 9 8 7 6 5 4 3 2

The Library of Congress cataloged the 2007 Skyhorse edition as follows:

Jacob, Heinrich Eduard, 1889-1967
    Six thousand years of bread : its holy and unholy history / by H.E. Jacob ; translated by Richard and Clara Winston.
        p. cm
    Originally published: Garden City, N.Y. ; Doubleday, Doran, and Co., 1944.
    ISBN-13: 978-1-60239-124-6 (alk. paper)
    ISBN-10: 1-60239-124-6 (alk. paper)
  1. Bread--History. 2. Bread--Social aspects. I. Title
    GT2868.J33 2007
    664.752309--dc22
                    2007015911

Cover design by Rain Saukas
Cover photo by grafvision/iStock/Thinkstock

Print ISBN: 978-1-62914-514-3
Ebook ISBN: 978-1-62914-829-8

Printed in China

CONTENTS

CONTENTS

FOREWORD BY PETER REINHART

I have a friend named Herbert Ernest who, as I write this, is a sprightly eighty-seven years old. Herb was a captain in the United States Army during World War II, in charge of the 110th Quartermaster Baking Company, a mobile bakery unit that marched across Italy during the final two years of the war, feeding the troops fresh bread and other baked treats. The 163 enlisted men and five officers moved their forty-eight ovens, along with mixers, pans, and small wares thirteen times. They tore down and reassembled their bakery approximately every two months, during which time the company baked, by Herb's reckoning and book keeping, nearly fifty million pounds of bread, as well as cakes and pastries. They fed not only the troops but also dignitaries such as Italy's Prince Umberto (later, albeit briefly, King Umberto), photographer Margaret Bourke-White, Bob Hope, operatic diva Lily Pons, Marlene Dietrich, USO entertainers, and countless others who remembered Captain Ernest and the hospitality his company provided. Shortly before the war ended, Prince Umberto called him to Rome and honored him with, in Herb's words, " . . . the Cavaliere della Corona d'Italia' ivory cross, encrusted with gold filigree. I was the first American officer to be knighted, but the generals soon followed." A few years after the war Herb saw Marlene Dietrich on Park Avenue in New York City during a taxi strike and offered her a lift. She jumped into his car because, as she said, she immediately recognized him as "the captain with the cake."

The work of Captain Ernest's 96th Quartermaster Baking Company begins, interestingly, at the exact time that Heinrich E. Jacob's *Six Thousand Years of Bread* ends, and it further illustrates the central point of the book: the importance, perhaps even the power, of bread in the unfolding march of civilization.

During the fall of 2004 I presented the keynote address at the first National Bread Symposium. My topic was: Is there a bread culture in America? The quick answer to the question, though much more developed in my keynote, was no. Compared to European and Middle Eastern countries we do not, in America, live in a bread-centric culture, but we may very well be on the verge of creating one. Ironically, though, when I was approached by media reporters in attendance the question on their minds was, "Is bread dead?" The low carbohydrate diet movement had just exploded on the scene and reducing bread consumption was one of its main targets. My response to the reporters, thanks to my recollection of H.E. Jacob's book was, "Bread has been with us for at least six thousand years, and it is not going away."

Within a year, the consumption and sales of bread returned to its former levels and the number of bakery cafes, both independent and franchised chains, increased dramatically. The public has spoken—bread is not going away. How could it, after all? It is inextricably woven into our cultural and personal histories, our orthodox and heterodox belief systems and world views, and into our deepest taste memories. It not only exists as a fundamental foodstuff, but as a vehicle for the transmission of knowledge from generation to generation. Bread does have its own story but it is also the metaphorical medium through which so many other stories are told: stories of escape from bondage; of historical and political battles for egalitarian legitimacy in societies built upon elitist hegemonies; of the intermingling of the supernatural and mystical into the natural world. Bread cannot go away lest the stories themselves go with them.

This brings us to the brilliance of H. E. Jacob, and his uniquely anecdotal approach to the history of bread. While the bakers of Captain Ernest's Quartermaster Baking Company, forty of them captured German soldiers from the North African campaign, were marching toward Germany, Mr. Jacob was escaping from Buchenwald and the Nazi regime. He tells us very little about himself other than in a brief prologue and even briefer postscript, trusting us to read between the lines. Remember that he wrote this book before the war ended, while Hitler yet breathed and still threatened to dominate the world, but his narrative themes reveal an intuitive and studied philosophy that tells us everything we need to know about him. As other writers before me have pointed out, this is not merely a book about bread as bread, the end result of grass seed ground into flour, but about bread as a signifier of transformation, both personally and historically.

The research challenge of such an undertaking, performed during stressful times in his native Germany and well before the limitless access that cyberspace and virtual research depositories afford, automatically begs the question of balance between factual versus interpretative historicity that is embedded within the author's speculations and leaps of imagination. He has surely done impressive homework, as the ample but now dated bibliography reveals, but he has done much more. Mr. Jacob has followed his six thousand year long bread crumb trail and connected their dots to tell us one big story by telling us many smaller stories. Is this method the only way to frame the march of civilization? Of course not, but by choosing the examples that he has in the relentless unfolding of his central image, bread, the author has captured a view of the world in a grain of grass and handed it over to us for pondering.

Without stealing his thunder, for he needs no help from the choir to make his points, let me explain what resonates so deeply for me in the bread-centered, eternally transforming universe that Jacobs so engagingly portrays, for it is in this very notion of transformation that bread's power resides. A seed grows into a grass that yields more seeds, some of which are harvested and destroyed, pulverized into a powder called flour. The once life-giving seeds are combined with water and salt to make clay and the clay is then leavened with yeast. With this act the baker has engaged the Promethean challenge; he (or she) has raised an Adam (which translated means clay) and brought that clay to life. The clay, now called dough, undergoes numerous transformations as its enzymes rearrange the starchy molecules and release hidden sugars; the sugars are then transformed by bacteria and yeast fungi into acids, alcohols, and gasses. The dough grows and develops character; the baker divides and shapes it and exposes it to various temperatures and environments in which it can achieve its optimum potential. But, as dough, it is still unable to fulfill its destiny; for this the yeast and other living organisms must make the ultimate sacrifice, enduring the fiery furnace, passing the thermal death point (the dreaded TDP, as my baking students call it), and in a dramatic, final surge and feeding frenzy, create one last carbonic push while the flour proteins coagulate, the starches gelatinize, and the sugars on the surface caramelize. Multiple and nearly simultaneous transformations take place behind the veil of the oven door until, at the appointed time, the dough emerges as something totally other. It has become a loaf of bread, the iconic staff of life. We then consume it and begin the cycle again.

That is the microcosmic, literal, metaphorical, analogical, and even anagogical story of one loaf of bread. You are now, courtesy of H. E. Jacob, about to embark upon the macrocosmic outplaying of this loaf as it reveals itself over a six thousand year series of cultural transformations, as it is acted upon and in turn, acts upon the actors.

When I met Herbert Ernest in 1995 I was a forty-four-year-old practicing baker and a first time author, and he was a retired elder, a trustee on the board of the most prestigious culinary school in America, and a passionate supporter of the culinary arts as a supreme expression of his truest passion, the art of hospitality (he was, in fact, a graduate in 1941 of the famous Cornell Hotel School). He told me that he had a book I might enjoy and gave me his copy, signed by him and dated March, 28, 1944. Thus, the first English edition of *Six Thousand Years of Bread* passed from Herb's hands into mine. He then told me about his many exploits with the mobile baking unit, and of the times he broke bread with and hosted the greats and the near greats of that era, and how they never forgot him, never forgot his hospitality, and never forgot the smell of 20,000 loaves of bread baking every day under the Italian sun. That bread fed over 300,000 soldiers and villagers through whose sacrifices the civilized world was granted yet another cycle to pursue its hungry search for continued acts of transformation.

—Peter Reinhart, May 2007
Charlotte, North Carolina

FOREWORD TO THE 1997 EDITION

"For a historical account of what bread had meant, in European tradition anyway, we strongly recommend a passionately written and engagingly idiosyncratic book written toward the end of World War II, *Six Thousand Years of Bread*."
　　　　　　　　　　　—Laurel's Kitchen Bread Book

From the first time I read what Laurel Robertson had to say about *Six Thousand Years of Bread: Its Holy and Unholy History*, by Heinrich E. Jacob, I was on the trail. I was researching the bread chapter in my own book, *Lost Arts*, and devouring every morsel of bread history that crossed my path. Although *Six Thousand Years of Bread* had been out of print for years, I finally located a lone copy at the main branch of the San Diego Public Library. The book turned out to be well worth the trouble it took to find. It was delicious. And then, like nearly everyone who reads this enigmatic book, I asked myself, "Who was this guy? Where did he live? And why did he write this book?"

First stop on the trail was Brinna Sands, owner of the King Arthur Flour Company, who seems to have encyclopedic knowledge of nearly everything related to bread. Brinna had never heard of the book, but she was fascinated when I told her about it. We both agreed that what I ought to do would be to find an old Deutsch baker who might have known Jacob or who at least might be familiar with his work. Since neither of us was acquainted with any old Deutsch bakers, I had to settle for a young Deutsch . . . who, as it turned out, was not Deutsch at all, but an Austrian Markus Farbinger. Farbinger was a fourth-generation baker from Austria, who currently teaches at the Culinary Institute of America in Hyde Park. Markus too was unfamiliar with the Jacob book, but was just as much a lover of good bread as Brinna and I. He gave me the address of the Deutsches Brotmuseum in Ulm, Germany, and said that if anyone would know anything about this book and its author, it would be the curator of the museum, whose father had been curator before him. Bingo! The staff at the Deutsches Brotmuseum had copies of the book in both English and German, as well as a number of articles and reviews in German on the book, and gave me the address of the executive director of Jacob's estate, one Hans Gerlach, living in Berlin.

My next step was to contact Gerlach. Fortunately, his number was listed in Berlin information, and with assistance from my friendly MCI German-speaking international operator, I managed to find him. Gerlach, it turns out, owns many of Jacob's original manuscripts. He has even compiled a brief biography entitled *Heinrich Jacob: In Two Worlds*, written in German. Gerlach supplied me with the name and telephone number of a colleague and friend living here in the United States who was an expert on early twentieth-century German writers. Jeffrey Berlin, the next stop on the trail, was an academic dean and professor of comparative literature at Holy Family College in Pennsylvania. Berlin specializes in German literature and is particularly conversant in the works of writers such as Thomas Mann and Stefan Zweig. I finally pinned him down to a half-hour telephone conversation in which I essentially asked him to tell me everything he knew about Heinrich Jacob. Now I had something to work with: a telephone conversation, a translation of a brief biographical sketch in the standard German reference book Deutsches Biobibliographie, a long string of titles, and a couple of articles Berlin had written on correspondence between H. E. Jacob and Thomas Mann in exile. The picture of Heinrich Jacob was beginning to take shape in my mind, and each step along the way had been a surprise.

Jacob was born in Berlin in 1889 to the family of a bank director. He was educated in German literature, philosophy, music, and history in Berlin and held the post of chief correspondent for the Berlin Tagesblattes in Vienna for several years. In his position as chief correspondent for an important European newspaper, Jacob was both socially and financially living comfortably. His parties were sumptuous and legendary, and provided him contact with "everyone who was anyone" in early twentieth-century Vienna. In April 1938, the Nazis made a surprise sweep of Vienna, arresting 150 of Austria's elite citizens. Jacob, a Jew, was among them, and he spent the next year of his life first in Dachau, then Buchenwald, until his release was secured in 1939 through the efforts of his first wife Dora and an American uncle who sponsored Jacob's bid for American citizenship.

Upon his release from Buchenwald, Jacob, like many of the more affluent European Jews, fled to the United States, where he lived in exile and relative obscurity for several years, maintaining close contact with other European Jews in exile. He did some of the research and much of the work on *Six Thousand Years of Bread* in New York.

At first, I had figured that *Six Thousand Years of Bread* would have been the lifetime work of a single-minded author. Imagine my surprise when Barbara Haber, curator of printed books at Radcliffe's Schlesinger Library and noted food historian, drew my attention to the fact that there were thirty-seven entries under the name Heinrich Jacob in the Harvard University cataloging system! Do not think for even a moment that Jacob's works were limited in scope or undertaking. Henry W. Brann, an American critic writing for The Jewish Review in 1960, called him "an outstanding writer whom we must consider one of the few great encyclopedists of the twentieth century, a dying species in our age of stultifying specialization." Jacob published more than forty works in his lifetime and edited many more. Here stands a real Renaissance man if ever there was one. Widely acclaimed biographies of Felix Mendelssohn, Johann Strauss, Joseph Haydn, and Mozart were interspersed with a biography of Emma Lazarus, the forgotten Jewish-American poet who penned the words that adorn the Statue of Liberty, a novel about the German film industry of the twenties entitled *Blood and Celluloid* (Jacob served for a time as dramatic adviser to Max Reinhardt), assorted poems, plays, novels, and an important work, considered to be the "mother" of a genre, entitled *Coffee: The Epic of a Commodity.*

Jacob claimed to have examined more than four thousand works over a period of twenty years in order to complete what was considered his greatest work, *Six Thousand Years of Bread.* He had begun work on the manuscript during the years before his arrest in Vienna and completed it after he came to live in the United States, doing much of his later research in the New York Public Library. During his imprisonment, his wife Dora Jacob had hidden the manuscript from the Nazis, who had blacklisted Jacob's work in 1933. Although the book was written in German, it was originally published by Doubleday in English in 1944, and finally in German in 1954. A truly graceful translation of the book was done by Richard and Clara Winston, top-notch translators of German who also translated a number of C. G. Jung's works into English.

Six Thousand Years of Bread was generally well received upon its publication. The *Chicago Sun* referred to the book as "the 'Golden Bough' of bread and wheat." A reviewer in the *New York Times,* March 1944, lauded, "Rarely has a book intended for a popular audience displayed evidence of more exhaustive scholarship . . . a broad social survey of Western civilization, which although it omits many fields of human endeavor and many epochs of human history, still includes a bewildering richness and variety of material. The amount of information Mr. Jacob has unearthed that will be new to most readers is simply astonishing." *The Wall Street Journal* commended the author, "In writing the story of bread, a colossal epic tale, Mr. Jacob has sketched world history—its folkways, its religion, its superstition and its plagues, all in terms of bread. The author appears to have missed nothing and neglected nothing from the ancient Egyptians down to 1943. This is a fascinating book." German poet and friend of Jacob's Stefan Zweig wrote, "What a daring venture to tell the story of bread, its religious, political, and technical evolution!" Franz Werfel, author of *The Song of Bernadette*, wrote that the book "ought to be read by those who are attracted to the deepest mysteries of life."

Perhaps the most poetic tribute of all was written for a trade publication, *The Baker's Digest*, in June 1944. "In this book, the author tells the story of the human race in terms of our most important food, bread. It is a fascinating story, full of wars, revolutions, religious conflicts, hunger, misery, progress, scientific enlightenment, triumph. And through this story, like a mighty river flowing through an endlessly varied landscape, runs the narrative of bread and baking, from its most primitive beginnings on the mud banks of the Nile to the completely mechanized mammoth plants of today, a single one of which may daily turn out tens of tons of enriched white bread 'untouched by human hand.'"

A few astute (or maybe just picky) observers suggested that, at times, Jacob's research was faulty, his conclusions unwarranted, and his narrative ungainly. Paul Sears, writing in *The Saturday Review*, April 1, 1944, first lavished praise upon the author, saying, "It is a much more serious task to write history in terms of bread than of battles. Unquestionably it is a better way. To undertake it requires poetic insight, over and above historical scholarship and skill. The author has these merits, and by their virtue has produced a book that is significant and vastly entertaining as well." Sears then went on to offer this somewhat curious observation: "So important do I consider this book, that I hope no pains will be spared to clear it of numerous and serious defects by thoroughgoing revision. Since it is in translation, and the subtleties of language are great, it is hard to fix the responsibility in all cases. Certainly there is room for clear-headed editorial work of a general character. The opening section on 'The Bread of Prehistoric Man' needs to be gone over jointly by competent students of biology and cultural anthropology." Sears does not clearly indicate the nature of these "numerous and serious defects," other than to suggest that they may have something to do with the translation (which was generally lauded by the critics) and that when it comes to the area of anthropology and biology, Jacob may not know his nuts and bolts. He gives us no indication which passages or ideas expounded in the opening section he finds suspect, so it is difficult for the interested reader to assess the validity of his challenges.

When a work has been translated from the language in which it was originally written, the translator has the solemn responsibility to render not only the words of the author into a new language, but his or her general tone and attitude toward the subject in question. And this is not always easy to do with great accuracy. I have, for instance, seen translations from French (a language that I can read) that I felt altogether misled the reader as to the author's true meaning. Richard and Clara Winston, the translators of Jacob's book, were considered top-drawer translators of the German language in their day. They had translated a number of works of C. G. Jung into English, and must have had some sort of feeling for the importance of myth and religion in the affairs of humankind, because I felt they conveyed the reverent nature of Jacob's work intact. Curt Reiss, a reviewer for the *Chicago Daily News* (whom I assume could read German), said, "A word about the translation, the work of Richard and Clara Winston. It is an excellent job. The Winstons have succeeded in turning the nervous yet powerful prose of the author into adequate readable English." And Walter Hendricks, writing for the *Chicago Sun*, observed, "Originally written in German, this book escaped destruction by the Nazis, and now enjoys the good fortune of having been sympathetically translated."

With the recent increased interest in artisan bread baking, *Six Thousand Years of Bread*, originally published in 1944, has developed a sort of cult following in the food world. The bibliographies of nearly every serious bread book contain it; and many good bread bakers and food historians either know about the book or own a copy.

Many thanks to Jeffrey Berlin for information, encouragement, and guidance; Hans Gerlach for stewarding the spirit of H. E. Jacob and sharing generously; Helen Mildner for scrupulous proofreading; Kersten Robers for being an incredibly intelligent and enthusiastic translator; and most of all to M., the very lead in my pencil.

—Lynn Alley
San Diego, 1997

PROLOGUE

PROLOGUE

I REMEMBER IT as though it were yesterday.

I was four or five years old and lived in a large city—the same city in which I was born.

I sat upon a tall chair, all alone, in my uncle's office. My uncle was a grain trader. But I did not know what that was.

I believe my parents had business elsewhere and had left me here, planning to come back for me later. I sat alone, and finally I slid down from the chair because I wanted to touch the yellow stuff that lay everywhere on the floor. The whole floor was heaped with this dry, crackling stuff.

It was not pleasant to hold it in my hand. In fact, it frightened me. Stalks which had looked smooth as silk felt sharp and raw. Their dry brittleness bit into my palm, and their smell was sharp. They had long, soft hairs growing from hard little heads.

It seemed to me I had often seen this on the street. Wasn't it the same stuff that spilled out of the feed bags of horses when they ate? I was afraid of horses—so I began to cry.

My uncle came back into the room carrying a box. He wondered why I was crying.

"Why are you crying, silly? Don't you know what that is?"

He held it against my cheek. It tickled. I pulled my head away.

"It's grass," I stammered.

"Grain samples, that's what it is," my uncle said. "There's no reason to cry about it."

I asked, "What are grain samples?"

My uncle smiled. "When you go home you'll find it on the supper table. Look at it closely. Then you'll see that you like it. . . ."

When I arrived home, very tired, there was nothing yellow on the table. My father, a tall, slim man, bent over and cut the bread. The crust of the bread was as brown and glossy as my father's sideburns, and inside the bread was as white as my father's quiet face. In the light of the lamp the bread seemed even quieter and more peaceful. Safety and a sleep-inducing stillness and loveliness emanated from the white bread and from my father's hands.

I forgot what I was supposed to ask him. It seemed folly to me to imagine that the strange yellow stuff had any connection with my familiar bread on the table. No, it did not even seem folly. I had forgotten the other thing completely; the bread was just there—it could not be any different.

Years later, in 1920, I recounted this childhood experience to the great botanist, Georg Schweinfurth. He laughed briefly.

"You were wiser than your uncle," he said; "and right on every count."

I can still see him vividly, this man of almost ninety, who was Livingstone's contemporary. The travels of his youth and middle age had illuminated much of the Dark Continent. From the heart of Africa he had brought exciting word of pigmy tribes and long-sought plants. His hair was white but his carriage still erect.

"It is legitimate to fear a stalk of grain. Even though one does not know its history, one knows that it is indeed a hero with its plume, a miracle of statics with its stone armor of petrified silicic acid. That is why grain crackles when the wind plays among the stalks. The wild Germans and Slavs were terrified by it when they entered the Roman Empire and heard this sound for the first time."

"How remarkable!" I exclaimed.

He made a gesture that seemed to say, "That is not the half of it."

"It was the most natural thing in the world, your not being able to identify the grain and bread. How unlikely it seems. It took man ten thousand years before he learned to make bread out of the grains he had roasted or eaten as a porridge."

"Who invented bread?"

"We do not know. But it was undoubtedly an individual of that unique nation which combined the peasant's patience with the curiosity of the chemist. Undoubtedly an Egyptian."

"Then since the times of the Egyptians bread has always had its place on our table?"

"Not at all; much too rarely," he replied hesitantly. "Often the farmer could not plant grain because his tools were taken away or he was too oppressed by taxes. It is a piteous tale. But there are also happier tales about bread. The most wonderful story I know is, perhaps, that this bread, thousands of years old though it is, is not yet finished in the baking. Botanist, farmer, miller, and baker are still experimenting with it. The entire story of bread goes very deep—its social and technical, religious, political, and scientific story."

"Religious also?" I wondered.

"Certainly, bread has played a tremendous part in the life of religions. Most of the great cultural faiths strove first to become and then to remain 'religions of bread. . . .' "

"Why don't you write the story?" I exclaimed. "The history of bread for ten thousand years."

His expression became very wise and very old. His tone changed suddenly to that of the great scholar or the retiring statesman: "Why don't *you* try to write it? All there is to do is to examine everything in human history from chemistry and agriculture to theology, from economic history to politics and law. Take notes for twenty years, and then you may begin writing!"

I can so easily call to mind his smile. It was kind—but not without irony.

"Why should I take up such a burden?" I thought to myself. "Who would ever finish gathering so much material?" But then I did take up the burden. And I gathered—without finishing.

And now, in the midst of the garnering, I begin the tale.

BOOK ONE

The Bread of Prehistoric Man

History celebrates the battlefields whereon we meet our death, but scorns to speak of the plowed fields whereby we thrive; it knows the names of kings' bastards but cannot tell us the origin of wheat. That is the way of human folly.

HENRI FABRE

THE RIDDLE OF THE ANTS

ON APRIL 13, 1861, the great Charles Darwin rose to address the Linnaean Society of London. Darwin, then fifty-two years old, was still youthful and his beard was not yet gray.

No one had ever seen Darwin agitated, nor was he now as he spoke to the assembled members: "I have received two letters from Dr. Gideon Lincecum, an American physician in the state of Texas, who writes that he has discovered the secret of the origin of agriculture. He asserts that agriculture was not invented by man; rather it is but another of the many prehuman discoveries. Lincecum declares that the first sowers and reapers of grain were the ants."

Some four years previously Darwin had published the *Origin of Species.* As Linnaeus was the "father of plants," so Darwin had become the "father of animals." Since the day that the Lord of the Book of Genesis led the animals before Adam that he might give them names there had been none to do what Darwin did.

Darwin read to the society the first letter on the ants:

"Around the mound . . . the ant clears the ground of all obstructions, levels and smooths the surface to the distance of three or four feet from the gate of the city, giving the space the appearance of a handsome pavement, as it really is. Within this paved area not a green thing is allowed to grow, except a single species of grain-bearing grass. Having planted this crop in a circle around the center of the mound, the insect tends and cultivates it with constant care, cutting away all other grasses that may spring up amongst it and all around outside of the farm circle to the extent of one or two feet more. The cultivated grass grows luxuriantly, and produces a heavy crop of small, white, flinty seeds. The insect watches the ripeness; then it harvests the crop, and after the harvest all the chaff is taken out and thrown beyond the limits of the yard area. This ant rice begins to grow in the early days of *November*. There can be no doubt of the fact that the particular species of grain-bearing grass mentioned above is intentionally planted."

In order to inquire more deeply into the matter, Darwin reported, he had written his correspondent of his prudent doubts. To these Lincecum had replied in a second letter. The American insisted that he had no doubts at all. "I have for twelve years watched the same ant cities during all seasons." The ants, he averred, sowed their grain deliberately, and as a monoculture.

"Not a green thing is suffered to grow on the pavement, with the exception of a single species of grain-bearing grass: Aristida stricta. . . . They also collect the grain from several other species of grass as well as seed from many kinds of herbaceous plants—but they never sow them. The species of grass they so carefully cultivate is a biennial. They sow it in time for the autumnal rains to bring it up. Accordingly, about the first of November a beautiful green row of the ant rice about four inches wide is springing up on the pavement, in a circle of fourteen to fifteen feet in circumference. In the vicinity of this circular row of grass they do not permit a single spire of any other grass or weed to remain a day. Leaving the ant rice untouched until it is ripe, which occurs in *June* of the next year, they gather the seeds and carry them into the granaries. . . ."

This detailed account of Dr. Lincecum's produced a momentous effect on the audience. Everyone rose and clamored for the floor. Could this truly be the solution to one of the great riddles of human civilization? All the scientists suddenly recalled significant scraps of their schoolboy theology and the classics. It had been known for thousands of years that the ants of the south, particularly those of the Mediterranean basin, lived by storing provisions, especially the seeds of wild grasses, against the winter. In the Bible Solomon had admonished, "Go to the ant, thou sluggard!" And Horace, the Roman poet, praised the foresight of the ants which *"haud ignora ac non incauta futuri* [took the future into their reckoning]." Virgil, too, one of the society members observed, had mentioned the ants in the Fourth Book of *The Aeneid*. He had said, in Dryden's translation:

> ". . . Thus, in battalia, march embodied ants,
> Fearful of winter, and of future wants,
> T'invade the corn, and to their cells convey
> The plundered forage of their yellow prey."

Others rose to refute them. "But that is something wholly different. These quotations merely assert that the ants store grain in order to consume it in time of want. But Dr. Lincecum is the first to maintain that the grain is also *sowed*."

"Quite true." Darwin nodded. "Between gathering and sowing there is a distance as great as that between Edinburgh and Peking. Consider the ramifications!"

They considered. If the ants understood the art of sowing, one could say they had embarked upon causal thinking to an extent and depth hitherto unknown in the purposeful activities of dumb creation. Or was such causal thinking unknown? The scientists who were members of the Linnaean Society naturally thought very highly of the animal world. The discoveries made by animals before man trod the earth were by no means trifling. In mathematics, architecture, and physics the "dumb creatures" were far in advance·of. man. How ingenious of the bee to construct its hexagon, the purest of geometric forms, without the aid of any instrument for measuring angles. Consider the swallow's invention of mortar construction—man needed only to analyze the work of this bird to learn the technique of building galleries and balconies. Or the activities of the beavers, the most powerful of all gnawing creatures, who transformed the face of the earth by building dams miles in length to control streams. In the case of the beavers, the great enigma was the question of time. The construction of such a dam required possibly two hundred years. For whom were they building?

And now it was averred that the ants had invented agriculture; that man, a hundred thousand years ago, had learned their secret by sharp observation.

But would it have been possible for primitive man to learn by observation .something that presumed the keenest understanding, a thorough knowledge of the relationship between cause and effect? Science had only recently established that primitive peoples did not possess reason, or, at best, possessed a reasoning faculty peculiar to themselves. The inhabitants of the Marquesas Islands refused to believe that the birth of children had any connection with the sexual intercourse of husband and wife nine months before. It appeared illogical to them that so trivial an act should have such vast and fearful consequences. Now scientists were asked to believe that *ants* sowed in order to reap; that they waited eight months, like a human farmer, for their crop to mature; and that meanwhile they took exacting pains to weed their field. Was this not claiming too much? It was too human, too "anthropomorphic."

And so, after a great deal of discussion pro and con, many members of the society suggested that Lincecum might well be a jokester. Had Darwin and the society been made sport of?

§ 2

For forty years no more was said or thought about this embarrassing tale, à la Mark Twain, of the agricultural ants, until another American exhumed it and inveighed against it. W. M. Wheeler wrote:

Lincecum is responsible for the myth that this Pogonomyrmex sows a certain species of "ant rice," protects it from harm and frees it from weeds while it is growing, for the purpose of reaping the grain. This notion, which even the Texan schoolboy has come to regard as a joke, has been widely cited, largely because the great Darwin stood sponsor for its publication. . . .

Since Darwin's day a new science had sprung into being, "myrmecology," or the study of ants. It was founded by great scientists like the Swiss physician, Forel, the Englishmen Lubbock and Romanes, and the Austrian Jesuit father, Erich Wasmann. These observers all contended among themselves over the interpretation of their observations. They suggested various explanations for the motives of the insects, the force that underlay their activity. The larger group of myrmecologists concluded that the ants, among all living creatures, came closest to man in intelligence—closer than the anthropoid apes. But some were horrified by this view. The pious Wasmann refused to believe that "the power by which man deduces one proposition from another, and proceeds from premises to consequences," man's *reason*, was a trait that could be shared by such creatures. Wasmann ascribed all the apparent miracles to instinct. Bethe, on the other hand, believed that the ants possessed neither reason nor instinct; that all invertebrates were merely reflex machines.

These disputations, however, in no way hindered the amassing of an immense amount of information about the ants. Before long virtually more was known about them than about the early history of mankind.

Biologically and sociologically the ants were a remarkable species. They produced an *odeur de contact*—a scent by which they recognized individuals. They had their own language, consisting of movements of the antennae, and had developed this language into an excellent means of communication. For the sake of their works they had renounced sexuality; that is, immediately after the nuptials they allowed the useless males to die of starvation and entrusted the welfare of the tribe to sexless workers. They waged wars with their neighbors, which they would arbitrarily conclude to make peace with those who a moment before were deadly foes—and they kept the peace. French scientists described their skill in road building; English scientists investigated their tunnels and bridges. The American, Mac Cook, studied their sleep, their yawns upon awakening, their toilet, exercise, and common gymnastics. Reverend W. Farren White examined their burial rites and their aid to the sick. Darwin himself described their slave hunts.

Darwin had early recognized that the various nations of ants lived under different conditions and had, consequently, different talents. Ants in England behaved differently from ants in Switzerland. Some ants dwelt in pastoral societies: they fed beetles which they pressed, causing them to yield milk. Even the principles of fermentation were not unknown to them. They cut leaves and chewed them into a crumbly mass. Through the enzyme contained in their saliva (similar to our own) starch was converted into sugar. The resultant material was then allowed to stand for a while before it was eaten by all. Were these things not miracles of civilization? According to Nordic mythology, fermented beer was first made of Kwasir's saliva, which he had stirred with grain in a vat. But what did the ants know of Kwasir, the Nordic hero?

The entomologist, Mac Cook, reports that one of the Pennsylvania nests of these mysterious insects is, in proportion to the size of its builders, eighty-four times as large as the Cheops pyramid. Could not so great a race have discovered agriculture, as it discovered fermentation? But Lincecum's "cultivated fields" had vanished in the course of the years. No one knew where they had been located—and neither the Texas ants nor any other ants seemed to plant grain.

On the contrary. The more scientists investigated, the more certain they became that the ants were sworn enemies of agriculture. This was only natural. The ants did their utmost to prevent the grain which was their provender from sprouting. They sprinkled the grain with formic acid or bit off the sprouts before they placed it in their storehouse; or they let the seeds lie in the sun until they were thoroughly dried out and could no longer germinate.

Had Lincecum been lying, or had he erred in his observations? This question was at last answered by Ferdinand Goetsch in 1937. Lincecum's ants were not fabulous, Goetsch found, but they had "actually sowed by mistake." From extensive observation of ants in Europe and South America, Goetsch discovered that most ant tribes are possessed of two contradictory instincts: the instinct to collect and the instinct to build. The first leads them to bring grain, wood, and other materials into the nest; the other instinct impels them to carry all these materials out of the nest again and use them for building. Among their building materials are seeds of grasses and grains. A period of drought stimulates the collecting instinct; moisture, the building instinct. Goetsch suggests that Lincecum's fields arose from such grains which were aimlessly (for they should have been used as food) carried out in the course of building activities. Thus they were unintentionally placed upon moist soil and germinated. Conscious sowing it was not. But if this "mistake" had been repeated millions of times in the history of the race, thereby becoming a part of the group memory, could not this in the end engender a sowing instinct? Perhaps Lincecum's particular ants had developed such an instinct; perhaps the physician had not been so misguided after all.

This much is certain: Stone Age man, when he discovered agriculture, discovered it against his will. In order to store a supply of the delicious grass seeds with which he relieved the pungency of the meat he customarily ate, he had sought out a dry spot in his cave. But the ground eventually became wet and the seeds began to germinate. Their taste was spoiled, and at last he threw them away, bitterly complaining of his lot upon this inhospitable earth. But, to his indescribable astonishment, eight months later the grain appeared once more.

THE INVENTION OF THE PLOW

§ 3

PRIMITIVE MAN did not have a microscope.

"Culture arises through imitation," Gabriel Tarde taught. But though primitive man was a mimic, he could not have imitated the ants because they were too small. Consider "the soul of the ant with its industry, its instinct of architecture, order, fidelity, and courage"—such is the tribute that E. Dubois Reymond paid the ants. But he, working in 1886, could observe their noble traits through his microscope. This was precisely what primitive man could not do.

The soaring flight of a handsomely plumaged bird—that was something else again. A bird's flight, its dances, its language—these were things that could be imitated. A bird could be considered (as birds were later by the Indians) as a god or the father of the tribe. But alas! the lovely birds neither sowed nor reaped.

No, man could not learn agriculture from any of the beasts. It was something he had to discover for himself. Or, rather, that his wife had to discover.

Man never would have acquired the art of cultivation without woman. We can, with a high degree of probability, conceive its origins thus:

In the oldest times man was a hunter.

If the fortunes of the hunt went well one day, he ate. But if, on the following day, no prey fell to his stone club, he went hungry. Soon he learned that he need not hunger if he preserved the remainder of his meat by passing it over the fire. Fire purified; the meat did not spoil and could be eaten for days.

The invention of roasting solved the problem of storage. (Cooking was not discovered until much later, for men had no vessels that could withstand the heat of a direct flame.) But after a few days hunger once more crouched to spring upon the hunter. Then, perhaps, the hunter's son suggested to his father: "Let us make a great hedge and capture the animals within it, rather than kill them. Let the he-beasts lie with the she-beasts, so that they will have children. Then we shall eat and not die."

Thus the hunter's son became a herdsman. He noticed that not all the animals he guarded ate the flesh of others; many of them fed on grass or plucked fruits from the trees. They seemed to him wise animals. The herdsman noticed also that he himself and his family were subject to mysterious diseases. Their gums grew foul in their mouths; they suffered from headaches and difficulty in breathing. Then the herdsman took grass seeds and sprinkled them on his roasted meat. He also ate of the fruits of the trees, and his diseases ceased.

Now the family divided the work. When the hunter grew old, he took his son's place as herdsman. The vigorous son hunted in his stead, bringing the finest animals within the fenced enclosure and killing others. The wife gathered grasses and fruits—those mysterious things of the earth whose origins none understood. But because she was alone a great deal, the woman had much time for reflection and observation. Not all growing things were alike. They were as various as the creatures that moved on the earth and begat their own kind.

And the woman became mightier than the man, because she knew the qualities of the various herbs. In these herbs dwelt powers that could change the minds of men. There were those that induced sleep and those that brought merriment, for the men were inclined to rage or melancholy when the animals caused them trouble. The men were also constantly frightened by strange phenomena in the skies. They trembled, for example, that the moon did not remain always the same, but sickened from a disc to the horn of a bull, or for a time vanished utterly. Therefore they took white cattle whose skins gleamed like the silver moon and whose horns were handsomely curved, and offered them up to the moon, which repaid them by growing fuller once more. These sacrifices were made amid tears and anxiety. But the woman possessed a way to lull the man's fear, for she had observed how beetles and butterflies clung to fermented sugar that the heat of the sun had made ooze from the bark of trees. Thus the woman learned to brew intoxicating drinks.

And the men arose after they had slept off their intoxication and returned joyfully to their flocks. The woman remained at home, meditating over her plants, which her husband needed for his well-being, but which, at the same time, he despised because no strength of muscle was needed to tame them.

One day, when the husband had returned from his pasture, he found that the woman had made a garden. She informed him that the earth bore fruit as did her own womb nine full moons after it was filled with seed. The man laughed incredulously. But soon he believed.

His wife had invented a tool with which she helped the earth to receive its seed: the grubbing stick. She bored holes in the earth and into the holes she placed the seed of "Father Millet." She lavished more love upon the children of the millet than upon the seeds of any of her other plants, for it nourished her own children and made strong men of them.

One day, however, digging holes with this stick became too burdensome for her. She requested her husband to bind a long stick to a short one at right angles, securing them with tough grass. With this tool she hacked at the ground, putting the weight of her body behind the blow. The womb of the earth opened more easily, and woman had invented the hoe. For many thousands of years she cultivated her garden with the hoe and raised her grasses and vegetables.

One day the husband and his friends came riotously home, their cattle following them. The sun god had covered the pastures thickly with juicy grass, and the cows had grown fat. The men wished to celebrate in honor of the god. They drank fermented drinks and sat under the trees of the garden. In his exuberance one man took the hoe and drove it so deeply into the garden soil that none could draw it out. Then, while all shouted and laughed, the master of the house took one of the bulls and tied him with stout fibers of grass to the hoe that had been driven half the length of its shaft into the ground. The bull stepped forward, pulled and pulled. But he did not pull upward. He drew the hoe horizontally through the garden soil, tearing it open. And suddenly he threw his head toward the sun and bellowed until the very horizons shivered. The men stood watching the earth being torn like a piece of hide. They began to fear the bull and the hoe, which continued to rip open the womb of the earth. They sobered, trembled that they had outraged the gods, and cut the bull loose from the hoe.

The following day they wished to fill in the furrow in the earth, to obliterate what had happened. But the woman interfered, saying: "Let us first place the male beside the female, put the male seed of the grasses into the womb of the Earth Mother." Thus the men did what the women had done for so long. But they did not feel safe in so doing. They begged the earth to forgive them for cutting her open, and gave her all sorts of presents. They feared the earth would, in her anger, open of herself and swallow them all. Nevertheless, nothing of the kind took place. The earth blessed those who had aided her reproductive powers; everything grew taller, greener, and richer. Thereupon they continued to help her. The hoe that had been drawn through the soil they kissed and sanctified.

§ 4

In some such manner man may have invented the *plow*. In all of history no subsequent invention vies with this in importance. The discovery of electricity, of the railroad, or the airplane was not of such far-reaching effect and did not so alter the aspect of Mother Earth as the plow. We shall never know where plowing was first discovered, but primitives used it from Ireland to North Africa, from western Europe to India and China.

This we know, however, that it was invented in some river valley, for only well-irrigated land would lend itself to the first crude plow. The oldest real culture was, necessarily, an oasis culture. Did the plow first come into being in ancient Mesopotamia, the valley of the Tigris, and the Euphrates? It was in this land that the bull, the symbol of the sun, was most revered. Or did the plow originate on the Nile? We do not know. In India, along the broad banks of the Ganges? Again we do not know. In China, then, in the fertile alluvial soil of the Yellow River? There, we are certain, it was not invented, for the Chinese plow is so highly developed that the plows of western Asia, those employed by the Assyrians and the Egyptians, would represent a wretched retrogression. The Chinese realized that a dragged spade would be more efficient than a dragged hoe. They created the modern plow, with the properly curved iron moldboard connected to the plowshare. This plow throws up the earth in a manner unlike that of the older, West Asiatic plow. An invention can decay, but its basic principle never proceeds from better to worse; therefore the origin of plowing can hardly be credited to eastern Asia.

Wherever men learned to utilize the plow, throughout the Orient and the Occident, it powerfully inflamed the sexual imagination. It resembled the instrument with which man overcomes woman, inflicting upon her the selfsame violence that the furrowing plow inflicts upon the earth. Much later Plutarch observed that "wounding is the principle of love." Plowing, too, was an act of love. There was no doubt that the earth was a woman. In her virtues and faults, in the whims that impelled her to yield or to deny, she behaved like a woman. She was the wife of the sky —the Greeks later believed that she was one of Zeus's wives. Zeus, to be sure, had many wives, and the earth avenged herself by taking the first plowman, Jasion, for her lover. Zeus, enraged, struck him down with his thunderbolts.

But Jasion's descendants did not cease to love the earth and to beget upon her with the *aratron,* the plow. Each year the peasant opened a certain familiar portion of the earth—not one place one year and another the following year. He learned to love it as long as it supported him— and this was an entirely new emotion, for the earth had been indifferent to him while he was still a herdsman tending his cattle. The plow gave rise to property and to the desire to possess the earth. Though much evil sprang from this desire, in the beginning it was something splendid, for without such an emotion men would not have continued to plow the ground. For the first time man had become the master of the earth. In the wilderness of plant life that previously had covered the earth man had been only a guest, never the master. But the plow transformed a part of the soil; the land became the soil of the plowman and sower.

Man gave to this new earth chosen seed. The plowed field ceased to be subject to the whims of the winds—and this was entirely new. Where man's plow sank into the earth, the promiscuous mingling of the sexes ceased; the field became monogamous. Man opened the earth to a single will. This is why, everywhere in the world, the gods of agriculture also became the gods of marriage. Conversely, the winds were the gods of adultery and thievery.

The righteous plowman, in his labor, conducts himself as a husband toward his wife. To symbolize this ethical relationship, the Roman monogamous marriage was solemnized upon a plow. And Hesiod adjured the Greek plowman to walk naked behind his plow. The sacred nexus between the man and the earth must not be impaired by clothing. When the harvest had been taken and the earth stripped of its blessing, the peasant was directed to lie with his wife upon the naked soil in holy copulation. They would remind the earth that it must bear afresh!

So, in earliest times, the tilling of the soil was surrounded by the aura of religious commandments. For none doubted that this great miracle—that man could beget upon the earth—was made possible only by the highest of heavenly blessings. Indeed, the priests insisted upon this daily.

From where did these priests appear? Originally every man had been his own priest, performing all his activities in a religious fashion. Later on division of labor made distinctions among priests, hunters, herdsmen, and peasants. Soon the priests claimed that all the great inventions that had transformed the life of man had been their work: first fire, then the plow, the wheeled cart, the castration of the bull, the breaking of the horse, and the arts of weaving and forging. All these techniques, they claimed, the gods had charged them to give to men. In return they demanded that their brethren feed and care for them.

They were distorting the truth, of course. It is unlikely that any inventions were made in honor of the gods. Religion was never creative of technology, nor could it ever have desired to be so. On the contrary, religion hastened after the invention and took possession of it. Religion established itself promptly as the guardian of each technical innovation. For the development of humanity, this was a necessary and valuable step. We must remember the feeble reasoning powers of early man, his faulty memory, his vast frivolity, and his constant state of drunkenness. Chance inventions would have been forgotten at once if they had not been re-enacted within the rituals instituted by the priest.

Every invention resulted from the passion to improve modes of living. Then religion came and guarded the invention from oblivion by sanctifying it. When men perceived the impracticability of having the plow dragged by the reluctant bull or the milch cow, they created the ox, the sexless worker. When the new creation proved its worth, it received the protection of religion.

The Hindus hold it blasphemy to eat the flesh of the ox, but not because it is a sacred animal; rather, the ox is a sacred animal because it is indispensable to plowing. Another element contributes to its sacredness: the bull had sacrificed its masculinity for the great civilizing work of plowing. Because of its enforced deprivation, it became an object of pious reverence not unlike the priest himself who, out of his concern for things spiritual, did not marry and beget children.

But technology was always sovereign and never subservient to religion. Wherever religion attempted to impose subservience upon it, conflict broke out. Such a conflict is recounted in the legend of Prometheus, who stole fire from heaven and taught men to forge metals. He was overpowered by the Supreme God, Zeus, and bound to a rock. But Zeus was forced to release him. Prometheus, the technician, was stronger, for he could foretell Zeus's future. . . . It is a legend of great profundity. Religion and technology fare better when they join forces rather than cross swords with each other. It can be said that technology made use of religion (as religion made use of technology) to protect its inventions. As today inventions are protected by patent law, so in the early history of mankind they were protected by religious law.

THE RIVALRY OF THE GRASSES

§ 5

MEN WERE NOW EMPOWERED to beget upon the surface of the earth; to increase, by the work of their own hands, the numbers and varieties of plant life. It gave them cause for unprecedented rejoicing; men became intoxicated with their own new-found powers. Many primitive peoples are still under the spell of this elation, as though their mastery over the earth were brand-new. They cannot imagine that new things originate in any other manner except by "planting." When the traveler, Karl von den Steinen, showed a Brazilian Indian chief a box of matches, the Indian joyfully exclaimed, "We must plant these things."

For centuries it has remained a moot question which grass was first sown by men. In all likelihood the question will never be answered with certainty.

The story of the rivalry of the grasses is one of the most tantalizing of the unwritten chapters in the history of human civilization. All grain was once grass. The grains favored by civilization were grasses whose seed pleased the taste of primitive man. But early man's crop of grass seeds was often pilfered before it could be harvested, not only by insects but by the force that propagated the waving meadows of grass—the wind. The wind shook the flowering heads of wild grasses so much that they cast their seed at the lightest touch. This was necessary for the perpetuation of the wild grass, but how was man to harvest ripened grain? The first task of man was, therefore, to break his favorite grasses of this bad habit. For millennia he cultivated only those individuals whose seed clung to the ear for an unusually long time, and he succeeded. The wild grasses he metamorphosed into cultivated wheat, cultivated rye, and all the other grains that became the great nourishers of mankind. These new varieties have fruit which clings so firmly to the pedicel that it can be removed only by trampling, shaking, or beating—that is, by what we call threshing. The threshing floor is the battlefield between the tenacity of the stalk and men's hunger for flour.

How prehistoric man accomplished such a miracle of selective breeding is a mystery. Such transformations, such operations upon the very source of life, were not again undertaken until the nineteenth century, by professional botanists working upon the basis of Gregor Mendel's laws of heredity. How did early man acquire such knowledge of the workings of nature? By what train of thought did he arrive at branding such knowledge as a secret science? One might perhaps remark that Gregor Mendel was also a priest. In early times the priests, who did not have other work, were excellent observers of all growing things. It is impossible to imagine that a priest invented the harrow, the plow, or any other tool that has changed the life of mankind. But it is extremely likely that it was the priest who interfered in the life habits of plants.

For fifteen thousand years the epic of grain has been one with the epic of man. We may say that man has transformed the wild grain into a domestic animal. It follows man everywhere because it needs the excrements of his economy—manures, phosphates, and nitrogen. And it would die at once without him. Grain is more dependent than is the dog upon the kindness of its master, for its seed adheres so steadfastly to the stalk that the wind can no longer sow it; it can reproduce itself only by artificial sowing.

The grain that gives life to man lives in its turn only through the grace of man. And yet the sower of grain for the past few thousand years has had the lot of the stepchild in human history.

§ 6

The species of grain eaten by men are brethren that have prevailed for millennia. If we omit rice—whose history is totally at variance with that of the other grains—there are six that man has used since primitive times. These are: millet, oats, barley, and wheat in the earliest period; rye since the late classic period; and maize or Indian corn since the discovery of America. These six brethren have fed the world for nearly ten thousand years.

The oldest of the group was probably "Father Millet," which fed men and their gods long before the invention of the plow. A courteous, pulp-faced ancient who had no liking for cold climates, he was, nevertheless, loyal and persevering and followed the peoples who loved him. The peoples with whom Father Millet dwelt were never rich or warlike. The Mongol and Khirgiz nomads of Central Asia are to this day lovers of millet. In China we find it had been cultivated around 2800 B.C. In primitive India a great deal of millet was eaten. When the Aryan master race descended upon India, it decreed that the food of the subjected race would not do for the food of their men. The Aryans brought their own grain: *djavas,* barley. A contest of taste began from which *djavas,* the grain of soldiers and strong men, emerged as victor.

Barley, in Egyptian, was called *djot*—the words are the same. Though there was no commerce of merchants or sailors between the two great empires of India and Egypt, a seed and a name traveled from one to the other!

Barley not only deposed millet from its throne, but also put a check upon the dominion of oats. Oats had never been too strongly established, for the oat had peculiarities which did not endear it to men. It was like a poorly trained dog, easily tempted to follow another master. It had atavistic inclinations to imitate its cousin, the wild oat, and allow the wind to sow it instead of the hand of man. It reverted to the tougher beard, the looser husk, and the smaller grain of the wild oat. Indeed, when it was not tended carefully, it behaved unconscionably like a weed.

This alone would probably not have made the oat undesirable. Its misfortune was that it was also an excellent livestock feed. In primitive times man loved and admired his animals. Later he despised them as servile creatures. Who would wish to eat from the same board as an animal? Homer's Greeks, who roasted barley and sprinkled it on beef, were contemptuous of the Scythians, who ate oats like their horses. The Romans cherished the same contempt for the oat-eating Germans. In vain the wiser physicians of the Roman Empire, who understood something of nutrition, attempted to popularize oats. One suggested cautiously that oats might be good for the sick. But the "price-ceilings" order of Emperor Diocletian (A.D. 340) mentions oats only as an animal feed. Long before Cato had characteristically recommended that it be exterminated as a weed. Saint Jerome says: *"Avena bruta pascuntur animalia* [only brute beasts are fed with oats]."

This contempt for oats was passed on by the Roman Empire to the Middle Ages. No French or English knight would have touched the food he gave his horse. The Irish and the Scotch alone, who did not live on Roman soil, were fond of the grain. Samuel Johnson in his famous English dictionary defined oats as "food for men in Scotland, horses in England"—to which the Scotch replied: "England is noted for the excellence of her horses; Scotland for the excellence of her men."

Oats were unknown to India and to Babylonia and the surrounding country. In these lands the strong-tasting, brownish-yellow grain of soldiers and peasants was barley. The heavy, consonantal names of this grain are descriptive of the grain's quality: in Greek it is called *krithe,* in Latin, *hordeum,* in German *Gerste.* Different varieties were cultivated in different periods and in different lands. In the territory of the Swiss lake dwellings six-rowed barley prevailed. In Egypt four-rowed barley was

EGYPTIAN EMMER WHEAT

found in a sarcophagus by the archaeologist Schweinfurth. We do not find a two-rowed barley until the third century B.C. in Greece and Italy. This barley, however, was not hardy enough to survive the winters.

In the river valleys barley never achieved the status of a monoculture. At first only in the richer lands, but presently everywhere, wheat began to appear. In Egypt both were cultivated. Both grains might have continued peacefully side by side but for the most important event in the history of grains. *Bread was invented in Egypt.* Barley was not well adapted for bread; it did not bake adequately. Barley had been admirably suited to the stage before the invention of bread, when men roasted flat breads. No sooner was bread discovered than barley fell off in importance and became the victim of snobbery. The Bible frequently mentions it in a deprecatory fashion.

Nevertheless, it was barley that symbolized the strength of the people of Israel. Nowhere—not even in Homer—is there written so forcible a tribute to barley as in the Book of Judges, where an Israelite dreams of a cake of barley bread tumbling into the Midianites' camp and destroying all of Israel's enemies.

Wheat, however, became the king of grains—and remains so to this day. Since its rise to the throne it has never been deposed. Schweinfurth and Legrain found wheat in the graves of the Neolithic age, which are as old as the sixth and fifth centuries before Christ. The Austrian scientist, Unger, found husks and grains of wheat embedded in the bricks of the Dashur pyramid, which was built around 3000 B.C. The Chinese cultivated wheat as early as 2700 B.C., and had developed elaborate rituals to honor it. Mention of wheat by the Assyrians and Babylonians is found on the stone ruins of Tello, which date from 3000 B.C. Who brought the grain to all these peoples and who developed it from its wild state? Was there a nation that acted as intermediary for the exchange of the seed— such as Syria, the land of merchants who traded between Egypt and Babylonia? Wheat, in Egyptian, was called *botet*, in Babylonian, *buttutu* —the same word. But then how are we to explain its progress to China? Perhaps at some time in the dim past there was a bridge of vegetation between the Near East and the Far East. Or perhaps the seed traveled in the crops or stomachs of migratory birds. All riddle, all surmise. He who excavates the soil of prehistoric times is eternally coming across older strata. His confusion is like that of Ibsen's Peer Gynt:

> What an enormous number of swathings!
> Isn't the kernel soon coming to light?
> I'm blast if it is! To the innermost center
> it's nothing but swathings
> —each smaller and smaller—
> nature is witty.

§ 7

But now we can say with fair assurance where the oldest wheat originated. It existed in Abyssinia, whence it descended into the hot river valley of the Nile from the high tableland which is the river's source. The seemingly insoluble problem of the origin of wheat was ingeniously solved in recent years by the Russian scientist Vavilov. Vavilov postulated that every living thing has a "gen center"—a definite source for the first specimen; and, further, that the gen center is to be recognized as the place where the greatest number of varieties have developed in the narrowest area. Let us imagine the man from Mars coming to earth and endeavoring to determine where the English tongue originated. He would properly narrow his search down to south and middle England, for there, in the smallest area, the greatest number of dialects exist side by side. The hypothesis has considerable validity when applied to languages and animals; it has even more validity for plants, which are incapable—or rather less capable—of movement. Vavilov reasoned from this principle and from a number of Mendel's laws of heredity. He concluded that the cradle of wheat lay in Abyssinia.

The wheat that grew in Egypt was hardly like the wheat that today covers the great fields of America, Canada, and the Russian Ukraine. It was an early form of it, emmer wheat. The Romans bred other wheats out of this original variety and planted these new varieties extensively in Egypt. The Romans established their perfected wheat as the predominant grain of the Mediterranean world. From Roman times on its history is lucid and without enigmas.

Rye came into the world suddenly, in the form of a revolt of the lowly. In Pontos, on the shore of the Black Sea—a city surrounded by excellent wheatland—grain ships were loaded to take seed to southern Russia. A few weeds that none regarded became mixed with the seed. But behold! when the time came for sowing, the soil proved too harsh for the wheat, and the weed flourished mightily. Rye abruptly had become a cultivated plant. The sowers intelligently exploited the accident, and within a few hundred years rye had spread to many soils that had been exhausted by continual crops of wheat. The rye yielded great harvests. In its swift course, with the ambition and exuberance of youth, rye also advanced into France and England—though in later times both these countries once more became wheatlands.

Within the territory of the Roman Empire, from England down to Egypt and northward again through the Ukraine to the Danube and the Rhine, the triumph of rye was not lasting. But eastward there begins the vast German-Russian expanse of rye, which stretches all the way into Siberia. The Siberian peasant is a man of cunning. He knows the old hostility between the seeds of rye and the seeds of wheat. It seems to him a case of feuding kinsmen; the Siberian peasant refuses to believe that they are two different species, and calls his rye "black wheat." At sowing time the peasant mixes the black and the white wheat in his seed bag (the mixture is called *sweza*) and broadcasts it. If the year is a raw, cold one, the yield is rye; if it is gentle and warm, wheat is harvested. "Fools!" says the peasant. "And I'm cleverer than you both!"

Raised bread cannot be prepared from millet, oats, barley, or corn. Therefore the history of bread revolves upon wheat and rye—and wheat far more than rye. Bread, in the technical sense of the word, is a discovery of man—one of his first great chemical triumphs. The Albanian proverb,

"Bread is older than man," springs from a poetic but misguided sense of history.

Bread is a product baked in a properly constructed oven from a dough that has been raised by yeast or some other leavening agent. Some of the gases produced by the leavening are imprisoned in the dough. The pores containing these gases are hardened and made permanent by heat. Only dough made of wheat or rye flour possesses the ability to retain gases; this is due to specific properties of the proteins peculiar to these grains.

Long ago Occidental man acquired a definite preference for raised bread instead of cooked cereals and flat breads. Bread reigned over the ancient world; no food before or after exerted such mastery over men. The Egyptians, who invented it, based their entire administrative system upon it; the Jews made bread the starting point of their religious and social laws. The Greeks created profound and solemn legends for their Bread Church of Eleusis. And the Romans converted bread into a political factor. They ruled by it, conquered the entire world by it, and lost the world again through it. At last the day came when Jesus Christ made consummate all the spiritual significance that had become attached to it, saying: "Eat! I am the bread."

BOOK TWO

Bread in the Ancient World

Pandarus: He that will have a cake out of the wheat must needs
              tarry the grinding.
Troilus: Have I not tarried?
Pandarus: Ay, the grinding; but you must tarry the bolting.
Troilus: Have I not tarried?
Pandarus: Ay, the bolting; but you must tarry the leavening.
Troilus: Still have I tarried.
Pandarus: Ay, to the leavening; but here's yet in the word 'here-
              after' the kneading, the making of the cake, the heating
              of the oven, and the baking; nay, you must stay the
              cooling too, or you may chance to burn your lips.
                   SHAKESPEARE: TROILUS AND CRESSIDA

EGYPT: THE DISCOVERY OF BAKING

§ 8

MEN OF ALL early cultures prayed to rivers. With vast, supernatural
limbs, the great streams moved forward, obedient only to their own will.
To be sure, men might outwit them for a time by digging ditches and
erecting dams, in imitation of those waterwise builders of the animal
world, the beavers. But in essence the rivers remained vast and invincible;
they devoured men, dwellings, and domestic animals as the whim moved
them. It was well to sacrifice to the rivers, to placate them by presents.

Men had prayed to the Rhine, the Rhone, the Euphrates. But to no
river had they prayed with more ardor than to the Nile. For to the people
who lived close to the Nile the god was not fearsome, but a benign father.
The Egyptian Nile personified the sensible *pater familias* who fed and
clothed his children.

Along the entire 3,473-mile course, from Lake Victoria to the Mediterranean, no important tributaries flow into the Nile. The skies, too, are
no more liberal in giving to the river, for it seldom rains in Egypt. All the
water in the land is Nile water. Consequently, the land of Egypt exists
only upon the shores of the Nile; it is an oasis with a width of no more
than a few miles.

Nowhere else upon the surface of the globe has there been such topog-
raphy: a river lined on both banks by a continuous chain of villages,
gardens, cities, and men—a land that is all length and no breadth. The
Egyptian's political mind could conceive of but two directions: north

and south. Eastward and westward a short camel ride brought him to the desert that separated Egypt from the outside world. What lay beyond either desert was a matter for metaphysical speculation: in the east the sun rose and in the west the dead dwelt. But as far as the living Egyptian was concerned, there was the Nile, which flowed north and south, bringing bread, bringing life.

The god of the Nile was a sensible fellow. Every year, since time immemorial, he had let his waters swell in June. They rose gradually at first, then more swiftly and powerfully in the latter half of July. In August the god overflowed his banks; in September he formed lakes which remained through October and began to recede at the same measured pace in the early days of November. By January the Nile god had returned to his old bed, but even here his waters persistently dwindled until June, when they began to rise afresh. Thus the god of the Nile worked all year for the Egyptians, with a precision unknown to mortal man.

But the god, in his yearly cycle from low water to flood, did not bring water alone. Above all, he bore earth within his waters: the mud of the Abyssinian plateau, washed out grains of slate, barium carbonate, gneiss, and a great deal of iron oxide. Every year the god lavished this "black earth" upon his right and left banks. The higher the Nile rose, the greater was the stretch of alluvial land that could be tilled. A nation that had experienced this kindness of the river's for thousands of years could not doubt that the Nile acted with conscious intent. The Greeks, however, the fathers of skepticism, did doubt. Hekataios of Milet, Theopompus, Herodotus, and Thales delved into the question of the Nile's source. Herodotus had a strong inkling of the truth: that the equatorial rains which fell between March and September in the vicinity of the Nile's source in Abyssinia were the cause of the annual flood. The Egyptians would have been aghast at this materialistic explanation of a supernatural phenomenon. Did the Nile have any source at all? It would have seemed blasphemous to them to search for the source, for the delivery chamber of the god. . . . The rising of the Nile was a gift of the divinity. The night on which begins the flooding of the Nile is still, after twenty centuries, celebrated as the "Night of Dripping." To this day Egypt maintains its Nile surveyor at Elephantine, upon the island at the first cataract, who proclaims the joyful tidings: "It is rising!"

In ancient Egypt men and women marched in solemn procession to honor this time of times. They sang:

Worship to Thee, Oh Nile!
Hidden one, Thou who bringest the things of the darkness
To the light!

Thou who drawest thy waters
Over the meadows of the Sun God!

Thou nourisher of the world of men and beasts,
It is thy path that everywhere quenches the land's thirst:
Heavenly Courser, Thou, for Thy oncoming—
Worship to Thee!

The Egyptians called themselves *chemet,* sons of *chemi,* the black earth. They traced their origin and their name to the divine act that brought them the rich soil in which they sowed. Thus they became a nation bound more intimately than any other to their grain.

They took as great pains to plan as the god seemed to take before his slow, deliberate rising. They would use his earth so efficiently that no handbreadth would remain unfruitful. A network of canals provided assurance that even a small flood would irrigate all the land. Next to the beavers, the Egyptians became the best builders of dams the world had seen. Along with the Nile canals in Lower Egypt they built a system of storage reservoirs in Upper Egypt to retain and distribute the water. What land was not irrigated by these basins and canals the peasants watered by hand. They erected hoisting mechanisms, the most common of which was known as the *schaduf.* It resembled the device for drawing water out of a well, and consisted of a pole that moved between two fixed posts. On one end was the bucket; on the other a large lump of clay served as counterpoise. The device is still in use. With its aid bucketfuls of the precious Nile water are still hoisted some three yards and distributed over the sloping fields that do not lend themselves to irrigation.

Gay-Lussac, the nineteenth-century scientist, observed that the Nile mud lacks one of our chief fertilizing agents, phosphate. But the miracle wrought by the Nile water is ascribable not only to the organic substances deposited, it is equally ascribable to the chemical and physical changes produced by the floods. Under the influence of the sun the wet clay topsoil cracks open. The sun itself acts as a plow; the torn soil is aerated. When the flood recedes, it leaves the unworked soil as receptive to seed as is a cultivated field elsewhere.

In the Egyptian representations of agricultural labor we notice an air of frivolity, of ease. Natural fruitfulness seems to prevail; the labor of men is a small concomitant. But this, of course, is a false impression. Egyptian aesthetics forbade any depiction of effort as such. Egyptian art was a conquest of the material realm. The reality was quite different. Once the flood was past and the fields reappeared, the Egyptian farmer labored mightily to plow the muddy soil.

The Egyptian plow underwent few changes; it consisted of a long wooden share managed by two slightly curved handles. At the end of the long shaft was a crosspiece that was placed in front of the oxen's horns. Their weight bore down against this crosspiece, for the strength of the oxen resided in the muscles of the head and neck.

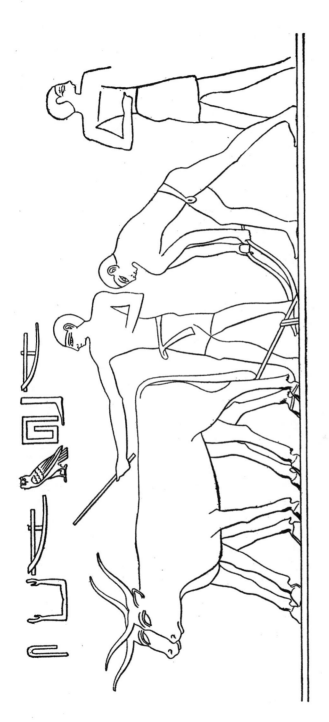

EGYPTIAN PLOWING
(Tomb painting)

Two men worked the plow. One threw his full weight upon the handles as he walked; the other drove the oxen. After each furrow the two changed places. The upturned clods were sticky and became baked together. It was therefore necessary to hoe vigorously to break up the clods after plowing.

Then came the sowing. The "grain scribe," like all scribes an important official in this bureaucratic state, where everything was a matter for record, inspected and made note of the amount of seed. Then sheep and swine were driven across the field to trample in the broadcast grain with their small, sharp hoofs. Later, when the grain burgeoned upon the stalk, the Egyptians cut the ears high above the ground with a short sickle. Unlike us, the Egyptians cut only the "fruit of the wheat," not the entire plant. There could be no scientific reason for leaving the plant, since all grains are annuals. This method of harvesting grain as clusters of grapes are harvested may, however, have been dictated by their emotional need to take no more of the plant than they needed for grinding and baking. Or was it that they rejected the straw because it made threshing more difficult?

The Egyptians were not familiar with the large sheaves we are accustomed to bind. They carried small, delicate sheaves to the threshing floor. The asses that carried the sheaves then trampled them. The flail, with its powerful leverage, they did not know.

Afterward the threshed grain and chaff were swept with a large wooden fork into a high heap. Then the women came to separate the wheat from the chaff by spreading the mixture out on small boards. A large, square sieve was also used for separating.

A small measure of grain was consecrated to the spirit of the fields, who protected the region; another measure was brought to the owner of the estate; and a modest festival was arranged in honor of the agricultural god, Min—the lord contributing beer to the festivities. The scribes of the granary and the grain measurers continued their work for a while, until the harvest was stored in the granary. This cylindrical mud structure was approximately five yards high and had two openings—one above, where workers standing on ladders emptied the sacks; and the other below, through which the grain could be removed. The lower opening was always closed to keep out rodents.

Such was the farmer's year. Little of the harvest was his own; often he complained:

> Shall we be granted no rest at all
> From bearing the grain and the white spelt?
> The granaries are already so full
> That the piles of corn spill out at the top,
> And the ships are already laden so low
> That they burst asunder and sink. . . .

§ 9

Who was the overlord of grain? He was the master of the greatest part of the soil, in whose person the state was incorporate. According to the custom of the ancient empire, as King Mena had developed it around 3000 B.C., the entire people, from the highest official to the lowest peasant, owed unconditional obedience to Pharaoh. Each paid for his existence through forced labor and taxes.

The word "taxation" was unknown; in its place a word meaning "accounting" was employed, because the size of the harvest, in the sense of the "count of the sheaves," formed the basis of the tax rate. An estimate of the harvest was made by the Nile surveyors, who were distributed everywhere throughout the land. These surveyors predetermined how large the harvest was to be by the extent of the flood. That is, the actual harvest was taxed, not the property owned, which was only reasonable, since the greater portion of the land belonged to Pharaoh.

The grain was paid into Pharaoh's treasury, whence it flowed to salaried officials and was used to maintain the royal household. Since the whole land of Egypt was Pharaoh's domain and since, by his ownership of the canals, he was also the granter of irrigation, he was able to organize these contributions with extreme strictness. We behold in ancient Egypt a large-scale agricultural industry, the "greatest manorial estate in history." The entire population filled the granaries of an omnipotent private estate, and these same granaries were in turn emptied to feed the entire people. Naturally, there were significant differences in the relation between influx and outflow. The poorest in the land, the serfs, contributed the largest part of the golden harvest to the royal granary; as the grain flowed back to the people, a considerable part of it was diverted to the "great ones of the land," to the governors of the provinces and other favorites of Pharaoh.

Thus every Egyptian lived in dependence upon the king, who indeed had to "give life" to every Egyptian. This fact was so obvious to all that no one felt spiritually oppressed by his serfdom. *Personal freedom had not yet been discovered;* personal lack of freedom, on the other hand, freed each individual from worry about his food.

Even the wealthy among the Egyptians were at best "administrators," or overseers. To keep these administrators in check, to remind them constantly that the state was the "house of Pharaoh," Pharaoh needed the officialdom. Officialdom in ancient Egypt was huge in numbers and impressive in powers. Indeed, all the bureaucracies of later date were modeled upon the Egyptian. This official machinery, however, was also a source of potential danger to the king. Independent princely houses sprang from the great administrative districts and waxed in might; it fell to Sesostris III, surnamed the Great (1860 B.C.), to restore the royal power by deposing all the old administrators and appointing new officials to the various districts. In the new empire he thus established every last foot of soil became the property of the Crown. Egypt now presented an appearance so astonishing to the author of the forty-seventh chapter of Genesis that he believed Joseph had *established* this agrarian constitution. With the exception of the fields of the temples, all the land belonged to Pharaoh. Since it was rented out to the peasants, they had to deliver a fifth of their crop to the Crown; the rest they were allowed to keep for their own needs and for seed.

In this new empire, the Egypt to which the Jews of the Bible came, the Crown shone with new radiance, and around the Crown like planets around the sun circled the officials, also radiant with reflected light. The scribe became more and more prominent. "He alone rules the world; he guides the labors of all people." As a tribute to his indispensability, the scribe was exempt from paying taxes.

It would have been fitting for this agrarian state (for this was what Egypt was) to heap all its honors upon the peasants. In fact it was the officials who received all the decorations and distinctions. When the "Great Warden of the Fields" in solemn audience presented to Amenhotep the "crop lists of the south and north" and respectfully reported: "The Nile was greater than it has been for thirty years," Pharaoh was moved to order that the official deliverer of the list be anointed before his eyes and adorned with ribbons.

Nevertheless, everything depended upon the peasant's year. The calendar was based upon it. Egypt's twelve months were divided into three seasons, each of one hundred and twenty days—not spring, summer, and winter, but "Flood," "Sprouting of the Seed," and "Harvest of Grain." The beginning of the flood was New Year's Day, which corresponded to the day when Sirius, the Dog Star, reappeared in the morning sky.

The Nile gave to its sons not only knowledge of the days, but also of the art of surveying. "The provinces of Old Egypt," writes Strabo, who traveled through Africa in 25 B.C., "were divided into districts; these in turn into localities; and the smallest segments of these parts were the tillable fields. They needed to be marked out with extreme exactitude, for the Nile River removes and adds land every year; it constantly changes the ground and also wipes out all signs that might serve to distinguish each man's property. Therefore the Egyptians must repeat their measurements each year. The art of surveying is said to have developed out of this need, as arithmetic was developed by the Phoenicians to serve trade."

Thus the Nile governed the science of Egypt. Egypt was in every sense "the gift of the Nile." The Nile gave the soil from which techniques and arts sprang. And one day the Nile gave the *art of baking bread,* an art

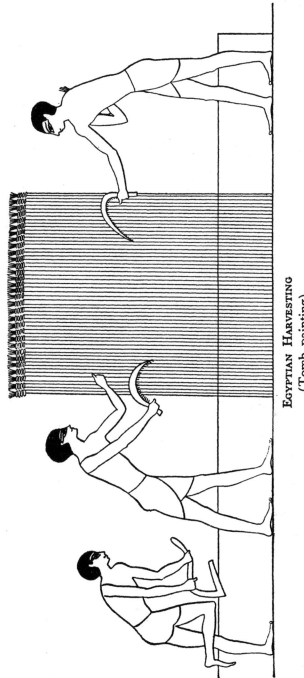

EGYPTIAN HARVESTING
(Tomb painting)

that at one stroke raised the Egyptians above the other peoples of the ancient world, who subsisted upon meal and flat breads.

§ 10

The inhabitant of the postglacial Swiss pile dwellings prepared his cereal food by roasting the grains on hot stones and mixing them with water to form a paste. If he pleased, he went a step further. He dangled a vessel of this porridge over the hot coals of his fire, or spread the paste on hot stones until it baked to a tough and hard sheet. This preserved it for a time—but also removed most of its taste.

Porridge and flat breads, flat breads and porridge, remained the menu for many centuries. Not of prehistoric man alone, but of even the civilized peoples of the ancient world for an astonishingly long time. But for the example of Egypt they would never have known real bread. Pliny says: *"Pulte non pane vixisse longo tempore Romanos manifestum* [For a distinctly long time the Romans lived on porridge, not on bread]." The Greeks, as urn paintings of the sixth century show, ate their "bread" in the form of flat cakes that were baked over wood coals and preserved rolled up, like a manuscript. The Germans at the time they encountered the Romans knew only oat groats; much later the Slavs had only their *kasha.* Even the Assyrians, the black-bearded contemporaries of the Egyptians, ate a breakfast of date syrup with hot slices of barley flat cakes.

But the people who, according to Herodotus, did "everything in a different fashion from ordinary mortals," made an enormous contribution to civilization by using their grain differently. While all other peoples feared lest their food decay, the Egyptians set aside their dough until it decayed and observed with pleasure the process that took place. This process was the process of fermentation.

Though fermentation has been known for thousands of years, its nature remained a mystery until the advent of modern chemistry. The air contains numberless bacteria waiting for nourishment, waiting for prey . . . Spores of yeast plants fell upon the traces of sugar contained in the mixture of Nile water and meal. They broke up this sugar into alcohol and carbonic acid. The bubbles of carbonic acid could not escape from the tenacious material; they remained imprisoned, puffing up the dough and loosening it. In the course of baking the acid and the alcohol did escape. The alcohol, so important for the making of beer, vanished completely. The carbonic acid left a trace of its presence in the porous texture of the bread.

Naturally, these chemical details were neither known nor named. They were not discovered until the seventeenth century, when Van

Leeuwenhoek saw yeast cells under his microscope. The Egyptians observed only the consequences: that when they baked their sour dough the resultant product was wholly different from anything that had been hitherto known. Moreover, this new product could not be baked in the coals of a fire. The Egyptians were led to invent the oven. They erected their cylindrical structures of brick made of Nile clay, the top narrowing to a cone. A flat partition divided the interior. The lower part had a firebox opening; the upper section a larger opening for the breads and for drawing off gases.

When they were about to bake, they took the soured dough from the bowl, salted it, and kneaded it thoroughly once more. They then spread bran at the bottom of the baking vessel, to keep the dough from touching it. With a scoop they distributed the fermenting dough, pushed the pan into the oven, and closed the oven door.

In awed admiration family and friends stood around to watch. In this chamber grew something which so far was the product of their familiar labors but which they had now entrusted to supernatural forces over which they had no control. The master of the household warned against untimely opening of the oven. But no one obeyed; the miraculous chamber was continually opened and inspected to see whether the bread was ready. Friends offered advice. One.suggested that it was needless to obtain the yeast from the air; a piece of the old sour dough could be saved in order to "implant" the leavening in the new dough. This would sour the dough more quickly and thoroughly. The suggestion proved valuable —and from that day on "reproductive sour dough" was as sacredly preserved in Egyptian households as was the hearth fire among other peoples. They dared not lose the precious primal stuff of baking, the stuff that "raised" the bread.

Who can trace all the inventions that followed upon the great primary discovery? For example, they learned to mix poppy seed, sesame, and camphor with the dough. Before long they had fifty varieties of bread. But they would have been sufficiently proud of one alone. The thing they took out of the oven hardly resembled what they had put into it. Flour, water, salt, and yeast had danced around in the roaring fire. When, finally, they emerged, they appeared as something entirely new. Indeed what had the puffy, crumbly inside or the dark, fragrant crust to do with these simple substances? Spirit hands had been at work. This was the kind of magic in which the Egyptians delighted.

"The. wise priests of Egypt," wrote Plutarch in his essay on Isis and Osiris, "call the black earth 'chemia.' " Just as unknown substances are mingled in this black earth that was once the gift of the Nile to form a soil of ultimate fertility, so known substances are coupled within the oven according to an unknown law. The oven was the womb of chemistry; for the Egyptians it was also the first magic cauldron. Curiously enough, while the other nations' gods had forbidden their people to employ magic, that "blasphemous infraction of the laws of causation," its use was expressly permitted to the Egyptians. Thoth, their monkey-headed god, had himself written a book of magic which was preserved upon a remote island, locked up in six stout chests. The Egyptians persistently searched for this island, although they already possessed a wealth of magic formulas.

For thousands of years the world trembled before the magical gifts of the Egyptians. As late as the tenth century A.D. Suidas, the Byzantine lexicographer, recounted that Emperor Diocletian, in the year 296, after having suppressed an Egyptian uprising, ordered all the Egyptians' chemistry books to be burned. Undoubtedly this struck them at their most sensitive point and destroyed the source of their power. In this same tenth century the Arabian author, Aln-Eddin, wrote that the pyramids had undoubtedly been "chemical.laboratories and the hieroglyphs alchemistic texts."

All this had its beginnings in the harmless oven. But the oven, with its uncanny resemblance to a woman's pregnant abdomen, was perhaps not so harmless after all. After thousands of years the comparison has remained. The German folk saying remarks, "The oven will soon fall in" of a woman who is close to confinement; and of a cripple, "He ought to be baked over."

No, the oven was far from innocuous. It was invented by a people who were also not innocuous; whose priests were chemists and who spent their days mixing, pouring, brewing, reckoning.

§ 11

It is curious how well informed we are of the facts of everyday life in Egypt. We have far scantier knowledge of the technique of baking which prevailed in English courts so many centuries later, but thousands of details of commonplace life on the Nile are familiar to us.

We owe this knowledge to Egyptian tombs and the murals within them. The historian Diodorus remarks of the Egyptians that they considered life short and death long; therefore they constructed their dwelling houses like temporary summer cabins and their tombs as permanent homes. Against the breakwater of these tombs time crashed ineffectually.

While modern man recalls his dead kin only on religious holidays, the lot of the dead was a daily concern to the Egyptians, for the dead as well as the living had their daily life. Popular belief had several versions of where and how he lived this life. Possibly the deceased had been transported to the faint stars beyond the Milky Way; or possibly he sat upon the tomb in the shape of an innocent bird and watched when one brought offerings to him. It was impossible to know whether he had crawled as a serpent into some hole in the earth or had been accepted as a son by the sun god and was helping to rule the heavens.

These, however, were only transitional phases. The goal of every dead man was to return to life. Therefore his shell, his body, was to be guarded against decay. It was treated with natron, mineral pitch, and resin. The limbs were wrapped in linen; over the face a mask of plaster was pressed to preserve the features, then the mummy was laid on his left side like a sleeping man—as though to protect the heart—and closed in a casket upon which a door had to be painted! The purpose of the embalming was to insure that the *ka*, the life principle, which had left the dead man, would find a body fully habitable when it returned. The devout Egyptian thus had two beings to tend: the body of the dead man and his ka. It followed from this that the life spirit (we prefer not to call it soul), if it were not to wither away, must be given the same care that a living human being would receive. Above all, the ka needed nourishment. Naturally, the great, new invention—bread—must be given to him, and the wealthy Egyptian also contributed wine and meat.

The Egyptians were constantly beset by the fear that their dead would go hungry. They called one of the dark islands of the sky the "field of viands," conceiving it as traversed by streams which, like the canals of the Nile, were opened at the time of the flood. Here, they believed, grew the "grain of the dead," which was reaped, threshed, and ground like the wheat of the living.

Presumably this field would provide for the dead. But what if the dead could not *find* the field? It was more prudent to supply him with provisions. The multitude of possibilities, the fear of committing some mistake, some omission, made the living eternally anxious. It is to this anxiety that we owe our knowledge of the minutiae of their lives.

It is true that the realistic scenes of labor that were painted on the walls of the tombs seem to have been intended principally for the amusement of the dead. They were a picture book for the ka, to while away the tedium of his stay. But most human activities have diverse motives. Had the Egyptians known with certainty where the realm of the dead was, where the dead actually went, their cult of the dead would have been simpler. But they did not know, and consequently each of their actions in caring for the dead sprang from a confusion of purposes. The painting in the tombs served not only to amuse, but also to ward off danger. There was the unfortunate possibility that the dead man (who daily made great journeys) might fall into the power of evil spirits, might become involved in other worldly wars and sieges, might be imprisoned or torn to pieces. To protect him from such vicissitudes, a "passport" was needed—the record of who he was. The tomb paintings supplied this record by refreshing his memory. "I am the ropemaker So-and-So. I know all about making ropes; I can explain each step in their manufacture. I can even tell jokes about my trade—how my apprentices brawled among themselves on the last day of each month. I may well demand that in the other world I be treated as befits a ropemaker. . . ."

Egyptian tomb paintings were also effective magic to preserve the dead man's identity; to, as it were, confirm it. To this motif the paintings in the kings' tombs added the capitalist element, for they counted up the king's

THE BAKERY OF KING RAMSES
(Egyptian tomb painting)

possessions, what he could lay claim to in the other world, permanent riches which he in no way forfeited by his temporary residence in the grave. It was as one of the king's assets that the *royal bakery* was painted on the walls of tombs.

We see first two men with long poles energetically trampling the dough. They seem to be dancing; probably they are working in rhythm, using the poles partly to keep their balance upon the yielding dough, partly to jump higher. (Centuries later Herodotus mocked a people "who knead dough with their feet, mud with their hands.") Next we see water-bearers carrying amphorae to a table where an apprentice begins tumbling the dough back and forth with his hands. The bottom of a baking dish is heated, and molded dough is placed upon the dish with the aid of large tongs. Next, another assistant arranges or turns the dough in the pan with the aid of a shovel-like tool. Near by a large oven is being filled with fresh fuel. This serves for the smaller molds, which are not handled as carefully as the large ones. The next pictures show that care is taken to make the small breads of equal size, so that all will be thoroughly baked.

Thus a dead king has given us a detailed report of the life of his meanest subjects. As for the lordly dead, it was required that they continue to lead a lordly life in their journeyings in the hereafter. And so the royal bakery accompanied them. The fact that Pharaoh received bread (a thousand breads a day a magic numerical formula informs us) linked him to the poorest of his people, all of whom were granted at least bread, water, and sacrificial barley.

The Egyptians were concerned lest their offerings of food to the dead would be stolen by spirits or destroyed by magic. What if the bread should wickedly commence to burn as soon as the dead man lifted it to eat? It was well to provide the deceased with spells to meet such emergencies. If, for example, an enemy challenged his right to bread, he must reply (in the words of the famous *Book of the Dead*):

> I am a man who has bread in Heliopolis,
> My bread is in Heaven with the Sun God,
> My bread is on earth with Keb.
> The bark of evening and of morning
> Brings me the bread that is my meat
> From the house of the Sun God.

After such a recital the dead man could not be denied his bread.

§ 12

In the ancient world the Egyptians were known as the "bread eaters." The term expressed almost equal portions of admiration and contempt. Certainly it expressed also a considerable portion of astonishment, for bread was not an incidental food but the principal food of all Egyptians. The lower classes in Egypt lived almost exclusively on bread. To this day their descendants tear open their round breads and stuff the hollow center with whatever additional food Allah has blessed them with—vegetables, chopped meat, or fish.

This "manufactured" product, bread, was much more than Egypt's principal food. It was a cultural unit and a unit of measure. "Number of breads" signified wealth; the ovens throughout the land were virtual mints. Flour baked in an oven eventually became the coinage of the realm. For hundreds of years wages were paid in breads, the average peasant receiving three breads and two jugs of beer a day. (The legendary hero, Dedi, on the other hand, received 500 breads and 100 jugs of beer daily.) "Do not eat bread when another is standing near without holding out your hand to offer some to him," instructed the Egyptian book of etiquette for school children. It was the foulest of sins to refuse a beggar bread. "In my time I gave bread to all," declared a soul in the realm of the dead, when his heart was placed upon the balance.

Bread's function as money made it the root of many—if not all—evils. Failure to pay breads on time was an early demeanor. Not a few letters have come down to us accusing the great lords or the priests of giving the bread late or not at all ("although they promised us that we would receive the bread"). A curiously modern story dates from the times of Ramses IX (1154–53 B.C.) A troop of laborers who had been sent to work in the country received fat and beer, but no bread. Thereupon they began "to lie down in their homes"—that is, they refused to work. A month later, when they were again refused their ration of bread, "they lay down" again, and sent petitioners to Thebes, the provincial capital. Here the strikers met with success; the governor gave them the bread that the private entrepreneur had twice refused. The leader of the "workers' delegation" made a significant entry in the troop's pay-roll book: "Today we were at last given the bread, but we had to contribute two chests of bread to the fanbearer." Probably the fanbearer was one of the governor's officials, who levied his customary bribe.

We have very exact knowledge of the payment of priests. A temple official received annually 360 jugs of beer, 900 fine wheat breads, and 36,000 flat breads roasted in coals. He also complained bitterly of the insufficient quantity of bread. During the reign of Ramses III, who was Pharaoh for thirty years, the king delivered almost six million sacks of grain and seven million loaves of bread to the temple. This was his largest gift, although the number of geese, fish, oxen, and legumes delivered was by no means small.

This whole land of Egypt has the aspect of one long oven whose function it was to supply both living and dead with nourishment. (And the brewery was not neglected, for yeast—in the proverbial phrase—is the midwife both of bread and beer.)

"Bread is a generous gift of nature, a food that can be replaced by no other. When we fall sick, our appetite for bread deserts us last of all; and the moment we recover the appetite we have shown a symptom of recovery. Bread is suitable to every time of the day, every age of life, and every temperament. It improves other foods, is the father of good and bad digestion. Eaten with meat or other foods, it loses none of its delight. It is so perfectly adapted to men that we turn our hearts to it almost as soon as we are born and never tire of it to the hour of our death."

These words sound as though they were copied from a medical papyrus of ancient Egypt. In fact they were written by the Frenchman, Parmentier, in 1772. The mood is significant, for if the Egyptians had not invented bread four thousand years before Christ, the French nation would certainly have done so. The two peoples are alike in their worship of bread, as in their general talent for daring and successful experiments in the chemistry of the cuisine.

Like the French, the Egyptians also wished their bread to be food for the eyes. On the walls of their tombs they delighted to paint not only the technique of baking, but the multitudinous shapes of their breads. What law or what wantonness governed these shapes? We see round breads; cubical breads with domed tops that resemble small trunks; high, conical breads like the woven straw hats of Mexican peasants; braided breads; breads in the form of birds and fishes; and breads like pyramids—miniature reproductions of the mysterious tombs of the kings.

Perhaps, however, no mystery was intended in these reproductions. Our traditional tendency to read metaphysical significances into the most commonplace acts of the Egyptians may be leading us astray. Shall we not rather ascribe to the Egyptians a hankering for pure amusement? The Egyptian child, molding houses and animals out of the Nile mud, imagined himself the Pharaoh, the owner of the world. The Egyptian adult, eating the clay of the universe, his bread, in many shapes, could also enjoy possession of all the world's goods. As the Chinese, with no symbolic intention, carved endlessly the images of what they saw in the world of nature in soapstone and jade, so the ancient Egyptians may have sculptured in bread. Such an amusement would be in keeping with the inclination to the rococo and the *précieux* that flourishes in many nations as a result of a long epoch of peace. An image of the divine cow, Hathor, goddess of fertility, found among Egyptian bread molds, may be of no more august significance than a little model of the Eiffel Tower standing in the show window of a Paris jeweler.

Let us, for the moment, imagine that our civilization should vanish like the Egyptian. Some future archaeologist, finding a mold or painting representing some product of our bakeries—say a snail roll—would be struck with astonishment. How mysterious it would seem. For even in nature the windings of the snail are a subject for deep thought. Of what use to the snail is this involved helix, this Archimedes' spiral? In shipmaking, in vehicles, the helix is sensible, for it cuts through resistance. But it is quite inexplicable why the slowest of creatures, the snail, should carry a shell shaped like a corkscrew. Now the archaeologist discovers that twentieth-century man baked rolls in the shape of snails. What could we have been symbolizing? Our love of slowness? Or our love of speed? Was the spiral one of our gods?

But perhaps the archaeologists of the future will be wiser than those of the present and conclude that we took a childlike pleasure in pretty forms. . . .

"We must reckon a great deal on our child customers," a baker once

said to me. "The children bring the parents. Whenever we bake something new the children scent it. Even if it's just a couple of raisins that
we put in a roll like eyes in a face. . . ."

ISRAEL: IN THE SWEAT OF THY FACE

I will insist that the Hebrews have done more to civilize men than
any other nation.

JOHN ADAMS

§ 13

THE PEOPLE OF ISRAEL learned to know what bread was through their
intercourse with the Egyptians. The Bible recounts how the scene un-
folded when the Hebrews and the Egyptians, the shepherds and the tillers
of the soil, for the first time stood face to face. Joseph, who had become
grand vizier of the Egyptian Pharaoh, sends for his nomadic kinsfolk and
instructs them in rules of conduct. If Pharaoh should ask them their oc-
cupation, they were to reply cautiously that they were keepers of cattle—
but from their youth; that, as it were, they had never learned any other
trade. For, as Joseph explains, "every shepherd is an abomination unto
the Egyptians."

Joseph does not explain why the Egyptians abhorred pastoral peoples.
This peasant folk could not have been annoyed merely at the nomads'
love of animals. Pharaoh, too, loved his cattle and preferred the fat kine
to the lean; and the gods of Egypt wore animals' heads. Perhaps their
abhorrence rested upon the obstinate conviction that all shepherds practice sodomy—a fantasy that persisted into modern times. In 1499, in the
war between the Swabian peasants and the Swiss herdsmen, the Swabians
placed cows before their battle line and dressed them in women's hats
and skirts. The Swiss, infuriated by the taunt, swept down upon the South
German army and utterly routed them.

In any case, the Egyptians considered the pastoral tribes unclean; they
looked down upon them as present-day Egyptians look down upon the
Hamites of the interior of Africa, the Dinka. Of these people Schweinfurth writes: "Everything that derives from cattle is considered pure and
noble by the Dinka tribes. The manure, burned to a white ash, is used as
bedding or is smeared upon the face as an ornamental paste. The urine
serves as washing water or as a substitute for cooking salt, which is scarce
among all African Negroes. . . ." To be sure, these practices would have
been wildly inconceivable to the Hebrews or the other Semitic nomads,

with their strict sanitary laws. But Joseph, who knew his Egyptians well, wished to be prudent. As a statesman he might well fear that his kinship with keepers of cattle would reflect upon himself. He took care that his father and brothers should not come too closely in contact with the bread-eating Egyptians; he settled them in Goshen, a province containing a great deal of pasture land.

It must have astounded the Hebrews, occasional tillers of the soil as they were, to find a people who devoted their entire day to the preparation of bread. The Hebrews learned to bake bread in Egypt; but they would not have done so had they remained shepherds. Bread requires permanence and patience. Abraham and his people, who lived in tents, had stores of flour—for a small amount of agriculture is possible in a nomadic society—but they possessed no ovens. The Egyptian ovens were made of brick and belonged to a permanent dwelling. There were, to be sure, other ovens that were portable, but they were extremely heavy—three-foot-high pots of stone or metal. A shepherd people, living in tents and hastily built huts, could not be bothered transporting such ovens through the land. The Jews baked no bread until they were settled upon their own soil.

From the habits of Bedouin tribes in the desert we can surmise how the Hebrews ate their grain in earlier times. Either they parched the grain, like the reapers in the Book of Ruth, or they set flat cakes to bake between layers of slow-burning camel dung, as we are told in the Book of Ezra. If they had a hearth, they roasted the dough in the ashes; but the result was still a flat cake and not bread. Similarly, the *panis subcineraria* of Roman armies on the march—bread baked *under* the coals—was also not real bread. A swiftly moving army had no time to allow dough to sour.

So it was with the Jews while they remained herdsmen. When, however, they began baking real breads, they baked very well. Their best bread was of wheat, made from a specially sifted flour (*kemach soleth,* the "essence of flour"). This flour was chosen for sacrifices to Jehovah; it was also used in making bread for the rich. Another excellent bread was baked of white spelt. Barley was used only by the poor; it also served as horse feed. The Jews were wont to behave as snobbishly toward barley as the Romans toward oats. There was some justification for this attitude; in order to make barley flour tasty, ground lentils, beans, and millet had to be added.

In the early history of the Jews the housewife herself tended the oven, perhaps with the help of one daughter. This we read in Genesis. But in Judges we find the larger households employing maidservants. Among the Jews baking was always done by women. Every family in Israel possessed its own oven; only in times of famine did two families bake in one oven.

As the Jews became more settled, became established as city dwellers, the men took over the baking. A natural division of labor gave rise to a new trade: that of the baker. It was not long before the baker's character fell into disrepute; metaphorically, at least, the prophet Hosea scolds the baker who cheats his customers. He "sleepeth all the night" and in the morning the bread "burneth as a flaming fire." In the age of Christ the trade of baker was enormously widespread. Every city in Palestine had its baker, as we learn from Josephus. Christ's extensive knowledge of the technique of baking strikes us as something remarkable. But in reality such specialized knowledge was not unusual, for all trades in the Orient were practiced virtually on the street. Jesus, like Socrates, liked to watch all artisans and learn from their precision. The city of Jerusalem possessed something not to be found in small country towns: a bakers' street. All the masters of the trade were located in one quarter. These masters were, however, more merchants than manufacturers, for the prophet Jeremiah speaks of a "tower of furnaces." Apparently Jerusalem had a "bread factory" to which the master bakers brought their flour to be baked into the breads they later sold in their shops.

The breads were round; they resembled flat stones slightly raised in the center, and were scarcely thicker than a finger. They were so small that at least three breads were necessary for one man's meal. When Abigail entertained David and his men, we find two hundred breads mentioned, but only two jugs of wine. This proportion bespeaks the smallness of the breads rather than any temperance on the part of David. The Jews' bread was, in point of size, rather like the modern roll.

If we keep in mind how flat these breads were, we will understand why the Jews *broke* their bread rather than cut it. There was no religious significance in their reluctance to touch their bread with the blade of a knife. It never occurred to the Jews to consider their bread as an organic living or supernatural being; this was the historic contribution of Christianity. To the Jews bread was one food among many others, although a well-beloved food. But men could live without bread; the story of the "manna" expressly stressed this to them. God was above caring for His creatures by sowing and reaping; if He chose, He fed His people forty years in the desert on a food that was *not* bread. . . . Nevertheless, the Jews in the desert so longed for their bread that they even debated a return to Egypt, the "house of bondage." This is an indication of how indispensable bread had become to them.

In Canaan, however, bread was not only their own food, but the food of their God, Jehovah. It was, to be sure, a very special bread. Thereby hangs a tale.

§ 14

The Bible tells us that the children of Israel departed from Egypt in such haste that they had no time to finish the preparation of their bread in the Egyptian fashion.

And the people took their dough before it was leavened, their kneading-troughs being bound up in their clothes upon their shoulders.

And they went forth out of the land in great haste.

And they baked unleavened cakes of the dough which they brought forth out of Egypt, for it was not leavened; because they were thrust out of Egypt, and could not tarry, neither had they prepared for themselves any victual.

Then Moses spoke unto the people:

Remember this day, in which ye came out from Egypt, out of the house of bondage; for by strength of hand the Lord brought you out from this place: there shall no leavened bread be eaten.

The day was to be celebrated each year in the week of the Passover:

Seven days thou shalt eat unleavened bread, and in the Seventh day shall be a feast to the Lord.

Unleavened bread shall be eaten seven days; and there shall be no leavened bread be seen with thee, neither shall there be leaven seen with thee in all thy quarters.

And thou shalt shew thy son in that day, saying, This is done because of that which the Lord did unto me when I came forth out of Egypt.

And it shall be for a sign unto thee upon thine hand, and for a memorial between thine eyes, that the Lord's law may be in thy mouth: for with a strong hand hath the Lord brought thee out of Egypt.

Thou shalt therefore keep this ordnance in his season from year to year.

The prohibition against eating leavened bread appears, then, to be no more than an "aid to memory." Every year some of the circumstances of the exodus from Egypt were to be reproduced. This seems quite obvious —and is quite wrong. The ritual was indeed more than an aid to memory.

"The concept of a memorial celebration is quite foreign to the Penta-teuch," declares the religious historian, Oscar Goldberg. Moreover, the custom of eating matzoth was older than Moses. When Lot was visited by the angels, he offered them unleavened bread, although he dwelt in a settled house and had time to finish baking his bread. Since Lot lived several hundred years before the Exodus, he could not very well have been celebrating it.

The seven-day period of eating unleavened bread which God and Moses imposed upon the Jews could, therefore, not have been a memorial of the flight from Egypt. This was essentially an etiological explanation of the custom. Of what, then, was it a memorial? Lot's behavior gives us the clue. At any time during the year and upon all occasions the profane yeast bread, baked in the Egyptian oven, could be.eaten; but in the presence of God or His emissaries, only sacred bread could be eaten—cakes that had not been made with sour dough.

God Himself would eat no other bread. When Jehovah received the offerings of his people in the tabernacle, he permitted only unleavened breads to be placed upon the altar. We hear again and again of this prohibition. Scornfully, the prophet Amos cries: "Offer a,sacrifice of thanksgiving of that which.is leavened." But why did God insist upon this? Did he wish to be reminded of something?

The solution is suggested by the fact that Jehovah, the God of the Jews, was worshiped in a tabernacle—that is to say, a. tent. This tent.had no resting place. The God of a pastoral, nomadic people disdained to eat the bread of settled peasants, bread that took a day to bake; he preferred, as more fitting, the hastily prepared flat cake of the Bedouins and warriors. God was unaccustomed to life in a fixed dwelling, in a cedarn temple. When David wished to build such a temple for him, God called upon Nathan the prophet and gave him these words to transmit to King David:

Thus saith the Lord, Shalt thou build me an house for me to dwell in?
Whereas I have not dwelt in any house since the time that I brought up the children of Israel out of Egypt, even to this day, but have walked in a tent and in a tabernacle.
In all the places wherein I have walked with all the children of Israel, spake I a word with any of the tribes of Israel, saying, Why build ye not me an house of cedar?

In the distant future, God declares, when the people of Israel "dwell in a place of their own, and move no more," will he desire a "house for my name."

The Jews had by now become thoroughly urbanized; by insisting upon unleavened bread it would seem that their God compelled them to flatter him, to stress that he was in reality the God of poor shepherds. It would appear to be the impulse of the rich man who remembers with pride his low origins.

But this, too, is an incorrect interpretation. Comparative religion has disclosed that in Rome also the *flamen. dialis,* the high priest of Jupiter, was forbidden to touch *farinam fermento imbutam* (flour mingled with leavening). The Romans had never been nomads; they were always farmers and cityfolk. The chief of their gods had no reason to insist upon their observing nomadic traditions in regard to the food they offered him. That such a custom should prevail among these two peoples argues for some common cause.

§ 15

The prohibition against bringing leavening into the presence of God is in fact one of those *taboos* that assert themselves in the cultures of primitive peoples. Something that is taboo may not be touched without unfortunate consequences. The anthropologist, Northcote W. Thomas, writes in the Encyclopedia Britannica: "Persons and things which are regarded as taboo may be compared to objects charged with electricity; they are the seat of a tremendous power which is transmissible by contact, and may be liberated with destructive effect if the organisms which provoke its discharge are too weak to resist it." Such a discharge was provoked by any man who brought leavening into the presence of God.

For God abhorred leavening. He rejected it just as he rejected certain animals and parts of animals in sacrificial rites. And when we read that Jehovah demands the death penalty for those Jews who eat bread or leavening during Passover week, it becomes apparent that the prohibition is not merely a matter of custom or of remembrance. The death penalty for a mere breach of custom would have been too disproportionate. The eating of leavened bread in the immediate presence of God (spatially speaking, in the tabernacle, or, temporally speaking, in the Passover week) was not a mere breach of custom; it was an infraction of a living principle, of a natural religious law; and such an infraction would injure the entire people.

Is not such a taboo concept a question of pure imagination? Frazer, who has explored to the roots of these matters in his *Taboo and the Perils of the Soul,* gives the ultimate answer to this question: "The danger, however, is not less real because it is imaginary; imagination acts upon man as *really* as does gravitation and may kill him as certainly as a dose of prussic acid." In the realm of belief the only criteria are effectuality or ineffectuality; faith is capable of producing profound changes in the make-up of the physical world. There is a strong similarity between the laws of religion and the laws of physics. Just as we do not know the causes of gravity or electricity, though we are familiar with their functions, so we do not know the rational cause for many taboos. But they operate among those who believe in them.

Chemistry holds it a mystery that two substances violently avoid each other. We see and hear the explosion, but we cannot determine the reason for the repulsion. Similarly, many taboos remain a riddle. However, there is an explanation for the taboo that prevented the Jew from bringing leavening into the presence of his God—the same leavening that he ate without qualms throughout the year.

The sin offering was considered food for God. Meat that was sacrificed to God was held palatable for only two days; on the third day it must be burned. This law also applied to vegetables. Now sourness and rottenness were one and the same thing. How could one offer God something that was in a state of decay, of fermentation, of dissolution? The scientific distinction between fermentation of dough and decay of meat was of no matter here. Transformation through the medium of bacteria (had the Jews known what this was) could not have appeared attractive to them; above all, they could never have considered the leavened dough as "living." With the Egyptian, as we know, it was otherwise; he worshiped endless change, the metamorphosis of all things. Therefore he paid homage to the transmuting sour dough. The Jew's sense of cleanliness and purity prohibited him from offering his God matter in dissolution. Consequently, he never brought milk as an offering, though other Semitic peoples, like the Carthaginians and the Arabians, did not hesitate to do this. Allah loved the yeast bacillus; more modern than Jehovah, he considered it not as a destroyer of life but as a giver of life. The Mohammedans in the Caucasus boast that Mohammed himself taught them to make kefir of milk, and their favorite drink for more than a thousand years has been this fermented milk. But the Hebrews had an aversion for sourness, the mysterious concomitant and the visible principle of dissolution. Instead they honored salt, the principle of preservation. All sacrifices were strewn with salt because it was healing and purifying. Even newborn infants were rubbed with salt.

What was astonishing about all this was that the Hebrew freely ate the bread he would not offer his God. He found it quite simple to maintain his life upon two planes. There was a sacred bread and a profane bread. Their coeval existence invited speculative thinking and sharpened his delight in drawing fine distinctions.

§ 16

The Hebrew had an attitude of remarkable sobriety toward the bread he himself ate. He did, to be sure, recall his God when he beheld it. And each day as he broke bread he spoke the *baracha,* the blessing of the bread: "Blessed art Thou, O Lord our God, who bringest forth bread out of the ground. . . ." The Protestant theologian, Friedrich Heiler, the historian of prayer, remarks that it was precisely this thanksgiving that elevated the Israelite above other cultures "wherein men believed that by sacrificial offerings they had coerced God into fulfilling their wishes, and consequently had no further need to be grateful to Him."

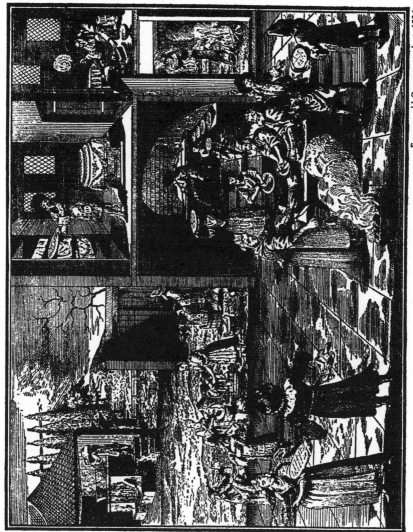

JEWS PREPARING MATZOTH

From an old German woodcut, 1726.

The Jew gave thanks for his bread; on the other hand, the sentiments of the Christian peoples of the Middle Ages, who always spoke of their "dear bread" or even of "holy bread," were quite foreign to him. In the Jewish writings, both sacred and profane, we find not a single remark analogous to the Egyptian "oven worship." The proverbial phrase, "the oven is the mother," which came to Byzantium from the Orient and thence proceeded to Russia, where it is still in use, would have been incomprehensible to the Jew. Indeed, he must have found the Romans ridiculous for worshiping an oven goddess, Fornax, who was included in the circle of *deae matres,* mother goddesses. He must also have taken exception to the Greek doctrine that men had lived like wild beasts before the discovery of agriculture. (The Greeks represented this tradition in the Eleusinian Festival in honor of Demeter: creatures wearing animal hides appeared upon the stage and threw stones at one another.)

The Hebrews, too, had their harvest celebrations. But why should they honor the fruits of the fields so excessively? A Jew striving for truth could but smile sadly when he saw how the neighboring peoples exaggerated the importance of agriculture, for he knew better. In the first book of the Bible it was clearly written that agriculture was a *curse.* How joyously had Adam and Eve lived in Paradise, needing only to hold out their hands to receive nourishment from the generous trees. But then man sinned—and was expressly condemned to till the soil.

No other mythology is so realistic. No other dared to say that the necessity of labor is a curse. Every other religion forebore to do so because the consequence would inevitably have been great social despair.

Was plowing and sowing a curse? Zarathustra-Serdusht, who gave the Persians their religion, taught precisely the opposite. Of Masye, the first man, he says:

The creator showed them the sowing of corn and declared: This is thine, O Masye, which is an ox; thine, too, is this corn; and thine those other appliances; henceforth thou shouldst know them well.

Thereupon he commanded the angel Hadisch to feed the first man; Hadisch would in the future be his guardian.

We see that Ahura-Mazda, the God of the Persians, refrained from telling his first man of the torment that lay sleeping in the soil. Only the Hebrew religion—trusting to the courage, the endurance, and the profound reasonableness of mankind—dared to relate that Jehovah spoke these words to Adam:

Cursed is the ground for thy sake; in sorrow shalt thou eat of it all the days of thy life;

Thorns also and thistles shall it bring forth to thee; and thou shalt eat the herb of the field;

In the sweat of thy face shalt thou eat bread, till thou return unto the ground; for out of it wast thou taken: for dust thou art, and unto dust shalt thou return.

How chilling this must have been! Was this knowledge not sufficient to lead every man to drop his hand from the plow and to deny all life? Yet there was a religion that viewed the lot of man even more pessimistically: the Buddhist religion. The Buddhist views the necessity of creating the bread that one eats as the height of suffering. The *Fo-Sho-Hing-Tsan-King* of Dharmaraksha (ca. A.D. 420), the Chinese life of Buddha, narrates:

As he proceeded to the gardens from the city, the road was well prepared, smooth, and wide, the trees were bright with flowers and fruit, his heart was joyous, and forgetful of its care.

Now by the roadside as he beheld the ploughmen, plodding along the furrows, and the writhing worms, his heart again was moved with piteous feeling, and anguish pierced his soul afresh;

To see those labourers at their toil, struggling with painful work, their bodies bent, their hair dishevelled, the dripping sweat upon their faces, their persons fouled with mud and dust;

The ploughing oxen, too, bent by the yokes, their lolling tongues and gaping mouths; the nature of the prince, loving, compassionate, his mind conceived most poignant sorrow,

And nobly moved to sympathy, he groaned with pain; then stooping down he sat upon the ground, and watched this painful scene of suffering; reflecting on the ways of birth and death!

"Alas!" he cried, "for all the world! how dark and ignorant, void of understanding!" And then to give his followers chance of rest, he bade them each repose where'er they list;

Whilst he beneath the shadow of a Gambu tree, gracefully seated, gave himself to thought. He pondered on the fact of life and death, inconstancy, and endless progress to decay.

To carry this to its conclusion meant the end of culture—culture in the sense that it is identical with tilling. If agriculture is synonymous with such poignant suffering, men must give it up, must return to the status of hermits, nourishing themselves upon the few berries they can pluck without pain. And this was what Buddhism taught.

But the Jews responded differently. They did not abandon culture. For culture's sake they took up the burden of pain; instead of fleeing it, they bravely admitted it into their life and their consciousness.

For the bitter knowledge could not be dismissed, could not be lived down. What must the Jews have thought when they saw Egyptian pictures of plowmen and reapers laboring with movements like the movements of a dance? Did God love the tillers of the soil? When the sons of Adam brought offerings to Him—Abel took them from his herds; Cain brought the fruit of the ground—the Lord took the firstlings of Abel's flock, "but unto Cain and his offering he had not respect." Why? How so? We do not know. Apparently the God of the Jews did not love those who tilled the soil. Not until after the Flood did He take pity upon them and make a covenant with Noah and his descendants.

I will not again curse the ground any more for man's sake; for the imagination of man's heart is evil from his youth; neither will I again smite any more every thing living, as I have done.

While the earth remaineth, seedtime and harvest, and cold and heat, and summer and winter, and day and night shall not cease.

But, in spite of this vow, God still did not extravagantly favor the tiller of the soil. The ear of wheat *changed*. Where previously the ears were large and filled with grain far down the stalk, God now made the ears smaller. After the Flood he placed the grain only upon the topmost part of the stalk! . . . The Jews did not write this version of the ancient curse into the Thora. But they remarked upon it among themselves, until at last it was included in the Talmud, whence it made its way into Polish legend. In any case, it had been indelibly engraved upon the hearts of men that they were condemned to till the soil. The work was sour, not sweet. The sweat of man's face dripped upon the bread when it was plowed, sown, reaped, threshed, ground, and eaten. Let man keep sourness from his God; it was sufficient that he himself had soured his bread with sweat.

Acting precisely upon this knowledge, the Hebrews erected the soundest bulwarks against the "pain of labor" that have ever been devised by man. These were the agrarian laws of Moses. If working the earth was a curse of God, let it not also become a fouler curse among men—this was the intention of the laws. Nine hundred years before Solon, the Greek, and thirteen hundred years before the Roman Gracchus, the great Jewish leader, prohibited agrarian usury.

§ 17

Moses, the legendary hero of the Jews, had been brought up in the Egyptian court. He was well acquainted with the profound moral weaknesses of the agrarian system under the Pharaohs. The soil belonged not to the people, but to a single man; and one third of the land was owned by the Church. Eternal servitude was the consequence. Such servitude might satisfy the Egyptians, for it assured them work and bread. But it did not satisfy the Hebrews. They were a people of nomadic shepherds who loved the land less than their own freedom of movement. If they consented to qualify this freedom, they certainly did not wish to cultivate their fields as servants of a king or a priesthood; they would have their own land.

This, however, was not simple. Moses needed only to look about him in the world to see how difficult it was. As a well-educated man, he must certainly have known how the other Oriental empires were organized. Were conditions better anywhere outside of Egypt? What, for example, was the situation in Babylon, which, since 1914 B.C., had been governed by the laws of Hammurabi? The land belonged to the King, the Church, or to very rich bankers whose policy was to allow the peasants no peace. Imprisonment for debt was a commonplace. To be sure, Hammurabi's code ostensibly had been decreed so that "the strong shall not harm the weak, and widow and orphan shall be consoled." But this was written only in the preamble. In reality, the law was hard indeed on the weak; of two hundred and eighty sections, sixty deal with the rights of landowners. Such a code could provide the Hebrews with no suitable precedent on which to found their corpus juris.

The Mosaic constitution was extremely wise. If every Jew in Canaan had been granted an equal portion of land, with free disposition over it (that is, with the right to buy and to sell), the rich cattle owners would very swiftly have obtained the land of the poorer Jews. For this reason Moses' constitution provided that none could permanently sell his land— for the owner was God, their Lord. They were tenants, and could only lease their land in subtenancy. "For they were strangers and sojourners with Jehovah."

There was, then, no private property; neither the few nor the many exclusively owned land. Land was given only to those who could cultivate it—priests were not permitted to possess any—and they stood in the position of tenants of God. The arable land was divided so that all fields were equal. Boundary stones stood between them. Whoever moved a boundary stone for his own profit incurred the wrath of God:

Thou shalt not remove thy neighbour's landmark, which they of old time have set in thine inheritance, which thou shalt inherit in the land that the Lord thy God giveth thee to possess it.

Cursed be he that removeth his neighbour's landmark. And all the people shall say, Amen.

Horace also speaks of agrarian usury (in Roman literature it was a subject near to home) in his odes. Of what use is it, he asks scornfully, to lay field to field when all must—alas! so soon be cast aside? But this melancholy observation refers only to natural death and the futility of living for one's heirs. The Jewish sense of justice went much further. To the Jews agrarian usury was not merely folly but one of the worst social sins. In a tone quite different from Horace's mild scorn is the curse of Moses' follower, the prophet Amos:

Forasmuch therefore as your treading is upon the poor, and ye take from him burdens of wheat: ye have built houses of hewn stone, but ye shall not dwell in them; ye have planted pleasant vineyards, but ye shall not drink wine of them.

The most fundamental proof that the land belonged to God was furnished by the legal provision that all debts on land would be wiped out every fiftieth year. This year was called the jubilee (from *yobel,* a trumpet blast) because its beginning was marked with the sound of the trumpet throughout the land. All debtors and tenants were freed of their obligations:

And ye shall hallow the fiftieth year, and proclaim liberty throughout all the land unto all the inhabitants thereof: it shall be a jubilee unto you; and ye shall return every man unto his possession, and ye shall return every man unto his family.

And in all the land of your possession ye shall grant a redemption for the land.

If thy brother be waxen poor, and hath sold away some of his possession, and if any of his kin come to redeem it, then shall he redeem that which his brother sold.

And if the man have none to redeem it, and himself be able to redeem it;

Then let him count the years of sale thereof, and restore the overplus unto the man to whom he sold it; that he may return unto his possession.

But if he be not able to restore it to him, then that which is sold shall remain in the hand of him that hath bought it until the year of jubilee: and in the jubilee it shall go out, and he shall return unto his possession.

This law eliminated speculation in land. Every sale of land was only an apparent sale; essentially it was merely a sale of the proceeds of the crops until the next year of jubilee. The price was scaled according to the distance from this year. "According to the multitude of years thou shalt increase the price thereof, and according to the fewness of years thou shalt diminish the price of it" we read in the third book of Moses (25:15). "For according to the number of years of the fruits doth he sell unto thee." That is, if there still remained forty years to the year of jubilee, the price of a given piece of land was four times as high as it would be were there but ten years to the jubilee. The agrarian reformers of the Henry George school studied the law and interpreted it to mean that every sale was only a lease; the length of the lease was expressed in the form of the sales price. The agrarian socialists of the nineteenth century abided by the law of Moses.

But did the Jews abide by it? The goal of the Mosaic agrarian laws was to protect all members of the Jewish people for all time against penury. Every citizen and his descendants were to be assured an unalienable share in the use of the soil; no one was to be allowed to increase his neighbor's "sweat of the face" by having him plow for others as he would for himself, or by taking away his land and casting him into misery. But the wealthy, with an endless variety of devices, prevented the enforcement of the law of the jubilee. They did not discharge their debtors, they made the soil breed them money (as though it did not belong to the Lord), and used the land according to their whim for cultivated fields, pastures, or as sites for buildings.

Nevertheless, the law *existed* (even though the daily life of the Jews admitted a series of violations of its promise), and it was a powerful instrument of conscience. It was a law that no other people possessed; a light that shone far in the misty twilight of the Orient. All the prophets till the time of Christ could hearken back to this law. Israel possessed the law of equal rights to the land—a law that Rome never had and whose lack there was the cause of centuries of strife between plebeians and aristocrats.

It was, to be sure, hated and sabotaged. But it was a law. And since it was never rescinded, it had force. It was as eternal as the square letters and the stern words: "In the sweat of thy face . . ."

GREECE: THE PASSION OF THE SEED CORN

Men will deal bitter blows to that which is the cause of their life.
(In Thrashing Grain.)

LEONARDO DA VINCI: PROPHECIES

§ 18

IF WE GIVE CREDENCE to their historians and poets, there was no nation with as great a gift for agriculture as the Greeks. This was by no means the case. The sober statistics of the national production show that their enthusiasm was rather the expression for a wish: Athens, for example, which called herself *Metropolis ton karpon,* "the mother city of the fruits of the field," in her most flourishing period had to import more than a million bushels of grain annually for her half million inhabitants.

The Greeks were not Egyptians because their land was not Egypt and because their soil was a bad one. It was essentially limestone, covered by an extremely thin layer of humus poor in clay. It was too thin to hold water, and so scarce that in leases it was expressly provided that none of this precious earth might be carried away. Grain grew sparsely upon it. The principal grain was barley, and most of the wheat was imported from Sicily. To be sure, some soils in the Greek homeland were better than others—the soil of the Peloponnesus was, for example, better than that of Athens; and Corinthian soil was superior to the Spartan. The worst soil was probably to be found on the rocky islands of the archipelago: these islands produced no more grain than the Norwegian cliffs of today.

The cities with large populations were consequently compelled to import grain from abroad. Grain could always be bought in Egypt, of course. And what could not be obtained from Sicily was brought from the eastern shore and probably from the northern shore of the Black Sea. When the Russians excavate the Greek cities east of the Crimea, their findings will possibly confirm the theory that the legend of the Argonauts was no more than a romanticized grain expedition. Jason and his heroes were armed grain merchants who hoped to bring the "golden fleece" back to their hungry motherland. The golden fleece is a symbol of a plain shimmering with golden grain, and Jason, who appeared with only one shoe (an archaic mythical symbol of man going naked to commemorate his intimate connection with the soil), was probably identical with Jasion, the lover of the Earth Mother, whom we know as the first plowman.

Some effort was made to improve the soil of the Greek homeland. But the Greeks, who possessed neither the theoretic mind of the Egyptians nor the practical mind of the Romans, were not the people to plan and execute vast projects. They brought forth important inventions; but their inventions remained things of the laboratory and were never translated into practical, civilizing forces. As regards the technique of agriculture, the Greeks created virtually nothing new; they beautified agricultural tools, but they did not improve them. They passed on the plow as they had received it. As late as the seventh century B.C. (as we learn from Hesiod's *Works and Days*) they were without the iron plowshare that the Hebrews had used back in 1100 B.C., in the time of Saul.

Furthermore, the Greeks knew nothing of the advantages of rotation of crops. Other peoples were well enough informed to sow their soil to different crops each year. The Greeks took the measure of letting their soil lie fallow every second year. Thus they deliberately surrendered half the potential yield. It was quite late in their history that they learned to use manures to contribute new life to the soil. Homer, as we know, was familiar with the custom of manuring; but the Greek landholders of the post-Homeric era neglected it utterly. Cato and Columella, Romans and consequently splendid observers, knew that agriculture is gravely dependent upon animal husbandry; but the Greeks were so unaware of it that they regarded it as very clever of Hercules to guide a stream of water through the stables of King Augeas. It did not occur to them that the manure might have been put to better use; that it was not common filth to be dredged away.

When the migrating Greeks settled their peninsula, around 2000 B.C., they were shepherds and warriors. And long after they had abandoned their nomadic life they remained loyal to the nomadic conception of honor. When Homer sings of the wealth of princes, he does not mention the extent of their wheat and barley lands. Quantity and quality of cattle are his standard. Odysseus possessed the greatest herds of swine in the ancient world; Nestor was a breeder of magnificent horses. All the Homeric heroes and their guests ate bread—mostly in the form of flat cakes; Homer never forgets to mention bread as an accompaniment of meat. But the heroes (though they are landowners) are not considered tillers of the soil.

A complementary reason for this was the Greek's traditional love of the sea. The dweller along the coast could easily stave off hunger; food was not a pressing problem. And the sea subtly moved the hearts of men with that restlessness which is the enemy of agriculture. Inviting piracy, warfare, and, later, trade, the sea called for an attitude entirely contrary to that stipulated by the slower, less-stimulating work of tilling the soil. Nautical instruments seemed to Homer the most fitting tools for the hands of men; he reveals this in the passage where he speaks of uncultivated men who were such "landlubbers" that they thought an oar a kind of hoe!

§ 19

It was only a vast political and social transformation that turned a people like the Greeks into real makers of bread. This transformation began in the seventh century B.C. and reached its height in the legal code of the Athenian, Solon (ab. 639–559 B.C.). Solon, virtually the first of the Greeks with a social conscience, possessing also the boldness of mind and the richness of language of a great poet, implacably reminded the wealthy landowners of their sins. They had rented out their lands to peasants, and later, when their tenants could no longer pay, had sold them into slavery. When Solon became head of the state he introduced a kind of "jubilee," the seisachtheia, or freeing from debt. This law was radical in the extreme. Not only were the peasants relieved of their burden of mortgages, but those peasants who had been sold into slavery were bought free with the money of those who had sold them.

Above all, Solon's law prohibited further extension of one-man estates and expropriated all landholdings above a certain acreage.

Once Solon had paved the way, the new political party of small landholders soon obtained power in the Athenian state. A man became eligible for election to the highest offices when he attained a certain standard of agricultural productivity. Formerly, the large landowners who had used their land primarily for pasturage had formed the strongest party.

Now the "party of Bread," those more prosperous farmers who "produced at least five hundred bushels of barley," ruled Athens.

Solon's constitution, which transformed Athens into an agrarian democracy, might have lasted for a century if it had not run afoul of that class which essentially represented the genius of the Greek people. The hostility of the nobility might have been withstood, but not the hostility of the artisans. The artisans, from sculptors to potters, who produced no fruits of the field whatsoever, now found themselves excluded from the government. They rebelled and forced a change in the constitution. Not long after the time of Solon, in the wake of a period when the state was governed almost exclusively by farmers, there was a reaction and five large landholders, three farmers, and two artisans were elected to the Supreme Council.

The experiment had failed in Athens. But Solon's revolution nevertheless resulted in a total revaluation of agricultural labor throughout Greece. Despite their poor soil and, indeed, despite their ideals, the latent cultural bent of the Greek people asserted itself toward the end of the sixth century. Without the blessing of a Nile or the command of a Pharaoh, the Greeks adapted themselves to their role as tillers of the soil because they recognized the necessity. Wisely, they cloaked this necessity in the mantle of religion. In reverence to the *cult of Demeter* the Greek became something he had not originally wished to become: he undertook a kind of labor that the free-born Greek scorned for its odium of sweat and of stubborn earth. All agriculture, from plowing to grinding and baking, came under the aegis of the Demeter cult. Every Greek who had any part in the sowing or the making of bread was held to be performing a priestly service. He was a *religious apprentice to Mother Earth*. This ennobled him within a society in which all "bending and sweating labor" had been considered shameful for many centuries.

§ 20

This new religion of Bread and Soil—strange as it seems!—was also helpful to repel the foreign foes of the Greeks. Two legends from the Persian wars are proof of it. The first:

Pausanias tells us that the Battle of Marathon (490 B.C.) would have been lost but for a miracle that occurred in the midst of the combat. A weaponless man of peasant appearance, in threadbare dress, appeared suddenly upon the battlefield. Holding a plowshare, swinging and dancing like one mowing a field, he advanced against the mighty army of the Persians. Immediately after the victory he vanished. When the Greeks asked the Oracle of Delphi who the man was, they received the reply:

"You may honor the demigod Echetlios, emissary of the goddess Demeter."

With more depth of feeling than Pausanias exhibited, Robert Browning, two thousand years later, interpreted this legend. These are his moving, dancing verses:

Here is a story, shall stir you! Stand up, Greeks dead and gone,
Who breasted, beat Barbarians, stemmed Persia rolling on,
Did the deed and saved the world, for the day was Marathon!

No man but did his manliest, kept rank and fought away
In his tribe and file: up, back, out, down—was the spear-arm play:
Like a wind-whipt branchy wood, all spear-arms a-swing that day!

But one man kept no rank, and his sole arm plied no spear,
As a flashing came and went, and a form i' the van, the rear,
Brightened the battle up, for he blazed now there, now here.

Nor helmed nor shielded, he! but, a goat-skin all his wear,
Like a tiller of the soil, with a clown's limbs broad and bare,
Went he ploughing on and on: he pushed with a ploughman's share.

Did the weak mid-line give way, as tunnies on whom the shark
Precipitates his bulk? Did the right-wing halt when, stark
On his heap of slain lay stretched Kallimachos Polemarch?

Did the steady phalanx falter? To the rescue, at the need,
The clown was ploughing Persia, clearing Greek earth of weed,
As he routed through the Sakian and rooted up the Mede.

But the deed done, battle won,—nowhere to be descried
On the meadow, by the stream, at the marsh,—look far and wide
From the foot of the mountain, no, to the last blood-plashed sea-side,—

.   .   .   .   .   .

How spake the Oracle? "Care for no name at all!
Say but just this: 'We praise one helpful whom we call
The Holder of the Ploughshare.' The great deed ne'er grows small."

Not the great name! Sing—woe for the great name Míltiadés
And its end at Paros isle! Woe for Themistokles
—Satrap in Sardis court! Name not the clown like these!

It was not the steel-armored heroes with their waving helmet plumes who saved civilization from the deluge of barbarism, but "the spirit of the unknown plowman." And precisely the same strange occurrence took place ten years later, when the second rolling tide of Persians was brought to a halt at Salamis. This time the danger was even greater; Athens, the

heart of the world, was occupied. All the inhabitants had fled. Few were
there among the Greeks who believed in the possibility of victory.

The day before the battle, the second legend recounts, two Greeks
stood in the camp of the Persians and looked out over the plain. They
were political emigrants, a Spartan the one, an Athenian the other. As
they stared gloomily over the twilit fields, they saw a cloud of dust
approaching from the region of Eleusis—a vast, dark-brown cloud whirling as though stirred up by the marching feet of thirty thousand men.

DEMETER INSTALLS TRIPTOLEMOS ON HIS WINGED CHARIOT
(From a Greek vase)

From the center of the cloud shrilled a *iakchos mystikos,* a mysterious cry.
The Athenian began to tremble. Fearfully he wailed to the Spartan:
"Oh, Demaratus, a frightful misfortune will strike the army of the Great
King! For today is September 20. In other times this day would have
seen the Greeks all gathered in Eleusis to honor the goddess of the grain.
When so terrifying and turbulent a cloud arises over the land, it means
that the goddess demands her festival and will take fearful revenge upon
those who have spoiled it for her!" Thereupon the Spartan grew pale
and gripped the Athenian's arm: "Keep silence, Dikaios; tell this to
no man, for if you should, the King of the Persians will surely strike off
our heads!" As they spoke the whirling mass of cloud swept on toward
the Bay of Salamis. Two days later, Herodotus tells us, Persian sea power
was destroyed for all time.

§ 21

Who was this almighty goddess who was after all not a warrior goddess
—this Demeter who rescued the Greeks in their direst need? In spite of
her Grecian name (for Demeter is equivalent to Demo-Meter, "the
mother who maketh the people to grow," or Ge-Meter, "Earth Mother"),
she was not a Greek, but a foreign goddess who had established herself
among the Greeks in earliest times. She came from Asia and was a cousin
of the Egyptian Isis and the Phoenician Cybele. Her cult was gentle, for
she wished to behold no blood, but it was a strange one.

More than one god had come to the Greeks from the East. But the
figure of Demeter was essentially more alien, for it was singular enough
that a goddess, not a male god, should be the teacher of agriculture because in Greek civilization the man was unequivocally supreme. Yet this
goddess was mistress not only of the fruits of the soil, but of all tools and
all labor connected with the soil. She possessed a court of assistants and
invisible heroes whom she sent forth as missionaries, like the "thrice-
plower," Triptolemos, whom she sent flying over the earth in a winged
chariot "to teach the art of tillage to all men in all the world. . . ."

It was something entirely novel for a woman to exercise such royal
sway over the heavy physical labor of men. Demeter sprang from an
older, un-Greek society, from an epoch of peace when it was not the warlike male but the fruitful mother who determined the fate of nations.
This period was the legendary era of matriarchy—first explored in the
nineteenth century by the great Swiss scholar Bachofen—an era not entirely legendary, for historical remains of the era have been found in
Crete, Asia Minor, and Etruria. Ridiculous as it seemed to the Greeks
that women should prevail over men in affairs of state, in the realm of
religion they understood well why Demeter, goddess of agriculture and
bread, was a woman.

Wherever Demeter came to land in Greece, she won the reverence of
men. To plant the first germ was a cultural event of profound significance. That one seed should engender ten others, as a man has ten children, would have been comprehensible. But the mathematics of fertility
is staggering: that a hundred ears should grow upon a single stalk, and
ten thousand stalks from a hundred ears—this miracle of geometrical
progression must have shaken the soul of every Greek. Moreover, he was
awed by the change that took place in the earth herself when men became
settled. The Greeks believed that before the arrival of Demeter men had
been hunters and cattle-raising nomads—as indeed the Greeks themselves
had been. It was only her coming that solidified the hitherto inconclusive
concept of the family and of property. Wherever there were cultivated

fields the tents that shook in the wind were replaced by sound and solid cities, and out of these cities arose states. Plato magnificently compares the growth of city walls out of the ground with the growth of grain. Thus the goddess of bread and grain became the Thesmophoros, the lawgiver and protector of settled living.

On the mainland and among the Greek islands there sprang up a host of Demeter's sanctuaries. As the local goddess of countless cities she had countless names and titles. In Boetia she was called Megalomazos and Megalartios (i.e., the mistress of the great breads); in Syracuse she was worshiped as Himalis (the baker). Cicero, centuries afterward, remarked that "the whole of Sicily belongs to the bread goddess Demeter." She protected her peasant people in defensive warfare, as we have seen, but in the main, wherever the bread goddess was worshiped, the prevailing spirit was that exemplified in the Biblical phrase: men shall beat their swords into plowshares.

§ 22

Sowing and reaping were men's work. The threshing was done by oxen who trampled the grain. But with the making of flour we enter the sphere of women's household work. Originally there were no male millers in ancient Greece—only miller women. In the islands of the Aegean Sea, in fair, flat Sicily, on the deeply indented coast of the Peloponnesus and in the Greek cities of Asia Minor—everywhere that the Greek language was spoken—it was the young girls who turned hand mills.

It was tedious, toilsome work. In earliest times the mill consisted of a fixed block of stone, hollowed out somewhat on top, upon which rested a second stone that was worked back and forth by the miller. Later on the upper stone was polished and provided with a handle, so that it could be moved with a circular motion. An enormous amount of physical effort was expended in the work. The instrument was stubborn—how stubborn we learn from the miller's song that Plutarch has recorded:

> *Alei, myla, alei*
> *kai gar Pittakos alei*
> *megalas Mytilanas basileuon*
> Grind, mill, grind
> For Pittakos also ground,
> Great Mytilene's ruler.

The accent of these verses shifts back and forth, pauses and grinds harshly, until the laboring hand has overcome the obstruction.

Homer makes it very plain that the crushing of grain was the unloved part of breadmaking labor. We refer to that passage in the *Odyssey* where Odysseus, disguised as a beggar, enters his house and bitterly looks on at the insolent behavior of the suitors. Weary and despairing of success, he implores the gods to send some sign to fortify his dwindling courage. Thereupon, shortly before dawn, Zeus thunders a greeting to Odysseus, and immediately thereafter brings to his ears the words of a girl slave who is working her mill unobserved near his beggar's couch. In Cotterill's translation:

> . . . Here were standing the mills of the prince of the people.
> These were worked by the women, a dozen in number, that toiled there
> Making the meal of the wheat and the barley, the marrow of mortals.
> All of the rest were sleeping, for ground was the whole of their wheat-grain.
> She was the weakest, and now was alone and incessantly toiling.
> Stopping her mill she exclaimed (to her master it came as an omen):
> "Father of all! Great Zeus, who art monarch of men and immortals,
> Loudly in sooth thou hast thundered from starry expanses of heaven,
> Nor is a cloud to be seen! It is surely a portent for some one!
> Also for me, poor wretch, accomplish the prayer that I utter:
> O for the last and the latest of all their delightful carousings
> Here in the halls of Odysseus to-day to be held by the suitors!
> Yea, for the men have loosened my knees with this pitiless labour,
> Grinding the grain—so now let them finish their feastings for ever!"

These verses—which in 1897 suggested to Samuel Butler that a feminine hand had written the *Odyssey*—are indeed extremely remarkable. Apparently the ancient world knew more social pity than it was later credited with cherishing. Triumph was, to be sure, the basic value of Greek civilization; victory of the nation or the individual, of a god or the tribal father. Greek art served to celebrate this value. Nevertheless, the artists were aware of the undercurrents, of the whispering voices from below. Even in a culture in which slavery was an economic necessity and in which only the strong and beautiful merited the name human, it was possible to express an emotion that is, in its essence, closely related to Christian pity.

Yes, pity! Although the Greek was no Christian, he was able to identify himself with the suffering of other creatures. He could not, however, achieve so deep or so lasting an identification as could the Indian, the Jew, or the Christian. The Buddha, who compared the dead elephant in the jungle to himself (*Tat tvam asi*—that is you!), or Hillel and Christ, who pronounced as a dogma that men must love their neighbors as themselves—such men would have offended the Greeks by their excessiveness. But the Greek felt very strongly the dignity of life itself, the irrevocability of existence. Since he, at the height of his glory, was above all an *artist*, he believed in the ability of art to give life to inanimate things. To him everything lived: an oar, a vase, a cave, a tree. And it lived because he himself lived, because his hand and his imagination would endure nothing dead in their presence. This animation which the Greeks conferred upon everything sprang from an impulse less religious than artistic; there was nothing ardent in that feeling; it was objective and truly serene—a "plastic coldness," as one scholar has called it.

The Greek people—and this we have to understand!—never treated an orderly religious system like that of the Egyptians, the Jews, or the Chris-

THE HAND MILL—TODAY AS 6,000 YEARS AGO

tians, for at the very apex of Greek culture each artist had the right to alter the myths as he saw fit—so long as he was a sensible man who did not overstep the bounds of moderation and order. The Greek truth did not consist in the communication of religious doctrine, nor in the unequivocal character of doctrine, but in the *form* of the communication. This form had little kinship to what is named form in our own formless age. Form, "the Olympic ring," as Bernard Shaw has named it, was, in the ancient world, the loftiest emanation of divine grace.

To the Greek everything was true that had this Olympic ring: When he objectified anything, molding it with his artistic hands, it lived for him, suffered and rejoiced before him. It was not "himself," but it was a life like his own.

It was due to this remarkable and unique capacity that the Greek could put himself in the place of a mill slave who represented not at all his ideal of triumph and beauty. But his capacity for objectivization and transference of feeling went still further. The Greek extended his *symphilein*—his admission of an amiable relationship—to the seed itself. He saw that not only the girl who slaved at the mill suffered, but the *grain* as well.

§ 23

It was crushed; it was tortured. Why should this be so? The wheat was, after all, the *"marrow of men"*—it was a kind friend of the human race. Nevertheless, it was mistreated—as the grape was mistreated before it became wine. There existed this strange contradiction that the grain could become bread only by previously being tortured and murdered by those selfsame men it would feed. One can scarcely say the Greek who first "perceived" this idea was thinking coldly and plastically. . . . And the perception ushered him into a religious realm in which nothing was cold—where everything burned and flamed. This was the realm of *bad conscience.*

In order to live, in order to maintain the life of his civilization, man murders without cessation. Even as a vegetarian, like the Buddhist who spares all animals, he incessantly kills plant life. What is more, in the further reaches of man's history he made extremely slight distinction between the two types of life. Were trees and grasses poorer in consciousness than calves and sheep? No Greek would have agreed that they were. Psychic sensitivity—not religion—accorded all living things the same degree of soul. The grain suffered when it was ground in the mill; the flax suffered when it was broken; the grape bled like an animal when the wine flowed out of the press. Men needed bread, clothing, and wine. Men must therefore torment and kill—but they must see to it (no matter how indifferently religious they were) that they *appeased* the souls of the things they murdered. The living soul of the wheat must be honored. It was honored in song and sculpture.

Robert Eisler, the historian of religion, has selected examples from the beliefs of many peoples which show that bad conscience is universal among men when they kill for the sake of food and clothing. This bad conscience transforms the creatures of the plant and animal world into gods, demigods, and heroes—according to the religious talents of the peoples in question. Peoples with little talent for religion, like the Greeks or the Teutons—who nevertheless possessed great genius in art—created myths of repentance in which the theme of atonement has become almost completely obscured, but whose sensuous, artistic splendor is immortal. As the grape was crushed, so Bacchus, the god of wine, is trampled and torn in immortal verse. Weak or strong, this theme of placation appears in the collective thought of all nations. "Forgive us, O flax!" the Lithuanian girl pleads. *"Rugens Pine"* (the sorrow of the rye) is a familiar fairy-tale motif among the Scandinavians:

> First they cast me into a grave,
> Then I grew to a stalk, then became an ear,
> Then they cut me, then ground me,
> Baked me in an oven,
> And then they ate me as bread.

In almost the same words a medieval poet, Johann von Krolewiz, speaks of Christ who "was sowed, sprouted, stood in flower, grew, was mowed, bound like a sheaf, driven to the threshing floor, threshed, swept with a broom, ground, thrust into an oven, and left therein for three days, taken out, and finally eaten by men as bread." Here we have the passion of Christ interpreted as the *passion of bread.* What unsuspected mysteries the Egyptian invention of bread bequeathed to the Middle Ages!

But even without the final cruelty of the "fiery oven" the passion of the grain was sufficiently tragic. If everything had a soul, then the "burying alive" of the seed in the earth was a crime for which men must atone. Even the Jews of the Bible felt this, although Jehovah had given permission for them to feed upon plants and animals. They felt that they were murdering vegetation. Thus Joseph manifests features of a martyred grain god when he is thrown into the pit by his wicked brothers, traded away to Egypt, and there is gloriously resurrected. The name Joseph means *he increases.* It is appropriate to his character as a bread god that, as the Bible states, he "gathered corn as the sand of the sea, very much, until he left numbering, for it was without number." And this provider, this giver of joy to mankind, had been offended against. Rue and repentance descend upon the brothers!

Yes, one must kill in order to live. With cruel jollity Robert Burns—a Scot who knew little of the Greeks but who nevertheless contrived to live like them—described the "passion of the seed corn." He based his song on a popular ballad, "John Barleycorn," beneath whose liquid surface we can see clearly gleaming the farmer's instruments of torture:

> There were three Kings came from the east,
> Their victory to try;
> And they have taken a solemn oath
> John Barleycorn must die.
>
> They took a plough and ploughed him in,
> Laid clods upon his head;
> And they have taken a solemn oath
> John Barleycorn was dead.

There he lay sleeping in the ground
Till the dew on him did fall;
Then Barleycorn sprung up his head
And so amazed them all.

There he remained till Mid-summer
And looked both pale and wan;
Then Barleycorn he gat a beard
And so became a man.

Then they sent men with scythes so sharp,
To cut him off at knee.
Alas, poor Johnny Barleycorn!
They served him barbarously.

Then they sent men with pitchforks strong,
To pierce him through the heart;
And like a dreadful tragedy
They bound him to a cart.

Then they sent men with holly clubs
To beat the flesh from bones;
The miller he served him worse than that,
He ground him betwixt two stones.

O, Barleycorn is the choicest grain
That's ever grown on land.
It will do more than any grain
To the turning of your hand.

It will put sack into a glass
And claret in a can;
And it will cause a man to drink
Till he neither go nor stand.

This great song smacks strongly of the mood engendered by whisky, and hidden in it is the theme of cannibalistic riot. To understand it is to understand also the bacchanals of the Greeks, which commenced with sorrowing for the death of the crushed god of wine but proceeded almost at once to a crass jubilation at his resurrection.

Similar to this was the festival of the bread giver Demeter and the daughter whom she lost and recovered; the celebration was a composite of profound mourning and unbounded rejoicing. In his sorrow that he must trample the living wheat seed into the earth in order to reap his harvest, the Greek composed the myth of Persephone, the seed, who for four months of the year must remain in the dark underworld, mourned by her divine mother. In time all Greece constituted itself the mourning mother.

GREECE: THE BREAD CHURCH OF ELEUSIS

Here is a story, shall stir you! Stand up, Greeks dead and gone.
ROBERT BROWNING

§ 24

OF THIS attempted "Rape of the Bread" by the jealous gang of the dead and of the frustration of this rape the Greeks were told by a solemn hymn of the seventh century B.C.:

Persephone, the beautiful daughter whom Demeter bore to Zeus, was plucking flowers upon a summer meadow. It was in the neighborhood of Enna, in the middle of Sicily, where Mt. Etna threatened and the gates of the underworld yawned. Suddenly a strange god in his chariot came rushing up to her and seized the girl. Persephone cried out to her father. But Zeus, though aware of all, had gone to attend a distant sacrifice and did not interfere. Persephone struggled in the arms of her captor. While the god continued to race across the upper world, Persephone screamed so loudly that the mountains and seas resounded with her cry. With her nails and teeth she struggled—but at last the god carried her down into the underworld.

Demeter heard the cries. She donned garments of mourning, lit a torch upon Mt. Etna, and set out to search the lands of the earth. She encountered the goddess of darkness, Hecate; but Hecate had seen nothing of the kidnaper or his victim. However, Helios, the all-seeing sun god, had seen both. From him, who spoke only truth, Demeter learned that the god of the dead had snatched away her child. He had made Persephone his wife and consort to the throne of the underworld. It was a marriage that could not be dissolved. Helios advised Demeter to put by her rage, for she would probably not find "a better son-in-law than the immortal prince of Hades. . . ."

Demeter was in no way pacified. She swore never again to set foot upon Mt. Olympus where Zeus, accomplice by neglect, dwelt. Disguised as a stooped old woman, she continued her disconsolate wanderings. In the neighborhood of Eleusis the daughters of King Keleos encountered the weary old woman and asked her to tell their fortunes. The goddess gave cautious, evasive replies and requested that she be admitted to the king's household as a serving maid. Metaneira, the queen, accepted her and gave into her care her infant son, Demophon Triptolemos. But the silent dignity of the strange woman, and a greatness that at times seemed to flash forth from her withered body, inspired doubt and fear in the queen. For days Deo—as the new serving woman called herself—sat by the fire without speaking or eating; until a bold maid named Jambe Baubo lured a smile from her by her crude jests. . . . When she was offered wine, she refused it, asking for a drink of mixed flour and water. . . . Demophon Triptolemos, the infant, waxed strong and hardy in the hands of his new nurse. She anointed him with ambrosia and apparently knew a good deal of magic. One night Queen Metaneira arose to spy upon the nurse; she beheld Deo holding the infant naked in the flaming hearth fire. Screaming, the mother rushed into the room to rescue her son. The stranger told her: "I did this to make him immortal!" A fair aura encircled her head; the wrinkles vanished and beauty returned to her body. She made herself known to the household and promised high honors to the king's posterity. For herself she desired a temple erected above the spring where Keleos' daughters had first met her.

The temple of Eleusis was built, and Demeter dwelt in it. Here, far from the gods of Olympus, far, too, from the life of mankind, she shut herself up with the king's family and worked the magic of her terrible revenge. She made all fields unfruitful; she would not let the seed rise out of the earth. Here was ultimate peril to all men and beasts, but also to the life of the gods themselves. For as men and animals could not live without plant growth, so the gods could not live without the sacrifices men offered up to them. To avert the extinction of all life Zeus dispatched the messenger of the gods, Iris, to command Demeter to appear on Olympus and speak with him. But in vain. Thereupon all the gods, led by Helios, visited the sorrowing mother and offered her the most precious gifts. But these, too, placated neither her mourning nor her anger. Once more she swore:

> prin g'epibesesthai, prin gaies karpon anhesein,
> prin idoi ophthalmoisin heen eupida kouren.
> Not to mount to Olympus, and not to release the grain
> Until with her own eyes she saw the face of her daughter again.

And at last Zeus was compelled to bow to her will, for otherwise all creation would have returned to dust. He sent Hermes, the "guide of souls," as a messenger to the underworld. Hermes donned his winged sandals, descended, and asked the god of the shades to release Persephone. For her mother, he declared, "was holding the seed back in the womb of the earth, and the sacrifices of the gods were vanishing!" Contrary to all expectations, the god of the underworld consented. Smiling, he raised his terrible brows and said:

> Ercheo, Persephone, para metera kyanopeplon!
> Go, Persephone, to thy sorrow-garbed mother!

Accompanied by Hermes, Persephone once more stepped forth on the upper world at a moment when Demeter was looking out of her temple. When she recognized her daughter, she cried out like a maenad in the forest. Intoxicated with joy, she received Persephone. But in the midst of laughter and tears a new anxiety overcame her. She asked Persephone whether she had eaten anything in the underworld. . . . The girl confessed that she had. Demeter was cast down once more. She knew that whoever ate at Hades' board must remain a third of the year in the underworld. But she soon took heart. A third of the year—that was four months. There were twelve months in the year—eight months of the twelve the seed could remain with her mother and mankind. Once more she wept tears of joy. When Zeus sent a messenger to invite mother and daughter to Olympus, Demeter, wholly reconciled, accepted the invitation. First, however, she recalled the curse of unfruitfulness from the earth and taught the kings of Eleusis how they were to celebrate in her temple the kidnaping and the return of the seed corn. She taught the men certain rites, secret procedures, that were never to be offended against or questioned. And she promised blessedness—a happy afterlife—to all who devoutly prayed to mother and daughter in this temple.

§ 25

The ancients believed that Homer had written this hymn. This was not the case, but it was probably written by one of those Homerides who took over Homer's conceptual world—his psychological attitude toward authority, family conflict, and the rivalries of the gods.

The narrative of this nameless poet acquired the force of *canon* among the people. The events of the Demeter hymn assumed the same place in the beliefs of the Greeks as the sufferings of Mary in the beliefs of the Christians. Although religious dogma was generally obnoxious to the Greek (his gods were like magnificent clouds in a turbulent sky, forever shifting and changing), he made a remarkable exception of Persephone's story. It meant so much to him that it became the central ecclesiastical concept of all Greece.

Characteristically, the sufferings of Persephone—the imprisonment of the wheat seed—were not what aroused the pity of the audience. A young girl kidnaped and raped did not touch the Greek so much as did the sorrow of the mother. It was Demeter's passion, her near-madness, and her release from this suffering, that made the Greeks ardently espouse the myth.

In this myth Demeter is not so much the goddess of the earth (in the seventh-century hymn she is certainly no longer that) as the personification of a force springing and thrusting out of the earth. The earth is blind

—this was apparent to the Greeks. She permits growth and withering without choice. But the goddess of agriculture exercises choice. She brings salvation to man—but in a sense akin to the Old Testament, men must keep their covenant with her. The divinity cannot give her gift without the aid of men who plow, sow, and prepare the bread.

The great stress that the poet placed upon the hospitality accorded to the bread goddess by the royal couple is thus wholly justified. King Keleos, whose descendants later became the hereditary high priests (that is, he had the same position in the Church of Eleusis as Peter later had in the Christian Church), won undying praise for sheltering the goddess. For there is a deep-rooted religious motif in this taking an alien old woman from the street and employing her as a nurse—a position that implies the highest confidence. The *Odyssey,* too, commends charity to beggars, for gods wishing to test men may well be among them. And in Hebrews 13:2 we find the whole of this classical precept in the sentence: "Be not forgetful to entertain strangers: for thereby some have entertained angels unawares."

Other elements in Demeter's life with the king's family, which seem at first glance romantic touches, have in reality a deliberate religious significance. Her holding the boy in the fire to make him immortal, for example, is perfectly intelligible. The Greeks considered Triptolemos the missionary of the plow; the iron of the plowshare is indeed made indestructible in the fire. Triptolemos' descendants, the high priests of Eleusis, in the seventh century B.C., acquired a dominion over the politically and geographically disparate Greeks such as was possessed by the priesthood of no other god. The cult of Demeter and the games in her honor outshone the worship of all the other gods—with the possible exceptions of Zeus and Apollo.

How was this possible? Only because Demeter, giver of bread and goddess of the fields, and founder of the law, the family, and the state, was assigned another and still greater capacity. She had power over the realm of the dead; she it was who decided the *resurrection or destruction of a soul.*

It was a masterpiece of astuteness on the part of the priests of Eleusis to have given her this attribute. Yet the emotional process was of the simplest: the earth in which the apparently dead seed was placed was the selfsame earth in which the bodies of the dead were laid. Was, then, the will that decreed whether a seed would germinate or wither away not the selfsame will that released a soul from the underworld or condemned it to remain there forever? In the Egyptian *Book of the Dead,* with which the priests of Eleusis were familiar, the soul replies from the hereafter: "The gods live as I, I live as the gods. I live as grain, I grow as grain. I am barley." Thus it was actually the same will that permitted the soul and the grain to germinate.

It is most difficult to convey to contemporary man the full force of this belief. For a modern man at most feels it as a metaphor, an analogy, that the power which rules over seeds should resemble that which rules over souls. But the Greek of the classic period was incapable of thinking in terms of resemblances; he did not see "metaphors," but *realities*. Either a thing existed or it did not exist. When the priests of Demeter showed him that the goddess of the bread, the founder of civilization, and the redeemer of souls from the realm of the dead were one and the same divine being, the believer did not perceive this trinity of traits as separable. The indivisibility was plain and reasonable. There were no Greeks who did not believe it.

§ 26

There has been a false conception of long standing that the Greeks cared only about this world. It is utterly wrong—the Greeks placed tablets in the coffins of their dead on which was written what amounted to a map of the underworld. There was an admonition to turn to the right upon entering, not to the left, for Paradise was situated to the right. Plato's dialogues show how concerned the men of his era were about a blessed afterlife. The secret Orphic Society had actually put out a small textbook for its members entitled *Katabasis eis Haidon* (*The Descent into the Underworld*). Those same Greeks who laughed at the Egyptians for having gods with the heads of birds were anxious disciples of the Egyptians in all questions of the afterlife.

What was it in the mysteries of Eleusis that inspired such enormous popularity for a thousand years? It was not the dramatization of the descent of the seed corn and its return to the upper world. Rather, it was the promise that the initiates (in Christian terminology, the *baptized*) would themselves be resurrected. It was with this that they were concerned, and it was of this state of happiness after death that the Greek poets spoke. Thus the Hymn to Demeter closed with the words:

> Happy is he who sees this, of men dwelling upon this earth!
> But who does not share in these rites, whose life is without them,
> Shall suffer a different fate in the mist-darkened underworld.

This is a curse, though a curse in disguise. Those who did not attend the rites were *damned*. The idea is expressed much more directly by Sophocles, the great Athenian dramatist (496?–406 B.C.):

> Oh, thrice blessed are those mortals
> Who beheld the rites, before their descent began!
> For them alone is there life in the underworld,
> For others only sore trial and distress.

Pindar, the great lyricist and hymnalist (522–448 B.C.), maintains that only initiates of Eleusis "know the end of life and the God-given beginning as well"—a further testimony to the identity between the grain that is forever being buried and resurrected and the human soul. This Eleusinian dogma—that the goddess of bread was also the intercessor in the realm of the dead—later caused intense hatred for Eleusis among the Christians. Even before Christianity had become the religion of state, Christian writers such as the great Clemens Alexandrinus (around A.D. 200), Asterius, and Julius Firmicus Maternus (around A.D. 347) inveighed against the "Eleusinian atrocities." For the mediator of eternal salvation could, of course, only be Christ! The other Greek cults of Apollo, Zeus, or Aphrodite offered no rivalry to Christianity. But the religion of Demeter was dangerous because it alone gave to its initiates a life of the soul after death. For this reason Demeter's church was Christianity's only significant competitor.

§ 27

When the pious Isaac Casaubon (1559–1614), Geneva's most famous scholar and greatest connoisseur of all kinds of faiths, first rediscovered the fact that there was a strong similarity between the resurrection of Christ and the return of Demeter's seed corn, he was stunned. Then he raised his hands: "God may have known," he exclaimed, "the reasons for giving those pagans approach to our deepest mysteries!"

Indeed, it was perhaps hard to conceive for the contemporaries of Casaubon that the frenzied joy of the faithful in the Eastern Orthodox Church and their cry, "Christ is raised from the dead!" had the same holy roots as Demeter's joy over her resurrected child. And also that the Roman Church, its popes and priests, its feasts and rituals, were anticipated in heathen times by the Bread Church of Eleusis . . . !

Never did a holy community undergo a more interesting fate. Internal dissension soon transformed the priest kingdom of Eleusis into a priest republic whose government was in the hands of six noble families. From these families were drawn the four highest officials, who were elected for life. The highest of these four was the *hierophant*, who showed and explained the sacred relics. The second was the *daduchos*, the torchbearer. The third and fourth were the *keryx* and the *epibomios*, the herald and the priest of the altar. These latter officials called the worshipers to services and ministered at the offerings. These four also had parts as performers in the mystery play that represented the death and resurrection of the seed corn. Throughout Greece the four enjoyed honors such as today are accorded only to the Pope and archbishops. Even their servants, who washed the images of the god, were persons to be envied and had seats of honor in the theater.

There were also, of course, female high priestesses of Demeter and Persephone. These priestesses were also members of the noble families. But their functions were severely limited. Greek decorum did not permit women to officiate in public; the power of the priestesses lay mostly within church circles.

Besides the priestly hierarchy, Eleusis also maintained a number of semi-secular officials: chamberlains who administered the temple area with its inns for visitors; and, most important, the guardians of the temple treasure. The treasure consisted of granaries to which all Greece voluntarily contributed, of money accumulated by the sale of this grain, of fees from those initiated into the mysteries, and of precious objects of gold and silver—gifts from all over the world. A ten-man financial collegium, composed of shrewd grain traders, sold the grain at good prices for the benefit of the temple treasury. The profit was used to defray the expenses of the great festival. Over all these spiritual and secular officials ruled a three-man directorate which administered the police and judicial powers of Eleusis and had the power to inflict punishment upon any Greek who disturbed the peace of the goddesses.

This priest state of Eleusis was a politically independent unit. In a territory no larger than a quarter of Brooklyn (today it is a marshy plain inhabited by impoverished Albanese) lived ten thousand people in a splendid temple city, ruled by spiritual authorities. And the administration of this tiny state possessed a political power comparable to that of the States of the Church until 1870, where genuine secular sovereignty was united with spiritual authority.

After centuries during which the gifts to Demeter from all Greece had enriched the bread goddess and her Eleusinian priests, there succeeded a period, around the time of the Persian wars, when the popularity and the income of the church began to decline. To combat this tendency the priesthood had the inspired thought to wed the mysteries with the destiny of Athens. They therefore offered this secular city-state supervision of Eleusis and a part of the temple income. Neighboring Athens had for a time attempted to compete with Eleusis. The Athenians had done their best to make their city goddess the goddess of agriculture and to transform one of their heroes, Erechtheus, into the missionary of the plow and the teacher of the farmers. But for obscure reasons the maneuver failed. Perhaps Athene, the goddess of "artisans of the mind and hand," was not a woman to lend herself to an earthy materialism and the slow processes of growth. Although she had brought the olive tree she was no goddess of fertility; her chaste, virginal nature repulsed such a burden. Demeter, on the other hand, was far from virginal: she was one of the wives of Zeus and had cherished, besides Zeus, many a lover—like that

Jasion whom Zeus struck down with his thunderbolts ("for," as a Cretan myth would have it, "who sleeps with goddesses must die").

When the cities of Athens and Eleusis became united politically, the jealousies between Athene and Demeter ceased. The cult of the bread goddess became the state religion of Athens—and the state of Athens lent its vast secular glory and its propaganda apparatus to the Eleusinian festival.

§ 28

This great "celebration of the Bread" was the proudest feast of the ancient world—and, we daresay, in its splendor and beauty, it is incomparable to any popular celebration in the later three thousand years. It began every year around September 20—that is, at the time when the seed corn was once more returned to the underworld, and it lasted nine days—the number of days corresponding to the time Demeter wandered mourning over the earth. Without distinction of class or position, everyone who spoke Greek could take part. The significance of this is that slaves were included, as well as women and children—though the latter participated only in the public part, not in that part of the festival which was reserved for the "initiates" and took place in the inner chambers of the temple. The festival did not begin in Eleusis, the spiritual center, but in the political center, Athens. To Athens the images of the bread goddess and her daughter had previously been transported. A whole month before the beginning of the festival noble youths were sent as messengers to all the cities of Greece to proclaim the peace of the god and to announce that the celebration would take place at the next full moon. All Greece obeyed their call; those who were to participate assembled in the inns of Athens. On the first day the highest Athenian official proclaimed that all who had blood on their hands were excluded from the ceremonial procession. Then the hierophant of Eleusis spoke, having come to Athens for the occasion. He concluded his speech with the famous cry *"Halade mystai* [Novitiates to the sea]!" At once a grand race began, with all who were to be initiated that year vying to be first to reach the purifying salt water. On the second day, in Athens, the first official sacrifice was offered, and this was repeated on the third day for latecomers from distant parts of the Greek world. The following day was taken up by the procession to Eleusis. Followed by thousands of chanting worshipers, the images of the gods were borne back to the city of the priests. Beside the images of mother and daughter there was a third image of Bakchos-Iakchos (the "loud-crying wine god"); for the priests of Bacchus had seen to it that in the fall of the year, the time of the grape harvest, their worship was merged with that of the popular goddesses of the fields. It was a stroke of wisdom. For not only are bread and wine naturally inseparable (as we see in the Sacrament of the Lord's Supper), but without the presence of the god of wine the autumnal procession to Eleusis would have been distinctly somber. For now began those four months when Persephone must once more rest in the arms of the god of death. However, the inclusion of the wine god cast a pleasant and pious mood of intoxication over the procession of the thousands. Among the leaders of the procession, for example, was a man disguised as a woman who bore the name "nurse of Bakchos" and carried on a cushion sundry toys of the wine god's childhood—dice, a ball, a whip, and a top. Behind her came the *kistophoros* (the chest bearer), who carried Demeter's sacred trunk, in which the cult objects were reproduced in the form of cakes—a baked plow made of wheat and honey and other finely wrought objects made of bread dough. Then came the holy fanbearer, carrying something that resembled a winnowing fan; in just such a basketlike fan Bacchus had lain as a child. This object had a role similar to that of the manger in Christianity. The sacred fan was covered with foliage; none knew its contents. Perhaps it represented the idea that as the fan separated the chaff from the wheat, so the Eleusinian mysteries purified man of his portion of sin.

Fourth in the procession came the basket bearer, holding the *kalathos,* the harvesting basket, which symbolically was to receive the first fruits of the fields for Demeter. Only after all these officials came the Eleusinian priests, the entire membership of the Athenian government, the novitiates, and the populace.

Police accompanied the procession, and along the sides of the road young men stood guard. But this protection was entirely superfluous; in a thousand years the procession was never attacked. No band of robbers would have ventured so unspeakable a blasphemy.

The pilgrims were modestly dressed: since the poor and the slaves also took part in the procession, good manners forbade the showing of any luxury. Those who had no gifts for the gods bore, at the least, sheaves of grain, agricultural or milling tools, very big breads, or burning torches. All went on foot—riding, except for invalids, was punishable by a severe fine. For Demeter, too, had gone on foot when she searched with burning torches for her daughter.

The road from Athens to Eleusis was actually a four-hour walk. But the pilgrims took ten hours, because they stopped everywhere to perform some of the minor rituals of the cult. In one spot, for example, the novitiates wound a scarlet ribbon around their hands and feet—like the prayer shawls of the Jews. At another place, where a brook was crossed, a lusty dialogue took place, in honor of Jambe Baubo, the maid who at King Keleos' hearth had lured a smile from the sorrowing Demeter. After much resting, praying, and noisemaking, the procession arrived by torchlight and the glow of the full moon in Eleusis. Here the sweat-soaked and dust-covered worshipers betook themselves to their rest in the inns of the temple area.

The next day was spent in making sacrifices. To forestall envy, rich offerings were made not only to the goddesses of the fields, but to all the divinities. On the sixth day the people began the dance in honor of Bacchus, the horse races, foot races, and the market fair. Within the sanctuary the novitiates were shown the passion play of the death and rebirth of the Sacred Seed Corn. This part of the festival was so secret that at one time two youths who for the lark of it had penetrated the temple were seized and put to death.

We can only guess what actually went on within the temple. The millions of people who were initiated in Eleusis between the seventh century B.C. and the fourth century A.D. all kept their vows of silence. Even such a writer as Pausanias, who gave an exact description of every stone in Greece, hastens to say, in reference to the innermost part of the temple and to the mysteries, that he must keep silence, for a dream had warned him against reporting these things. It is due only to the insane animosity of the older Christian writers who hated Demeter as a goddess of bread and immortality that we are acquainted with a number of details of the mysteries. These men probably let themselves be initiated in order to spy out the secrets of the cult.

As with the Freemasons, there were three degrees among the Eleusinians—apprentice, journeymen, and master. Half a year before the Eleusinian festival the apprentices were convoked in an Athenian temple and requested to put off their outer garments and their shoes, and to remove all metal ornaments. Then they were given wreaths of myrtle and their faces were covered, so that they might hear the better. In this condition they were instructed in the fate of Persephone. Then the blindfolds were removed and the priests gave them a password by which they could identify one another until the next festival. The terms of this password, which was strictly secret, have come down to us. It ran: *"Have you eaten bread?"* This challenge called for the reply: *"I fasted, drank the mixed cup of water and flour; I took bread from the chest, I tasted, placed it in the basket, and replaced it from the basket to the chest."* It is an obscure formula, comprehensible only when we see it as an incident from Demeter's life, something that happened at the Court of Keleos, re-enacted with a kind of slow-motion precision.

The novitiates were required to make two pilgrimages to Eleusis. They did not receive the initiation until the second year. As the *mystes* marched into the courtyard of the temple they sprinkled themselves with holy water. When they entered the temple itself they became *epoptes,* beholders. First they were blindfolded, then lowered by an ingenious contraption into stony basement rooms. Holding the hands of priests who seemed to lead them over raging torrents, past the snapping teeth of ravenous beasts, through showers of stones and tumultuous noise, the imagination of the novitiates experienced all the terrors of the underworld. Here a geyser of hot mud menaced them, there the *empusa,* a gluttonous, man-eating spirit. After hours of groping about in darkness, the frightened novitiates were taken to rest and recover upon mystic beds. Suddenly a tremendous light broke. The blindfolds were snatched away. A door sprang open; in the radiance of glowing torches the exhausted group of novitiates beheld the host of older "brethren," who jubilantly greeted them: *"Welcome to the Sanctuary, bridegroom!"* The novitiates were then given seats and handed the mixture of flour and water that Queen Metaneira had once given Demeter to refresh her after her long wandering. All were clad in white garments. When the novitiates raised their eyes, they beheld a smiling little girl standing at the altar of Demeter. It was a child who performed the priesty services! Behind her stood the hierophant, guiding her uncertain hands. Then this scene sank into the earth and the play began—of which not a single scene or line has been handed down to us. We know only how it closed: at the end the stage was flooded with light; the full midday sun of harvesttime bathed all in its warmth. A new backdrop showed green meadows, and a blissful fragrance spread over the room. The peace of the divinity entered the souls of the "beholders." They knew now that they were in Paradise. Demeter, who had accomplished the resurrection of her daughter from Hades, had also saved their souls from the terrors of damnation.

§ 29

The cult of the bread goddess of Eleusis is almost entirely lucid to us today. The agitation of elevated emotions, the Shakespearean trick of surrounding the tragedy with clownish jests—these are readily understood. Only one element is not so clear—why was the most important part of the ceremony secret? If Demeter was the goddess of bread, and if her protégé, Triptolemos, the "thrice-plower," was sent over the land in a winged chariot to teach agriculture to men—why were these teachings at the same time kept secret?

This love of secrecy was derived from Egypt. There, as Plutarch recounts, the son of the earth-goddess was pictured "with his finger pointed to his mouth, a proper emblem of that modest and cautious silence we ought to observe in these matters." How strange this seems. On the one hand the priests wished to spread Demeter's work over the entire world, and on the other hand every Greek, when her name was mentioned, felt a superstitious scruple, a dread of committing blasphemy. In our view, these two facts are paradoxical.

This view is not solely a modern one. There were a number of contemporary minds who considered Eleusis and the mysteries with a certain degree of irritation. Epaminondas (418?–362 B.C.), the great Theban general, refused to accept the Eleusinian initiation. Demonax, the philosopher, asked: "Why should I permit myself to be initiated? How am I to take a vow of silence? Should I find that what is taught there is useful, I should consider it my duty to spread the knowledge abroad; if it seemed harmful to me, I would warn all against it." This was the moralist's view. The power of Eleusis was, however, so great that few ventured to speak so boldly. And after Greece lost her independence and sank to the status of a Roman province, the importance of the mysteries grew rather than declined. Cultivated Romans, the Greek-speaking officials, army officers, and philosophers of the world empire, now began streaming to Eleusis to take the initiation. Partly from true devoutness, partly from snobbishness, they zealously guarded the principles of the secret society. All Roman emperors, from Augustus to Marcus Aurelius, were initiates of the bread goddess. Although the cult of Eleusis was by no means the state religion of the Roman Empire, as it had been of Athens, the Romans identified their native goddess of the fields, Ceres, with Demeter. The sanctuary and the sacred relics of Eleusis were considered by all Romans as the seat of the mother church. The proposal of Emperor Claudius (A.D. 41–54) to transfer the Eleusinian festival to Rome caused widespread horror, comparable to the horror that would be aroused today if it were proposed to change the seat of the Pope from Rome to New York. For Eleusis was the place where the wandering goddess had first revealed herself in human form! The Emperor was forced to abandon his plan.

However, far more minor things were considered blasphemous. The youth Alcibiades, Socrates' spirited friend, committed blasphemy one night at a party in a private dwelling in Athens. He donned priestly garments, a white-sleeved gown and a beribboned tiara. Then, before his uproarious companions, he imitated some of the rituals performed by the high priest of Eleusis. When the affair leaked out, all the spectators were arrested. Alcibiades, who at this time was fighting in Sicily as an Athenian general, was deprived of his command and taken back to Athens in a government galley. En route he succeeded in escaping. He was tried in absentia and sentenced not to prison, but to *death*. Only his successful escape saved his life. Since in blasphemy trials no uninitiated judge was permitted in the courtroom, the trials were in practice secret and the accused was almost certain to be found guilty.

Secrecy is a peculiar matter. Not only in the field of religion but also in our social life. When the priests of Demeter created the Eleusinian mysteries, they knew very well what they were doing. After hunger and love, the gravest of social forces is probably human curiosity. The priests enlisted this curiosity in their cause. Human society is so constituted that men will allow their neighbors to possess millions in gold, but not a paltry secret. Society abhors gaps in its knowledge as nature abhors a vacuum. The might of social curiosity overpowers the secrets of individuals and communities. The pressure comes from all sides, like that of water upon a diving bell—either society will compel its own admission to the secret, or it will avenge itself upon the holders of the secret by turning them out of society, making them outlaws. Society's reaction to any exclusion from knowledge is: "What is concealed from me must be unclean."

The priests deliberately aroused the curiosity of their world, but they saw to it that the pressure of the secret would bring no baleful storm upon Eleusis. By the payment of an initiation fee, anyone could be inducted into the secret. Anyone who was not a murderer or an illiterate could become a full-fledged member of the Bread Church of Eleusis, sharing with others the secret and the promise of life after death.

Nevertheless, we would be mistaking the case to brand the actions of the priests as the workings of ordinary greed. As with most human actions, the desire to make a mystery of the religion sprang from a mingling of self-interest and the highest ideals, for the significance of the religion was reinforced by the secrecy. Goethe once remarked upon the increased force that secrecy confers upon an idea:

If men are always informed at once of the nature of things, they think that nothing lies behind. Certain secrets, even though they be public secrets, ought to be paid their full due of silence and veiling, for this acts upon the sense of shame and good morals. . . .

In this wise Macoy defends secrecy in his *History of Freemasonry:*

The mighty labors which clothe the earth with fruits and flowers are "wrought in darkness." The bosom of Nature is a vast laboratory, where the mysterious work of transmutation of substances is perpetually going forward. There is not a point in the universe, the edges of which do not touch the realms of night and silence. God himself is environed with shadows, and clouds and darkness are around his throne; yet his beneficence is felt, and his loving spirit makes itself visible through all worlds.

Although the sacred, then, has a right to be secret, we saw that humanity has rudely mishandled almost all secrets precisely because they strove to remain secret. Though millions of human beings were initiated in Eleusis between the seventh century B.C. and the fourth century A.D., the number of millions who remained uninitiated was incommensurably greater. All these people were gnawed by a curiosity that inevitably became hatred; for this is the fate of unrequited curiosity. In later centuries, whenever secret societies (like the Templars, the Rosicrucians, the Freemasons) attempted to preserve their secrets, terrible persecutions broke out; the curious sought to destroy the holders of the secrets.

Eleusis, too, lies destroyed. Hatred and calumniation urged on the hands that broke down its walls. The older Christian writers, such as Julius Firmicus Maternus, had ascribed the most frightful atrocities to the Eleusinian ceremonies. Reasoning from the principle that "what is concealed from me is unclean," he had asserted that upon the stage at Eleusis the hierophant and priestess dramatized Demeter sleeping with the boy Triptolemos by copulating in public. . . . At the time such calumnies represented no direct danger to Eleusis. The accumulated hatred could not be discharged until an event of the greatest importance took place in the "Eastern Roman Empire," at that time ruled from Constantinople. This event was the *invasion of the Goths* in A.D. 394.

§ 30

The Goths, a German tribe, had not actually come as enemies. They were a standing Roman auxiliary army in the service of Emperor Honorius; but after they had entered imperial soil in Greece they began plundering for themselves. Giving the pretext that his people had been attacked by mountain peoples in northern Greece, King Alaric began a vengeful march to the south.

The barbarian chief wore a suit of red fur; but, unlike his long-maned warriors, his blond hair was cut short. He would not permit his men to call him by his proper name, Ala-reiks, but insisted officially upon the Romanized form, Alaricus. Like so many Roman officers of German origin, he spoke excellent Latin; in addition he had learned Greek and was an admirer of the Greek philosophers.

The Goths marched southward, followed by a host of wagons. Even more terrible than the fires that flamed in the night sky were the name and reputation of the king. The magistrate of the city of Athens prepared for defense. But how could Athens defend herself? No imperial troops were in Athens. Sighing, the citizenry fetched out their anachronistic weapons and their ancient helmets and greaves. The hoofbeats of the Goths' horses would have sufficed to scatter this regiment of armed merchants, teachers, and students. . . . Then came an incredible message from Alaric. For the payment of a ransom (and not a particularly large one) he would spare the city. No Goth would set foot in it; he would lead his entire army past Athens and pitch camp in the port of Piraeus. He made only a single condition—that he be permitted, as a private person, to spend a day after his own fashion in Athens. For, the message declared, he had a boundless reverence for the city which was the cradle of art and of humanity.

The Athenians agreed gladly. To their astonishment, the following day a lone man, dressed in white, appeared upon the road. He was wearing the ancient dress of nearly a thousand years ago—the garments of the time of Pericles. The man was Alaric. He greeted the gaping crowds with the Greek salute "Chaire [Rejoice]!" And they had reason to rejoice. The guards upon the walls, who stood with bows bent, lowered their weapons, and the magistrate brought the strange guest into the open city. In excellent Greek Alaric expressed his happiness that Athens had not been destroyed by the earthquake of A.D. 375 which had wrought destruction to so many cities. He attributed this to the protection of the goddess Athene—a remark that sounded strange upon the lips of a Christian. But it was intended philosophically.

It was a beautiful autumnal morning. First Alaric asked to be led to the Acropolis, where he looked at the temples and monuments. Then he went to a banquet in the Prytaneion, where flautists and singers entertained him. At his request a reader began to recite Plato's *Timaios*. Finally he asked that Aeschylus' *Persians* be performed for him in the theater. Twilight was nearing. With tearstained face, Alaric listened to the immortal verses that celebrate the victory of Hellenism over the barbarians. From the masks of the actors proceeded what seemed to him supernatural voices that recounted the indestructibility of the classic world. The hosts hoped that the drama would weary the foreign king; but Alaric wanted more. After the theater he asked for readings from Homer, selections from the *Iliad* and the *Odyssey*. In utter boredom the magistrate, to whom the classic period was a thing of the dull past, fell asleep. But Alaric arose from his seat at dawn and returned fresh as ever to his army.

The army received the tourist, who returned in a white *chlamys* and wearing a wreath on his brow, with silent mockery. Some even ventured to laugh outright. Alaric grew angry. What had he done? He withdrew to his tent to meditate, and when he emerged he understood that there were not many more cities in Greece that he dared spare.

The sparing of Athens was the destruction of Eleusis. The disappointed horde of Goths had scarcely left Piraeus when they beheld, beyond the road and the forest, the treasure-filled temple. The state religion of Rome was already Christianity; no Greek would have dared openly to sacrifice to Demeter. But a cultural peace had been concluded between the new era and the old; the priests of Demeter were permitted to remain in cloistered seclusion, although the sacrifices and the games had long since been banned.

Alaric stood rooted to the spot when he saw the city in the twilight. But his warriors rode, hoarsely shouting, past him. They dismounted and stormed the gates and secret chambers of the temple. The golden holy vessels, the silver tankards, and the bronze tablets—the gifts of ages— soon stuffed the chests of the plunderers and the feed bags of their horses. Whatever they could not take was destroyed; the paved floors were horribly soiled and the holy vessels desecrated. In the midst of the destruction the last high priest stepped toward them. He had ceased to perform his office long ago. The priest was the aged Nestorius, a neo-Platonian of subtle mind. As a philosopher, not as a priest, he reproved the barbarians for plundering. He attempted to tell the shouting men who Demeter had been—protector of agriculture and friend to men. But in vain. The Christian monks with the Goths urged on the hesitant soldiers. Infuriated by the sight of the demi-nude statues, the monks encouraged the barbarians to strike down everything in sight. Under the blows of a dozen swords, Nestorius sank to the ground. Dying, he saw the priests of the Goths encouraging their horde to rush into the interior of the temple. He heard their cry of *Christus panis, Christus panis* (Christ is bread!), and died, knowing that a mightier bread god than the holy mother Demeter had come into the world.

ROME: BREAD IN POLITICS

Soon shalt thou pass from each fair purchased field;
From home, from seat where yellow Tiber rolled,
Thou'lt pass; and all thy treasured gold
Thou to thy heir shalt yield.

HORACE

§ 31

WHEN, in the year A.D. 79, the city of Pompeii was buried under the ashes of erupting Vesuvius, the priests of Isis remained longer than others in their sanctuary. They were still sacrificing to their goddess when the destruction approached its end. Only then did a priest take up an ax to cut his way to the outside world. But the ashes smothered him.

The religion of Isis was, like that of Demeter, identified with the earth. Perhaps the priests expected that their goddess's relationship with the raging underworld would save them. But the torrent of glowing stone thickened and buried temple, houses, and markets. It not only buried, but preserved. After eighteen hundred years the spade uncovered a city that seemed to have fallen asleep the day before.

In November 1923 I went walking through Pompeii with a young couple, the husband a Belgian manufacturer. They were on their marriage trip. The young wife was, perhaps, a little disappointed. A very fashionable young Parisienne, she had probably expected to find Pompeii similar to the museum at Naples. She missed all the rings, plates, and bottles, the miniature implements of life that had been found in Pompeii and brought to Naples.

The husband seemed better disposed. He felt foundations and walls, appraised the gates of the houses, the baths, the sewage system. He seemed to hope to find machines. He asked for the house of the weavers. The industry of the city interested him.

We stopped before a half-shattered courtyard. A large oven was visible. To one side of it we saw several stone towers about two yards high, in the shape of an hourglass—wide at top and bottom but narrow in the middle.

"Those are mills," the Belgian said at once.

"How do you know?" Then I glanced at my guidebook. This was the Casa di Salustio, and the bakery had indeed been situated here.

"So they had mechanical mills! In pre-Roman times flour was ground in handmills. What bad flour the Greeks must have had! A high percentage of stone splinters."

He walked around the stone towers, which now took on the shape not of hourglasses, but rather of dolls wearing a long blouse above a wide skirt. Shyly at first, then with familiarity, he placed his hand on the hip of the tower. I watched as he read the invisible writing of a vanished civilization.

"Splendid machines, by God! Three men must have worked here, and let us hope mules, not men, were used to set this mill in motion. Look how ingeniously it is worked out. This tower with the narrow waist is made of two pieces, not one. The lower part is the fixed millstone. This other hollowed cone is placed on top of it and is movable. Here you see the handles. Here the animals drew on the pole. When the animals rotated this stone chamber around the lower, fixed stone, the grain that had been poured in from above was crushed. The flour trickled out from under the 'blouse.' You see how it worked? It was not even very heavy. The material is tuff, a volcanic stone, which the beasts could turn easily."

I stepped closer to him. "Easily? I'm not so sure. I recall reading in the Greek Anthology the 'Complaint of an Old Horse':

> "Now I drag the heavy millstone
> of Nisyros around in a circle . . ."

He looked at me, touched and embarrassed. "But people want bread. So it must be ground. What do I care about your old horse! The machines were good—that is the principal thing." Somewhat nervously he tapped his index finger against the stone. "See how closely the lower cone fits the upper, so that it would turn with a steady motion. There was grinding, there was a delicacy those dilettante Greeks never possessed. Those Romans!" he exclaimed suddenly. "The Americans of their day."

Now his wife also exclaimed. She had seen the oven, the fine, modern oven that the people who dwelt in this place two thousand years ago had cleverly constructed. French, and loving white breads and cakes, this was something she understood. With what care the Roman masters had surrounded the inside of the arched oven with a square hollow space to insulate the hot air. There was a draft for the smoke, a container for ashes, and a container for the water with which the crust of the half-baked bread could be moistened, in order to impart a fine glaze. Adjoining the oven were two rooms for the bakers, with stone tables for molding the dough. This pleased her. And then she saw on the wall above her head the picture of the oven goddess, Fornax. Not one of the great goddesses, to be sure, she was more of a serviceable divine assistant. But still this Fornax had her own festival in Rome, the Fornacalia. Originally, ears of grain had been roasted over open fires at this festival. It had been founded by the ancient King Numa Pompilius. Later, when the Egyptian practice of baking bread was instituted in Rome, it became an important popular and national festival. For even to the sober, practical Romans—the Americans of their day—the growth and transformation of bread in the oven seemed something mysterious, like the growth of a child in his mother's womb.

§ 32

Out of the mills of these practical Romans, whether driven by criminals, by animals, or by the flow of water, flour trickled soundlessly—flour which was the mortar of life; which held the nation together because it satisfied the stomach; which was eaten by rich and poor; which the Roman soldiers carried in sacks on the ends of their lances when they conquered the world.

The Romans were by nature no gourmets, and it took them a long time to learn that bread was better than roasted grain or meal. But once learned, they learned it thoroughly. Wherever pictures of their bread-making are lacking, their writers have filled the gaps for us. Athenaeus tells us that many bakers had their apprentices work with gloves and masks of gauze, so that no sweat or bad breath would spoil the dough. For those Romans who had developed elegant tastes, many things were done to this dough. Besides the ordinary bread, which was shaped like a bomb, there was *panis artopticius,* which was turned on a spit. The *panis testuatius* was baked in an earthen vessel. One delicacy was known as Parthian bread; it was allowed to swell in water before being baked. It was required to be so light that—in contrast to the ordinary bread—it would float on the surface of the water.

The shapes of their bread were even more artistic and more arbitrary than those of the Egyptians. The rich always desired something new. When a poet visited them, they ordered breads in the shape of lyres; at wedding suppers there were breads in the shape of joined rings.

Besides the bread bakers there were the bakers of sweets, the milk bakers, and the pastry bakers. Cato and Pollux tell us a great deal of what the cakes contained. There was honey, imported from Greece and Asia Minor because it seemed better than the Italian honey; oil from North Africa; rice, milk, cheese, sesame seeds, nuts, almonds, peppers, anise, and laurel leaves. In so far as the number of ingredients was concerned, the cake bakers of Rome seem to have surpassed by far the bakers of our day.

At the beginning no specialized class of Roman bakers existed. Bread, the basis of all other foods, was prepared by the housewife of *siligo,* the variety of wheat which even in those days was known to be the most nourishing. But then the Roman woman became a lady. She who had long been the wife of the peasant and the warrior and had been proud of her household work learned from the East that it was good for a woman to spare herself during the hot hours of the day. Mirror and rouge preserved youth; leavening and baking brought on age. The ladies of the Orient knew this, and now that the husbands of the Roman women began conquering the Orient, the Roman ladies soon learned it. Until the year 172, when Aemilius Paulus conquered Macedonia, we find no professional bakers in Rome. But around this time they began to relieve the burden of the housewife by offering baked goods for sale in shops. These bakers were also millers.

Their work was considered a highly skilled craft. They were classed in the popular mind not where they are classed today, but perhaps at the rank of tailors. Craftsmanship was considered unique and individual; people spoke of the *ars pistorica,* the art of baking. The owners of bakeries were for the most part freed slaves; they were highly respected men who had fair opportunities to rise to wealth, like one Vergilius Eurysaces whose tombstone has been preserved in Rome. A painting upon it shows him instructing his kneaders, young men with intelligent faces. Syrians and Phoenicians were especially prized as apprentices; the Romans knew that the peoples of the Orient had a refined sense of taste and more delicate hands for the work of baking.

The self-consciousness of the bakers soon made itself manifest. They established guilds whose rights were guaranteed by the Roman state. The bylaws of the guilds prescribed their relationship to their slaves and free apprentices. The guilds had considerable importance in the religious life of Rome. The festival of the oven goddess was given the fixed date of June 9, when the ovens and the baking tools were wreathed in flowers and everyone ate and drank copiously. The *corpus pistorum* was a unified organization with which Italian cities had to reckon in municipal elections. To say of a baker *"bonum panem fert* [he delivers good bread]" was equivalent to giving a reason for electing the man to a municipal office. And bakers often were elected. Paquius Proculus, who belonged to the bakers' guild, became the second mayor of Pompeii.

The emperors confirmed these rights and gave special privileges to the bakers, as "people important to the welfare of the nation." There was a purpose to this favoring, and at last the day came when the purpose was accomplished—the bakers became civil officials. This was an evil development, good neither for the bakers nor for Rome. It is a phenome-

CERES ENTHRONED
(Pompeian mural painting)

non that shows us that the Romans were only apparently a practical people; they did not understand their real problems, or they could not master them. Bread made the Roman Empire great; but bread also destroyed it.

§ 33

The long era of Roman decline begins with the words of Pliny, "*Latifundia perdidere Italiam* [The great landholdings have destroyed Italy]." Nor has any historian who has examined the fall of Rome evaded Pliny's addendum: "*jam vero et provincias* [and later the whole empire]"—neither the Englishman, Gibbon, nor the German, Mommsen, nor the Italian, Ferrero, the Frenchman, Glotz, nor the Russian, Rostovtzev. Barbarian invasions on the pattern of Alaric's would not alone have destroyed the empire, nor would the federalism of Emperor Diocletian have done so, had not the masters of the Roman Empire pursued the worst agrarian policy in all history. The empire would have survived if Rome had not made a political football of bread!

In the oldest period the Romans had good laws, which protected the farmer. All land that was conquered belonged to the state—at first to the king, later to the Roman Republic. There was, therefore, virtually no private property. The state, however, had the right to give land to the poor. This was what it did. When meritorious soldiers returned home from the wars, the state settled them as farmers. By tilling the soil the soldiers became the owners of it. Other land was given away in a different manner. It was rented—to the rich, of course—because the Roman state needed money. The wealth of the rich at that time consisted not of land, but of cattle, herds, and of slaves.

Why was it that the poor man had no luck with his gift of land? He had nothing but his own two hands, his plow, his oxen, his wife, and his half-grown son. He had scarcely manure enough to improve his land. But the rich man had everything he needed to grow farm produce better and cheaper—slaves, better plows, and as many animals as he needed. When the small Italian farmer drove from his fields to market to offer his grain for sale and perhaps his fowls and milk, he found that the country town had been taken over by the sales organization of the owner of the *latifundia*. The millionaire gentleman farmer produced everything more cheaply and could therefore offer everything at cheaper prices. The poor farmer could not compete; his income vanished away. He returned home with so little money that he could not continue to till his soil. With false sympathy, the rich man then came to him and bought his land for a ridiculous price. The farmer then moved to the city, became a plebeian, loitered in squares and in taverns, and looked with hatred upon the state that had cheated him. Why, he asked, was Rome making farmers of soldiers, if she could not protect the livelihood of her new farmers?

There were, to be sure, statesmen who perceived the danger in time, and laws were made to combat it. Plutarch tells us:

When the wealthy man began to offer larger rents, and drive the poorer people out, it was enacted by law that no person whatever should enjoy more than five hundred acres of ground. This for some time checked the avarice of the richer, and was of the greatest assistance to the poorer people, who retained under it their respective proportions of ground. But the rich contrived to get these lands again into their possession under other people's names, and at last did not hesitate to claim most of them publicly in their own. The poor, who were thus deprived of their farms, were no longer either ready, as they had formerly been, to serve in war, or to be careful in the education of their children; inasmuch that in a short time there were comparatively few freemen remaining in all Italy, which swarmed with workhouses full of foreign-born slaves. These the rich men employed in cultivating the ground from which they had dispossessed the citizens.

Thus the laws were evaded, and the misery of the farmers increased. The abandonment of the land for the city likewise increased. There were repeatedly men who saw the danger to their country. Even members of the oldest Roman noble families considered the situation intolerable. The grandsons of the greatest of Roman generals, Scipio Africanus the younger, who had conquered the Carthaginians, founded a reform movement that aimed to help the farmers. These men were Tiberius and Gaius Gracchus.

One day Tiberius Gracchus arose at a public meeting and spoke words that no Latin ear had heard before. "The wild beasts of Italy have their caves or nests. But the men who fought for Italy, who were ready to die for her as soldiers, have at most a share in her air and light, but neither house nor roof to shelter them. They must wander about from place to place with their wives and children. *Kyrioi tes oikoumenes einai legomenoi* (These warriors are called the masters of the world), but not a square foot of earth in this world belongs to them!"

To our ears these words ring even louder than they did to the Romans. For Tiberius Gracchus began his speech with words almost identical to Christ's: "Foxes have holes, and the birds of the air have nests; but the Son of Man hath not where to lay his head." How did Tiberius Gracchus know what the Nazarene would say one hundred and fifty years later? Or how did Jesus (an uneducated man who would know nothing of Roman history) know what the Tribune of the People, Gracchus, had said? . . . The same situation evoked the same words.

There began a parliamentary conflict in which Gracchus sought to renew an ancient law that limited possession of land to five hundred acres. Gracchus won, and graciously granted each rich man's son an additional two hundred and fifty acres. But the large landholders procured assassins who killed Tiberius as he was about to speak to a popular assemblage. Strangely enough, although Tiberius Gracchus had been a wholly secular figure, the Romans had the feeling that they had committed an act of blasphemy. They said: "*Cererem vetustissimam placari opportet* [The ancient goddess of the fields had to be placated]." For the agrarian reformers were considered to belong to Demeter as intimately as, in mythical times, had the missionary of the plow, Triptolemos.

After a drought in 496 B.C. the *Sibylline Books* had commended the cult of Demeter to Rome (the name Ceres, which the Romans gave to her, means Creator). Ceres had always fought on the side of the Roman democratic party. The worshipers of Ceres in Italy were almost entirely plebeian. It is curious to note that in the same year that the "plebs Romana" founded the Temple of Ceres on one of Rome's seven hills (490 B.C.), Demeter was winning the Battle of Marathon for the Greek peasants. She did not do so because the Persians were contemptuous of agriculture. On the contrary, they were probably far better tillers of the soil than the Greeks. ("Their soil is so particularly well adapted to corn that it never produces less than two hundredfold," Herodotus wrote enviously. "In favorable seasons it will sometimes rise to three hundred, and the ear of their wheat is four digits in size. . . .") But the Persians were *douloi,* serfs of a despotic king, not free landholders. It was because of this that Demeter aided the Greeks at Marathon and Salamis. . . .

The assassinated Gracchus was mourned by the "people's party" as a "missionary of Ceres," and his funeral procession was so vast that the Senate felt compelled to confirm the agrarian laws. Eighty thousand new farmers were placed on the land that Gracchus had taken from the rich. His younger brother, Gaius, continued the tradition of the elder. But he, too, was assassinated or driven to take his own life. And the vengeance of the great landholders swept aside not only the work of the Gracchi, but all the old traditions of the state as the owner of the land. Now all the land of Italy belonged to a few hundred families who sat idly in their country homes and let their slaves work. Neither Marius nor Caesar, both men of the popular party, was able to check this evil. The state deserted its farmers and bowed in submission to the rich.

The first consequence was that the Italian landowner gradually left off raising grain. He found it more lucrative to use his lands as great pastures, because cattle and sheep were far more profitable than grain. The rich man, to be sure, sold grain. But it did not grow in Italy. It was brought in ships, at extremely low freight rates, from Rome's overseas possessions.

§ 34

As soon as Roman policy had wrought its worst and had reduced Italy from its position as a bread-producing country, it became necessary to import grain from abroad. This was not difficult, since all the land abroad belonged to Rome.

By a quite fortuitous course, the form the empire took was one favorable to this state of affairs. Conforming to Euclid's proposition that "the center of a circle is equidistant from all points on the circumference," the city of Rome, the legal and military capital, was situated in the center of the webwork of empire. It had befallen this way through instinct, not reason—a geometric instinct such as the spider possesses. This creature— *Arachne diademata*—constructs a web out of the juices of its own body, which harden in air. Taking into its calculations the strength of the wind and the weight of its own body, the spider suspends its web between twigs, and waits. Where does it take up its post to wait? Long before Euclid it arrived at the theorem that "distance is equivalent to time," and hence waits in the center. Should a fly become entangled in the web and struggle against the sticky threads, the spider must reach it in the shortest time, which always corresponds to the shortest distance. For if the fly is not stunned quickly, it will tear the web, and the spider will not only lose her prey, but will have a torn web to repair. Therefore, she sits in the center.

Rome emulated the spider. The world web of Rome was so woven that *potestas, impetus,* and *ictus* (might, drive, and striking power) always came from the middle, from the geometric center. The Roman Empire avoided the error of Alexander the Great, who attempted to build an empire from the outer circumference and unite all the land from Macedonia to India. The impetus did not come from the organic center. Neither the Macedonian army nor Greek philosophy could permanently gloss over this defect in structure, and it was not long before Alexander's empire fell into dissolution.

On the other hand, the map of the Roman Empire shows that its growth from the earliest period was consistently concentric. The military ideal—ability to strike out promptly at all possible threats—would permit no other fashion of growth. Hence, Macedonia was conquered at almost the same time as Spain—for they are situated at equal distances from Rome; soon after Dalmatia, a campaign was launched against the South of France. Caesar did not only conquer England but also, for the sake of concentricity, conquered Egypt six years afterward. Military instinct forbade extending the boundaries too far. Rome followed the sagacious policy of not going too far north; walls and rivers served as barriers against the Germans and the Sarmatians. Equally, no attempt was made to conquer in the far south and east. All the Roman emperors, from Caesar to Diocletian, acted in consonance with the Chinese saying that "there must be an outside of a wall, as there is an inside."

When Italy began to decline as a grain-producing country, she commanded sufficient sources to guarantee the safe importation of grain for hundreds of years. The modern reader is somewhat astonished to learn which countries were Rome's chief sources of supply. Egypt, of course. But also Spain and North Africa; in addition, though to a lesser degree, Sicily, Sardinia, and, finally, England!

For strategic reasons it was necessary for Rome to possess the Spanish Peninsula so long as the Carthaginian Empire existed, for Spain was the territory through which the Africans marched upon Italy. Besides her strategic value, Spain was a treasure for her mines. Then, suddenly, in the imperial period, the Romans abandoned the mines. Since Italy's agriculture could no longer fill the Roman stomach, grain had become more important. Although the soil of Spain is poor in humus, luxurious wheat fields were established in the river valleys. Cartagena and Taragona were important export centers, but the richest export traders were located in Cadiz. Strabo, the geographer, tells us that most of the millionaires of the Roman Empire lived in Cadiz. Yet as early as the time of Nero this commercial prosperity was threatened; the grain traffic to Rome was cut off. The wild tribes of the Sahara crossed the Straits, tempted from their desert by the green gardens and grain-covered fields along the coast of Spain.

The Roman capital could, to be sure, live without Spanish grain. Together with Sardinia and Sicily, Spain delivered only a third of the grain required at the time of Augustus. The second third was supplied by the province that was then called Africa: Algeria and Tunis. These lands today are very different from what they were in Roman times. Originally the Romans had a deep grudge against Algeria and Tunis for serving as springboards for the power of Carthage; they did not intend to permit these lands to revive after Rome had subdued them. But Julius Caesar was more generous and more ambitious. He planned cities which were established in North Africa, and the land was subjected to intense cultivation. Not only the Roman immigrants thrived, but the native population quickly regained its prosperity.

After twelve hundred years of Mohammedanism it is hard to imagine that in the second century A.D. Africa from Tunis to Tangier was one vast Roman field of wheat. The great accomplishment of the Romans consisted not in their introduction of Roman law or Roman police, but in their making farmers of hundreds of thousands of nomads. They compelled the Berbers to dismount from their horses and gave into their hands sacks of seed and the handles of the plow.

These tribes were not so heavily exploited as were the Egyptian fellahin; they remained loyal to the Roman Empire and defended it bravely against their own brothers who still dwelt in the desert. At a time when the Moroccans were invading Spain and hampering sea traffic with Rome, Roman Africa flourished. The ruins of the country palaces where landowners and leaseholders lived; the number of small Roman courtyards; the place names—all these things prove that at one time Romans infiltrated all of North Africa. In a single century of labor the Romans contrived to conjure fruits and bread out of a land that is now only waste and parched plain. It was not that they found springs that today are unknown. Their miracles were accomplished through the erection of aqueducts and, above all, of cisterns. The Romans practiced a stern thrift upon the water that fell from the heavens. In villages that archaeologists have excavated, every house was found to have a cistern. Probably the storing of water was mandatory. This artificial irrigation allowed for great density of population. Six cities sprang up in an area of six hundred square miles. One authority believes that in North Africa the cities were as close together as are the villages around modern Paris.

This bread land, conquered in the classical manner of the Romans, was lost in the classical manner. A province that owed its entire existence to the farming population and paid a natural tax of grain to the Roman Empire permitted itself to ape Italy and discriminate against its own farming class. Very soon after the conquest, the state declared the newly won land *ager publicus,* and rented or gave most of it away to deserving veterans and citizens. After a short time the rich began buying up the land of the poorer peasants; a great expropriation of the peasants began. The familiar *latifundia* economy set in. Around the year 50 B.C. half of North Africa belonged to six rich Roman families, and only some two thousand dirt farmers were left. (Cicero speaks of this in his essay "On Duty." It is, by the way, wholly false to imagine that the ancient writers did not see these abuses. But they had even less power than writers today have to repair abuses.) At last the farmers were living merely as lease-holders upon their own land. The small leaseholders were oppressed in turn by the large leaseholders. Over the large leaseholders in Rome stood the Roman senator or the capitalistic head of the state, the billionaire emperor.

The predicament of the small Roman farmer in Africa became intolerable; he began thinking about armed revolt. But before any uprising was set off, another revolution overwhelmed him. There descended a foreign enemy: the Vandals. A German tribe that had sped across Europe from Hungary to southern Spain at breath-taking pace, the Vandals crossed the Straits in A.D. 429 and took possession of Africa. The Germans allied themselves with the Negroes, "the untamable men of the south," who were the other sworn enemies of Roman civilization and who had cause to revenge themselves for many a raid into their country to secure slaves and loot. Haters of agriculture, the Germanic warriors and the black nomads not only destroyed the leaseholders and the rich landowners, but the small farmers as well, who had hoped to revolt. This was the end of the wheatland and the culture of North Africa. It never revived.

For the Euclidian structure of the Roman Empire, it was a misfortune that the grain-producing lands were located on the circumference, and were therefore the first to be lost. But why did Italy depend on grain from overseas and not on European grain? For France is, after all, the classic wheat country of Europe. But the Gaul that Julius Caesar won was not wheatland at all, nor did it become so later on. Only in the South of France were there figs and wine; in the center and North France was a country of forests and pastures. The wealth of the Gauls consisted of their cattle; and for centuries the Gallic aristocracy remained interested only in horses, hunting, and fishing. Flour for bread was ground from acorns, and was bitter indeed.

But a great many Roman soldiers were garrisoned in France; of what did they bake their bread? The answer to this question completely overturns the modern picture of Europe's agrarian setup. All the grain for the Romans in France, Holland, Belgium, and the lower Rhine came from *England*. Grain ships brought it from Sussex and Kent. "For Gallia and the Rhineland towns," we learn from Ammianus Marcellinus (A.D. 330–395), "it was usual to rely on the harvests of British corn" (i.e., wheat). Once more it was a misfortune for the Roman Empire that the English granary was located on the periphery, so that it could easily be cut off.

As long as Egypt remained, however, there was sufficient bread in Rome. The struggle for Egypt had been the struggle for the greatest of bread lands. The sober Romans were interested in the Nile because of its grain. Alexander had gone to Egypt to be crowned a divine king and have himself declared the "son of the sun." But Caesar and Antony felt no such twinges of glory when they ascended the Nile. They wanted nothing but grain. This, too, was what Augustus wanted. It was to have consequences of the greatest moment that Augustus, after the death of Cleopatra (30 B.C.), did not ascend the Egyptian throne, but took possession of Egypt. The kingdom of Egypt was placed under his personal administration. It became—as we would say today—his domain. And from then on the mastery of the Roman emperors over Rome inseparably depended upon their possession of this richest of domains. Since in contrast to all other provinces Egypt did not belong to the state, the income from it belonged not to the state but to the emperor. He could do with it what he wished. Thus was established the profitable relationship between the billionaire emperor, the greatest landowner in the empire, and the Roman unemployed, the poor man of the capital. Egypt was the magic wand that linked Caesar to the proletariat and the proletariat to Caesar. The one gave bread, the other fists.

Emperor Augustus jealously guarded his exclusive and unchallenged rule of the Nile. Roman knights and senators were forbidden to travel in the bread land. This precaution was necessary because in the wars for the throne that Augustus fought with Antony, Egypt had constantly been upon the side of the pretender. This must be avoided in the future. Therefore, the first emperor saw to it that Egypt was administered by his privately appointed officials. For if a Roman party of opposition should obtain control of the bread land, the Roman emperor in power was lost, for he would not be able to feed the proletariat and his own bodyguards.

The administration was not bad. Egypt still was, as it had been four thousand years before, "chemi"—black earth—and the gift of the Nile god. Since there was nothing to cavil at with the old, the old was permitted to remain. Through the elimination of the native court, the costs of administration were considerably decreased. The golden cup which the Pharaoh had formerly thrown into the swelling Nile in June, at the Egyptians' most important festival, was now cast by the Roman viceroy—he, too, called "beloved of Ptah and Isis." From this inexhaustible Nile Valley came a full third of the bread required by Rome and all of Italy—and the wheat was so cheap that it could literally be given away.

Egypt was bread. He who owned the bread could also be emperor. It was this highly practical consideration that made Egypt the spot where most of the revolutions of the intermediate imperial period began. This was the case, for example, with the revolt of Vespasian (A.D. 69.) Vespasian's plan splendidly comprehended Roman conditions. The plan exhibits perfectly the indissoluble trinity of imperium, proletariat, and bread. Vespasian decided to seize the grain fleet which regularly delivered grain to the Roman capital; the Romans would go hungry until they recognized him as emperor. By this logical device the Flavian family came to power in Rome.

§ 35

It was the Flavians who made civil servants of the bakers. Gradually the bakers ceased to be a class of free artisans. They retained their guild privileges—no one could set up as a baker unless confirmed by the guild —but they were made subordinate to the Minister of Food Supply (*prefectus annonae*). The two hundred and fifty-eight shops kept by the bakers of Rome ceased to be privately owned. They were not expressly expropriated, but they became "places of state" in which the bakers and their apprentices remained as officials of the state. No one was permitted to sell his shop or to discontinue his license; every baker's son had to become a baker; the profit of the bakeries flowed into the treasury of the corporation.

The state, of course, paid its bakers from the *fiscus frumentarius* (the funds of the Ministry of Food Supply). But many of the bakers were ill-pleased with the new order. Some of them had become very rich and owned vast enterprises, like the Latini brothers, who daily ground and baked almost a thousand bushels of flour. Such men were now employees of a state that was anything but socialistic. They did not like it, but they could do nothing about it. A painting in the catacombs shows us a Roman baker standing at a table and holding in his left hand the symbol of the guild, the *modius* (bushel measure). His right hand, however, is holding a basket of bread toward the *plebs frumentaria* (people who were not proper customers, but recipients of the national dole).

This *plebs frumentaria*, the army of the urban unemployed, was the terror of the national treasury. Through the ruthlessness of the large landowners, who were depopulating Italy, ever greater hosts of jobless were driven into the city. In 72 B.C. the number of people receiving free grain was already 40,000. But the number grew. Soon Sallust (86–34 B.C.) spoke of *largitiones, qui rem publicam lacerant* (largess that was rending the nation). Julius Caesar found himself required to feed no less than 200,000 recipients of grain. Augustus attempted to reduce the numbers of the proletariat by refusing the dole to those "whose need was pretended." But he soon gave up this reform. In order to rule securely he had to meet three requirements. The first was to provide grain for the *plebs frumentaria* in the manner to which it had been accustomed. Then he must feed his own bodyguard. Third, he must always be prepared to dump a large amount of grain on the market so that private grain speculators could not force up the price of bread.

Rome was not a socialistic state, and there was great grain speculation. Only in Egypt, the imperial domain, were the traders banned. In all the other provinces they could buy grain and gamble with it. Suetonius (A.D. 70–140) mentions it as a special virtue of Augustus' that he succeeded in "reconciling the interests of the capital's population with those of the grain dealers"—something that was certainly no easy task, for the grain dealers complained eloquently of the risks involved. They could not lower their prices, what with freight rates, pirates, wrecks, and crop failures. It is a familiar song. One time, when several African dealers were assassinated, the police did not trouble to pursue the murderers.

The principal thing was that Rome remained quiet. The *prefectus annonae* and his bakers saw to this. To conduct the dole in an orderly fashion the *tessera frumentaria*, a grain-control stamp, was introduced. It was made of bronze and carried the portrait of the ruling emperor and dispenser. Whoever could present this identification was entitled to the monthly government dole. Later the distribution was made weekly, and lead coins were provided. Under Emperor Aurelian (270–275) distribution of bread rather than grain was introduced, with each member of the proletariat receiving two breads daily. Some 300,000 people thronged before the bakeries in the narrow streets of Rome, blocking traffic. Under this emperor the right to receive the dole was declared hereditary. Thus the unemployed were encouraged to multiply, for they and their descendants would be maintained by the state in perpetuity. In order for the state to feed people, it also had to support a vast number of officials in the ports of entry and in the most distant provinces.

The kindly goddess who gave this largess—originally she had not been a goddess at all, but an economic measure—was soon worshiped fervently by the people. Wherever the portrait of the "Annona" appears upon coins, she is shown as a young woman related to Demeter and Ceres, holding in her left hand a cornucopia, in her right a sheaf of grain. Often she is accompanied by symbols of shipping, to indicate that her grain did not grow in Italy.

It did not, and in lands distant from Italy the "Annona" was scarcely worshiped. The *provinciae frumentariae* (the bread countries) stripped themselves to send their basic food to Italy. In the peripheral lands of the Roman Empire a great many people suffered hunger.

ROME: THE BREAD GOD, JESUS CHRIST

§ 36

INTO THIS WORLD of the Roman imperium came Jesus Christ. It was, as we have seen, a world of real distress, of physical hunger; a world in which the grain speculators withheld the grain and the emperor misused bread for political purposes by feeding only those who supported his power. Into such a world came Christ. And said that he was the Son of God.

This world was also fecund with metaphysical hunger. Countless people felt that it was not the right world. The Roman genius for rule spent itself in perfecting administration, but it gave nothing to the soul. Wherever the Romans went, everything was organized—but simultaneously men could feel tangibly that everything had died. Values were at a low ebb. Even in the realm of religion, Rome conducted herself like a filing clerk. The *flamen cerealis*, for example, the high priest of agriculture, was required to appeal to the following "gods" at the great sacrifices:

> *Vervactor*, the god of the fallowing
> *Redarator*, the god of the second plowing
> *Imporcitor*, the spirit of furrowing
> *Insitor*, the spirit of sowing
> *Obarator*, the genius of plowing in
> *Sarritor*, the genius of hoeing
> *Subruncinator*, the genius of weeding
> *Messor*, the divine assistant in mowing
> *Convector*, the divine binder of the sheaves
> *Promitor*, the god who distributed the grain

This is the list given by Fabius Pictor in his *Jus Pontificium*, the "law of sacrifices." Both priests and laity knew that this was not religion, for the divinities to whom the high priest appealed were, of course, not divinities, but necessary activities that had been clothed in religion so that the farmer would not forget them.

Rome's juridical rule literally disenchanted the earth. Aside from local religions (the Jewish, for example), which were not overcome by Rome, however, certain great spiritual forces still existed throughout the vast empire. There was, first of all, Greek culture; the artistic heritage of Athens and the teachings of Epicurus and the Stoa. These teachings were the philosophical consolation of all cultivated men. But only of cultivated men. The noblest gift of the Greeks was an artistic skepticism. But the people did not enjoy doubt; the people demanded positive belief.

Consequently, the Egyptian priests of magic were far more influential and powerful. The prestidigitators from Alexandria who traveled through the whole Roman Empire demonstrating transubstantiation—changing water into wine—were far more important to the people than the pallid intellectual culture of the Hellenized salons. Here was something direct. From the Egyptians one could learn to make magic scientifically. Papyri and formulae were sold which were alleged to extend the powers of the will. With them one could compel fate, could practice spells and magic upon one's foes. This fad even extended into the salons of the intellectuals. Ovid, for example, the fashionable poet, was nothing else but a depicter of "magical metamorphoses," painting in splendid verses the transformation of a man into a cloud, a tree into a nymph, or a woman into stone. The "consolation" that most people sought was power over matter.

There existed side by side with the Egyptian magician a force more powerful than he. This was his opposite, the Assyrian astrologer. Although the empires of the Assyrians, the Babylonians, and the Persians had been destroyed utterly, the national religion, the belief in the stars, persisted among the people. And the same Roman subjects who had but recently believed that the will of man strengthened by magic was capable of all things now believed they were playthings of cosmic forces. The destiny of each individual was dictated by the position of sun and stars at any given time. Even the lives of great heroes had been lived out in obedience to the nocturnal heavens. The twelve labors of Hercules symbolized the progression of the sun through the zodiac. After the death of Jesus Christ, Mark the Evangelist, who was himself probably an astrologer, arranged the events of Jesus' life so that they corresponded to a sun year and to the "adventures of the sun." The astrological parallels with the life of Jesus were worked out to the very minutest detail. The account of John the Baptist at the beginning of the narration is explained by Aquarius, the constellation of the Water Carrier who appears above the horizon at the winter solstice. The two fish in the zodiac correspond to the fishermen, Simon and Andrew, whom Jesus made his disciples. When the sun entered Virgo, the "Constellation with the Corn Ear (Spica)," the disciples gathered ears on the Sabbath in order to clear a path through the wheat field for the master. The salvation from the tempest at sea took place as the Milky Way retired from the sun. The miracle when five thousand were fed with seven loaves and two fishes took place when the sun was in the sign of the Fishes. Many men would not have accepted Jesus as the Saviour if his life had not been symbolic of cosmic events. His fate seemed like that of the sun: dawn, rise, culmination, descent, and setting.

But if one sweeps all this aside and attempts to find the real life of Jesus amid the layers of Greek, Egyptian, and Babylonian mythology and to see it as it actually was: the life of a great prophet who revolted against the theology of his people, the Jews—even then there remains in his life much that is unreal. The evangelists who portrayed his life seem inordinately concerned with symbols of agriculture. Where they do not transform him into a sun myth they connect him at every step of his way with the year of vegetation. Consider, for example, the significance that this son of Joseph and Mary was born in Bethlehem. "Beth-Lehem" means "house of bread"; and in order that there be no suspicion that Jesus was a dispenser of bread, like Emperor Augustus, he was born in a stall: a poor child who was warmed by the breath of the beasts of the field, oxen and asses. (The vegetation god Bacchus, we remember, was placed in a grain fan.) Even the hill of Gethsemane has a place in the agrarian passion, for it means "oil press." These things are in themselves remarkable. But it is even more remarkable that Jesus, in the period from solstice to solstice in which his destiny was enacted, clothed his ethical teachings in a number of parables taken from the art of cultivation. It is remarkable because he himself was not a farmer, but the son of a carpenter. Yet with few exceptions—like the parable of the beams and the splinters—his parables are concerned not with structures and cabinet work, but with the subtle processes of plowing, sowing, harvesting, cattle raising, herding and shepherding, cutting grapes, and baking bread. Obviously a large number of people were interested in placing him in the realm of the agrarian and limiting him to this realm. That is, they would accept his ethics and his prophecies for the other world only if he founded an earthly realm of plenty, a realm of bread.

Jesus felt that these interests were just; on the other hand, he resisted them—therein lay the heroism of his life. For we must not forget that the chief problem of the times was hunger. It was virtually a new problem, considered only rarely by Roman writers because the ruling caste as yet had not perceived it. Ovid, for example, speaks of hunger in purely rhetorical fashion as a mythological horror dwelling somewhere in the underworld beside "cold" and "fear." Mass hunger seemed something unreal. It was still too new to be seen clearly, for before the Roman Empire organized the world, only local hunger, of short duration, had existed—when a city was besieged or when a plague dealt widespread death among the reapers. Such small misfortunes were repaired by the next harvest. For example, in 430 B.C. the Athenian orator Lysias delivered an oration against the traders who cornered grain. But how small a matter was it that Athens received more or less grain from the Black Sea coast during a season. Thirty miles from the city the shortages were unknown.

The Syrians, to be sure, had dedicated a temple in their city of Smyrna to the goddess of famine, Bubrostis. But the temple was rarely opened. The problem of worked-out soil did not exist in the older period—nor was there the insidious political handling of bread, with the bread provinces being stripped to feed other provinces. Since most areas fed themselves, there were also no transport crises. But overnight all this had changed. Hunger coursed through the provinces of the Roman Empire— natural hunger, and along with it the artificial hunger produced by Roman administrative measures. It was no wonder that a man who wished to "save" mankind would encounter first and foremost the question: "What do you bring us for this world?"

§ 37

In earlier times Eleusis had magnificently combined two solutions. The mysteries promised felicity in the other world; but at the same time the farming class is granted great honors in this world. But the elevated rank of the Greek farming population was a thing of the past. On the contrary, Rome was hostile to the farmer. The goddess of agriculture "had been offended" by the assassination of Tiberius Gracchus. Two Roman officials now sat in the highest collegium of the Eleusinian world church; but the Eleusinian ceremonies were now practiced only for the sake of the promised other world. The celebration of the plow and the harvest had long since become petrified into mere forms. Five hundred years before, Eleusis had been a vital force in agriculture; now it stilled only metaphysical hunger.

In the year 1890, when Demetrios Philios was guiding a number of visitors through the excavations at Eleusis, an American tourist asked: "Where was the agricultural school located?" The question was very natural. The American was a student of Seaman A. Knapp, who reformed agriculture in the South after the Civil War. The American tourist thought he recognized in the legendary Triptolemos the type of the "teacher"; the director of the excavations, however, replied that Eleusis had hardly been the place for an agricultural school, for it was not necessary. At the time Eleusis was founded the problems of agriculture had not been difficult. Religious memory was sufficient guide in cultivating the fields.

In Roman times, however, more learning was necessary. With the exhaustion of the Italian soil and the concomitant plundering of the provinces, the Eleusinian church might well have made some practical contribution—either of technical or social reforms. But Eleusis did not, of course, intervene.

The masses could expect no help from this ancient church. The mysteries still attracted the curiosity of a great many people; but though the salvation of the individual was a great consolation, "heavenly bread" was not enough; earthly bread was also needed. Therefore, the people asked one question of each new prophet: Was he concerned about the price of bread? And did he have food for them?

The day came when the province of Judea had to deliver *ton tetarton tu situ* (a fourth part of its grain) to the Roman state treasury.

§ 38

No wonder Jesus Christ encountered bread as soon as he began his calling of prophet! It was the devil who suggested that if Christ were really the son of God, let him remove the evil that most plagued his contemporaries: let him destroy famine. And as Matthew and John tell us, the devil chose the moment that was psychologically apt for his plan. Jesus had gone into the desert, to prepare himself for his work as a saviour of men. "And," we read, "when he had fasted forty days and forty nights, he was afterward an hungred. And when the tempter came to him, he said, If thou be the Son of God, command that these stones be made bread. But he answered and said, It is written, Man shall not live by bread alone, but by every word that proceedeth out of the mouth of God." He was here referring to Moses' explanation of the miracle of the manna.

In *Paradise Regained* Milton has written a magnificent exegesis of this scene. Here the devil approaches Jesus in the form of a curious wanderer. He declares he has already heard a great deal about Jesus and finds it dreadful that he should be walking about in the desert:

> So far from path or road of men, who pass
> In Troop or Caravan, for single none
> Durst ever, who return'd, and dropt not here
> His Carcass, pin'd with hunger and with droughth?

Would it not be better, he suggests, to find some town or village (though the nearest one is still far off!) where Jesus might teach and others listen to him?

To this Christ replies dryly:

> . . . Who brought me hither
> Will bring me hence, no other Guide I seek.

This would be possible, the devil interposes cleverly, only by a miracle.

> What other way I see not, for we here
> Live on tough roots and stubs, to thirst inur'd
> More than the Camel, and to drink go far,
> Men to much misery and hardship born;
> But . . .

With great tact Milton's devil leads the conversation around to where he wishes it:

> But if thou be the Son of God, Command
> That out of these hard stones be made thee bread;
> So shalt thou save thy self and us relieve . . .

It is only then that Christ is at a loss. But he recognizes whom he has before him, looks at him, and hurls truths at his head. Angrily he begins:

> Think'st thou such force in bread? Is it not written,
> For I discern thee other than thou seem'st,
> Man lives not by bread only, but each word
> Proceeding from the mouth of God, who fed
> Our fathers here with Manna? In the mount
> Moses was forty days, nor eat, nor drank;
> And forty days Elijah without food
> Wander'd this barren waste, the same I now.
> Why dost thou then suggest to me distrust,
> Knowing who I am, as I know who thou art?

Jesus recognized the danger. If he solved the chief problem of the earthly Roman world; if he removed hunger by turning chance inanimate objects into nourishing bread, he would have become king of this world. The small round stones of the desert which so closely resembled the bread of the Jews could very well be transformed by the fevered imagination of a famished man into bread. But if Christ had followed the suggestion, he would have undone the spiritual and heavenly part of his mission. This was what Milton's devil desired when he tempted him so softly and with such natural gentleness. . . . Thinkest thou such force in bread? Bread did indeed have such force in an age where it was lacking. And—Dostoevski, too, perceived this—if Jesus had actually placed his hand upon this instrument of force, this lever, he could have lifted the earthly world out of joint. He would have become emperor of the opposition and won the victory over Augustus.

This he did not desire, although he loved men also in their earthly guise and would have liked to free them from hunger. He had a precise and realistic understanding of the real value of bread as a human food. When your son asks you for bread, you cannot give him a stone, he says—

this is the reverse side of the temptation in the desert. The need for bread is also more weighty than the comfort of one's neighbor: if a friend has come to us from a journey and we wish to borrow three breads to set before him, then we knock at our neighbor's door even at midnight, when he is already asleep (Luke 11: 5–8). Bread is also more important than the law—like David who took the sacred bread of the temple when he was hungry, the disciples of Christ plucked the ears of grain on the Sabbath. To the Syro-Phoenician woman who asks the Lord to heal her possessed daughter, he replies, after glancing into the house, with the astonished question: How was it that she gave the dogs in the room bread, but none to the children?

And she answered and said to him, "Yes, Lord: yet the dogs under the table eat of the children's crumbs."

Jesus praised her for this answer, and seconds her thought: no creature of God can be excluded from the enjoyment of bread. When he teaches his disciples the Lord's Prayer, he asks above all for "daily bread." That is, he asks for the very thing which he desires his followers not to be overly concerned with. He knows that concern for bread stupefies men. Who looks after the ravens and the lilies of the field? he asks. The goodness of God provides for them. Such words, spoken to men, are intended to soothe their minds. But when he speaks to his Father, he reveals his own deep concern for bread. For bread is the only earthly thing for which Jesus, otherwise wholly spiritual, asks. He does not plead for bread in general, but for *daily* bread. He is not afraid, like the Roman poor, to ask for the *panis quotidianus,* for bread as the Roman emperors distributed it. But his request is addressed to one infinitely greater than the Roman emperor. This plea is so moving that one must have a heart of stone in order not to weep when repeating it. It is, we repeat, real bread, daily bread, for which Jesus asks. Saint Cyprian (A.D. 252) is wholly wrong when he says: "It was unnecessary for Jesus to ask his Father for *real* bread. Bread has a figurative meaning; it signifies heavenly wisdom. Jesus was a righteous man. The righteous man can suffer no lack and can never hunger. He possesses all!" This view is a distortion; it overlooks the spirit of community which Jesus felt toward all men. He wished to be not only the God of the righteous, but of the sinners also.

§ 39

When Jesus Christ declared that he was the Son of God, that his dwelling was in Heaven, and he was only a guest upon earth, the impact of this statement upon the men of his day was wholly different from what it would be upon modern men. The ability to decide whether "something is true" derives from the sum total of education acquired by observation and reasoning. Present-day education virtually prohibits our believing that someone whom we can see with our own eyes is also the Son of God; but the judgment of men in Jesus' day, even of cultivated men, was of a wholly different order. Seneca, for example (4 B.C.–A.D. 65), speaking of the dual nature of phenomena, says:

As the rays of the sun touch the earth, but truly belong in the place whence they spring, so it is with the great and holy spirit which is sent down into the bodies of certain men so that we may become more closely acquainted with the Divine: the spirit dwells among us, but it clings to its place of origin. It depends upon this origin, and thither it gazes and strives, remaining among us only as some noble guest.

Seneca did not know Christ; but probably, like countless of his contemporaries, he would, if he had met him, readily have believed in the moral and physical dual nature of Jesus.

If the educated class did not consider the contemporary residence upon earth of a god in human form an impossibility, how much less so did the people! The people of the Near East did not believe in a single, invisible god—as the Jews insistently and fervently demanded—but in a number of gods who succeeded but never wholly suppressed one another. The Near East had been politically part of Egypt for a long time; then, for centuries, it was ruled by the Persians and Greeks; later Roman mercenaries from all parts of the world brought their diverse beliefs into the receptive country. The people drank them up gladly. A dozen living religions circulated through Asia Minor, a variegated cup of mixed wines. The intellectual atmosphere of Palestine which the Jew, Jesus, breathed, was by no means purely Jewish. If the artisans and farmers to whom he preached his doctrine had actually been pious Jews, people who knew the Scriptures and the law, he would have been put to death far sooner. He would scarcely have been given time to travel about for a full year.

Whatever the mass of the people believed, in one respect they were agreed: if a new god were to appear, he must bring them some easing of their lot. This he could do in many ways. He could start a revolution, a nationalistic war, and undertake a just redistribution of all goods. In the parable of the penny (that one must "render unto Caesar the things that are Caesar's") Jesus rejected this course. But there was still another open to him: to allow the political order to remain, but to revolutionize the order of nature by means of a miracle. It was the second course that men entreated. They followed him, they importuned him, they asked for individual salvation from material evils. Some desired the healing of diseases, some desired more food. They demanded the miracle of created bread—precisely what Jesus had refused to do when the devil tempted him in the desert.

THE MIRACLE OF THE LOAVES
(Woodcut by Schnorr von Carolsfeld)

Then why did he grant their request? He did so from the noblest motive: because—as the evangelists stress again and again—he "had compassion" for them. It was easier to resist the devil than to resist pity. These people suffered from terrible diseases; they were helpless, hungry, and died too young. And, therefore, out of love for men, he did what was perhaps not best for the purity of his teachings—he cured them and gave them bread. Certainly he should not have done what was done by an unscrupulous charlatan like Apollonius of Tyana, who traveled through Italy and Spain awakening the dead. It is scarcely likely that Apollonius did this out of pity for the bereaved; he was looking for power. But Christ immersed himself so deeply in the sufferings of others that it seemed intolerable to him not to help. The consequence was that men believed in him. *This* was a consquence he desired, but he made a mistake in choosing the means. He, who had come to prepare a more perfect society for the kingdom of Heaven, became ever more entangled in the *miraculous*. If he were a God in human form, he must do something to prove himself one to the people. He forgot that the consequences for him, the giver, were greater than for those who received. They listened to him only when he produced miracles for them. They wanted him as a God of earthly bread. As such they worshiped him. So long as he failed to see the danger, he fell in with this compromise.

With the greatest psychological insight the evangelists describe Jesus' innocence in performing his miracles and the growth of his understanding of the danger. The transmutations of matter began, according to the account of John, at the marriage in Cana, where the celebrants had no wine and Jesus transformed water into wine. Here he behaves like a Greek god, like Bacchus; a dispenser of joy, using his talents to provide a festival.

Then he feeds five thousand men. He and his disciples had betaken themselves to a desert (he was compelled to do this because John the Baptist had just been beheaded and Jesus was in danger). Many people followed him, however, to hear his preaching. Soon they begin to be hungry.

He saith unto them, How many loaves have ye? go and see. And when they knew, they say, Five, and two fishes.

And he commanded them to make all sit down by companies upon the green grass.

And they sat down in ranks, by hundreds, and by fifties.

And when he had taken the five loaves and the two fishes, he looked up to heaven, and blessed, and brake the loaves, and gave them to his disciples to set before them; and the two fishes he divided among them all.

And they did all eat, and were filled.

And they took up twelve baskets full of the fragments, and of the fishes.

And they that did eat of the loaves were about five thousand men.

We must remember that feeding the people in distress was of old one of the functions of the Jewish prophets. Thus the prophet Elisha, who apparently provided the model for Jesus, fed a multitude with little at a time of sudden famine.

And there came a man from Baal-shalisha, and brought the man of God bread of the firstfruits, twenty loaves of barley, and full ears of corn in the husk thereof. And he said, Give the people, that they may eat.

And his servitor said, What, should I set this before an hundred men? He said again, Give the people, that they may eat: for thus saith the Lord, They shall eat, and shall leave thereof.

So he set it before them, and they did eat, and left thereof, according to the word of the Lord.

If we read this story from the Book of Kings attentively, we see that no physical miracle necessarily took place: the bread may not have been increased at all. Rather, the multitude were sated because they were psychically prepared to be sated. A multitude who received not only bread but the Word that proceeded from the mouth of God could be satisfied with little. Similarly, Jesus, too, may not have multiplied the bread; perhaps he created only the psychic readiness for satiation, which was sufficient unto itself.

This interpretation would make the miracle an "inward," psychological one. But this was precisely what the multitude did not want. They wanted the crudest of *physical miracles*, the transmutation of matter. They did not consider that they could be sated because, in addition to the five loaves and two fishes, they were fed upon the Word of God. They saw only that they had been sated—and the consequences were immediate and undesirable, for not only the common people, but the disciples also were incapable of comprehending what had happened. They did not see that their hunger had been satisfied "in concordance with the divine will, which Jesus consummated by prayer." They saw it only as a breach of natural law and were terribly frightened of Jesus. They were frightened also when, in the night, he walked across the water to their ship. How was this possible? "For," adds Mark, "they considered not the miracle of the loaves." The first great bread miracle, then, had worked negatively upon Jesus' followers: they saw in it only magic.

This should have been a warning to Jesus. It may almost be considered an intellectual fault that he did not act in accordance with this warning. Moreover—and this is so hard to believe that, characteristically, the Apostles Luke and John omit the tale—he shortly afterward repeated the miracle for four thousand men, who, in the same fashion, had listened to him preach for three days, until they no longer had anything to eat. This time it was seven breads which he transformed into bread for four thousand. But perhaps Mark recounts this story for the moral in it. A realm of plenty would begin as soon as God entered upon actual rule, and to the average man God's kingdom upon earth would be marked by much eating and drinking. The miracles of the bread were, as it were, rehearsals of what would be in the realm of plenty. Perhaps the historical Jesus spoke even more often of bread, of the pleasures of food in the afterworld, than the Biblical text indicates. Papias, one of the fathers of the Church (ab. A.D. 140), has ascribed the following apocryphal words to Jesus Christ:

The days will come in which vines shall spring up, each bearing ten thousand stocks, and on each stock ten thousand branches, and on each branch ten thousand shoots, and on each shoot ten thousand bunches, and on each bunch ten thousand grapes, and each grape when pressed shall yield five and twenty measures of wine. And when any one of the saints shall have caught hold of one grape another shall cry, "Better grape am I: take me; by men, bless the Lord!" Likewise also a grain of wheat shall cause to spring up ten thousand ears of corn, and each ear shall hold ten thousand grains, and each grain ten pounds of fine, pure flour. And so shall it be with the rest of the fruits and seeds and every herb after its kind. And all animals which shall use those foods that are got from the ground shall live in peace and concord, in all things subject to man.

In ecstatic moments Jesus had probably spoken similar words—and now, after the second miracle of the bread, the doors were wide open for misunderstanding. The common people no longer doubted that a man who had the power to make thousands of breads out of air was the new "god of bread" whom all men fervently longed for. Not because the earth was unfruitful—it was not at all; enough wheat and barley grew in Palestine—but because a curse lay upon bread which all men wished to have lifted—the curse of "In the sweat of thy face . . ." Miraculous bread was food that need be neither sowed nor harvested; therein lay its magnificence. Whoever gratified this dream of eating without labor was certainly the new god.

His was a tragic entanglement in miracles. Even his foes, the Pharisees, no longer able to escape the profound impression of his personality, demanded a miracle, a sign, from him. Naturally he refused. Everything that he had previously done he had received by asking God for it. How, in their presence, could prayer establish the necessary harmony between himself and God? We find him in this distressed and sorrowful mood when the disciples, who are embarked on a ship with him, once more ask him to create bread because they "had forgotten to take bread." This is too much for Jesus. He retorts angrily: "Why reason ye, because ye have no bread? Perceive ye not yet, neither understand?" When he broke five breads among the five thousand, did they not take up twelve baskets of fragments? And when he broke seven breads among four thousand, were there not seven baskets remaining? Yet they repeatedly ask him to perform the miracle again!

Thus Saint Mark describes Jesus' rising bitterness and his growing consciousness of the danger. John, however, tightens up the account of this story, cutting here, adding there, and building up the whole to a great climax. According to him, there was just one miracle of the loaves, when Jesus feeds five thousand. But immediately thereafter it became necessary for Jesus to conceal himself from men. He perceived "that they would come and take him by force, to make him a king," and withdrew again to a mountain. They would give him a kingly crown as the creator of bread, and that was the most drastic misunderstanding of his doctrines. The emperor in Rome was a bread king, for he was head of the bakers' guilds that distributed the *tessera frumentaria,* the bread stamp for the poor. Were they to make Jesus a king like this? A bread king and a bread god against his will? Already the people were going everywhere through the land searching for him; were sailing the sea in ships. Finally they found him and surrounded him in the synagogue at Capernaum. Then Jesus turned to them; like a wild creature that cannot escape, he hurled the truth in their faces: that they were seeking him not for the sake of the spirit, "but because ye did eat of the loaves, and were filled. Labor not for the meat which perisheth, but for that meat which endureth unto everlasting life." They asked him, "What shall we do that we might work the works of God?" And Jesus replied: "This is the work of God, that ye believe on him whom he hath sent." Shouting, they retorted that if they were to believe him, they would do so for the sake of the miracle of the loaves—just as they believed Moses when he gave their fathers manna in the desert. This was not the proper bread, the bread of heaven, Jesus told them; he alone could give them the true bread: "the bread of God which cometh down from heaven, and giveth life unto the world."

The people pricked up their ears. Was he going to create bread for them once more? They pressed close and cried flatteringly: "Lord, evermore give us this bread." But Jesus remained inexorable: "I am the bread of life: he that cometh to me shall never hunger; and he that believeth on me shall never thirst." The crowd did not savor these words. Had he struck awe into them with one of his miracles, they would at once have fallen on their knees before him. But Christ abandoned miracles—he began to emphasize spiritual values and spiritual gifts. They pressed close to him once more, staring into his weary face and murmuring because he remarked: "I am the bread which came down from heaven." They said among themselves: "Is not this Jesus, the son of Joseph, whose father and mother we know? How is it, then, that he saith, I came down from heaven?"

§ 40

In general Christ intended his sayings and teachings to be understood in the form of comparisons. He made great use of descriptive parables which he derived from rural and domestic life. If these simple parables were not understood at once, he customarily made good exegeses of them and offered thorough explanations. For he desired to be understood.

What, precisely, is a parable? The name itself is metaphoric. The word comes from the geometrical writings of Apollonius of Perga (262 B.C.) and denotes a conic section. It is a line that manifests itself in acts of shooting and throwing: the parabola is the curve described by a projectile which moves in a non-resisting medium under the influence of gravity. In rhetoric the word (entering English through the Old French form as *parable*) denotes a form of narration which after a long excursus returns to the plane of its outset—the understanding of the listener. The peoples of the Orient and of Greece were masters of this form of discourse. The rituals and the festival of Eleusis, for example, were parabolic: passion, death, and resurrection of the seed. The writers of the Old Testament employed parable, and Jesus was their successor and their brother.

Jesus, however—who knew that the ultimate things could not be spoken and therefore disguised them in metaphor—had a fateful trait of personality. He, who confessed to the disciples that they alone understood his secret ("Unto them that are without the kingdom of God all these things are done in parables") was like most of the prophets of the Jewish people in that he easily fell into rages. When he sensed in the listening crowd an obstinate resistance, a wicked refusal to comprehend, he became furious. Then he no longer spoke in parables, but in *hyperboles*.

Here again we have what etymologists call a doublet—a word that has split into two forms to express a literal and a figurative meaning. A hyperbola is a conic section consisting of two open branches, each extending into infinity. Translated into rhetoric, this signifies a figure of speech which overshoots itself and *does not return* to its point of origin. The passage in the Gospel of Saint John where Jesus says: "I am the living bread which came down from heaven: if any man eat of this bread, he shall live forever," is still parabolic; it conforms on every point to metaphorical reality. But immediately afterward he perceived that the Jews did not understand this parable; they strove among themselves and said: "How can this man give us his flesh to eat?" Up to this moment Jesus had said not a word about eating flesh. Now we can imagine his eyes flaming with anger. Against this rock of incomprehension his speech breaks into foam. He abandons the logic of parabolic speech and hurls out his rage in hyperboles. He tells his listeners things he could not, originally, have meant; things which, moreover, no longer conform to the metaphoric meaning of what he wishes to say. With emphasis he cries: "Verily, verily, I say unto you, except ye eat of the flesh of the Son of man, and drink his blood, ye have no life in you. *Whoso eateth my flesh, and drinketh my blood, hath eternal life;* and I will raise him up at the last day. For my flesh is meat indeed, and my blood is drink indeed. He that eateth my flesh, and drinketh my blood, dwelleth in me, and I in him."

These were words of anger—delivered to people who had not understood the simple parable that he, as the bread of heaven, was a warranty of eternal life as earthly bread was of earthly life. How simple and comprehensible that had been—and these wretched men did not understand it. How, then, did they behave when Christ denounced them in hyperboles, lashed at them with words that no longer contained any degree of logic? The Gospel gives us the answer: "Many therefore of his disciples, when they heard this, said, This is a hard saying; who can hear it?" But Jesus by no means checked his fury or returned to the simple, comprehensible parable. He spoke even more sharply. "Doth this offend you?" he replied. "What and if ye shall see the Son of man ascend up where he was before?" Thus he heaped a new hyperbole upon the old, and repelled those men who would have preferred to consider him either an innocuous moral teacher or a charlatan miracle worker. He did not need them. And Saint John reports: "From that time many of his disciples went back, and walked no more with him."

§ 41

The belief that there existed a "bread of life" which assured immortality was one that had long prevailed in the Orient. The Greeks called this bread ambrosia; they had taken the idea from the Babylonians. During their Babylonian captivity (597–537 B.C.) the Jews had learned from cuneiform inscriptions of the "bread of life" and had become familiar with the legend of the hero Gilgamesh, who desired immortality. Utnapishtim, the ferryman of the gods, bakes seven divine breads for Gilgamesh, in order to keep him awake during the "period of probation for immortality":

> For one bread the dough is mixed,
> A second bread is already kneaded,
> A third bread is already moistened,
> A fourth bread I have dusted with flour and put into the oven,
> A fifth bread is already brown,
> A sixth . . . But Gilgamesh, you are asleep!

By falling asleep (sleep is here considered a preliminary to death) Gilgamesh has lost his chance for immortality.

Thus it was no alien concept to the multitude when Jesus spoke of a bread that assured the one who ate of it eternal life. What was so monstrous was his claim that he himself was that bread! Christ lost not some hundreds or thousands, but most of his followers through this speech. Consider, after all, what he had said! With terrifying directness he had commanded his listeners to eat his flesh and drink his blood. The news of this spread like wildfire through the Jewish countryside. Was he insane? In any case, he was blasphemous. For though most of his listeners were not pious Jews but Jews open to the motley influences of the pagan world around them, they were united in one feeling: their abhorrence of human blood. The Jewish dietary laws prohibited altogether the eating of blood. In the Third Book of Moses we read:

And whatsoever man there be of the house of Israel, or of the strangers that sojourn among you, that eateth any manner of blood; I will even set my face against that soul that eateth blood and will cut him off from among his people.

And in another passage we read:

Ye shall eat the blood of no manner of flesh: for the life of all flesh is the blood thereof. Whosoever eateth it shall be cut off.

For the soul itself dwells in the blood—the soul and the blood are of God. God established blood as an offering of atonement; to use it for other purposes was sinful.

To be sure, the Pentateuch was concerned only with the prohibition against drinking animals' blood. The drinking of human blood was not mentioned because it was inconceivable. As is well known, there was no law against patricide in ancient Rome. Who would kill his own father? It was unnecessary for such abominations to be declared by law as forbidden—the deepest emotions of men made them impossible. And now there came this carpenter's son demanding so horrible a toll for salvation. Eating human flesh, drinking blood! If he had wished to be rid of his followers, there could have been no more effective means. As they had come in crowds, so they now fled in crowds.

Christ lost not only the Jews, he lost the finest minds among the pagans. He erected a wall between the urban cultivated people, the philosophers of reason, and himself. Such a man as Seneca, who, as we have seen, believed in the possibility of a god's manifesting himself in human form, would have been horrified by the command to "eat the flesh of a god." And the finest, most moderate mind of the times, Marcus Tullius Cicero, wrote the following words to elucidate a dispute in Eleusis which apply equally well to the Christian blood mysticism: "When we call corn

Ceres and wine Bacchus, we use a common figure of speech, but do you imagine that anybody is so insane as to believe that the thing he feeds upon is a god?" (From *De natura deorum*—"On the Nature of the Gods.") Cicero's writing undoubtedly reached far more of his contemporaries than Jesus' sermons. All educated men looked to Cicero. To the cultivated Roman the concept of eating a god was patent absurdity or the ravings of an insane mind. Yet Cicero's cool reason would have been operating upon a far wiser plane had it perceived that the lasting powers of renewal in the wheat seed and the grape were a divine mystery. Modern science is conscious of this. One of the historians of bread, Adam Maurizio, says: "We must not forget that the giver of our life itself lives." From the womb of the earth to the mill—and beyond—the seed that makes bread is a living creature.

But though Christ lost his contemporaries; though, as Paul said, his teachings were "unto the Jews a stumbling block and unto the Greeks foolishness," his vigorous speech won him countless men yet unborn, when neither dietary laws nor reason could quell the worship they felt for something which was beyond their understanding.

§ 42

When the time was fulfilled, Jesus desired to eat the Easter lamb with his disciples. He knew his fate, knew that this was his last meal in their midst. He was sorrowful and agitated at once; and when he saw the wine upon the table he broke out with the words that, while he yet remained upon earth, he would "not drink henceforth of this fruit of the vine." But he said more than this. Before, something of vital importance had happened, as Saint Matthew tells us:

And as they were eating, Jesus took bread, and blessed it, and brake it, and gave it to the disciples, and said, Take, eat; this is my body.

And he took the cup, and gave thanks, and gave it to them, saying, Drink ye all of it;

For this is my blood of the new testament, which is shed for many for the remission of sins.

Once more he proclaims this hyperbole! It is like some mountain cliff which Jesus had reached through going astray, and from which he could never descend again. But this is not so; he had often descended since the time he told all in the synagogue of Capernaum to eat of the bread of his body. Since that time he had frequently dealt with men and things with the greatest realism. What was it that once more brought on the state of fearful excitement in which his suffering spirit saw bread and wine as something they were not to other men? We know that those who are condemned to death have a feeling about their own bodies peculiar to their state. They see their bodies, their flesh, and their longings caught up in the midst of their transgressions, as already scattered amid lifeless nature. Christ looked upon the bread and the wine and saw how white and red they were. Like human skin and human blood. And he thought: these will live on while I must be extinguished. The torment of this thought—perhaps—made him desire to be not a man, but bread and wine. . . . Perhaps this was it. Or did he see the breads on the board and the eleven disciples sitting with him? Since Judas had gone out, there were only eleven, and he himself made the twelfth. Twelve breads were the number in the Jewish tabernacle. They were the shewbreads which were also, profoundly, called "bread of the face" or *lechem panim,* that is, the bread of the Presence—for Jehovah was present as soon as the twelve breads—the number of the tribes of Israel—lay on the table before him. The Presence! Perhaps Jesus thought: as my Father is present in the temple of the Jews, so shall I always be present among these disciples whom I love when the bread is upon the table. . . . Perhaps these were his thoughts. We shall never know.

We know indeed very little of the greatest *mysterium* that ever took place among men. Strangely enough, Saint John does not record the entire scene of the Last Supper, which should logically have been an interesting theme after he had so vividly described how Jesus offended the people with his flesh-and-blood speech in the synagogue at Capernaum. What is still stranger: although the other three evangelists recount the story of the Last Supper, none of them say a word about the reactions that Christ's words aroused in the disciples. The disciples do not rebel when Christ once more urges them to do what he admonished earlier in anger before the crowd at Capernaum: to eat his flesh and drink his blood. They are *not* disturbed about it, and Saint Luke reveals why. Luke, the physician, the natural scientist, says that Jesus added to his words: "This do in remembrance of me!" Here we seem to have the clue to the problem of the quietness of the disciples. Their Lord was asking of them nothing horrible, but something deeply moving and sorrowfully beautiful—an act of remembrance.

Undoubtedly the earliest Christians were careful to take this in no other sense. Thus we find in the *Didache* (the church book of the Greek Christians, which was found only a few decades ago in Constantinople) that the priests said when they gave the cup to the community at mass:

We thank Thee, our Father, for the Holy Wine of Thy servant, David, which Thou hast made known to us through Thy son, Jesus.

And when he broke the bread he said:

As this broken bread was strewed on the mountains and being collected became one, so let Thy church be brought together from the ends of the earth into Thy kingdom.

Here the words are plainly symbolical, and flesh and blood are not even mentioned. The earliest Christians anxiously avoided giving cause for any other impression. They had to be cautious so long as the state religion was still pagan. For they were accused—as we learn from a writer who did not hate them, Minucius Felix—of making "Thyestean meals" at their meetings; of eating the flesh and blood of murdered people, particularly of murdered children. (Such wild accusations are the price that all mystery religions must pay from time to time. We have seen similar things in Eleusis.)

If this view of Luke is correct (and it is supported by Paul in the First Epistle to the Corinthians), then Christ merely employed a harmless parable when he gave his disciples the bread and wine; he asked them to remember, when they saw bread and wine, this last meal they were having with him. And to remember that he had been broken as men broke bread; and that his blood had been spilled as men spilled red wine. If, however, Matthew and Mark have recounted the true story when they add no other words, "This do in remembrance of me," then Christ did say and did mean: "The bread that ye eat *is* my body; the wine that ye drink *is* my blood." For there is only one possible truth: the two accounts are irreconcilable.

With boundless eagerness men have set about interpreting these words for two thousand years. Millions of them have contended about the scene. How Jesus took leave of his disciples and what his words really meant will never be learned. The ambiguity has brought vast misery upon mankind and upon Christianity in particular. Armies of men have died in wars, falling for the words: "This is my body!" Indeed, at the threshold of modern times Christianity itself, as we shall see, was rent apart into three and four new Christianities, and the mystery of the bread was the source of the dissent. English Christianity parted from the Roman church of the Popes, and the Swiss church from the Germans. This was the incalculable ferment that Jesus introduced into the world by the phrase that none understood—the phrase that *the bread was his body*.

§ 43

Today it is obvious that it was not the lucidity of his doctrine that made Christ a conqueror of the world after his crucifixion. On the contrary, it was the *mystery*, the incomprehensibility, the force of secrecy, that won him the world. It was not his easily grasped parables, but the inexplicable hyperbole of his existence that conquered the earth. Christ is the Middle Ages. But it seems also as though he had absorbed the entire ancient Orient into his teachings and all the dark conceptions of prehistoric times. Stamped with the power of Christ's personality, these ideas were bequeathed to the Middle Ages. Within the broad folds of his teachings Christ unwittingly gathered up all that men had believed before him. In Babylonian, astrological terms, he ascribed his being to the cosmos. He is the Osiris of the Egyptians—murdered, torn to pieces, and rising again into the world as the spring. He himself is the Passover lamb of the Jews and the Messiah promised by the prophets. He is the lord of all seed, the redeemer of the dead; he is the bread of this world and of the hereafter. He is the wine stock; he is Bacchus bound to the wood, tormented in the press, and resurrected in the wine to march in a divine processional of victory to Persia and India. He is the second coming of Adonis, the youth who was felled by the boar, who spilled his blood among the roses, and was lamented by the Syrian women. He is Tammuz, the spring god of the Sumerians, who is sought by his mother, Ishtar:

> His mother wailing begins the lamentations for him;
> She wanders bringing a burden of tears;
> She sits and puts her hand to her heart;
> She wails; her sorrow is bitter.

As Ishtar wailed over Tammuz and Demeter mourned Persephone, so the *Mater dolorosa* approached the sepulcher of Jesus Christ. And behold, he was arisen! The entire Orient which rejoiced at the risen Osiris, Bacchus, and Tammuz, now rejoiced with Mary at the resurrection of Christ.

He is the "Lord of Vegetation"; at the same time he is the victim, the seed. From remote Persia and India Christ absorbed these conceptions. Persian *homa,* Indian *soma* is a climbing plant resembling the ivy in appearance. "Homa is the first of three gifts planted by Ahuramazda in the fountains of life. He who drinks of its juice never dies. *Homa* gives health and generative powers and bestows the gifts of life and resurrection." At first merely a drink, *soma* later becomes a god filling and penetrating those he loved. The communion with *soma* is the same for the Indians of the Vedas as, for the Christians, the communion with their God in bread and wine. All these ideas from the very frontiers of the inhabited world Christ carried over into the Middle Ages and transmitted to the victorious barbarians from the north. Even his last and perhaps mightier foe, the Persian god Mithras, the god of the soldiers, he overcame—although the sun-god Mithras had long outshone all other gods. Mithras felled the bull of fertility, in whose body the force of all plants and animals mysteriously slept. The soldiers called Mithras the "mediator between man and eternity" and prayed to him in grottoes into which no women were admitted. Like Saint Paul, they considered women lesser creatures who must be silent before the god. . . . But what became of

Mithras? By the earliest Middle Ages none remembered him or his omnipotent cult. He was merely a fold in the mantle of Christ.

To the peoples of the Middle Ages, Christ became the God of all gods
and the king of all kings. Peoples who had never seen him rose out of
their seats when they heard of his death and drew their swords to avenge
him. The Germans of the year 830 heard the gospels recited to them in
their traditional verse—the Old Saxon *Heliand* (Saviour). When they
heard that Saint Peter attacked the bailiffs with his sword, striking off the
ear of the servant of the high priest:

> so that cheek and ear bloodily broke from the bone
> and the blood sprang forth, welling out of the wound,

they lifted their own swords to save Christ, whose vassals they were. Yes,
this was what they were—his vassals. For the separation of church and
state which characterized the Roman Empire, the separation which Jesus
himself recommended when he commanded that men render unto God
the things that were God's and unto Caesar the things that were Caesar's
—this separation did not exist in the Middle Ages. Christ himself was a
ruler of the world. The Pope, ruling in Rome, and the Emperor in Germany were at best his right arm and his left arm; and the people of the
Middle Ages were not more than the footstool under his feet.

BOOK THREE

Bread in the Middle Ages

Thinkst thou such force in bread?
MILTON
There is not a thing which is more positive than bread.
DOSTOEVSKI

NEW PEOPLES ON OLD SOIL

§ 44

WHAT brought destruction down upon the world empire of the Romans
—that miracle of superb organization?

Helmholtz once observed that the great Saurians of prehistoric times
passed away because of the difficulties of guiding such a vast living mass
from a single central nerve organ. The transference of nervous impulses
to the extremities took too great a time, which hampered the adjustment
of the body to the needs of living.

The Roman Empire died from a similar cause. In the year 300 after
the birth of Christ the requirements of life were far more difficult than
they had been in the times of Emperor Augustus. For the world encircling
the vast body of the empire had changed altogether. Its dimensions were
still the same, but the Imperium Romanum stood in a space of different
quality, in another "national climate" whose tempests had grown fiercer.
The Germans and Sarmatians, the northern Gauls and Scots, the Arme-
nians and Persians of the time of Diocletian were peoples much altered
from what they had been three hundred years earlier, at the time of
Augustus. But this was only half of the truth. The other half was that
the Romans themselves had altered.

It was weariness of empire. A hitherto unknown feeling overcame the
best men of the time. "Since we must fight simultaneously on various
fronts against the barbarians at our frontiers; since the administration of
the provinces is constantly growing more expensive and difficult, why
should not each province provide bread and soldiers for itself?" men
asked themselves. "Is it practical to protect Spain with Armenian mercenaries and send the soldiers born in Spain into the valley of the Nile?
Should we continue to import South Russian grain from the Crimea to
feed the city of Rome when famine and revolt spring up at the mouth
of the Dnieper?" When the best men of Rome began harboring such
thoughts, the Roman Empire was ripe for federalization.

Emperor Diocletian (284–305) consciously formulated these ideas. His fanatic dislike of the position of Rome as the capital city sprang not only from rational grounds. Probably he remembered the humiliations that had been inflicted upon the emperors by the Roman Senate since the time of Augustus. "If Rome does not exist, neither will the Senate," Diocletian must have reasoned. And apart from his personal convictions, he regarded Rome as a bloodsucking and impractical administration. She took unto herself the ridiculous privilege of being fed and protected by all the rest of the world.

Diocletian replaced the ancient centralization of Rome with a federalized administration by moving the seat of the emperor from the city on the Tiber. In place of the emperor, a police commissioner ruled Rome. And instead of the capital, Diocletian chose to rule from a "traveling court," residing now in Dalmatia, now in Asia Minor. He himself retained the eastern half of the known world to administer and to defend. Over the west he placed his friend and disciple, Maximian.

This federalizing "New Order" strengthened first the self-consciousness of the Roman provinces. When they fended off the barbarians, they would no longer be doing it for Rome, but for their own *cultura,* which they had gained from Rome. But it was already too late. Once the division of the empire had been made new divisions appeared. Under Constantine the Great (324–337) history observes not two but four Roman empires. In addition to west and east, an independent administration rose in the north, and one in Africa. The chief reason for these divisions was not, as one might imagine, the aspirations of pretenders, but the fear of *famines,* which always led to dreadful provincial uprisings. As soon as the provinces were made independent, they had no need to export grain. If they did not export grain, they could manage to feed themselves. Rome's struggle for the bread lands ended with her giving these bread lands their freedom. In many cases, however, freedom was too tardy; the once-thriving provinces had already suffered so from the onrushing barbarians that they could no longer feed even themselves, let alone the empire.

A touching aspect of the decline of the Roman Empire is the manner in which the provinces were separated from it. They did not tear away in order to fight against or with the barbarians and form independent nations; they were torn away against their will. The island of England did not wish to lose touch with the empire; she implored the Roman Empire for help against the Saxons. That hour when Emperor Honorius (395–423) replied to the Britons: "Help yourselves; I can no longer help you," the Roman world empire crumbled.

§ 45

Let us examine the cultural level of the peoples who invaded the Roman Empire. Caesar says of the Germans: *"Agriculturae non student* [they have no interest in agriculture]"; and he adds the reason. Agriculture would be a softening influence on the tribes; they would accustom themselves to the possession of a definite piece of land. They would build permanent dwellings and cease to be warlike. But war, Caesar observed, was the fundamental ideal of the Germans.

A similar account is given by the Greek geographer of Emperor Augustus, Strabo. He says of the German tribes of his time: "It is common to all these people that they emigrate with facility because they practice no agriculture and gather no stores, but live in poor huts from one day to the next. Their food comes for the most part from domestic cattle, so that they can easily load their few belongings upon wagons and drive their herds whither they will."

Three hundred years later, at the time of the great migrations, the wild tribes who had lived on the frontiers of the Roman Empire had already learned the advantages of modest agriculture. When they shifted to a new dwelling place, they always remained for a full year. Near their pastures they set aside some acreage for the cultivation of oats, and they waited for the harvest before moving on. They not only liked oatmeal, as Pliny testifies; oatmeal became a kind of national symbol and milestone. Here was a new way of living for them. If they had believed formerly that agriculture weakened their military striking power, they learned by now that, on the contrary, agriculture strengthened it. Only peoples of very small population can subsist on their herds. For a people that wished to increase, cattle raising was impracticable.

According to the studies of Russian scientists, among the central Asiatic nomads a family of six needs three hundred head of cattle in order to live in moderate circumstances. They make their clothes and shoes of the skins, and can sell hides and horns to merchants in exchange for flour, brandy, and woolens. But with only a hundred animals, the family would live wretchedly, if they lived at all.

Thus the barbarian hordes who poured into the Roman Empire, with their numbers constantly growing, would have needed billions of head of cattle (for which there was not sufficient pasture land) if they were not to starve in the midst of their victory. It was logical that they should change their economic pattern and abandon cattle raising for agriculture.

But they did not do this unscathed. For a thousand years the instinct of the Germans, Kelts, and Slavs rebelled against the necessity of this transformation. Eternal wandering, sleeping in the open air, proud endurance of hardships—such a pattern seemed to them like some lost paradise. The German king, Ariovistus, had once said to Caesar: "You will see what warriors can do who have not slept under a roof for fourteen years." The history of the Middle Ages and of modern times, with its eternal struggle between the instincts of the warrior and those of the farmer, between the nomadic cattle raiser and the dwellers in towns, is preluded by these words.

§ 46

When the peoples of the north, very much against their will, were forced to exchange the life of the warlike herdsman for that of the farmer, the land they took along the Roman frontiers was placed under the common administration of the entire tribe. It was a form of agrarian communism, somewhat perverted by the fact that the military leaders had a greater share in the captured land than the ordinary warriors. At first probably no one possessed land; parcels of land were merely distributed annually by lot, according to the number in a family. The fields were cultivated and the entire harvest of grain was then distributed among the families. With tillable land went, of course, rights to use pasture, water, and woods. The only inviolable possessions of the individual were, in all likelihood, his sword and his shield, and perhaps his agricultural tools.

The Germans' dislike for agriculture, together with the unequal fertility and unequal yields of different parcels of land, soon led to a wholly unequal distribution of labor. The tribe realized that the contribution of grain from one warrior-farmer was not equal to the contribution of another. Probably the first consequence of this was the decree that each must feed himself; that is, the soil became the possession of the man who plowed it. The man who tilled his soil well had food; the man who preferred to drink and while away his time was faced with hunger soon; he sold his tools, and then, finally, his land to someone more competent or diligent. At last—perhaps not the original farmer but his grandson—he was reduced to selling the strength of his arms to his neighbor. He gave up his freedom, but by so doing he bought the right to be fed and protected against the insecurities of economic life.

However, this was only one root of unfreedom on the land; and it was not the most important. Before the German tribes took possession of Roman land they had scarcely known slavery. They shrewdly preferred to kill their prisoners of war rather than entrust the tending of their herds to them. But in the Roman fields the economic form of slave labor had prevailed for many centuries. The worker was "fettered to the soil." The northern people had no taste for "bending, sweating labor," and this presented a ready-made solution: let the soil be tilled by the grandsons and great-grandsons of the enslaved Roman colonists.

But there was Christianity to be considered. What position did the Christians take on the question of slave labor? As a "religion of the oppressed" Christianity should have forbidden it. But when Christianity became the state religion under Constantine the Great (A.D. 313), it could no longer commit the impropriety of denouncing the Roman economic form, and instead accepted the curse of work as Adam's portion.

PLOWING ON AN ENGLISH MANOR

At the same time it did something else that, working slowly through the centuries, was dangerous to slavery: it ennobled the concept of slavery. In the Holy Scriptures not only all Christians are referred to as "bondservants of God"; more, Christ himself took the form of a bondservant, becoming enslaved to God like Israel in Egypt. The implication of this was that the slave had his right to honor and pride of station. This was not only a consolation; it expressed something real. The Roman slave was a thing; the serf of the Middle Ages, though possessed of very few rights, was a *person*.

Moreover, in the early days the serfs were not treated at all badly by the landowners. In order to do good work, a man must be well fed. The man who owned the soil was, in the Anglo-Saxon view, the *hlaford*, that is, "the man who gives out the bread." Later the word was contracted to *lord*. His wife was the *hlaefdigge*, that is, "kneader of the dough"—the *lady*. The history of the language thus testified that these landowners were not of the type of the factory owner, who pays his workers and has no further concern for them. The landowners were themselves foremen; their serfs were a family over which they exercised the powers of a father. The lord of all the lords was the king.

Everywhere in the economic life of these times the idea of reciprocity prevailed. There was much that spoke for it. "Protection of the lord" was not an empty phrase; many farmers continued to enter voluntarily "into the protection of the lord." Alfred the Great, King of the West Saxons (871–901), considered every peasant as an "outlaw" without a protector who would guarantee him bread and justice. The exchange of freedom for security seemed indeed a very good trade. The free man had to give military service, which included supplying his own horse and weapons. The man who surrendered his freedom could save himself this expense and, moreover, did not place himself in peril of his life.

When the lords came back from wars in which they had vented their brutality, their serfs felt the effects of their intoxication with victory. But in spite of roughness and violence, tradition and language still regulated the relations of person to person. The crude warmth and simplicity of patriarchal economic forms forestalled any great exploitation of the serving class. It was not until around the year 1000, when the young Germanic empires swelled through continual conquests into large, Roman-scale organizations and the serfs became much greater in number, that the lot of the bread grower worsened.

MONKS, DEMONS, PEASANTS

To have a judgment over the thoughts your grandfather's grand-father used to think you must know them before. Then you may decide how stupid or how clever he was . . .

DIDEROT

§ 47

IT WAS a magnificent work of the Christian priests to transform the northern peoples into eaters of bread and tillers of the soil. Undoubtedly the Germans at first considered it a mild madness of these priests to be everywhere clearing woods, doing most of the work themselves to transform pasture into cultivated fields, walking beside their oxen with tucked-up women's clothes. Why were they exerting themselves so, when everyone would soon move on?

But the people did not move on. That was it!

And indeed the monks might have asked themselves whether it was worth while teaching such men to use the plow. They themselves had, after all, not invented it. They would have greatly preferred to sit in their monasteries over their books and study agriculture theoretically. There was, for example, the noble Cato (234–149 B.C.), describing with precision all conditions as to how a farm must be laid out to prosper, or the tremendous Terentius Varro, who had lived from 116–28 B.C. This Varro had written six hundred books; the book on agriculture was achieved in his eightieth year. It informed posterity what agriculture was and how the character of soils, water, climate, and labor affected it. Could these monks impart even a little of such knowledge to men with whom they had almost no communication?

This was not a matter of the natural gap between the educated and the uneducated. The new nations of the early Middle Ages had bodies and senses different from those of the Greco-Roman people who had settled around the Mediterranean. These Greco-Romans had absorbed into their very blood elements of the Egyptian, Persian, and Phoenician races, and the Christian priests were in many ways their spiritual heirs. But the Nordic nations came as from another planet. The first reason why no understanding could be with them at all was as peculiar as important: The Teutons were *wind worshipers*. The chief of their gods, the wind god Odin, rode upon an eight-footed horse and was accompanied by flying ravens. Only men whose great-grandfathers had never seen a house could believe that the world had been created by a wind god. In ancient times the Greeks and the Romans also had honored the wind—but Hermes and Mercury were of minor importance in their pantheon. The Mediterranean world was unfamiliar with the tempests that raged in northern Europe. Only the Germans considered the tempest the creator and changer of the world. They would have shaken their heads at the civilized, rationalistic explanation of Hippocrates (460–359 B.C.): *"Anemos rheuma kai scheuma aeros* [wind is a flowing and pouring of air]." The power that broke forests and rocks; the force that heaved the waves of the North Sea—this could not be merely "air"!

They knew better. The Mediterranean peoples lived in their "culture," in their little portion of the world, as though nothing else existed. House, hearth fire, and field were the center of the world to them. They no longer had eyes for the kingdom of chaos, wherein the storm god Odin, the thunder god Thor, and the cloud goddess Freya reigned.

And now these peoples were pressed by urgent necessity to settle down in one place forever and to eat their bread from a tilled earth! Long they resisted. For it was one of their most fundamental beliefs that free, uncontrolled nature was more than mortal man; and that it was sinful to impose great changes upon the earth. Yet large-scale farming—plowing and sowing—was that not the greatest compulsion, the most dire control, men could exert over nature? It was characteristic of the Nordic religions that they always defended the rights of nature against the rights of man. More, these barbarians considered agriculture as "theft," and believed really that in winter the demons of the earth "entered the storehouses of men and took back the stolen grain or flour." When the new nations tilled the soil, they did so with a bad conscience. The thousand customs that surrounded every act of plowing, sowing, harvesting, and baking were spells calculated to ward off the vengeance of the offended spirits of the earth. But they feared the heavens as well. Therefore, they also put agriculture under the protection of the heavenly foe: of the wind god Odin, the cloud goddess Freya, and the thunder god Thor. Thursday was sacred to the latter. Consequently, the Germans began all agricultural labors on Thor's day.

They considered the field a living creature which had to be tamed, before cultivation was begun, by magic spells. Some tribes rode horses furiously over the field, to imitate the storm and commend the field to the good graces of Odin. Since the horse was sacred to the wind god, they also placed the skulls of horses on the four corners of the field. Similarly, boars' teeth and bristles were plowed into the field, since swine, as animals which root in the earth, had an older right to the field than usurping man.

The act of plowing filled the Kelts, the Germans, and the Slavs with intense fear. To avert the anger of the earth, they pretended that the plow was not a machine, but an animal with its own will. Therefore, the Anglo-Saxons called the plow "pig's nose," the Letts called it "bear," and the Rhinelanders called it "wolf"—as though to put the blame on the animal for having dug up the earth. These fears never ceased. Wood from a plow that had been struck by lightning could not be used to make a new plow, for this would have turned Thor-Donar's rage upon the new plow. It was well to singe a few hairs off the ox that drew the plow to protect him from the lightning. At the first plowing an egg was laid before the plow; if it broke, the earth was willing to accept the sacrifice. If a man forgot a furrow while plowing, someone in his household would die. Dreaming of a plow meant death, for the earth thrown up by the plow was akin to the graveyard earth turned up by the spade.

After plowing came the sowing. The ancient enemy of sowing, the wind, must be placated if the sowing were to succeed. The Bible expressly forbade men to pay attention to the wind while sowing, for the man who had God's blessing was stronger than the elemental forces. The German felt just the reverse: the wind was stronger.

When the young seed began to sprout, more magic was necessary to compel sun and rain to favor it. Taboos were observed to guard the health of the earth. Women who had just given birth and people with lung sicknesses were not permitted to approach the field. When bodies were taken to the grave, the procession must not cross any cultivated field.

When the grain finally appeared on the stalk, the tribulations of summer began. It was necessary to pay close attention to the figures the wind stirred up in the waving fields of grain. The spirits of vegetation, fore-seeing that their death was near, were bent on mischief.

The yellow field of waving grain—to modern man a symbol of peace—in those times concealed terrors. In the waving of the ears, in the low hissing of the tufts, dwelt offended spirits. The grain "welled, wafted, wove, wended," or it "swelled, quivered, smoked, steamed, puffed, and ground." The northern peoples heard "riders hunting through the corn" or "a witch twisting." But above all animals seemed to be at home in the grainfield, animals with a cap of invisibility. The effect of their motion could always be felt. There were, first of all, gigantic swine, or the tracks of foxes; a restless, gusty wind was called a "buck." When the wind descended a sharp curve, people said "the hares have run through there." And when the ears, pack upon pack, with yellow hindquarters and flanks, pressed panting against the ground, it was said: "Now the wolves are running."

But even more than the movement of the grain, the people dreaded the deathly silence of the noon hour: the hour of the "granny of the rye" or the "noontide ghost." When the air shimmered as in an oven over the silent ears, the German farmer was seized by profound dread before an alien natural phenomenon. These grainfields had come from Asia and Africa. Only two or three hundred years before sacred *forest* had stood in this place, cool and richly watered. The murmur of the twigs had been familiar, not uncanny like this silence of the grain. The forest had always been the friend of the Teutons; it had been hostile only for the Romans when the Germans slaughtered them in the Teutoburger Forest. The brightness of the noonday sun upon the fields was again the "corn mother," going about her field and searing the Germans' hearts with her fiery breath.

In spite of the "wicked corn mother" and the invisible animals, the day came each year when the superstitious pagan began to sharpen his sickle. Shouting, he ran amid the grain, cutting and slaughtering the ears. He had no feeling of this as peaceful work; it was an act of war that he performed when the tufted stalks of the rye sank before his blade. Thinner and thinner grew the ranks of the foe, and finally the entire strength of the field fled into the "last sheaf." The last sheaf was the subject of many rituals—rituals that were a compound of fear and triumph. Among some tribes it was not cut, but "taken prisoner," placed upon a wagon, dressed in clothes, and the women danced around it, mocking it. Among other tribes it was honored: it was brought to a barn, but not threshed like the others. A traveling stranger must be given it to take along—perhaps this wanderer was Odin?—or the sheaf was untied and then strewn over the field to placate the earth. Everywhere, as soon as harvest was safely in the storehouse, the rites of appeasement began. The more violent the autumn winds, the more the bread growers trembled before the anger of Odin-Wodan. By raising pillars of dust, the wind indicated that he wanted his portion of flour.

> *Da hast du, Wind!*
> *Koch Brei fuer dein Kind!*
> There you are, wind!
> Cook meal for your child!

the people said, and from the roofs of their houses they emptied a sack of flour into the raging wind. When, during the nights of the last part of December, the tempestuous winds roared with fearful noise, flour and salt were placed before the threshold. If the wind took this offering, or if he dried out an offering of moistened barley meal, the prayer would be heard.

And all this man must do for protecting his daily bread! This whole cycle of blackmailing and bribing the demons of the earth, the agonized anxiety with poisoned Kelts, Germans, and Slavs, was a serious problem of mental cure for the Christian missionary priests. The priests argued at first that no activity could be evil whose end product was *Christus Paniformis, Christ in his form as bread*. When the barbarians did not understand this, the priests sought a roundabout way to teach them the Jewish view: that the earth was the slave of men and man God's governor over the earth. There was no need to worry about plowing, sowing, harvesting, and baking. They were taking nothing away from the earth.

Some of the demons of the field whose activities were plainly disturbing because they robbed men of their harvests, the priests transformed out of hand into devils. For the sundry gods they substituted saints, saints of agriculture, who were baptized and thenceforth helped the people, as the illustrious Saint Martin of Tours.

The original Saint Martin had been an army officer. One day, meeting a freezing beggar at the city gate of Amiens, he tore his riding cloak in two and gave one half to the beggar. Thus he gave rise to a figure of a saint who helped the poor against wind and weather. The fiercer forces of nature he mastered under the spell of the cross. It was inevitable that Saint Martin, in order to oppose Wodan, himself took on some of the features of a wind god. He acquired a holy day in October, the month of tempestuous equinoctial winds, to hold the vicious storms in check. On the day of this Christian hero all Christians ate Saint Martin's bread. But when astonished priests inquired why they preserved pieces of this bread for the entire year, the peasants replied: "So that the thunder god will not strike the house!" The new teachings were nothing but a gloss upon the old beliefs; out of the marriage of pagan and Christian the people created an intermediate world in which security and anxiety could both flourish.

The greatest success of the priests was their disposal of Freya, the cloud goddess. In her place as a mistress of the fields they substituted the Mother of Christ, Mary. She, who "walked amid the ears," who was represented in a dress of cerulean blue embroidered with the fruits of the fields, became a Christian symbol for the mildness and generosity of the earth. In the middle of harvesttime, on August 15, fell the day of Mary's Assumption, as though she, the true "corn mother," had now given the human race all she could give and could depart from the earth without anxiety for her children. Everywhere in the Roman Empire the Holy

MEDIAEVAL WEEDING
(From Loutrell Psalter, A.D. 1340)

Mother replaced the cult of Demeter-Ceres. Often this took place too quickly, so that large parts of the old ritual remained in the ritual belonging to the rural Mary. But the priests were in a hurry, in northern as in southern Europe, to plant the new religion in the soil of the old. On Annunciation Day, March 25, the peasant drove the first furrow in his field, to open the womb of the earth and make it receptive for the seed, just as the Immaculate Mother Mary received the "heavenly wheat seed of Christ." And on September 8, Mary's birthday, the winter sowing was begun—after the seed had been sanctified. Around this time the festivities in Eleusis had also begun, the celebration of Persephone's descent into the underworld.

Thus, from plowing to harvesting, paganism and Christianity waged an intellectual struggle for the governance of the fields. The Germans and the Slavs wished to leave this governance to the universe of unreasoning Nature. The priests would not permit this. Man, as the image of God, must rule the forces of creation. We cannot sufficiently praise the great accomplishment of these priests. Without them the fragments of the Roman Empire would have been utterly destroyed for all time.

Nevertheless, this intellectual struggle produced also *ill effects*. In the course of the century-long war in the soul of Western man, with the bread god, Jesus Christ, fighting against the wind gods and the water gods for the fields and the cultivation of the fields, the whole of Roman agricultural technique was lost. Nordic people were neither able nor willing to study a book of Columella's, the great Roman teacher of agriculture (A.D. 70). The British historian, Hallam, rightly observed that the barbarism of the Middle Ages began when men ceased to speak Latin—when Latin declined to a professional language of the educated, and the mass of the people could no longer share in the treasury of the ancient world's knowledge.

Culture is tradition, a remembrance of practices. Only a part of the practices is passed on without the written word; remembrance entirely unwritten is worth little. Knowledge was very swift to evaporate. Amid the dogmatic struggle between faith and superstition, the soil was cultivated with increasing ineptitude, for men were no longer certain of their tasks. The war to drive out the demons, to decide whether Jesus or the old gods would guide the plow, was necessary, for the gods of the barbarians, Odin and his companions in the wind, would in the end have let the plow rust. But the struggle confused the reasoning powers of the peoples who experienced it. They became so ignorant in technical matters that they did not have the slightest idea of how to cope with the terrible hygienic perils that marked the beginning of the Middle Ages. One day it turned out that the devil had really come to infect bread. But not a theological devil; one wholly different.

§ 48

Once, in the time of the empire of the Franks, the city of Limoges was ridden by rumor. A witch had been seen at noon in the fields, the "corn hag," with tangled hair and bony arms. Her breasts were pitch black. (This detail of blackness emerges in all the accounts.) She had lured children into the field and given them bread that was smeared with tar. When they refused to eat it, she had clamped them to herself with an iron grip and smothered them. The children had died of fright or suffocation.

Limoges was a town in Gaul. "Lem" was a Keltic word meaning stag. Like stags, the people of Limoges once had lived in their free forests and eaten their acorn meal until Caesar and the Romans came. Then the forests were cleared; towns, markets, an amphitheater, temples to the bread goddess, Ceres, and to Vesta, goddess of the hearth, were erected. Later Saint Martial came to Limoges to preach Christianity in the theater, and to convert the people. Monks of this new bread god Jesus Christ made their way with cross and plow into the stony wastes where the land was *rude et facheux et tout hérissé d'épines* (rude and angry and torn by thorns). No sooner had the land become cultivated soil when the wild Teutons came, flying before the Huns, and drove the rightful inhabitants into caves in the earth. For centuries no peace existed. In the midst of all these conflagrations and revolts, grain was poorly sown and bread poorly eaten. That a few children should be turned black by the corn hag, or smothered, was no great catastrophe in this tragic France.

But in the early fall of that year of travail A.D. 943 more dreadful things began to happen. Shrieking, wailing, and writhing, men collapsed in the street. Many stood up from their tables and rolled like wheels through the room; others toppled over and foamed in epileptic convulsions; still others vomited and showed signs of sudden insanity. Many of these screamed, "Fire! I'm burning!"

This was the case. Those who did not recover at once seemed to burn alive. It was an *"invisibilis ignis, carnem ab ossibus separans et consumens* [an invisible fire that separated the flesh from the bones and consumed it]," the chronicler wrote. *"Cum intolerabili cruciatu,"* with intolerable, excruciating pain men, women, and children perished. In the town of Limoges every house resembled a pyre in which, day and night, the victims were burned. The cries were heard, the limbs of the burning people were seen, but there was no fire. First their toes turned black, then their fingers burst open, their arms and legs convulsed and broke off. *"Tamen desiderantibus mortem tantum remedium denegabatur* [nevertheless, the last consolation was denied to those who longed for death]," *"donec celer ignis invadet membra vitalia* [until the seat of life itself was attacked by the fire]," the chronicler, Hugo Farsitus, wrote. *"Ignis hic tanto frigore glaciali perfundit miserabiles, ut nullis remediis possint calefieri* [it is remarkable that this fire permeates the wretched people with such cold that no means suffices to warm them]." A *horrendissimus ululatus,* a horrible roar of pain, could be heard for miles, and the indescribable stench hung for weeks in the streets.

The order of nature had been overturned. Hell seemed to have broken forth out of the depths of the earth, consuming men in an invisible fire whose nature resembled that of ice. Infectious plagues were known. But this was not one of them. The undertakers who carried the thousands of rotting and twisted bodies to a pit, where they were all thrown together, remained healthy. And, on the other hand, in villages where there had been no deaths, the entire population died in a single day. At the same time, the bread of the people of Limoges became transformed upon their tables. When it was cut, it proved to be wet, and the inside poured out as a black, sticky substance.

Did the plague spring up from the bread? The despairing populace fell to their knees before the altars. They called upon Mary and Christ for help; they also implored Genevieve of Paris, the patron saint of good grain. She had been dead only a few hundred years, and the great-grandparents of the plague-stricken people had seen the saint in her person, tall, blonde, and helpful, a sort of Valkyrie, as she brought grain ships up the Seine to the beleaguered Parisians. Since that time the Frankish peasants had honored Genevieve as a guardian spirit against cloudbursts and famines.

But Genevieve was unable to put out the invisible fire. Nor was help to be had from Saint Gertrude of Nivelles, the renowned mouse saint, who had spoken so persuasively to the rodents that they forebore to gnaw the roots of the rye. The pestilence did not cease until the bishops fetched the bones of Saint Martial. But 40,000 people had died in a single year.

Today we know what the plague was. The unfortunate people of the Middle Ages had forgotten about *ergot,* which makes grain black and sweet-tasting. In their fields they had thoughtlessly chewed such grains and later ground them up in their flour. Ergot, a dangerous poison, is a fungus disease of rye (*Claviceps purpurea*). Actually it contains two poisons, one producing convulsions of the limbs of men and animals (*ergotismus convulsivus*), the other causing the limbs to rot (*ergotismus gangraenosus*). In the earliest history of the disease, both symptoms appeared at once.

Since ergot imparted a sweet taste, insects visited the "honey drops" which oozed out of the infected ear. Thus the fungus spores were rapidly spread, and the rain did the rest. Yet these black, waxy grains could be seen with the naked eye. No farmer in the Roman Empire would have threshed such grain; no miller would have ground it; no baker would have baked bread out of it. Columella had instructed the Romans why and how the disease must be fought. Even without the assistance of hydrochloric acid, iodoform, and the microscope, with which the modern chemist detects and separates ergot from the flour, the Romans knew that *cleanliness* was essential to the preparation of bread. Only in times of great emergency, as when Caesar was besieging Marseilles and the troops had to eat poorly threshed grain, had there been occasional cases of ergotism among the Romans. Never were there any such mass disasters as this one of the Middle Ages.

The new nations had lost the old conscientiousness in the arts of tilling and baking. Their knowledge of technical procedures had declined greatly. Medicine and the natural sciences were in the harness of the Church, and the Church held the checkrein tightly. Generously, the Church erected hospitals to care for those who were attacked by the disease. (The sick were entrusted to the guardianship of Saint Anthony, and the disease became known as "Saint Anthony's Fire.") But at the same time the Church banned medical research as magic. It was not until the late Renaissance that physicians—Lonicer in 1582 and Kaspar Schwenckfeld in 1600—discovered the true cause of the dreadful disease and began the battle against it.

THE MILLER WAS AN EVIL MAN

§ 49

WE HAVE SEEN that the Nordic peoples felt disapproval and mistrust for the cultural and technical inheritance that suddenly came their way. Among the most remarkable objects that the barbarians found in the Roman Empire were the *water mills*. Wherever streams were to be found, in the Alps or in Spain, in Greece or in Asia Minor, these rapid, highly complicated machines whirled busily. They were all built according to a single plan which Vitruvius, a famous engineer writer of the Augustan age, had described. This plan was so good that its fundamental principles have scarcely changed to this day. The Roman wrote:

Water mills are turned by a wheel that is struck by the current of the river. A drum with teeth is fixed into one end of the axle. It is set vertically on its edge and turns in the same plane with the wheel. Next to this larger drum is a smaller one, also with teeth, but set horizontally, and this is attached to the millstone. Thus the teeth of the drum which is fixed to the axle make the teeth of the horizontal drum move, and cause the mill to turn. A hopper hanging over this contrivance supplies the mill with grain, and meal is produced by the same revolution.

This ingenious structure, devised by Roman engineers and produced by the thousands, was incomprehensible to the barbarians. They hated such instruments. It was blasphemous to compel the spirit of free streams, of wild brooks, to work as a slave of the mill. They let the mills rust and decay. Where mills continued to be used, where the wheels rattled on, the people tried to appease the elemental power by sacrifices, by throwing flour or breads into the river. It was, after all, convenient that they did not have to turn the millstone themselves, or hitch their animals to it.

As formerly, the entire race of Egyptians had been considered privy to magic, so now the Roman miller was looked upon as a magician, and the mills, in which the water was tortured upon the wheel, became uncanny places. Whoever lived in a mill had cause to fear the wrath of the mistreated element. Moreover, the water spirits were in league with fire, so that frequently the mills exploded. Nobody knew what can be learned today from any handbook of milling: that as soon as more than some twenty grams of flour dust are distributed in each square yard of air, there is the danger of an explosion which may be set off at any moment by the frictional heat of grinding. Purifying the dust-laden air was unknown in the Middle Ages. Possibly the Romans knew about it, but in the decline of all technical knowledge during the period of the migrations such precautions were forgotten. In any case, during the fifth century the habitual mill fires aroused superstitious horror. They were considered a proper punishment for the sin of compelling the water to work for man. And almost twelve hundred years later (in 1671) peasants in Esthonia deliberately burned down a water mill "because it had offended the brook and was responsible for years of drought!"

Thus these water mills were occupied and used by the barbarian nations only with the greatest reluctance. Yet these Roman machines were milestones of civilization. They represented the path for human development: machine labor in place of slave labor; elemental power in place of human power. Once more the priesthood intervened to instruct the fearful people that it was no sin, that indeed it was a matter for pride, to make nature work for man.

Christianity won its victory slowly. It was a hard lesson to teach these heathens: "The mill makes your bread, and bread is Christ." By this token the Russians long believed that a splinter from a mill wheel could cure children's diseases. Another Slavic nation, the Serbs, was convinced that water caught as it was hurled off a mill wheel could cure "swiftly developing diseases"—ulcers and the measles. The priests opposed these beliefs, but were at last forced to yield and give their assent to them. The mill, whose end product was flour, had, after all, an intimate connection with Christ; therefore, its parts were sacred.

The millstone was a great problem. Many Germans, for example, refused to be convinced that the millstone had no magic powers, for its thunderous noise reminded them of Thor-Donar, the thunder god. The priests combated this belief cautiously by introducing a saint of the miller's trade, a woman at whose command the heaviest stones became light and well behaved. This woman was Saint Verena. She came from old Switzerland, where the inhabitants had set up little idols in their mills, to which they made offerings. Verena threw the idols into the millstream. At first there were floods, but afterward the mills ground better than ever. When she desired to leave the inhospitable forest dale where this occurred, the demons smashed her wagon and boat. Thereupon the saint took a millstone, placed it upon the water, and floated upon it out of the dale. . . . For this deed, the Swiss depicts her, still today, with a millstone under her arm. . . . The legend shows how the Christian priests labored to convert the old pagan fears into orderly Christian beliefs.

Against one superstition, however, they strove long without success. This was the notion that the mill wheel could *speak*. This was sober fact. One has only to listen to a mill wheel for a few hours to know that it does not produce soulless, mechanical noises, but alters the tempo and pitch of its tones with independent will. The Germans, sharp listeners that

they are, were once more in danger of hearing oracular pronouncements
—and from heathen oracles!

> *Was sag' ich denn vom Rauschen,*
> *Das kann kein Rauschen sein!*
> *Es singen wohl die Nixen*
> *Dort unten ihren Reihn*

sang Franz Schubert in the nineteenth century, when these things were
no longer matters of religion, but of sentiment. . . . In the time of the
great migrations, however, it was a matter of dead earnestness. Did the
mills which ground the bread belong to Christ or to the devil? Notker
Balbulus (died 912), the great monk of the Monastery of Saint Gall, told
the people: "Certainly the mill wheel can speak. But I have heard clearly
what it said today: '*Sanctus spiritus assit nobis* [May the Holy Ghost be
in our midst].'" On this theme he composed a sequence which was sung
by the monks.

§ 50

"To intrust valuable mills to the mercy of that violent element, water,
demanded no small boldness," wrote John Beckman, a scientist of the
eighteenth century, in his *History of Inventions and Discoveries*. "But it
was still more adventurous to employ the wind, no less violent and more
untractable and always changeable, for the same purpose. Though the
strength and direction of the wind cannot be in any way altered, means
have been devised by which a building can be moved in such a manner
that it shall be exposed to neither more nor less wind than is necessary,
let it come from what quarter it may."

It seems strange that the Romans did not invent such a machine; for
what is a windmill but a machine driven on the gear principle by the
force of wind, rather than of water? The Romans were competent sea-
farers; they knew precisely how to set sails to catch the wind, "let it come
from what quarter it may." Nevertheless, they left the great invention of
the windmill to the barren centuries after them. The age was excessively
proud of this new invention. A scholar of the Middle Ages exults:

I cannot pass over in silence what is so wonderful that, before I saw it, I
could neither believe nor relate it, though commonly talked of, without in-
curring incredulity. But a thirst for science overcomes reticence. In many
parts of Italy, therefore, and here in France, there are mills which are turned
round by the wind!

For a long time scholars held that the Crusaders had brought the
knowledge of wind motors from the Orient. This is incorrect. Neither

Syria nor Palestine (which in Roman days had many ox-driven and water-driven mills) has any windmills. But probably the Crusades first transmitted knowledge of the existence of such windmills from nation to nation. For the Crusades were a form of traveling and exercised a "broadening" effect upon the people of the Occident who had hitherto been limited to their towns and manors. The French knight made the acquaintance of the English and the German knight. On the long pilgrimage Christians saw what practical experience their neighbors had acquired. Thus knowledge of the windmill was spread.

In lands whose waterfalls were weak, no innovation was of greater importance for the production of bread. This applied especially to England. England would have had the greatest difficulty in establishing water mills. Feeder ditches would have had to be dug and artificial falls constructed; the mills would have had to be sunken mills, so that the water could fall with sufficient strength. These problems were now irrelevant; with the windmill placed at a sufficient elevation, the windy lands of northern Europe always had enough wind to operate the mill.

Nevertheless, the construction of windmills in the Middle Ages began very hesitantly. In the German city of Speyer the earliest windmill was erected in 1393—and the people of Speyer had to send to Holland to find a builder. This fact is significant. Holland, a land of slow-moving waters, quickly perceived the national importance the windmill would have, and engineers arose whose knowledge of these new machines was unsurpassed. The Dutch developed the mill with a movable head that could be turned so that the arms were in a position to catch every smallest puff of wind. The Germans realized the necessity of this quite late; for a long time they built fixed, immovable mills. Thus Holland rapidly became the center of European windmill construction, and the windmill became the insignia of the land—as we recognize in every picture of a Dutch landscape.

Curious legal disputes arose in connection with the building of windmills. When the monks of the Monastery of Saint Augustine in Overÿssel wished to build a windmill in 1391, the neighboring count ruled against it because the wind passed over his territory. But the Bishop of Utrecht, highly incensed, affirmed that the wind of the whole province belonged to him only, and the monks built their mill. Nevertheless, the Count of Friesland extracted a yearly tax for the use of the wind from his millers; and a Nuremberg jurist, Kaspar Klock, noted dryly in 1651: "It is the privilege of the authorities to sell the wind to the mills."

A world wherein windmills could exist was certainly a thoroughly Christianized world, for the ancient Gauls and Germans would never have dared to exploit the prime cosmic genius, the wind, to drive mills. Nevertheless, even among the Christians the mills retained their element of the uncanny—windmills no less than the water mills. The poets, framers of the unconscious thoughts of the people, saw to it that the old beliefs did not die out. When Dante in the 34th Canto of *Inferno* entered the lowest circle, he saw the arms of a windmill turning in the dusk. The mill looked like a menacing bird.

> Beneath each came forth two great wings, of size befitting such a bird. Sails of the sea never saw I such. They had no feathers, but their fashion was of a bat.

It is, however, not a mill but the devil himself, who has transformed himself into a mill and is grinding the souls of sinners. They are bound to the arms, from which he hurls them into his mouth. For Dante to have conceived this dreadful vision (which is painted by Orcagna in the "Last Judgment") he must occasionally have felt the familiar shudder of fear that overcomes us when we see a mill looming out of the November mists, its vast, naked bat wings turning and groaning. The Romance languages do not reproduce this sound of lamentation, but in Swedish and Norwegian the mill is given the onomatopoeic name of *qvärn*. Cervantes experienced similar feelings. He, the serene skeptic who lived on the divide between the Middle Ages and the Renaissance, did not wish to speak of the fear the windmill aroused in him. But he placed an image of this fear in the mind of his mad Don Quixote—the knight sees the arms of the mill as the arms of a giant whom he must assault with his Christian lance. It was not a notion peculiar to Quixote that the devil dwelt in the mill.

§ 51

All the peoples of the Middle Ages had a hatred for the miller's trade. English, German, Spanish, French—each nation speaks only bad of the miller. That they felt the mills as uncanny is only half the reason. The miller did not belong to the "town." Probably this was one reason for despising him, as the peasants were despised who were also not townsfolk. But the miller was not only despised; he was feared and abhorred as though he were the devil himself. He was involved in an economic drama.

What was it that the miller actually did?

When the Roman water mills fell into the hands of the Germans, they remained for a time private property. But it was soon realized that these magnificent machines had a value which extended far beyond a single family. Whole villages were established for their sake, or established near them. The law began to give them special protection. Injury to a mill was heavily punished; a man who stole the iron handle with which the mill was set in motion was punished with thrice the usual fine for theft. To build a mill was a matter of considerable expense; the village had to contribute to the building of the dam and the sluice and to the securing of the iron parts. The upkeep was also frequently more than the miller could manage. Thus, as the value of the mills rose, the miller's property rights in it declined. At last he was merely leasing the mill from the community.

Above all, the millers lost their property rights to the mill when the Germanic territories began using Roman law. According to the Roman law, *"cuius terra, eius molina* [who owns the land, owns the mill]." As the land passed into the hands of the aristocracy, the formerly independent miller became an employee of the lord. To protect himself and his tenants, the landowner introduced two restrictions under his *soke,* or right of local jurisdiction. One provided that within the neighborhood of an established mill another mill could not be erected; the second ordered the lord's tenants to grind their flour only in the lord's mill. This latter provision, which excluded all competition, was felt by the villagers to be extremely oppressive, and for centuries was the source of many local revolts—especially when the landowners broke into the villagers' homes and confiscated the private milling tools.

The mill—from the water of the brook to the last bag of flour—now belonged to a landowner, a count or a duke; and the miller who worked it became either an official who was paid by the lord, or in most cases a tenant who had to pay tenure in order to keep the mill. To enable him to pay his rent, he had to find some source of additional income. Where did he find it? Here lies the root of the popular hatred for millers.

In order to live the miller *had to* steal grain. The peoples of the Middle Ages were convinced that every miller stole. Every one, without exception. There was little use in making laws to prevent the miller from stealing. The city of Munich compelled the millers to permit their customers to weigh the grain once more before grinding, and to take the grain from the mill leat with their own hands. But the millers of the thirteenth century paid no attention to such laws; they shut the door in the faces of peasants and bakers. "Beside every mill stands a hill of sand," laments a German proverb. Nothing suspicious in the weight of the grain which the milling had transformed into bran and flour, but behind closed doors the miller had taken his share and mixed fine sand into the flour. "No miller can enter Heaven," declares a saying of Normandy. When a miller came to the Heavenly Gates, "merely seeking his cap, which the wind had carried in," Saint Peter threw him out with the words: "One who on earth has been a miller tells nought but lies afterward."

But on earth it was not so easy to get rid of the miller. To run a mill without ruining it was considered a rather difficult art. Jakob Grimm tells us how difficult it was to inspect a mill. The outer wheel consisted of a central oaken beam, into which was secured a double set of spokes or "arms," joined by "curves," and strengthened by iron bands and stays to form a large double wheel. Between the outer rims a series of trough-like ladles were arranged to catch the current of water. If a part of the external apparatus failed, the damage might be repaired. But when the inner gear broke, or the vertical spindle that was the whirling soul of the mill, it was more difficult. The full weight of the upper stone lay upon this spindle of soft iron, and the continual friction severely tried the brass pivot at its base.

Among the technically ignorant men of the Middle Ages, the miller was, then, one of the few engineers. His responsibility was great—to himself as well as to others. His profit or his loss, even his fortune or his ruin, depended upon the exact adjustment of all the various parts of the machinery in operation. His ear, by day and by night, was directed to the note made by the running stone in its circular course over the bed stone, and his hand was constantly placed under the meal spout, to ascertain the character and qualities of the meal produced. The thumb, by a particular movement, spread the sample over the fingers: the thumb was the gauge of production value—and hence may have arisen the saying of "Worth a miller's thumb."

Besides his powers as a technician, the miller also exercised police powers; he was the official spy who saw to it that the peasants of the entire neighborhood did not disobey the *soke*. He crept about peering through cracks in walls to see whether some peasant was not grinding his flour in a handmill, for they must come to the miller, who as an official of the lord not only took the third part of their flour—this was his regular payment—but also stole a fraction of it. This was one of the causes that led to the peasant wars.

§ 52

Scarcely anywhere in Europe was the hatred for millers greater than in England. The Chronicle of Bristol praised King Edward I for his merciless treatment of the millers. The most trenchant judgment of them, however, is to be found in Chaucer's *Canterbury Tales,* which paint the culture of the times.

In Trompington near Cambridge stood a mill whose owner was wont to "steal meal with a golden thumb." He was known as impudent Simon. He had married a parson's daughter who was as haughty as he:

> A ful fair sighte was it upon hem two;
> On halydayes biforn hire wolde he go
> With his typet bounden aboute his heed,
> And she cam after in a gyte of reed;
> And Symkyn hadde hosen of the same.
> Ther dorste no wight clepen hire but "dame;"

The unpleasant couple had a pretty grown daughter and an infant child. Among the advantages of the mill was the fact that its *soke* extended to the university at Cambridge; the university was obliged to have its grain ground in Trompington. One day the rector of the university fell so ill that he could no longer devote himself to the business of grain and meal.

> For which this millere stal bothe mele and corn
> An hundred tyme moore than biforn;
> For therbiforn he stal but curteisly,
> But now he was a theef outrageously,
> For which the wardeyn chidde and made fare.
> But thereof sette the millere nat a tare;
> He craketh boost, and swoor it was nat so.
> Thanne were ther yonge povre scolers two.

The two young scholars were named Alan and John. They wagered that if they carried a few sacks of grain to the mill with their own hands, not an ounce would be stolen. The rector considered this impossible, but finally permitted them to make the attempt and lent them a horse to carry the grain. They arrived at the mill, where Simon promised to grind the grain at once, and asked them how they intended to spend the time while waiting.

> "By God, right by the hopur wil I stande,"
> Quod John, "and se how that the corn gas in.
> Yet saugh I nevere, by my fader kyn,
> How that the hopur wagges til and fra."
> Aleyn answerde, "John, and wiltow swa?
> Thanne wil I be bynethe, by my croun,
> And se how that the mele falles doun
> Into the trough. . . ."

But the miller outwits them. As the grinding begins, he secretly unties their horse, which is hitched outside. The horse runs away, and the miller's wife, who is in league with her husband, shouts the news into the mill. The students run after the precious animal, the flour forgotten. Late in the evening, long after dark, having at last caught the horse, they return dripping with perspiration to the mill—to find that a large portion of their rector's meal has been stolen and used to bake a cake. But they have no proof and must courteously ask the miller to put them up for the night. The cheating miller, who is amused by the learned stupidity of the students, retorts:

> ". . . Myn hous is streit, but ye han lerned art;
> Ye konne by argumentes make a place
> A myle brood of twenty foot of space.
> Lat se now if this place may suffise,
> Or make it rown with speche, as is youre gise."

However, Alan and John—who are afire with the desire for revenge, though as yet they see no way to accomplish it—give the miller money and ask him for a good supper. So much beer is drunk that the miller falls into bed in a stupor. All, the guests included, sleep in one room. The light is put out. A roaring snore resounds through the house, mingled with the noise of the mill. Alan lies awake. His fury at the stolen flour and the lost wager becomes transformed into another emotion; he hastens to the bed of the miller's daughter,

> Til he so ny was, er she myghte espie,
> That it had been to late for to crie.

Soon afterward the cunning John, who has been unable to sleep for envy of Alan's good fortune, moves the cradle, in which the miller's infant son lies, close to his own bed. The mother, who wishes to quiet the child, does not notice the change in the room and sleepily crawls into the student's bed instead of the miller's. Before dawn the master of the house awakens and sees what has happened to his wife and daughter. An uproarious brawl ensues, in which the miller's wife takes part. She helps her husband, but by mistake she strikes the miller's bald head with the handle of her broom. He falls unconscious to the floor, and the two students return to Cambridge with their flour and the horse, taking also the cake that the miller's wife had baked of the stolen flour. They had won their wager.

All England laughed at this jest—laughed for centuries. People laughed in the cities and in the manors, in market places, in monasteries, and in the boudoirs of English ladies. In the taverns where Shakespeare and Ben Jonson drank their ale they toasted the memory of Chaucer. The story was one on the millers, and a touch of its color remained clinging to the mills themselves. The mills were secretive places that promised lascivious adventures. Long before Chaucer's day, and long after him, they stimulated in men the memory of forbidden things. Sixteen-year-old Goethe proved it, in his first book of poems, *Annette*. The rumbling of the mill, which vibrated in all other rooms of the building; the flow of the flour; the warm atmosphere of mingled spray and dust—these things made the mills places of untrammeled sexuality. In consideration of this, Ethelbert's lawbook of the sixth century provided: "If anyone molest a maidservant of the king he shall pay fifty shillings amends. Or if she be the maid who grinds at the mill, he shall pay only twenty-five shillings."

AND THE BAKER STARVED US

Now speak to a craftsman—he'll tell you better the job!
SOCRATES

§ 53

PERHAPS no one protested more fiercely against the miller than his compatriot, the baker. The bakers stood socially far above the millers. They were, first of all, townsfolk. *"Town air makes a free man,"* goes the medieval saying; those who dwelt within the narrow cages of the towns were subject to no lord. The bakeries in the towns belonged to the bakers —something the millers could not say of their mills.

It is perhaps difficult to understand what these bakers and the other townsfolk in the Middle Ages were so proud of. A Roman of the year A.D. 200 whose ghost had returned to earth around the year 1000 would not have recognized this world. The classic world at its peak had beautified the earth—with broad market places, open towns, well-kept highways. In the Middle Ages the land was sown with stone; with walled-in towns that, until around 1400, propagated ugliness. Between these towns lay the expanse of muddy, uncultivated fields of the peasantry.

No architecture was uglier than the town architecture of the Middle Ages. It was based upon the animality of man's nature. Its fundamental conception sprang from *fear,* the common, creeping fear of attack by one's neighbor. In each town and dwelling there was no retreat from care, no place of freedom. Everything served the end of defense. Every dwelling was armored against balls of stone and iron, and blinked into the light through tiny cracks. The windows were merely holes through which to shoot and which would fend off arrows and fiery brands. The same principle of the fortress dictated the building of a low, narrow front door. One man could defend it.

This was the logic of the cave. Although they lived above the ground, the men of the Middle Ages lived as though they were in dens like their remote ancestors. A history of terror compelled them to do so. The security of the Roman peace had long since vanished; those who did not live within the shadow of a city or a castle wall were in constant peril of their lives. Merchants were attacked upon the roads; peasants in their fields. For centuries only the towns and the castles could guarantee a continuance in this life.

For description of life in a castle it is better not to read Walter Scott or other Romantic writers. Rather let us turn to the letter of a contemporary who lived at the dawn of modern times. Ulrich von Hutten writes:

> Whether the castle stand upon a mountain or in the flat land, it is never erected for comfort, but for defense. Surrounded by moat and wall, it is oppressively narrow inside. Crowded within are cattle stalls and dark chambers holding the arms of war. Everywhere rises the stench of pitch and sulfur, nor do I think the odor of dogs and their leavings the more pleasant. . . . And what din! Here the sheep bleat and the neat-cattle bellow, there the dogs bark—and we, who live near the forests, even hear the wolves howl. Each day one is troubled about the next; each day one is moving and restless. . . . When the year's harvest is poor, as is often the case with us, fearful distress and poverty prevail. In these times there is always something every hour to confuse and to dismay, to irritate and vex. . . .

The towns were no more than castles inhabited by burghers. The psychological and sanitary consequences of these conditions were evil indeed. We shudder at conditions in the Jewish ghettos. In reality every town of the Middle Ages was a ghetto for Christians. They could not leave it at will. At the gate sat the gate clerk, keeping a record of all who went out, and admitting no strangers. Five hundred yards beyond the town began foreign land. Here the townsfolk's money had no value, for each town minted its own coins. It was senseless, and meant the death of all trade relations; but the desire of each town to close itself off from the world was stronger than the desire for profitable commerce.

Thus for centuries men felt their home as a "prison," but nevertheless they remained in it voluntarily. These were the unhappy descendants of nations like the Saxons described by Tacitus, who had considered towns "as the defenses of slavery and the graves of freedom. They preferred to live in the center of their open fields!" "Very well, but where shall we bathe?" the Quades had asked Emperor Marcus Aurelius (A.D. 161–180) when he punished their tribe by forcing them to live in towns, where they could be supervised. And we must not forget that a Roman town was no medieval town!

Among these people who were artificially retained within a closed "town economy," behind walls, there arose a curious local pride—the town patriotism of the Middle Ages which flowered into strange and wonderful blossoms. In Roman times it was a matter of indifference whether one had been born in Cadiz, in Spain, or in Odessa on the Black Sea, so long as one was a Roman citizen. In the Middle Ages there was a world of difference between having civil rights in two neighboring Italian cities. To be sure, this hysterical local patriotism also produced ambition and a revival of art—in both culture and life narrowness has ambivalent consequences. Out of the close quarters of the medieval town the Gothic cathedral thrust its way to the stars. And scholasticism grew in the confines of the monasteries. Goethe, who understood perfectly the wretchedness and the pride of the Middle Ages, the miserable narrowness of the towns and the mystical transports of love that such closure induced, gives these words to Faust:

> Ah, me! This dungeon still I see,
> This drear, accursed masonry!

But in another passage he confessed:

> Ah, when within our narrow chamber
> The lamp with friendly lustre glows,
> Flames in the breast each faded ember,
> And in the heart itself that knows.

§ 54

Community life became split up into tiny isolated cells; similarly national feeling perished. In every town in England prevailed a spirit of jealous exclusiveness, and it was immaterial whether the stranger within their gates was an Englishman from a neighboring town or a foreigner from beyond the sea.

The towns considered that the ruthlessness with which they treated the outside world was an assurance of happiness for their own people. But this was precisely what it was not. In the "Christian ghetto" of those towns men and the trades oppressed one another. Grudgers and spies tormented their neighbors. Few could engage in the work they enjoyed and for which they had talent because the membership of the guilds was strictly limited. In order to ascertain that every producer would find a buyer, a host of prohibitions were established. For example, a "black founder" was not permitted to be at the same time a "yellow founder" —that is, an artisan who made iron ware was not allowed to work with brass. "The tanner of leather must not make shoes, nor vice versa." This principle of extreme division of labor led to awkward and ridiculous regulations. For example, there was a dogma: "Where a brewery stands, no bakery may stand." Precisely the opposite was natural. Bakers and brewers could use to advantage the same structures, for both worked with grain and yeast. In ancient Egypt (as the Egyptian paintings show) bakers and brewers always worked in adjoining rooms.

This compulsory division of labor struck most harshly against those who prepared bread for the people. For the first time the baker and miller were parted. All through classic antiquity the baker had his slaves, his animals, or his water mill to grind the flour. Even in the later classic age (in A.D. 364) a law passed by Emperors Valentinian and Valens provided that a baker retiring from office must deliver the entire organization of the bakery, the animals, slaves, *and the mill* to his successor. All Roman economic thinkers would have considered it highly impracticable to separate the trades of miller and baker. Why risk the precious flour by transporting it between the mill and the bakery? The Romans felt that grain should be converted directly into bread.

The Middle Ages, however, banished the mill out of the town. Since all grain was now ground by water power or by wind power, there was no other choice. The town wall cut across the middle of the trade, forcing the baker *intra muros;* the miller and his factory, which had to be situated near flowing water, of necessity remained outside the walls. The wind, too, ceased within the walls.

Thus the miller was excluded from the center of cultural life, such as it was. This separated him from his customer, in so far as these customers were townsfolk. Suspicion and animosity grew between the baker and the miller. Each depreciated the other's abilities.

§ 55

Of the town guilds, the baker's guild was generally the oldest. In consequence of this the guild had a great sense of independence. As we know, the incorporation of the artisans into guilds was not an invention of the Middle Ages, but of the later Roman Empire. In the course of the great migrations and the barbarian invasions, the institution was lost, until at last it was revived and extended by the later Middle Ages. A memory of the baker's status in the Roman Empire—where bakers were officials of the state—is to be found in the *Sachsenspiegel,* a Germanic book of the common law. Here the murder of a baker—as a man important to the community—is punished by a fine three times as great as the murder of ordinary men. And Louis XI of France (1461–83) decreed that no bakers be ordered to stand sentinel, so that if their bread were bad, they would not have the excuse that their baking had been disturbed. In other countries, however, the bakers were anxious to perform military service: It was a baker's regiment that saved the life and the crown of the German Emperor Ludwig the Bavarian in the famous Battle of Mühlberg (1322).

What kind of life did these bakers have, these men who prepared "the mortar of life" in a cellar chamber? They employed the selfsame instruments that had been used in the age of the ancient Egyptians. No changes had occurred in the technique of baking. The bread molds looked as of old; so did the table on which the bread was kneaded; the oven cast its glow over the entire room, illuminating the sacks of flour and the trowel. The bakers wiped their hands on their aprons; the sweat ran down their ruddy faces. For the rest, they were free men living in towns where the

ordinary man had advantages over the nobility. They could become coun-
cilors and help shape the political destiny of their fellows with their
bakers' hands.

It was not at all easy to become a baker. The apprentice who chose
to enter the trade had to be of legitimate birth. After a brief period of
probation he signed his articles. The period of apprenticeship ran from
two to three years. Then the indentures were signed, and the apprentice
became a journeyman. As a journeyman he was required to travel at least
three and often five years to become acquainted with other lands and
new techniques in the art of baking. These were the reasons officially
given—the true reason was quite different. Journeying was an economic
measure imposed by the town master bakers upon their successors. Its
purpose was to hold off competition for as long as possible. There is no
doubt that the masters hoped some of the wandering journeymen would
grow disloyal in foreign lands. Indeed, such defections happened quite
frequently, though we do not know as much about most faithless journeymen as we do about Claude Lorrain, who traveled from his birthplace in
Lorraine to Rome as a journeyman baker and remained to become a
great painter.

But most of them returned. They could show their indentures and the
record of the places they had visited in their journeyman's book, yet they
had still to wait until some house that possessed the "baking privilege"
was vacated. There must be a vacancy—that is, some baker must have
died. The new man was obliged to enter the special branch of the deceased baker, who might have been a white baker, a black baker, a sweet
or sour baker. After giving a banquet to the entire guild, the young master went to the town hall to take the "oath to the town bread ordinance."
This was a solemn and grave act; the baker had to swear *"that he would
always bake enough"* (this guarantee was, of course, extraordinarily important, since free competition was excluded), and that he would be
conscientious about the quality and weight of his goods. In some towns
the baker was also required to give bread in exchange for pledges. This
made great trouble for the bakers, since the role of pawnbroker was
odious everywhere. The poor people could never understand that pawned
goods might be forfeited forever.

The towns not only protected the manufacturer against unfair competition, but attempted also to protect the consumer's rights. Bread weighers
and bread inspectors who were chosen from the members of the guild
itself examined the weight and quality of the bread. According to the
Hamburg Bakers' Law of 1375, the weighers could immediately confiscate a bread that tasted bad and weighed too little. The baker would be
hauled at once before the town council, where he was required to pay a
fine that same forenoon. If there were a succession of such incidents with
a baker, the town handed him over to the populace. With angry shouts

and mocking laughter, the people placed him upon a baker's gallows—a large basket suspended over a puddle. In this the baker sat. He was not dropped into the puddle, but forced to jump into it himself and run home, dripping with mud. In 1280 a baker of Zurich named Wackerbold, to whom this was done, set fire to half the town. Fleeing in the early morning, he encountered a townswoman. "Tell the people of Zurich," he yelled, "I wanted to dry my clothes, which were still wet from the puddle. . . ."

The baker's life was not a happy one. The trade exacted a severe toll of the baker's health. Flour is, to be sure, not so heavy as the miner's ore; but throughout the Middle Ages, again and again, the complaint is heard of how frequently bakers fell ill. There was, first of all, the long hours of standing before the hot oven. Nightwork was prohibited in the Middle Ages, but not for the bakers, for the burghers wished to have their bread and rolls in the early morning. When the townsmen arose yawning in the amber dawn, the bakers were usually just putting out their lights. A master did not have many apprentices or journeymen; fourteen to eighteen hours of labor was not unusual. (As late as 1894 an English baker died of a heart attack after twenty-one hours of uninterrupted work.) The result was that the bakers often worked in a doze. They were always tired and usually poverty-stricken; they ate too little and too irregularly. They also slept in their bakery—the characteristic of the Middle Ages is lack of room—and so breathed flour dust even in their sleep. Baker's asthma or a bronchial catarrh was the consequence. In France bakers were called geindres, the groaners. "Les gémissements qu'ils poussent a chaque effort pendant le démêlage de. la pâte, ont pour but d'empêcher la farine de pénétrer dans les voies respiratoires [The sighs they emit while kneading the dough are intended to prevent the flour from penetrating into the lungs]."

Far worse was a skin disease, baker's eczema, attacking the bakers. It remained mysterious for centuries, until in 1817 its cause was discovered by the physician, William. The blocking of the sebacious glands by flour dust or yeast spores (and perhaps also by chemicals that the miller smuggled into the flour to make it look whiter) was responsible for this disease, which attacked principally the baker's naked chest and biceps. Even if the baker could avoid these diseases by ventilation and extreme cleanliness (which did not exist in the Middle Ages), decades of standing gave him "baker's knee," a deformity and stiffening of the legs. Many bakers hobbled in the guild parades, their legs shortened through years of standing—these veterans of the wars that the towns fought against hunger.

The chronicles never reveal any gratitude toward these sufferers. Far more frequently the baker was hated, though not with the profound hatred that was accorded the miller. "When the poor man weeps, the baker laughs," declares a Spanish proverb. The English chronicles say nothing of the countless honest bakers who were long-suffering servants of their fellow citizens. But "a baker did skillfully and artfully cause a certain hole to be made upon a table of his pertaining to his bakehouse,"

THE TALE FROM THE BAKER AND THE DEVIL

we read in Riley's *Memorials of London*. "And when his neighbours and others who were wont to bake bread at his oven came with their dough, he used to put the dough upon the table and over the hole to make loaves therefrom. Meanwhile, one of his household lay concealed beneath the hole and carefully opening it, piecemeal and bit by bit, he craftily extracted some of the dough, to the great loss of all his neighbours . . . and of others who had come to bake, and to the scandal and disgrace of the whole city."

Just as every miller stole flour and grain, the medieval burgher was convinced that every baker gave false weight and took excessive charges for baking bread. "It is difficult," declares an English historian, "to determine how much truth there was in these accusations, and how far the stringency of the regulations forced upon provision dealers an inevitable recourse to evasion and fraud. Municipal ordinances must frequently have lagged behind the constant alternations in the market supplies, and the consumer was probably unable or unwilling to distinguish between a natural and an artificial scarcity."

In fact, the public could never understand that the price of bread was subject to change because the price of grain did not remain fixed. The edict of King John (1199–1216), fixing a bread price that was in accordance with the price of grain, was the oldest English price law. It was replaced in 1266 by the *assisa panis* of Henry III, which remained in force for more than five hundred years. This law fixed the baker's net profit at 13 per cent. This was not much—and he had a sharp struggle to make this much profit.

In London the people took pleasure in putting "unfaithful bakers" in the pillory; or else the bread that had been found too light was hung around their necks and they were dragged through the streets. They might even lose their master's privileges. The London bakers, however, found a way out by "bribing the authorities to allow them to bake deficient loaves at their pleasure, a third or a quarter lighter in weight." Breaches of the assize, as the law governing standards was known, were the commonest of medieval offenses.

Distrust of the baker increased when the bakers began to fill municipal offices; with the baker holding power, the assizes were still more apt to be honored rather in the breach than in the observance. To guard against connivance on the part of the magistrates, the *Statute of York* (1318) provided that no officer responsible for the maintenance of the assize should be engaged in the baking trade during his term of office. As the Danish saying had it, "Where the mayor himself is a baker, the breads are always small." And a German couplet went:

> Where bakers in the Council swarm
> The whole commune will come to harm.

But it was not necessary for the bakers to have seats in the council for the common people to hate them. During famines their shops were stormed and many of them were killed, for to the medieval masses (and this persisted even to the French Revolution) the millers and the bakers were the cause of hunger.

THE CENTURIES OF HUNGER

If thou weepest not now, wherefor wilt thou weep?
DANTE

§ 56

HUNGER has always existed.

As they died of old age or disease, men had died of lack of food—when the grain became moldy or a war interrupted the cultivation of the soil. But the famines were always limited in time and area. In the Middle Ages this changed. For the first time hunger appeared everywhere and as a permanent phenomenon. It showed its fleshless mask now in England, now in Germany and France. Eastern Europe was almost always hungry. As soon as famine seemed to have left one place, it arose in a neighboring region, fed for a while like an infernal fire, and returned once more to the land it had left.

The twelfth century in Germany saw five long, terrible famines, and in the following century England underwent a true hundred years' war of hunger in which the brief intervals of peace passed unnoticed. Life in Europe was like the human body in illness, when, after successive terrible attacks, it presents the deceptive appearance of recovery, only to relapse again. Demeter had fulfilled her threat never again to send forth the fruits of the earth. It is difficult to understand how Europe lived at all during these centuries.

Not many could seriously believe that a few poor devils like the millers and the bakers were really responsible for such a disaster—although the technique of the artisans was to blame for some of it. The millers in the Middle Ages had lost the art of *bolting* flour—with the result that the burghers consumed about four pounds of stone meal per capita annually. This unpalatable flour was so puffed up by the baker's yeast that the people "were eating air instead of bread." The Middle Ages did not suspect that the problem of dealing with famine began with the plowing, although Cato had known this. (Plowing two inches deeper would have changed the history of mankind.) Nor had the people of the Middle Ages any understanding that the earth had a biochemical life of its own which could be influenced. Columella had a presentiment of it, but then this great idea lay waste until 1840, when its rediscoverer Liebig developed it scientifically.

To the people of the Middle Ages famine had supernatural rather than physical causes. Usually famines were preceded by warnings, urging them to repent in time. Terrifying cosmic phenomena ushered in each famine—there were many eclipses of the sun and moon, and above all there were comets. *Stella cometis, fames acerrima* (Comet—bitter famine) is a phrase frequently found in the contemporary chronicles. Comets were rods that God cracked in the skies as a warning to man.

Succeeding these heavenly warnings floods broke out; crops were ruined by hail; cattle plagues deprived the peasantry of their work animals; permanent wars—such as that between England and France— caused western Europe to forget the tilling of the fields. Even the wind, the old enemy, was often blamed for the famine. So intelligent a man as Gottfried of Viterbo ascribes the great famine of 1224 to a storm which raged all over the world and "shook the grain from their ears." The Christians had not yet ceased to believe in Odin-Wodan, the old god of the storm.

The economy of the Middle Ages was highly sensitive to all the vagaries of nature. People virtually lived upon what they grew in their own fields. The peasant paid his taxes and made an effort to keep enough to live on. He never had surpluses; had he any surplus, he would not have known how to transform it into money. The great land estates, especially the monasteries, might be in a better position, but their prosperity, too, rested not upon the money but upon land. It is, of course, not necessary to explain that the poor in the Middle Ages hungered more than the rich. But still it was not only the lower classes who suffered. In the Chronicle of Gembloux we find a simile that is hardly false, in which hunger is compared to the siege apparatus of the ancient Romans: "As the battering-ram crashes thunderously against the walls of towns, so hunger strikes the houses of rich and poor alike."

The state helped not at all. Men of vision, rulers who took the situation in hand, who conceived and executed emergency policies, were rare indeed in the Middle Ages. One of the first such men was Charlemagne. He issued an order that seems commonplace—that no grain was to be exported from the country. (When we see, however, how in the late Middle Ages the English kings shamelessly favored the export of grain because they made a profit by it, Charlemagne's law seems less a matter of course.) Charlemagne also forbade anyone to sell his grain *nimis care,* too dearly, and established a maximum price. One bushel of oats was priced at one denar, barley at two, rye at three, and wheat at four. At the same time the emperor ordered that his own estates sell oats and barley at half this maximum price, rye at two thirds of it, and wheat at three fourths of the maximum. He commanded the holders of royal offices to "see to it strictly that their people do not die of hunger." Another order read: "The poor who, tormented by hunger, leave their homes, must be gathered together again. *They enjoy the same royal protection as the ambassadors of foreign nations;* no one durst commit any crime against them or enslave them; they must be brought to a place where they may enjoy the emperor's protection." In consonance with this order, the king established welfare stations where the poor were cared for. He also provided for a poor tax: each abbot and each count had to give the equivalent of an English pound as alms to those in want.

The clergy did not wait upon such statutes. The monasteries not only gave of their goods: they sold their treasures abroad in order to feed the starving people. In some of the monasteries in France the people were so grateful that they declared that Christ's *miracle of the loaves* had been repeated—five breads were transformed into three hundred. For years the "guests" of the monasteries lurked around the refectories and were fed thrice daily. In the Rhineland and in Belgium conditions were so precarious that the Brothers in many monasteries rebelled against the prior and deposed him because they feared they themselves would go hungry if the giving of alms was not curtailed.

§ 57

Ezra Parmalee Prentice in his book on the influence of hunger in the history of man perceives correctly that in no age, not even in the most wretched of times, does the luxury enjoyed by certain individuals entirely fade. For luxury is far more than a habit: it is an *ideal* to which people will make sacrifices. To be sure, it is others who are sacrificed. And so we see in the Middle Ages the sacrificial fires burning with peculiar harshness and glare. Where almost all suffer want, some live in abundance.

The French courts, for example, naïvely maintained that the presence of the divinely appointed monarch made magnificent luxury an obligation. Illuminated manuscripts show us gentlemen and ladies whose precious costumes carried waste of materials to wild extremes (in a time when 95 per cent of the people possessed at most a pair of trousers and a linen blouse). They wore drapes of silks and furs, buckled shoes of Morocco leather, ornaments of precious stones and golden chains. And in the banquet halls peacocks were a standard dish. The banquets were a delight to the eye; the meat was carved to represent buildings and gardens. Often there were exhibitions of the plastic arts, in whose preparation not only cooks but sculptors in food participated. Thus, during the great war with England, a banquet was graced with a model of the winter siege of a city with frozen trenches of cake, siege machinery of sugar, and fish ponds of jelly. At such boards the knights sat down with their friends, courageously resolved to show no mercy to the city they were required to eat.

The bread the people starved for lay heaped in baskets on these tables.

Du Cange, in his *Glossaire de la Basse Latinité,* speaks of no less than twenty varieties of bread of the twelfth and thirteenth centuries. There was *pain de cour, pain de pape, pain de chevalier, pain d'écuyer, pain de paire*—all eaten at the court table; then there was the *pain de valet,* the lackeys' bread, which was eaten only in the servants' room, but which was still much better than the bread of the common people. For the people, if they had any bread at all, ate the *pain de boulanger*—bread that was shaped into a sphere, like Roman bread. *Boule* means ball in French, and from it comes the modern French word for baker, *boulanger.*

Countless hordes of paupers thronged before the doors of the court. They waited to be given the tablecloths, which were made of bread dough. This is one of the most incomprehensible customs of the Middle Ages, one that has often been explained as an act of cynicism, a deliberate abasement of the food sacred to Christianity. This, however, was not at all the case; the erroneous theory is but another example of how difficult it is to understand the past. The tablecloths were made of dough because there was a lack of linen tablecloths. The meat was cut upon these table-cloths of dough—therefore the French court protocol they named *tranchoirs*—and the dough, which became soaked with meat drippings and wine, was eaten by the diners at the end of the meal, or given to the poor who waited at the door (which seemed more Christian). This was, however, a precious gift, for these tablecloths of dough were far from small; Froissard has told us that they were *"demi-pied d'ample et quatre doigts de haut* [half a foot in width and four fingers thick]."

The luxury of the court was a permanent state. But even among other classes, who were far from excessively wealthy, there were insane excesses. Thus in the city of Augsburg in 1493 an artisan's family who had made a fortunate speculation, or come into sudden wealth in some other man-ner, consumed a fortune in a single week-long wedding feast. The chron-icle tells us that Veit Gundlinger, when his daughter was wedded, invited 720 guests. They consumed in a single week 20 oxen, 49 goats, 500 hens, 30 stags, 15 pheasants, 46 fatted calves, 900 sausages, 95 hogs, 1,006 geese, and 15,000 fishes and mussels—besides various salads. "And there-with," the town scribe noted, "the young couple was wedded. God bless them for all these things." He did not note that such a feast must have been accompanied by scenes similar to those of Trimalchio's banquet as the Roman writer Petronius Arbiter described it—with people vomiting and lying half choked on the floor until they were ready to eat again. Such things were the subject of gossip for centuries. They were excesses that showed garishly against the black background of the times.

§ 58

In spite of their savageness, these awful times showed a tenderness toward bread which is very touching. In their *German Tales* the Grimm brothers relate the following story:

The child of a townswoman died. It had been the apple of her eye, and she did not know what last kindness and love she could show to it before it was put under the ground and she would never see it again. As she was polishing and dressing the coffin as well as she could, it seemed to her that the little shoes were not good enough for the child. She took the whitest flour she had, made a dough, and baked the child shoes of bread. In these shoes the child was buried, but it gave its mother no rest nor peace; lamenting it appeared before her until its coffin was disinterred and the shoes of bread were taken from its feet and other, proper shoes put on in their stead. From then on it remained quiet.

The Grimm brothers considered this a legend. But it was a historic anecdote, something that could easily happen in the fourteenth century. There was nothing more precious to give the dead than bread. On the other hand, it was a "bread sin" to place the bread on the feet of the soul, for in the hereafter the dead person would have to walk on it.

Many legends deal with this matter of bread sin. In Tyrol a Frau Hitt who rubbed her child's clothes with bread was turned to stone. In the Baltic the city of Vineta sank into the sea because the godless inhabitants stuffed ratholes with bread. It is Shakespeare in his *Hamlet* (Act IV) who refers to the baker's daughter who was turned into an owl for refusing bread to the Saviour. In the German provinces, long ago, all bakers would avoid standing with their backs to the oven—for this alone was an act of disrespect. In Rumania, today, if a man drops a bread, he kisses it when he picks it up.

Why was bread so sacred? Had the rarity of bread given rise to these fables? This economic explanation is too facile. Bread was sacred not for its rarity, but because Christ in the Lord's Prayer had asked the Father for it; and because at the Last Supper he had said: "Eat! This is my body." The Bible, to be sure, had been written in Latin and large parts of it were unknown. But these things were known. Every village priest demonstrated them when, in mass, he transformed the loaf of bread into the body of Christ.

In every bit of bread dough that was prepared was latent the body of the Lord. All bread dough could become a holy wafer. For this reason, even when the bread was intended as ordinary food, three crosses were baked into the back of the bread, and it was forbidden to lay the bread on its back. Nor should it be placed on the uncovered table; those who could afford cloths laid it only on a tablecloth, "so that the friend of man would not have a hard bed." For, as a Swiss song of the times lauded:

> There came three things from heaven to earth,
> The first was the sun, the second the moon,
> The third thing was our Holy bread
> Which struck all ailments dead.

But, where was he now, man's friend? Where was this most beloved of all things—the bread?

It seemed gone, perhaps back to heaven.

§ 59

That misery serves a useful human purpose is a theory now held only by extremely suspect educators. Civilization can develop only where there is a certain surplus. Constant want enfeebles men's minds. The famous phrase from Persius' (A.D. 34–62) *Satires, "Magister artis ingeniique largitor venter* [The stomach is the teacher of art and the giver of ingenuity]," must not be understood in the sense that it is an empty stomach which produces art and ingenuity. If constant hunger is productive of ideas, the men of the Middle Ages would certainly have perceived how to increase their tillable land or to improve their plow. Instead, they perceived only how to make their bread worse. They continued to think they were eating bread long after they had only the meagerest of imitations.

This is quite understandable. In times of famine men ask themselves, "Why must my bread be made of wheat or rye? I have accustomed my stomach to these grains, but I have sufficient free will to break the habit." He forgets that his choice was made after thousands of years of trial, because the gliadin content of wheat and rye was larger than that of all other bread plants and the "bakability" of its flour superior. And thousands of years of habit for a certain food is also a biologic factor to be considered.

Even if the people of the Middle Ages had succeeded in finding something that would have provided a perfectly nutritious substitute for existing grains, their food difficulties would not have been solved. But they did not succeed. The potato (which is far from being a complete substitute for grain) grew on the other side of the world in a land still undiscovered. When the famines came, however, the people of France remembered man's ancient covenant with the acorn. Before men knew grains they had lived from the trees (even the Bible confirmed this), and there was no tree fruit better than that of the oak. Moreover, it was healthful, for otherwise the ancient Gauls would not have been able to live on it.

Russell Smith says that at all times the human race has eaten more of acorns than it has of wheat. Quite true. But the primitive peoples knew a splendid method to remove the bitterness of the acorn. For example, the Indians of North America carefully broke open each single acorn and dried it in the sun. Then they set to work with pounding stones, wicker trays, wooden sieves, and brushes. A sandy pit was dug, with steep walls that were lined with acorn flour. Twigs of cedar were placed over it, and through these twigs the Indians dripped hot water for days.

The patience these primitive peoples exercised to obtain their acorn flour—patience that was an organic part of the technique—was lost later on. Therefore, it was not so simple for the hungry Frenchmen of the Middle Ages to bake their bread from acorns. The food neither suited their taste nor bodily needs as it had their Gallic forefathers. The Bishop of Le Mans, René du Bellay, was properly indignant when he protested to Francis I (1546) that the people of his diocese were compelled to live on such food. Thousands of years of habitual grain-eating were no illusion. The archbishop perhaps recalled Virgil's words in the *Georgics* that man deserved a better fate:

> First Ceres taught the Ground with Grain to sow,
> And arm'd with Iron Shares the crooked Plough;
> When now Dodonian Oaks no more supply'd
> Their Mast and Trees their Forrest-fruit deny'd.

Here Virgil indicates that the oak forests were declining. Moreover, acorns had long been used as a feed for swine, and men felt it as a humiliation to live like swine.

Still, the acorn bread was better than the bread that the Germans obtained from grasses which resembled grain as the apes resemble man. In northern Europe, for example, there grew varieties of shore grass and wild, sandy oats (*Psamma maritima Linné* and *Elymus arenarius Linné*). The seeds and roots were ground, and people were convinced that they possessed nutritive value. Reeds and rushes were also processed; unwittingly, men were turning back infinite thousands of years to the stage of primitive man, who gathered whatever plants he came across. The head of the reed and the panicle of the rush were something utterly different from the crown of a wheat stalk. The Greeks had realized this; Greek myth recounted the competition between uncultivated grass and the human development of cultivated, fruit-bearing grain, personified as the struggle between Kalamus and Karpus. But the people of the Middle Ages were forced to live, and cut across this distinction.

The best they could do was to bake a great many vegetable seeds into their bread. For this they could refer back to the Bible. God had revealed various breads to Ezekiel, saying to him: "Take grain, barley, horse-beans, lentils, millet, vetch, these six things, and make bread from them which may last till the time that you shall sleep." As nourishment such bread was, of course, not bad. The worst did not arrive until men, to deceive their eyes and teeth, mixed into it materials which gave nothing at all to the stomach. The most monstrous breads that were ever baked in time of famine came from Sweden; they are preserved in museums to this day. These breads consisted of 90 per cent pine bark and straw. A moderate addition of pine bark was considered quite healthful even in normal times in the northern lands, which never produced enough grain: it was a preventive against scurvy—but never a bread flour!

The starving masses of Europe used every kind of plant matter imaginable. Anything that looked like grain was welcome to them in their hunger. In Hungary, Thuringia, and Denmark the peasants plucked straw from their roofs and placed it in their ovens. Others, driven by hunger, could not wait for grass to dry—they ran out into their meadows, ate like oxen uncooked grasses, and died of dysentery.

In France in the year 843 men mixed earth with a little flour and ate this in the form of bread. Did not the strength of the grain come out of the earth? Was not the earth the mother of all things? The historian Martin von Troppau asserts that in Hungary men ate the earth of a certain hill—a fine clayey soil—and lived upon it for a long time.

But the instinct of men looked for better things to keep their bread nutritious. The primitive custom of baking dried meat blood with flour revived. In northern Sweden reindeer blood was mixed with a very little barley and a great deal of water, and the dough was cooked on a stone slab until it was hard. These cakes were cut round; a hole was stabbed in the center and they were hung up to dry. In Esthonia a similar bread was made of rye and pig's blood. These flat cakes remained edible—though hardly palatable—for decades. All over Germany such "blood cakes" were eaten; men descended to a level which the early Jews and Greeks had despised.

§ 60

Man is not exclusively an eater of plants. The formation of his teeth shows that he was created to eat both plants *and* animals. However, the years of grain famine in the Middle Ages were also years when many cattle died. The first result of the famines was that all the beasts were slaughtered in order to sustain life for a few months. It became a kind of natural law that when the granary was empty, the barn was soon empty also. The opposite was also true: when cattle plagues killed the oxen, the plow enjoyed a holiday.

But Hunger, which Homer had called the "Humbler of man," whispered: "Where is it written that only the flesh of cattle, swine, goats, and chickens is nutritious?" And so—in the famines that stretched from the

eighth to the fourteenth centuries—men were like wolves and ate everything they could catch—from horses down to rats. Moreover, their thinking was like that of the wolves. Never since the beginnings of history—
despite Crusades, chivalric ideals, Gothic architecture, and minnesong—
was the morality of the masses so low as it was in the Christian Middle
Ages.

No wonder that *cannibalism* became a vice of which we have ample
testimony. Primitive peoples had and have a religious apology for cannibalism: they believe that eating their enemy increases their own strength.
Polyphemus, the giant who ate the Greeks in the *Odyssey,* acted out of a
naïve and joyous open-mindedness. But the peoples of the Middle Ages
were Christian; consequently, they were conscious of the deadly sin. Out
of the confines of their bad conscience sprang the many popular legends
of werewolves and cannibals. In all these stories there is a horrible smack-
ing of lips, a gruesome, ghoulish pleasure in the eating of human beings.
And legends and fairy tales do not lie; the people sublimate in them only
the things they have experienced—whether things of gladness or of
horror.

In France and Germany cannibalism is mentioned for the first time by
the chronicler Rodulfus Glaber as occurring in the year 793. From then
on the unnatural horror increased steadily, until it ceased around the year
1000. Bands of killers fell upon merchants traveling alone or journeymen
in the forests. Occasionally families of jongleurs who were traveling from
town to town were killed, together with their children, slaughtered,
cooked, and their flesh sold at the nearest market. Peasants were attacked
more rarely; they were known in the vicinity, and their disappearance
would have caused a great stir among their kinsmen. However, in these
times of distress there were also wandering peasants. They abandoned
their huts to look for food elsewhere. With the strength of desperation
they marched for weeks, until they fell half dead by the roadside. Like a
cloud of vultures the "hunters of men" tracked these bands of starving
peasants. When the murderers came across stragglers, they beat out their
brains and sold their meat to the unsuspecting people of the nearest town
or village.

From about 1032 on the wave of cannibalism died down in western
Europe; but it remained very high in the East. Otto von Freising (1114–
1158) considers it an example of "Slavic barbarism" that the Slavs ate old
men and children. In Bohemia, Silesia, and Poland cannibalism did not
cease until the end of the Middle Ages. Yet in England in 1314 there
were men who "from hunger secretly ate the flesh of their own children,
and thieves in prison who tore to pieces new prisoners and consumed the
still-smoking flesh of their comrades." We cannot today understand how
this came about, how it was that those who ate human flesh did not afterward kill themselves from horror. But Dante, great moralist that he was,

understood it. In the Thirty-third Canto of *Inferno* he describes the sufferings of Count Ugolino.

Ugolino and his three small children had been cast into a tower by a political opponent. They were faced with starvation. The soul of the count tells Dante:

And I heard the door below of the horrible tower locking up; whereat I looked on the faces of my sons without saying a word. I wept not, I was so turned to stone within. They wept; and my poor little Anselm said, "Thou lookest so! Father, what aileth thee?" Yet I did not weep; nor did I answer all that day, nor the night after, until the next Sun came out upon the world. When a little ray entered the woeful prison, and I discerned by their four faces my own very aspect, both my hands I bit for woe; and they, thinking I did it through desire of eating, of a sudden rose, and said, "Father, it will be far less pain to us if thou eat of us; thou didst clothe us with this wretched flesh, and do thou strip it off." I quieted me then, not to make them more sad. That day and the next we all stayed dumb. Ah, thou hard earth! why didst thou not open? After we had come to the fourth day, Gaddo threw himself at my feet, saying, "My father, why dost thou not help me?" Here he died: and even as thou seest me, I saw the three fall one by one between the fifth day and the sixth; then I betook me, already blind, to groping over each, and two days I called them after they were dead; then hunger had more power than grief.

What Ugolino's hunger did—Dante preserves the eternal dignity of man when, shuddering and forgiving, he does not describe the dreadful final scene, only hinting that hunger killed pain. But even after six hundred years the great poet's question remains: *"E se non piangi, di che pianger suoli* [If thou weepest not now, wherefor wilt thou weep]?" These words might stand as a motto of the humiliation of the human race during the Middle Ages!

§ 61

After centuries in which the level of popular welfare and health declined steadily, the year 1300 ushered in a crisis from which it seemed impossible for mankind to emerge by its own strength. Those who tilled the soil no longer knew how to till it rationally; and the states did nothing to help distribute what little was produced. What more disasters could come to bring Europe to the point of death? Something so monstrous came that its horror can no longer be comprehended. It was a disaster worse than hunger; but it collaborated with hunger to rule the world.

Pestilence overran Europe.

It was utterly unknown when it first arrived. To be sure, many humanists knew that there had been plagues in classic times. In a besieged city, for example, or after a year of crop failures, townsfolk and peasants had died of mysterious diseases. But always, like starvation, these plagues had been restricted to a local area, and they had passed very swiftly.

But now it was different. In remote India Pandora's box had opened and sent its poisonous vapors into the Western World. The plague landed in Sicily and at once fell upon northern Italy, southern France, Spain, and England; Germany and Russia soon followed. The first wave lasted four years. After a brief respite there were renewed surges; the plague shook Western man with the violence of an earthquake.

The American bacteriologist, Hans Zinsser, in his fascinating book, *Rats, Lice, and History,* advances the thesis that the history of humanity would have taken another course had men known the true foe at the time. The foe was the rat. Inconceivably vast hordes of rats were migrating westward. They were invisible, as they are today—for even now for every million people that dwell in a large city there are a million rats whose life is an underground counterpart of human life.

These rats, gnawing and crawling in the foundations and waste pipes of the Middle Ages, carried the plague. The people of the times had come to realize that the plague came out of the ground. But they believed that the soil itself was poisoned. The great agricultural religions (of Isis, Demeter-Ceres, and Christ) had instructed men that their health was dependent upon the health of the earth. The medieval people now reasoned that the infection, which spread from animal to man and then from man to man, was a "misty poison" which was breathed forth by the earth.

Physicians and scientists were agreed that the source of the disease— before it infected men—poisoned first the earth, then the water, and finally the air. Thus they were surrounded without hope of escape and without defense. Locally, some few measures could be taken: the evildoers who had hold of the poison and were infecting their wells with it (the Jews, for example) could be killed. Mass murders began first in Avignon, later throughout Europe. In addition, they could arrange mass pilgrimages of flagellants and penitents who traveled howling across the Continent to avert the wrath of Heaven. Neither method helped. Even where Jews had been burned and the blood of the flagellants spilled on the ground, the plague continued its march.

It continued, and its fury remained unchecked. The people of the Middle Ages had great experience in suffering. There was St. Anthony's fire, the ergot poisoning which killed off hundreds of thousands in the rye lands of Europe. There was leprosy—today only a tropical disease—which was a constant companion of European life. In northern Europe alone there were twenty thousand leper houses—islands of the damned that were avoided by all, where the lepers wore bells to warn of their approach. This was a tremendous number, when we consider the small total population of Europe at the time. Typhus and dysentery, diphtheria, malaria, and rickets were all far more widespread than they are today. These diseases depopulated Europe. But none of them compared in strength and horror to the plague, which often wiped out entire sections of towns within a few hours. It was not merely the outer aspects of the disease—the strangling of the stricken, the appearance of the blackened corpses, the impossibility of helping the suffering—it was not merely these things that destroyed men morally. Equally terrible was the destruction of all human bonds.

The Frenchman De Mussis wrote: "The sick man lay alone in his dwelling. No kinsman ventured near him, no physician entered his home; even the priest would give him the Sacrament only at a distance, and with horror. With heart-rending pleas children called to their parents, fathers and mothers to their sons and daughters, wives to their husbands. In vain! The people dared to touch the corpses of their loved ones only when they could find no one who would take pay for performing the last service to the dead. . . ." All piety came to an end, all human ties were dissolved. A Russian writer of the fourteenth century, speaking of the famine in Novgorod, wrote: "We were all in a fury of irritation; a brother rose against his brother, a father had no pity for his son, mothers had no mercy for their daughters; one denied his neighbor a crumb of bread. There was no charity left among us, only sadness, gloom, and mourning dwelt constantly within and without our habitations. It was a bitter sight, indeed, to watch the crying children, begging in vain for bread, and falling dead like flies." These words were applied to famine, not to the plague. But the two were brothers, and their effects were the same.

There are various estimates of the total mortality caused by the plague. In many towns in northern Europe—Luebeck, for example—90 per cent of the populace seems to have died. Hecker, a nineteenth-century historian, calculated that the plague of the Middle Ages killed twenty-five million Europeans out of a population of a hundred million. That is, about one fourth of the entire population. In England, it is believed, four million out of eight died—one half the population. This mass death exercised an enormous influence upon the economic history of the country. The social condition of England—the condition of the survivors—changed overnight. According to a contemporary, "no shepherds tended the flocks, and no reapers appeared at harvesttime."

The lower classes of the population were swept away more rapidly and in greater numbers than the upper classes. The feudal world—the world which had given all its esteem to the landowning nobility and none to the poor—found it suddenly necessary to place a somewhat different value upon the labor of men's hands. The labor supply, once so great, sank to a minimum. On many of the estates of great lords all the peasants had died, without exception. If the nobleman wished to find helping hands, he had to look around and to pay for them. The honor of labor and the wages of labor rose.

THE MAN WITH THE HOE

§ 62

THE pestilence of 1350 had enforced a revision of economic relations, but the feudal states still did not want to draw the full logical conclusions. The disastrous shortage of labor first caused a rise in wages, but this increase in the value of labor, however, was more favorable to the unpropertied townsman than to the peasant. In the towns wages of men rose 50 per cent, of women 100 per cent. But in the rural areas wages were paid in goods, not in money. Despite the great change the peasant continued to receive only the barest necessities of life. Although after the plague his labor was needed more than ever before, the Middle Ages still allowed itself the luxury of despising this labor.

Hatred and defamation of the peasant were for centuries typical of Occidental thought. Varied as were the forms of public life among the English, French, Italians, Germans, and Poles, this contempt for the bread-producing class was universal. There were small changes. At one time the "lord of lords" would succeed in depriving the nobles of their estates and giving out new fiefs as he pleased (as happened in France). At another time the noble landowners would succeed in limiting the powers of the king so that he ruled in name only (England); or the nobles whom the king had weakened formed an insignificant alliance with the small farmer; or the wave surged back again and in the Slavic lands agrarian communism arose afresh, flourished for a while, and failed in the face of human greed or certain men's dislike for agriculture which they would not practice except under economic and legal compulsion.

Compulsion is the keynote. According to Richard Hildebrandt's pessimistic view, agriculture is never practiced voluntarily; the peasant exists only because of economic need or compulsion by force. From free hearts, Hildebrandt maintains, neither nations nor individuals become farmers. And Karl Bücher believed that men created rhythmic music to make labor bearable. Greek terra-cotta groups show that when kneading dough, women had their flute players to make music for them. All work was done in rhythm, because otherwise it would not have been done. Pasturing cattle was not considered work, nor was warfare. But tilling the soil was work, and a form of work which men tried to escape with all the cunning at their command. The chivalric ideal which ruled the

culture of the Middle Ages for half a millennium was essentially a flight
from the labor of the peasantry.

An American or Russian farmer of our century would scarcely understand such a claim: that farming is obnoxious to man. But we must not
forget that we live in the midst of the greatest of industrial revolutions, a
revolution whose great founder was McCormick. *Agriculture has become
mechanized.* The Biblical curse has been lifted; the sweat of the face no
longer drips. Hatred for labor is no longer our compensation for the expulsion from Eden. In the Middle Ages it was very different; the difficulty
and insecurity of agrarian life inspired in the "better men" the desire to
remain completely aloof from it and let others do the producing of food.

§ 63

What was the origin of this mysterious contempt all other classes had
for the peasant?

Christ had often spoken his mind concerning the tillers of the soil. In
the parable of the sower (Matthew, 13) the peasant is a man who exercises almost divine wisdom in sowing the seed where it will best grow. In
Saint John, 15:1, Christ called his Father a husbandman, and ordered
his followers to obey the words of the Preacher (Ecclesiastes, 7:16):
"Hate not laborious works nor husbandry enjoined by the Most High."
Paul demands social justice for the peasants in the Second Epistle to Tim-
othy (2:6): "The husbandman that laboureth must be the first partaker
of the fruits." It is clear, then, that the spiritual poets and spokesmen of
the Church were aware of the "divine right" of the peasant. According
to the monk Berthold von Regensburg (1220–72), he who served was
as noble as he who was served. The mystic writer, Johannes Tauler, went
even further, declaring: "He who earns his bread in the sweat of his
face acts as well as he who attends a mass."

But literature which in the early Middle Ages only was written by the
monks was later written more and more by the knights and by the burghers. When the priest still felt that an aura of grace surrounded the poor
man, the sentiments of the knights, who had a bad conscience with regard
to the peasants, were wholly different. Even the most impious noble
wastrel held to the dogma that God had put the curse on the peasantry to
earn its bread in the sweat of the face. The peasants were the ones to
atone for Adam's sin in Paradise—not the other classes.

The creature that lived far below these other classes was the *villanus,*
"the village man," which later took on the meaning of our modern word
"villain." In many districts a *villanus* could not enter the town; like the
Jew, he had to employ a middleman for his trading. When Parcival
wished to ride to King Arthur's Court, a peasant showed him the way as

far as the city of Nantes. Here, however, the guide had to turn back; for
as the great German poet, Wolfram von Eschenbach (ab. 1165–ab.
1220), remarks:

> Behind these walls
> Reigns joy in measure and fine manners
> If any villein went inside
> These good things could not long abide.

So argued the knight. And what thought the townsman? The arrogant
burgher was free with his contempt for the peasant. Since most townsfolk
never left the walls of their towns, they knew nothing at all about the
peasants and conceived caricatured images of him: a long-haired creature armed with a club, living in a straw hut and scarcely speaking the
speech of men. (Medieval tapestries picture the peasant as a savage.)
Other burghers, with equal lack of knowledge, were convinced that many
peasants kept concealed treasures, lived in revelry, and held back their
grain until the townspeople paid outrageous prices. In literature the peasant was portrayed either as starving to death and living in Godforsaken
poverty, or as an enemy of the people and a blustering scoundrel. The
two classes knew virtually nothing of one another. If the clever artisans
of the towns had condescended to relieve the tool crisis of the rural districts, the towns would not have gone hungry. In ancient Rome there had
been a street called "Inter falcarios." Here hundreds of sickle smiths had
worked for their rural customers. In the Middle Ages no such thing was
possible. No town wheelwright or smith ever entered a village; and the
consequence was that soon the peasant was tilling the soil with his bare
hands.

The peasant could not read. But he needed no letters to feel the general
contempt. The knight on the highroad would give him a wide berth to
avoid being soiled by the peasant's breath; the townsman would portray
him in the carnival play between the devil and the fool. The peasant
knew well what was thought of him. The very agricultural work he did
was considered—as Coulton in his *Medieval Village* puts it—"unworthy
of an honorable and self-respecting man."

But, at last, what thought the peasant about himself? Could he agree
with his despisers?

§ 64

He could not agree. He couldn't at all!

Every peasant looks down at the ground as he works. What he sees
is *gleba,* the clod: cultivated soil; a plot of land furrowed into waves by
the plow, loosened, aerated earth softened by the rain and baked by the
sun. It is strong-smelling, rich, swarming with small creatures. This is the

true womb of the earth into which the farmer, sowing and sifting, places the paternal germ of the grain. It is hard to conceive that any peasant, no matter how dull, was not conscious of the dignity implicit in such labor. He did not have to be a Christian and know the parables of Jesus; he needed only to know *that no grain grows by itself*. Without the aid of man all grain would die, and soon afterward man himself would die.

The Latin word *gleba* is one of the primitive root words of human speech. It is a word tactile in origin, expressing the sensation of the earth; the moist, fat loam of the cultivated field is described in the consonantal combination *glb*. *Gleba* later gave rise to the word globe, which signified not any sphere but a sphere made of earth from a cultivated field. In

MEDIAEVAL HARVESTING
(From Loutrell Psalter, A.D. 1340)

Jewish cosmogony God blew his breath into earth which he had molded with his hands, and created man. And in the Greek cosmogony Cadmus sowed the seed of the human race into the soil.

The delicate, fecund consonants of the word *gleba* occur again in the words for the beginning and the end of the agricultural process. The mysterious word *hlāf* (loaf) which the Anglo-Saxons used for bread is no etymological riddle as soon as we examine it more closely; the law of the consonantal shift shows us that *glb* is the same as *hlf*. The word "bread" is of very late origin; it does not appear before the eleventh century and meant "something that had been brewed." Here we see again the traditional close relationship of baking and the brewing of beer. Perhaps, too, it is connected with "break"; bread is something that is broken.

Hlāf, however, was the older word for bread. This intimate relation of bread with the rich, dark soil is still present to the Russians; their *only* word for bread is *chleb*. Here we have no reminder of brewing or baking; bread is simply the soil. All Slavic peoples employ for bread this word, whose root is the same as the root of *gleba*. In Polish and in Czech bread is also *chleb*. The Letts use the derivation *kleipä*.

The Germans, too, before they had the word *Brot* employed *Laib* for bread. Jacob Grimm, great and scrupulous etymologist though he was, so misunderstood this word that he thought it came from *Leib,* body, and signified the form of the bread. The tactile origin of the word did not occur to him, for *Laib* means principally a "sticky mass." (In the Alps, when milk curdles, the people call the curd *Laab.*) Therefore, he did not realize that the end product, the *bread loaf,* is faithful to its origin in the *gleba,* the cultivated soil.

Etymologically, then, bread is a child of the soil. Should not that class of men who made the soil fertile have enjoyed more rights than any other class? Did not the peasant have a greater right to bread than—to name but two of his enemies—the burgher or the nobleman?

§ 65

The hostility of these two chief enemies did not arise from the state of freedom or servitude occupied by the peasant. The number of free and unfree peasants throughout Europe remained unchanged for a considerable time. The "persecution of the peasant" did not begin until the secular landowners—soon imitated by the Church, who was the greatest landowner of all—realized what an excellent source of income was the agriculture they hated. Then they set to work to expropriate the free peasants with every means at their command. The same development took place that had once before taken place in the Roman Republic: great estates were more efficient than the estates of the small farmer.

The farmer of the Middle Ages practiced the so-called "three-field system." He divided the field into three strips. On one he planted winter grain, on the second summer grain, and the third he permitted to lie fallow. This rotation was necessary to prevent exhaustion of the soil, but it was not lucrative; the small, free peasant was never able to raise more than enough for his own needs. The large estates, the *latifundia,* could raise more than their own requirements, and by good organization could sell their produce to the town markets. (At a later period the large estates became unproductive because they grew too large.) When the lord saw that the land in his own possession produced more than when it was owned by the small peasant, the lot of the small peasant was sealed. A responsible and capable peasant was set over the others as steward. These stewards became a sort of rustic nobility and extracted from the peasant what little he had not already yielded.

The free peasant was driven off—by perversions of the law and by violence, by forged letters, and by force of arms. The campaign lasted for hundreds of years, but the nobility emerged victorious—a nobility that had long since lost touch with their "protégés," for the nobles no longer lived in the midst of their vassals, but in castles and at the courts of princes.

Although the old statutes of the villages guaranteed to all the rights to wood, water, and pasture land—the *common*, without which the peasant could not live—the lord now seized these common lands. With the loss of their common right to the woods, the villagers also lost their right to hunt and to cut wood—which was bad indeed, since the peasant had only wood to heat his home from October to April. He now had to buy his wood, which in the memory of man had been his own, from the lord.

Yet even this was not the worst of it. The lord of the estate not only cultivated much hitherto uncultivated land—which was commendable— but invented a new obligation for the free peasant: in addition to his own land, the peasant was required to cultivate the lord's new land—to spend his time and strength on another's land without the slightest reward. So that he should not be deprived of his serfs, the lord established limitations on marriage: each peasant was required to marry within the lord's domain. Since he could not remove to another district, his children inherited the duty of service to the lord.

The lord's extortion of unpaid serf labor was not only devoid of humanity, but of all economic rationale. The peasant was required to pay the lord a tithe of his corn. But of what did this tithe consist? The peasant, overburdened with compulsory labor, could not till his own strips. Moreover, the land was perpetually laid waste by the absurd and injurious practice of hunting. Hunting in the Middle Ages was a sport, an exercise, and a ceremony. To protect their fields against injury from wild animals, the farmers had formerly surrounded their cultivated land with hedges and ditches. This was now forbidden. Even so just a man as Emperor Maximilian I (1493–1519) was willing to issue such a ban, so that there should be a clear field for shooting. Stags, boars, horses, and hounds sped through the cultivated fields.

> Revealing the bloodthirsty wolf to our lances,
> The boar vainly roots in the shimmering corn,
> A princelike pleasure lies laughing before us,
> That strengthens our manhood, that nobles our race

sings the hunters' chorus in *Der Freischütz*. The privileged class had no patience with hunting practiced from self-defense or necessity. If the peasant attempted to help himself, he was punished terribly. The monstrous Ulrich von Wuerttemberg (1503–50) had the eyes put out of peasants caught poaching.

But the nobles could eliminate the free peasant class without resorting to atrocities. Rights which the nobles took upon themselves destroyed him. There was, for example, "escheat," the curious law under which, upon the death of a childless peasant, all his movable property reverted to the lord of the fee. That is, in the midst of a world wherein everything was based upon inheritance, the peasant was fundamentally without property; he was merely "enfeoffed" for his lifetime. This death tax early aroused the indignation of many just men. When the knight Hugh of Lincoln saw his stewards taking away the cow of a weeping widow in payment of the "heriot," he forbade them, saying: "This woman had but two workfellows; death hath robbed her of the better and shall we rob her of the other? God forbid that!" Whereupon one of his servants, a cook, had the boldness to reply: "Sir, in this fashion you shall preserve neither your rights nor your property!"

Was it indeed better to die than to live the life of a peasant? The little grain he produced he could not, we will remember, use as he pleased. The lord was also the lord of the mill and the bakery. H. S. Bennett in his *Life on the English Manor* tells us: "Then the peasant would arrive at the mill, only to find the miller overwhelmed with work, or with his mill out of repair, or his head of water weak, or the wind feeble and variable. With the best will in the world (and the miller was notoriously not over-burdened with good will) much of the corn must wait many days before it could be ground. But at home the family could not wait. . . ." Once the villein received his flour, there arose the question of baking it. The presence of an oven in his hut of straw and mud would have meant inevitable fire. But the lord had not established an oven on his manor for reasons of safety: the bread was baked in the lord's oven in payment for an additional tax (the peasant had just paid one tax to the miller); baked by the lord's baker, whom he hated as much as the miller. In his description of conditions in the French feudal state, Champion says in indignation: "What rendered these monopolies so odious was not so much the fixed tariff or the prohibition against crushing one's own grain with a hand mill or between two stones, and baking this meal at home, as the compulsion to carry the grain for long distances, over abominable roads, and then wait two or three days at the door of a mill where the pool had run dry; or, again, of accepting ill-ground meal, burned or half-baked bread, and of enduring all sorts of tricks and vexations from the millers or bakers."

Vexations do not kill. The final blow that destroyed the free peasantry came with the onset of the *tool crisis*. Inadequacy of tools was detrimental to all classes, but it hit the poorest class hardest. The Middle Ages were, to be sure, centuries of master craftsmen; but this was true only of the towns. And even in the towns all crafts that did not serve the art of war or of ornament were pretty much neglected. The rural areas attracted only the poorest technicians. To keep a mill in repair became a thorny problem; and soon the process of degeneration attacked also the iron parts of the plow. When we study medieval miniatures and illuminated manuscripts showing peasant life, we are struck by the infrequent representations of the plow. Almost universally, more primitive tools are pictured. Had the plow begun to be forgotten? Or did only the rich lords, who could afford to maintain a smithy and buy iron, possess plows, while the farmers cultivated their fields with the hoe, like Stone Age man?

In the year 1862 the great artist, Millet, painted a picture which the Paris of his day at once acclaimed. He called it "The Man with the Hoe." The artist himself, whose name, "Father Millet," was the oldest name in agriculture, had painted a silent accusation: a man of indefinite age in indefinite clothing was shown hoeing in a mood of inconsolable despair. Did Millet, the peasant's son, intend his subject to stand for the tiller of all ages?

THE BLEEDING BREAD

> Error! Let free my blinded eyes!
> GOETHE

§ 66

DESPAIR! The culture of the Middle Ages would have had the possibility to recover if man was able to solve the question of the land and the daily bread socially or, at least, technically. Instead, a bickering began there about the holy nature of the bread—a very costly bickering.

Besides the secular cares that bread brought to the anarchistic age, there were the spiritual trials. The spiritual tribulation brought by bread seemed no less painful than the hunger. It caused the clergy and laity not only much trouble and dismay: it laid even the foundation to a grave mental disease of the whole society.

It was the function of the Church to explain to its children what Christ had meant when he said, "I am the bread." To explain and to appease. Neither explanation nor appeasement was easy. When he broke the bread for his disciples, had he performed a symbolic act, or had he actually taught that in the bread they ate his body was really present? This question was not put as an amusing riddle; it was of terrible importance. It was a spiritual and physical reality which men of our materialistic age can scarcely conceive of. Finally, the Church decided this question which for a thousand years had smoldered unextinguished. The question was decided in the year 1204—one of the fateful years in the history of humanity—by the *Lateran Edict*.

What circumstances led up to this edict, which forbade the individual from arriving at his own decision? The greatest of the church fathers, Tertullian, Augustine, and Origenes, had argued that the bread *represented* the body of Jesus Christ, not that it *was* the body of Christ. This representation was accomplished by a mental act, by "recalling to memory" the passion of Christ. At the Last Supper, they said, Jesus had offered his disciples only the *form* of his body and blood in the bread and wine—that is, that he had spoken figuratively, parabolically, metaphorically.

While he spoke, Christ could not possibly have meant that the bread was transubstantiated into his flesh, for in another passage he said: *"Caro non prodest quicquam* [The flesh profiteth nothing]." After such a statement, how could he have required his disciples to eat his own transformed body in the bread?

By far the greater part of the church fathers—who incorporated the theologic and philosophic culture of the times—held that in the Eucharist *no* transubstantiation took place; that Christ had rather asked the world to remember him in this ceremony. They pointed out that the Last Supper had taken place in an atmosphere of Biblical customs against an Old Testament background. "With desire I have desired to eat this paschal [lamb] with you before I suffer." Is Christ himself the paschal lamb? Certainly not, for he would have been eating himself. But he created an electric, fateful atmosphere in which he, quite naturally, was inevitably compared to the lamb. Till the end of the world, whenever this innocent creature was seen, it was to be a reminder of him. Thus at the Last Supper he proceeded from symbol to symbol. As he was now breaking bread and distributing it to his disciples, so would he soon be broken himself and his teachings go out over the whole world (for he knew his destiny). This was believed by most of the church fathers in the first few centuries after Christ, and bread was sacred to them because Christ had chosen it to serve as the symbol of his fate.

A smaller group among the church fathers, however, held different views, and advanced cogent reasons for them. First of all, the passage in which Christ offered the bread and wine and added, "This do in remembrance of me," was to be found only in the Gospel according to Saint Luke. The others do not mention this request. Then, too, these church fathers felt instinctively, and quite correctly, that when the end of his life was approaching, Jesus could scarcely have felt himself a rabbi, nor would he have adhered to such Jewish ideas as the Passover and the paschal lamb. Third (assuming that the physician Luke's phrase, "This do in remembrance of me," was merely an arbitrary addition), the bread that Christ ate *really became transformed into his body at the moment he ate it.* "When we see bread," declared Saint Gregory of Nyssa (331–394), "we may, as it were, see the human body in it, because bread, when it enters the body, becomes itself the body; similarly the bread that was eaten by Christ later became one with Him." It was not the uneaten bread upon the table that was sacred, nor the undrunk wine; both substances were worshiped only *after* the Lord, by eating and drinking, had incorporated them into his own substance. . . . This is Gregory's argument, and if we condense the thousands of pages that were written on the subject of transubstantiation in the early Middle Ages, we will find that all those who took Christ's words literally considered themselves *realists*. By eating and drinking he actually transformed bread and wine into his flesh and blood. How could this be denied? In the face of this, how thin and abstract seemed the reasoning of all the *symbolic* interpreters. In the Orient particularly the speech was taken literally. Saint Chrysostom, in order to explain the complete identity between the bread and Christ, employs the crudest of expressions: "He gave us His body pierced with nails, that we might hold it in our hands and eat it, as a proof of His love; for those whom we love dearly we are often wont to bite." There is no need, Chrysostom argues, to shrink from eating human flesh and drinking human blood. "For," he continues, "in order that the disciples should not be horrified, Christ first drank His own blood and so led them without fear or dread into the communion of His mysteries. . . ." The most important word here is "mysteries." To Chrysostom, as to many others, Christ was not much more than Mithras, the head of just another of the Oriental mystery religions. The Orient, laden as it was with Asiatic conceptions "that gods and men ate one another and gave of their substance to one another to preserve their energies," found nothing strange in Christ's command that his followers eat his flesh and blood.

However, if the Christian Eucharist was *not* an act of remembrance—and the realists insisted that it was not—a very difficult problem was raised. Christ had been sacrificed *once*. This sacrifice had redeemed the world. How could any human being presume to repeat this sacrifice, even if he were an ordained priest? Could the congregation come to the Sacrament as often as it pleased to sacrifice anew Christ's flesh and blood in the form of bread and wine? This was impossible. Therefore, Luke must have been right when he attributed to Christ the explanatory words, "This do in remembrance of me." The majority of Christians felt that Christ in the Sacrament of the Eucharist was not physically present in the bread, but spiritually present in the faith of those who ate of the bread.

Two currents of belief and thought ran parallel here, for a time without conflict. Symbolic interpreters and realists both had the best of grounds for believing what they believed. Their dispute could not be decided; for a time, therefore, no great contention was raised about it. If we glance back at Eleusis, we find that the earliest believers were wholly convinced of the complete identity of the wheat seed with Persephone. Later, when the skeptical Roman, Cicero, demurred that gods were certainly not present in the bread and wine that were eaten, no one in authority thought of bringing charges against him and threatening him with the stake. Undoubtedly this tolerance was the wisest course to pursue. How, then, did the Catholic Church come to disrupt this convenient harmony of tolerance by making a choice between the symbolists and the realists, accepting one and rejecting the other? The Lateran Council declared for the most extreme form of transubstantiation: at the Last Supper Christ had required his disciples to eat his own flesh and blood, and the Catholic priest had the power to perform the same transformation. In the Holy Eucharist—each and every time it was performed—Christ was actually present. Any other belief was *heresy and deadly sin* and would bring upon those who cherished it the punishment of eternal damnation.

§ 67

The Lateran Edict in reality established only an illusory peace. It drove the opponents underground; but the dogma of transubstantiation became an infernal machine that exploded beneath the Church three hundred years later and wrenched the greater part of the Nordic countries and England and America from the house of the Pope.

But this did not happen for three hundred years. Transubstantiation produced other cares for the thirteenth century. The religious revaluation which the newly imposed belief lent to bread at once confronted the clergy with the difficult technical question: Of what dough, in these times of hunger, shall the Host be made? Earlier no one had worried about this, but around 1250 Saint Thomas Aquinas insisted that under all circumstances the Host must be made of *wheat,* for in the Bible the Saviour had compared himself with wheat: "Except a corn of wheat fall into the ground and die, it abideth alone."

This was not quite true. Since only rich people in Palestine ate wheat, barley being the grain of the poor, it is scarcely credible that Christ was wont to eat wheat. The miracle of the five thousand was certainly done with loaves of barley bread. But Saint Thomas Aquinas, who was born in the vicinity of Naples where wheat bread was prized above all other breads, felt it almost blasphemous to imagine that Jesus ate anything but the bread of a great lord. Nevertheless, Saint Thomas did courtesy to the distress of his age when he added hesitantly: "A moderate mingling with other flours does not change the nature of the Host, because a small quantity of such flours is immediately assimilated by the wheat, but the mixture must not be in proportions of half and half." Obviously, this was purely a theoretical requirement; how was the Host to be prepared in the rye countries, for example? The Spanish Jesuit Suárez suggested the painful doubt that for hundreds of years in the Nordic countries the body of the Lord might not have been dispensed at all.

In the first centuries after Christ the breads of the Eucharist were extraordinarily large, shaped like a wreath, with a hole in the center. Probably most of the congregation was fed with *one* bread. Then in the eleventh century the priests commenced to bake small, flat breads no larger than a large coin. This was historically more accurate, since the breads of the Jews had been no bigger than our rolls. But the most important innovation began some time after the year 1000: only *unleavened* breads were used. This dogma was the subject of a dispute that was never settled between the Roman and the Greek Christians. Greek orthodoxy refused to abandon the view that the bread must be leavened (that is, in no way different from men's daily bread); the Roman Pope objected— quite justifiably—that in the Passover week Christ must certainly have eaten unleavened bread. Among the Jews there was a death penalty for leavening bread in the week of the Passover. How could he have obtained any leavened bread? A great deal of ink and gall was spilled over this question. Throughout the centuries there was never a reconciliation between Rome and Moscow—chiefly because of the dispute over the kind of bread the Lord had broken for his disciples at the Last Supper.

The Roman Catholic Church prescribed that the Host could not, of course, be baked in an ordinary oven—where it would have been at too close a proximity to leavening; it must be baked on a waffle iron (*ferramentum characteratum*). Any priest could do the baking, but it was often done in a convent. Three crosses were drawn on the small, round wafer; or the picture of the kneeling lamb; also the letters Alpha and Omega, to show that Christ was the beginning and end of all human knowledge. These wafers were then kept in the tabernacle; if the church were a rich one, the tabernacle glistened with gold and silver.

The wafer was not yet sacred. It had to be consecrated by the priest to become the Host. But since the wafer was the future body of the Lord, it was considered a "middle stage between the flour and the Sacrament." No wonder these little wafers were anxiously guarded by the priests. Nevertheless, some were always disappearing—especially in the rural areas.

The numberless trials for sins against the Host in the Middle Ages revealed that the wafers were, for the most part, stolen by peasants who wished to feed them to their cattle. They did so with utter naïveté, as much out of love for the Host as for their animals. We must remember that the Biblical assertion that man was created to rule over all animals was a relatively late idea. Primitive human society was, as we know from observation of primitive tribes, a mixed society of man and animal in which man felt himself at best a sort of *pater familias,* or an older and wiser brother to his creatures. Otherwise he admired the beasts that lived with him in his cave and could frequently do many more things than he; flying, climbing, and laying eggs were certainly matters for amazement and admiration. In all rural regions such conceptions never died out entirely. When Christ was born, the ox and the ass pressed close to the manger wherein he lay to sniff wisely at the newborn king. It was therefore not so strange that the peasants, in their innocence, secretly took the holy wafers to mix them with their calves' feed or (what was still more popular) to lay them on the floor of their beehives—for then the honey would certainly be sweeter.

It was forgivable for ignorant peasants to do such things. But for centuries more invidious treatment was given to the holy bread. Magicians and witches evinced a growing interest in the Host and attempted to use the great concentration of power within the round wafer for their own purposes. To be sure, the practice of magic was forbidden to all Christians. As among the Jews, it was considered a crime punishable by death, for it was an interference with the course of nature. But this was precisely what hundreds of thousands of people longed to do—and Christianity itself was chiefly responsible for this longing. The Catholicism of the Middle Ages had introduced the "daily miracle" into the religion of Christ. Masses were read daily for the living and the dead, and at each of these masses the priest, with the permission of the Pope, transformed the profane matter of bread and wine into the body of Christ. Was such a transmutation of matter in the power of only the ordained? A religion that was based upon diurnal repetition of a miracle inevitably provoked the desire among the laity to practice magic. Acquiring the power, conjuring up treasures, flying through the air, becoming invulnerable—these were things that millions believed possible. A religion that officially, with extreme dogmatism, proclaimed itself a miracle religion, fatally gave rise to its own negation: the belief in magic and magicians. The Egyptian religion also believed in miracles, and in consistency did *not* persecute the magician, but permitted every Egyptian to make as much magic as he pleased and could. The Christians and Jews thought differently.

In Schiller's ballad, *The Count of Habsburg,* the hero gives away his best horse because the day before he had lent it to a priest who was taking a dying man to receive the Sacrament. When the priest asked in astonishment why he did not wish to take it back, the count replied with these words:

"God forbid that in chase or in battle," then cried the Count with humility
    lowly,
"The steed I henceforward should dare to bestride that hath borne my
    Creator so holy!
And if, as a guerdon, he may not be thine,
He devoted shall be to the service divine,
Proclaiming His infinite merit,
From whom each honor and earthly good
I've received in fee, and my body and blood,
And my breath, and my life, and my spirit."

Hye stylt Cristoff acht partickel des sacrmēt auß der kirchē. legt das in sein calchē. hatt dy darinnē drei tag behaltē

Hye schuet er die sacrament den juden auff den tisch die vnuermayligt gewesen sein. darumb sy im ein guldē gaben

Hye teyltē, sy auß dye sacramēt schicken zwen partickel gen Prag. Zwē gen salczpurg. zwen yn die Newenstat

Hye verprenten sy die sacramēt versuchen ob vnser glaub gerecht wer floge auß dem offen zwen engel. vñ. ij. taubē

Ihye zereyst man den pfeyl vnd vettel die das sacramēt bebyltē. dz darnach gestochen vnd verprant haben.

Ihye verprent man sy mit sampt dē juden. die yn yrem glauben blyben. vnd vmb das sacrament gewyst haben.

ALLEGED HOST CRIME AND MARTYRDOM

Hye tragen die iudē vil ſchulklopffer.
die ſacrament yn ir ſynagog. vnd vber
antwurten oye den Juden.

Hye ſticht pfeyl Jud das ſacrament
auff irem altar. iſt plut darauß gangen
das er vn ander iuden geſehen haben.

Hye vecht man all Juden zu Paſſaw
die dy ſacramēt gekaufft verſchickt ge
ſtolen vnd verprant haben.

Hye furt mã ſy furgericht. verurtaylt
die vier getaufft. fackel man d. kolman
vnd walich. ſein gekopft worden.

Hye wirt der Criſtoff des ſacramentz
verkauffer. auff einem wagē zeryſſen
mit gluenden zangen.

Hye hebt man an zu pawen. vnſerm
herren zu lob eyn gotzhauß. Auß der
iuden ſynagog ꝛc.

The corollary is evident. If the devout considered the Host of such tremendous importance, the devil, too, must have felt it highly worth while to obtain one of the wafers. For this reason, the witches and magicians stole wafers. They were then offered up to the Lord of Hell in Black Masses, and in payment Satan granted them their desires: the rich man's money never would run out, the thief would succeed in his robberies, the hunter would never miss a shot.

Sometimes, however, the wafer defended itself against the robbery. It clung so firmly to the tabernacle that the thief broke his fingers. Or it escaped from the robber's sack and hastened back to the church. A defiled wafer—or one which someone had sought to defile—also possessed the faculty to reveal the attempt to all men. It *bled!* This wafer blood—red or brown encrusted blood—was seen by thousands of people throughout Europe; and wherever it appeared a terrible fear overcame the people. In Germany, France, Spain, Italy, everywhere, the horror appeared. Secular and spiritual authorities went on the hunt for the guilty.

§ 68

Of all the people of the Middle Ages, the Jews were certainly those least to be suspected of practicing magic. For no religion more vigorously condemned such "aping of God" than the religion of Israel. But there was something that did make the Jews suspect. They hated Christ. It was obvious that they hated him, for had they not crucified him? And must they not, from their inexorable hatred, crucify him again and again? They could not do this. But the incarnation of the Lord, the sacred Host, was present for them to attack. Indicted by this cruel logic, which seemed plausible to countless people, the Jews were at once suspected of being responsible for the bleeding Host. Since they themselves were not admitted into Christian churches, they must have thieves in their hire; and indeed thieves were found who confessed all under torture. What would men not have confessed upon the rack?

It is hard to understand how any educated Christian could believe these confessions. For the most fundamental difference between the Christian and Jewish faiths was that no Hebrew ever believed God could be incarnated in a loaf of bread. Why, then, desecrate the Host? The simplest reasoning showed that the accusation of desecration of the Host was based on the false hypothesis that the Jews, like the Christians, identified the Host with the true body of Christ. Since the Jewish mind forbade such an idea, what interest could the Jews have in piercing a holy wafer? Even the Jewish mystics of the Middle Ages, the cabalists, whose speculative nature often led them to extreme Pantheism, never dreamed of speaking of a "divine nature of bread." Men to whom such an idea was inconceivable would never "stab" the Host. But such reasoning did not touch the aroused Christians. The defendants were Jews, and as Lessing put it with bitter wit: "No matter! He is a Jew—and must be burned!"

There remained one question: Why did not the Jews get rid of the *corpus delicti?* Why did they not so destroy the wafer that it could not even bleed? The reply was given that the Host could be wounded, but it could not be destroyed. For example, had the Jews taken it to some distant field and attempted to crumble it, the pieces would have flown off in the shape of butterflies, lighted upon the eyes of a blind man and given him sight. Was it not known that angels and doves had flown out of an oven in which some blasphemers had tried to burn holy wafers? And in some places wafers were heard to weep like children.

A fearful psychologic epidemic seized the world. In the town of Beelitz near Berlin in 1253 the entire Jewish community was burned. In 1290 this was repeated in Paris; eight years later in Korneuburg, a suburb of Vienna. Then followed burnings in Ratisbon, Cracow, Güstrow, Deggendorf, Posen, Prague, Breslau, and Segovia. When the terror came to Poland, the Polish sovereign, Casimir, declared with angry laughter that he did not believe in any such thing as a "bleeding wafer." . . . His skepticism did not help. The clergy and the people demanded torture and the stake. The cruelty employed was merely the correlative of fear. People whose testimony was above reproach had seen the Host giving forth blood. What frightened people most was that the spots of blood did not remain fixed; they spread from day to day. An unnatural sin had been answered clearly and sharply by a sensational miracle. The instigators of the sin must be eliminated, lest the world come to an end.

In 1370, in Enghien, a rich Jewish banker was murdered by a band of thieves. His wife and son moved to neighboring Brussels. The murderers, who did not feel safe, immediately spread the rumor that holy wafers had bled in Brussels' Church of Saint Gudula. The populace fell upon the Jews, demanding that they confess to secret night meetings where they stabbed the wafers with daggers and then brought them back to the church. Despite torture they did not confess! Therefore, on May 22 hundreds of Jews were burned and all others in the city driven out. The Church of Saint Gudula was presented with a series of eighteen paintings which showed in frightful detail the stabbing of the wafers and the punishment of the guilty.

Exactly five hundred years later the Belgian clergy prepared to celebrate the anniversary of the miracle. In May 1870 there was a church procession through the streets of Brussels which would display to the people twelve wafers ornamented with gold and precious stones. At the eleventh hour the Belgian archbishop received a telegram from Pius IX forbidding the parade and the exhibition of the wafers. The Pope's action created a great stir of surprise; it was rumored that an examination of the archives had revealed a falsification in the documents. Instead of the words *pro sacramentis punice et furtive captis* (because of criminally stolen wafers), a chronicler had written *pro sacramento puncto* (because of pierced wafers), and the mistake had given rise to the legend. Since, the rumor went, the wafers had, after all, not been stabbed, they could not have bled and the miracle had not happened at all. It was quite true that the wafers had not bled. But the celebration was called off not because of a mistake in the chronicle but because two contemporary scientists, Christian Ehrenberg and Ferdinand Cohn, had proved that the wafers had *never* bled.

§ 69

It fell to the destiny of Professor of Natural History Christian Gottfried Ehrenberg (1795–1876) to clear up one of the strangest riddles of human history. Ehrenberg was the kind of quiet scientist who spent his life looking into a microscope, examining the soil or the water of his native city Berlin; a man eternally on the hunt for vorticellae and infusoria. Nevertheless, he did not know what a bacillus was, although he had had many dealings with the bacilli. His most significant trait was that he was a student of Goethe and Humboldt and realized that all things must be connected; that particular researches had, as their sole purpose, the explanation of the cultural whole.

On October 26, 1848, this Christian Ehrenberg appeared before the Academy of Sciences in Berlin and told his colleagues the following scientific tale:

Some six weeks before a friend had brought him a potato peel covered with a mold that was reddish rather than gray. This man had known Ehrenberg would be interested because thirty years before, at the age of twenty-three, the scientist had written his doctorate thesis on mold fungi. Ehrenberg examined the peel and found that it was indeed thickly layered with mold; but the red coloring mystified him. There was no such thing as red mold. While Ehrenberg pondered on this, he recalled having read in his youth the story of a Paduan physician named Vincenzo Sette.

In 1819 a peasant, who lived in Legnago, near Padua, had discovered red, rapidly spreading spots in his bowl of yellow polenta. Disgusted, he had thrown away the spoiled corn meal. But the following day the spots reappeared in another bowl of the meal. And then in the peasant's closed cupboard half a cooked fowl became coated with a thin, blood-colored jelly. The peasant told his tale to his neighbors, and great excitement spread through Legnago. The village priest read a sermon against the peasant, who was well known as a miserly cheat and who had held back his grain during the famine of 1817. The peasant turned for help to the University of Padua, and the university faculty detailed Vincenzo Sette to investigate the matter. Accompanied by a police commission, he appeared in turbulent Legnago and sealed the stocks of food. He called the phenomenon the effect of a harmless coloring matter of vegetable origin, which should be further studied because it might well be useful. These remarks of the free thinking physician infuriated the priest. Only in the house of a godless man, the priest raged, could food *bleed!* Thereupon Vincenzo Sette had one of his policemen smuggle a bowl of innocuous corn meal into the priest's home. The following day this meal also turned red. The witch hunt stopped at once.

In his student days Ehrenberg had been much amused by this story. Now he remembered it as he thoughtfully examined the blood-encrusted piece of potato peel. That evening he happened to be reading the classic writer Cornelius Nepos to his small son. He came across a passage to which hitherto little attention had been paid—a passage describing how Alexander the Great, while besieging Tyre (331 B.C.), was badly frightened because spots of blood appeared in his soldiers' bread. The army was on the point of abandoning the siege, but Aristander, one of the priests of Demeter, encouraged the soldiers by explaining that since the blood was *inside* the bread, the curse referred to the Tyrians shut up within their city. Cheered by this, the soldiers stormed Tyre and took the city.

"Can there be a connection," Ehrenberg asked himself, "between the potato peel in my hand, the Paduan anecdote, and the passage in Cornelius Nepos? Is this, perhaps, the solution to one of the most terrible mysteries of the Middle Ages, the bleeding of holy wafers?" Commanding his rising excitement, the scientist set to work. He succeeded in raising cultures of the red coloring matter and transferring colonies to unaffected potatoes. He found that the matter consisted not of fungi, but of infinitesimal bacteria which became visible as individuals only when magnified three hundredfold. With thousandfold magnification he saw that they moved energetically. Now there could be no doubt of what he had discovered. With the quiet scorn of the scientist he named the new bacterium *Monas prodigiosa,* the miracle-working monad.

"It was a monad, you see," he exclaimed to the members of the Academy, "which frightened Alexander when he was besieging Tyre, and only the priest's rhetoric inspired the soldiers to the assault. It was rhetoric, too, that caused thirty-eight Jews to be burned in our native city of Berlin in 1510. These people were burned to ashes—and the sentence was passed on them—because they had tormented consecrated wafers until the blood flowed. . . ." As he spoke, Ehrenberg removed a cloth from the speaker's stand. He revealed three white breads; all three had the bloody mark of the *Monas prodigiosa,* with which he had himself infected them.

The effect was instantaneous and enormous. This meeting of the Academy assembled everyone of any distinction. Philologists as Jacob Grimm, mathematicians, astronomers, philosophers, and chemists—all shook hands with Ehrenberg. And in the city of Berlin itself, where but recently street battles had been fought between the people and the king's soldiers, and where ordinarily the Academy was little regarded, the news of the discovery spread like wildfire.

How strange it was that for centuries men had trembled because bread bled. An inconceivably tiny creature had made fools of all mankind!

Scientists now set to work to find conditions under which this *harmless* micrococcus (for bleeding bread was as digestible as any other bread) could thrive and strike fear into men's hearts. Ferdinand Julius Cohn of Breslau (1828–98) found that the bacillus—which textbooks name after him as *prodigiosus Cohn*—excreted its red coloring matter only in warm temperatures with a certain degree of humidity. Should not men have noticed that the miracle of bleeding wafers never occurred in winter?

Cohn found the explanation for the rapid spreading of the color, the continuous bleeding which so frightened men, in the high powers of reproduction possessed by the bacillus. A cubic centimeter of water containing 47 billion bacteria very soon contained 884 billion. And as Sette had suspected, the bacillus did not appear most frequently in flour at all. It could often be seen on coagulated egg white, on the surface of milk, on veal. If the men of the Middle Ages had only had eyes to see . . . But they were lovers of abstraction, not observers, as the great scientists of Pliny's day had been. It was not until the eighteenth and nineteenth centuries that the years of blindness came to an end.

LE PAIN SE LÈVE—THE PEASANT REBELS

§ 70

THE CHARACTERISTIC of the Middle Ages was fear, an overwhelming fear of things which today even the savage scarcely fears. And on another plane the Middle Ages was governed by arrogance—an incomprehensible arrogance of class which sought to drown out the fear.

It is quite understandable that in these frightful times nobody rushed to help, when a Jew or a witch was put on trial. But it is less understandable that neither a statesman nor a thinker tried to make an end to the worries of the peasantry. Arrogance, then, barred all reason. The social ethics of the Middle Ages were formed by the Gaelic romances and the Arthurian legends. Their ideal was the mounted, sporting young man who engaged in adventures against enemies or monsters. The tiller of soil was far below him. *Rustica gens, optima flens, pessima gaudens* (The peasant who weeps is the best peasant; one who laughs is the worst). Most men of the times believed this spiteful proverb. We have not to overestimate that a great English poet, William Langland (ab. 1330– ab. 1400) made the farmer in his *Piers Plowman* the active and contemplative type, and that his disciple, the German-Bohemian poet, Johannes von Saaz (1360–1414), followed Langland's example. They, probably, never spoke in their life with a true peasant; their love was

TYING UP SHEAVES
(From the Loutrell Psalter, A.D. 1340)

only a metaphorical one. But the hate Shakespeare displayed against the peasantry was a real one. We see with a deep sorrow how Shakespeare took the wrong party in the most fateful struggle of his time.

Yes, they were not pleasant fellows. The peasants of this time had the trait common to all persecuted and oppressed people: they were mimics who tried to pretend they were not peasants. In the Middle Ages the peasants were permitted to wear only dark gray or dark blue. This was reason enough for the villager who still possessed a small independent farm to borrow money from a usurer and buy clothing of red Flemish cloth and a velvet cap. Then he sat before the village inn eating and drinking as though he were a lord. Afterward he threw up, and the dogs fed on the rich vomit. Behaim, Breughel, Schongauer, and other burgher painters have portrayed such scenes. The town artisans, who often went hungry in their self-chosen ghettos, were stirred to fresh envy and hatred by such scenes of gluttony.

The feudal state postulated that each man held his position and his property as a personal fief from God—the emperor his empire and the other classes, knights, burghers, and peasants, their possessions. According to Saint Augustine the occupations of the classes had been chosen *voluntarily. Cum divina providentia unus elegit unum officium, ut agri-*

culturam, alius aliud. (With the help of Divine Providence one man chooses one employment, such as agriculture; other men others.) Trying to leave his class was a *sin.* The Christian poets reproached the peasant particularly for that. In a famous German epic which has unjustly been considered friendly to the peasantry—the *Meier Helmbrecht* of Wernher der Gaertner (ab. 1250) the hero, a rustic good-for-nothing, finally becomes a robber and meets with a wretched death. This would have happened to the lazy young man in any case—even if he had started out as a knight, a student, a merchant, or a monk. To the highly moralistic poet —he was probably the gardener of a monastery—the crime from which all Helmbrecht's other crimes spring is his ambition to rise out of the peasantry. Whatever his fate, the peasant *must* stick to his soil. Even before the new scholastic law of the fifteenth century decided that the peasant himself was a "part of the soil," it was unanimously felt that the peasant belonged on the land. Belonged there morally, not merely legally. On this point all the Christian writers were as obstinate as the lay thinkers.

Into the latter class Shakespeare falls. In his Jack Cade he embodied all his notions about a rebellious peasant. ("This man seems to have been sadly slandered by Shakespeare," remarks the 1923 edition of Chambers' Encyclopedia.) Cade, the son of an artisan, led the revolt of the peasants of Kent in 1450 against the English nobility. An extremely gifted soldier, Cade succeeded in storming London and holding the city for a few days. In the Second Part of *King Henry VI* Shakespeare introduces him and his bread program to the audience in the following manner:

. . . There shall be in England seven halfpenny loaves sold for a penny: the three-hooped pot shall have ten hoops; and I will make it felony to drink small beer: all the realm shall be in common; and in Cheapside shall my palfry go to grass. . . . There shall be no money; all shall eat and drink on my score; and I will apparel them all in one livery, that they may agree like brothers, and worship me their lord.

It is only at Jack Cade's death that the dramatist saw him with a little more charity. The peasants have disbanded, tricked by the king's promise of grace. Jack Cade hides in the woods for five days, then climbs into a garden to find a "sallet" to stay his hunger. He sees the owner approaching, challenges him to combat, and falls. Dying, he says proudly that *famine* and no other has slain him. "Give me but the ten meals I have lost, and I'ld defy them all."

Here Shakespeare spoke the tragic truth. In a peasant war not only the better-armed, but the better-fed were victorious. The poet had experienced this. For Shakespeare knew, of course, of the great Peasants' War in Germany, which had flared up only three quarters of a century before. Some notes in the play seem to be derived from German reports rather than from English sources. When the peasant leader commands his followers to inspect men's shoes:

> We will not leave one lord, one gentleman:
> Spare none but such as go in clouted shoon
> For they are thriftly honest men . . .

it becomes clear that Shakespeare knew of "Poor Coontz" and the *Bundschuh* uprising.

§ 71

For it had happened at last—the event feared for centuries. The man with the hoe had risen. It had begun as early as the second half of the thirteenth century, and in the land where the "most peaceful people of Europe" lived: in Holland. The feudal system had not been instituted there; but the peasants reasoned that the nobility, influenced by the French policy, would attempt to confiscate all common land. They revolted, and a civil war lasting for decades was the result.

In France itself, where barons and king had been almost ruined by the English, they indemnified themselves by plundering and setting fires in the villages. In the spring of 1358 the peasants rose in revolt against this terrorization, and the famous *Jacquerie* began. (Jacques was the nickname of the French peasant.) Although the peasants were supported by the burghers of Paris, whose merchants were also oppressed by the feudal state, they were defeated when their leader was taken prisoner through treachery. The English, who were enjoying the difficulties of the French, took alarm when the conflagration that had begun in France spread to their own island.

"Le pain se lève"—this was the watchword of the French peasants. In England it became "The bread will raise!" when, weary of the fourfold oppression of lord, bishop, king, and townsfolk, who "cut his heart like the devil's harrow," the English peasant arose to win the right to "knead the dough for himself." The leader was Walter the Brickmaker, called by his contemporaries Wat Tyler. Froissart tells us that he had been a soldier in France. Consequently, he understood the art of war. On June 10, 1381, the peasants took Canterbury, leading the archbishop away as a prisoner; on the thirteenth they were in London. They opened the prisons, plundered the home of the treasurer, Hale, who was hated because he had shortly before established a poll tax for the peasantry, and locked him in the Tower with the Archbishop of Canterbury. On the fourteenth, King Richard II, then a boy of fourteen, rode out to the suburbs to parley with them and asked Wat Tyler what he wanted. Tyler demanded immediate abolition of serfdom, the rights to grind, bake, and

brew for all peasants, and, of course, a general pardon for the rebels. The king agreed. But when Wat Tyler demanded trial and punishment for the oppressors of the people, in particular the hated Lord Hale, the king broke off the negotiations. The peasants believed they had been betrayed and began anew to plunder London. Some broke into the king's castle, went to his bedroom and upset his bed, alleging that they wished to find "whether a traitor was hidden there." A few lusty fellows, smelling of manure, molested the queen mother, who fainted and later was taken away by her pages. All this was still half jesting. But in the Tower things were in earnest; the peasants informed Archbishop Simon that he must die. He requested permission to read a last mass. At the words *"Omnes Sancti orate pro nobis!"* the mob fell upon him and dragged him and the chancellor of the exchequer away. Hale died at once; a clumsy executioner hacked at the archbishop's neck eight times before the head fell from the body.

That very night London awoke from its terror. Citizens' guards were formed. The following day the peasants again demanded an interview with the king. Richard, with a large following, rode out on a field to meet them. Tyler ordered his men to wait and rode toward the king alone. He grasped the king's hand and shook it so familiarly that both parties were impressed. Then he demanded abolition of the estates of Church and Crown and general social equality. None was to be permitted to possess more than any other. The boy king said he would consider it, but that he would not divide the crown estates. Tyler was extremely dissatisfied. He began to shout that he was hot and wanted a mug of beer. When the beer was brought, he put it to his mouth at once and threw his head back to drink. At that moment a baron in the king's retinue cried: "I know him. This is a robber whom my neighbor condemned to death!" Wat Tyler threw the mug aside, drew his sword, and at once sprang upon the defamer. At this the mayor of London, Sir William Walworth, cried: "Save the king!" and spurred his horse before the king's horse. Tyler changed his direction and struck at the mayor's breast, which was protected by armor. Then Sir William Walworth and another knight ran him through. Dying, barely able to cling to his horse, Tyler reached his own line. A shower of arrows from the peasants answered the attack, but the king's knights succeeded in escaping. During the following days the leaderless rebels were scattered and order was restored.

There was still one real leader left: the eloquent priest, John Ball. For decades Ball had inveighed against the English bishops for their love of ornament and their un-Christian lives. The peasant was the rightful ruler, he declared, and the rightful preacher, for no other class had regarded and worshiped Christ like him. "We are men formed in Christ's likeness, and they treat us like beasts!" The Archbishop of Canterbury, shortly before, had imprisoned Ball in Maidstone. The peasants freed him, and he spoke to sixty thousand people in the open fields. In the course of this speech he coined two lines of verse which have outlived his memory:

When Adam dalf and Eve span
Who was thanne a gentilman?

But John Ball lived only a month after this triumph. On July 15th he was hanged, drawn, and quartered.

Although the peasants of the Continent had no ambassadors in England, the universities, where religion and politics were hotly discussed, maintained close relations with one another. An English brickmaker had shaken hands with the king, and a rebellious priest had thundered at the bishops: "It is written in Saint Matthew, 'Do not possess gold nor silver!'" These were unheard-of occurrences—revolutionary events that could well revolutionize the age. The news waxed greatest in the heart of Europe, in Prague. Restless, mystic Prague, the city halfway between Moscow and London, had never entirely abandoned the Slavic fondness for the peasant. Russian agrarian economy was communistic: the land and his bread, *chljeb,* belonged to the *mir,* the village community. (It was not until 1597 that Czar Boris Godunov abolished the peasant's freedom of movement and thus founded serfdom.) The German and Italian conceptions of rule and of property were never compatible to the Czechs. The University of Prague became a center for the propagation of revolutionary doctrines. John Wyclif (d. 1384), who had been expelled from Oxford for his hostility to the Pope demanded gravely "evangelical poverty." His doctrine had force among the Bohemians. Even the higher Czech clergy began to take the part of the peasantry. Archbishop Jentzenstein of Prague said ominously: "According to the Christian view, the estates of the Church are estates of the poor; the function of the bishops is merely to administer them." And the Czech priest Kunes von Trebovel inveighed against the "all-devouring Church." "The peasants are not slaves, nor usufructuaries of their land; they are the true masters! *Illi rustici benedicti*—they, the blessed producers of bread from whose sweat all of us live!" The Pope would have none of this; the divisions grew until Wyclif's famous and unhappy disciple, the peasant's son Jan of Husinetz (1369–1415), called John Huss, brought the situation to the breaking point. He preached against the landowning Pope and was forced to flee from Prague. His German and Italian enemies challenged him to attend the Council of Constance, and the emperor gave him a safe-conduct. When at the council he refused to abjure his doctrines and those of Wyclif, the safe-conduct was treacherously disregarded and he was put to the stake. The Czech word "Huss" means "goose," and the goose is the bird of Saint Martin, the saint of European peasantry. When the enemies of Huss saw him burning at the stake, they said jokingly: "Now the goose is roasted!" But they were completely mistaken, for this goose "hissed for a long time."

Indeed, the flames that rose around Huss ignited a long war. The Czech people rushed forth from their square mountain fortress of Bohemia like a torrent of lava. They marched in all directions: an army of peasants that none could resist, demanding freedom for the country and freedom of religion. For sixteen years the killing lasted, until at last they were defeated. But the very air continued to vibrate with the noise of their weapons and the sound of their sermons. Soon unrest gripped Hungary, and the wave lapped against the frontiers of Germany.

§ 72

All the rest had been prelude. In Germany the principal drama began. The cow that centuries before had been taken from the English peasant widow; the blood that the Czech people had but recently spilled; the Spanish baron's miller who cheated the people; the servitude of the Italian tenant—all the injustices of feudal society were reckoned up and the reckoning laid upon the table in Germany.

Why was Germany the battleground?

The German peasant was, in practice, as poor of rights as every other peasant. But theoretically his pre-feudal rights had never been written off from the letter of the law. He could still hope that someday all the oppressions he suffered would be exposed as great injustices.

This hope was now taken from him when the emperor and his councils, toward the end of the fifteenth century, hit upon the tragic idea of introducing *Roman law*. This system of law, which had been codified 1,200 years before, was based upon the slave economy of ancient Rome—and officially the Christian Middle Ages no longer sanctioned such an economy, though practically, of course, it still existed. Now, however, the peasant was to be made a slave in the letter of the law as well. He was to become a *glebae adscriptus,* a creature bound to the land. He would no longer be a subject, but an instrument of the economic order, a *thing*. No longer was the question one of degrees of property, honor, just wages, riches, or poverty; it was a question of whether one was a human being. When the bread-producing class of Germany was denied this title, the German Peasants' War began.

Nevertheless, the peasants would never have risen had they not felt at their backs the wind of the Reformation. "From the very first he was close to the little man," says Ernst Bloch of Martin Luther. The translation of the Bible into the German vernacular was an act whose effect cannot be calculated in the too puny terms of literature. What the peasants wished to do to the Roman law Luther in Wittenberg had

already done to the Roman Church: he had destroyed it and founded
a German Christianity. He was the natural ally of the peasants, whom he
justifiably considered the advance guard of the Reformation. And he
spurred the peasants to attack by reproaching the secular lords for their
sins and abuses more sharply than he did the spiritual masters:

> The common man can no longer endure it. The sword is at your throat;
> ye still think ye sit so tight in the saddle that ye cannot be pulled down
> therefrom. Such security and vicious audacity will break your necks, as ye
> will see. . . . Ye must become different, and live in fear of God's Word.
> If ye do not do it willingly, freely, ye must be compelled to do so by force
> and hurtful ways. If these peasants do not do it, others must. And though
> you killed them all, God would raise up others.

The peasants, on their part, were profoundly concerned about the
Biblical justification for their platform. They wanted to establish anew in
earthly law Moses' agrarian laws and Christ's love for the tillers of the
soil. To be sure, there were a number of low charlatans and cheats among
the peasants, like those "leaders" who led their comrades to the Neckar
River, threw heavy weights into the water, and declared: "If they float
on top, the princes and lords are in the right; if they sink, the common
man is in the right." But the majority of the peasant leaders were honest.
When Thomas Munzer cried to his men to march unafraid into battle,
for he could catch the bullets of their enemies upon his sleeves, he believed his own extravagance. He felt that God's might watched over him.

From Luther's translation of the Bible Thomas Munzer knew the
warning: "The children asked for bread, but there was none who broke
it." The bread would be had for the children, he determined. The *Twelve
Articles* of the peasants demanded bread in the spiritual and the material
sense. These "fundamental and correct chief articles of the peasants,
relating to the matters in which they feel themselves aggrieved," provided:

1. The villages were to be free to elect their own pastors.
2. The grain tithe was to be paid not to the lord, but to the pastor.
3. Serfdom was to be abolished—which was not to be interpreted as
the abolition of authority, for authority must, by God's commandment,
be obeyed.
4. Return to the peasants of the rights of hunting and fishing.
5. The right to use wood to be divided among the lords and the
peasants.
6. Those who so desired might continue to serve the lord, but:
7. Only for just compensation.
8. The fields were to be taxed only according to what they produced.
9. Trials were to be conducted according to the old common law, not
under the new Roman law.

10. Common meadows which had been the property of the village in ancient times were to be restored.

11. "Heriot" was to be abolished; in the future no peasant must be made to pay for his own death.

The twelfth article provided that the other eleven were valid *only* if their righteousness according to the Bible could not be contested. Here was an evangelical manifesto. Until this day the bread-producing class had had no mouth to make even a complaint before its oppressors. Now this program, drawn up by Balthasar Hubmeier and Sebastian Lotzer, appeared and was first peaceably presented to the authorities of the empire. When neither princes, towns, bishops, nor parliaments gave an answer, the war began.

The peasants had a great numerical superiority. Also they were tougher and more courageous than the hired soldiery of their opponents. But they were unaccustomed to bear arms. Centuries before they had voluntarily surrendered the right to carry weapons, and had preferred to pay for military exemption rather than be dragged to foreign parts by their lord. This fact now turned against them.

Above all, the peasants were not equipped to cope with the strategic problems of large-scale warfare. A unified plan was needed; preparations had to be made for month-long sieges of fortified places. The peasants had not the training for this. And so they came to form an alliance with their deadly foes, the lower nobility. The petty knights had no love for the princes, still less for the towns, whose bankers exacted outrageous usury from them. These knights were willing to throw in their lot with the peasants. Thus men who, as a class, had for centuries followed the trade of robber knight became the military leaders of the peasant army. Some of these apostates from their class, like Florian Geyer, were loyal to the peasant cause; others, like Götz von Berlichingen, helped to defeat their new friends by equivocation and treachery.

How the peasants lost battles and fell into traps that any other group would have avoided is an ofttold tale. Great writers like Goethe and Gerhart Hauptmann have told it. In the beginning they burned all the monasteries and castles in their path; but instead of marching on, they sprawled among the ruins and drank themselves blind. At first prisoners were treated like butts at a carnival, but their lives were not taken. But this changed when the peasants marched upon the town of Weinsberg, which was defended by a certain Count von Helfenstein, a son-in-law of Emperor Maximilian—a pious and moderate man. When shots were fired—without the count's orders—from the battlements of the city, the peasants stormed the town and slaughtered everyone. Count von Helfenstein was forced to run the gantlet while his wife, the emperor's daughter, looked on. Throwing herself at the feet of the peasant captain, she lifted her infant child and begged for the life of its father. In reply a peasant woman struck at the child and wounded it in the throat. The emperor's daughter was placed half naked upon a dung cart and, amid mocking laughter, taken to Heilbronn, which, like other Swabian towns, had surrendered to the peasant forces.

After the victory of the nobles, the "white terror" surpassed the "red terror" by far. All the peasants who had participated in the slaughter at Weinsberg were searched out. One of them, Nonnenmacher, a musician who had often played for the murdered count at table, was tied to a tree by a length of rope and the rabid victors then set fire to the tree. The unfortunate man ran around in a circle like an animal for half an hour, "being roasted with fine slowness. . . ." The commander of the victors, Georg Truchsess, burned down every peasant home in sight, drowning the guilt of the fathers in the blood of women, children, and grandchildren. The valleys of Swabia and Franconia smoked; in Bavaria and Austria thousands of peasants were dragged to the executioner's block; in Alsace and the Black Forest their hands were cut off if they were found to have subscribed to the Twelve Articles, or they were blinded with red-hot irons and the populace was forbidden to give them shelter or any help. For weeks the Main and the Neckar, the Danube and the Rhine ran with blood. Never before in the Christian era had any people so raged against their fellow countrymen. Fifteen years earlier, in Hungary, the peasant leader Georg Docza had been captured by his enemies and sat in a fiery chair. His subordinates had been forced to eat of the half-roasted flesh of the still-living man. But this had happened on the frontiers of Christian culture, "where the people were almost Turks." Now, in 1525, such atrocities were done in Germany, in the heart of Europe. Of this same Germany Enea Piccolomini, the humanist who later became Pope Pius II, had written: "Among the Germans everything is serene and pleasant. No one is robbed of his estates; each is secure in his inheritance. The German authorities act only against criminals. And there are no partisan struggles, as in the Italian cities. . . ."

Scarcely less felling than the artillery which eventually defeated the peasants in battle was the attitude of Luther. Trusting to his aid, they had marched to war. This man, who had given them the original Word of God in all its purity, must inevitably help them. But when the peasants began to confiscate private property, Luther was afraid that the estates of the Church—once expropriated—might revert to secular princes. He stabbed the peasants in the back, and in a way that horrified his closest friends. Perhaps he was tormented by the obscure fear that he would be held responsible for their bloody acts. Moreover, he violently hated the many "little Luthers," like Thomas Munzer, Andreas Karlstadt, and the other preachers who marched with the peasant army and seemed to be aping his words. He saw his life work endangered and feared for the

Reformation. And so he produced the vile pamphlet, *Against the Thievish, Murderous Hordes of Peasants*. He called upon the princes to exterminate the peasant bands:

> It is the time for the sword and for wrath and not for pity. So, then, the authorities shall go ahead and with a good conscience knock down and kill so long as they have breath left in their bodies. Therefore, whoever may be killed on the side of the authorities is a real martyr before God, before whom he may appear with a clear conscience, for he walks in the Godly word and obedience. But whoever of the peasantry perishes, is of the eternal brood of hell, for he carries the sword against the Word of God and obedience, and is a branch of the devil. Such are these present times that a prince can more easily attain the kingdom of heaven by bloodshed than others by prayer. Stab, murder, strangle, whoever can! If you perish in doing so, so much the better, for you can never die a more blessed death, for you die in obeying the Divine Word and command and in the service of love to save your neighbor from hell and the bonds of the devil.

So he raged, Luther, the miner's son, who knew well the life of the poor. This fury is the fury of the renegade; and even when the best minds of the country had turned away in horror from the bloody vengeance of the princes, Luther continued in his delirium—though the peasants had originally desired nothing more than his gospel and the bread that Christ had promised to men. With terrible tragedy the cry of a young peasant sounds across the centuries. As he stood in the market place of Stuttgart before the executioner's sword, he cried: "Alas! Now I must die, and in all my life *I have not twice eaten my fill of bread!*"

§ 73

Only the poverty of the defeated peasants put a limit to the fury of the victors. When, afterward, new punishment taxes were imposed upon the surviving peasants, the victors discovered that "the peasant home in Swabia had become a stable." The inhabitants possessed neither furniture nor blankets. They slept upon the bare earthen floor. For two hundred and fifty years, until the French Revolution, this defeat weighed upon the European peasants; it did incomparable spiritual damage. The year 1525 marked the beginning throughout Europe of what has been called the "peasant character"—the dark, cunning, taciturn, misanthropic habits of the peasant; the avarice, secrecy, and stubborn deafness that sprang from instincts of self-defense. Even great and unprejudiced writers like Balzac, De Maupassant, and Zola feared the peasants and doubted that their souls could ever recover.

Paintings have strange destinies. All his life Jean François Millet (1814–75) painted the dulled, crushed people of the peasant scenes he had known in his youth. How could he expect the public to love them? Who could like "The Man with the Hoe," which expressed the poverty-stricken dismalness of the Normandy landscape? And the other paintings of this peasant's son were no more cheerful: "Man Spreading Manure," "The Sower," "Harvesters Resting." But within a short time these pictures rose to heights in the art market. The painter, who had lived in

CARTING CORN
(From the Loutrell Psalter, A.D. 1340)

poverty and debt like his forefathers, enriched the art dealers. (He sold his famous "Angelus" for 1,800 francs—a canvas that a few decades later fetched 800,000 francs.) And soon America began to buy. Cities, museums, and millionaires, who knew nothing of the misery of the past that Millet's pictures expressed, hung them in costly frames on paneled walls, surrounded by marble and light.

It came about that Edwin Markham, America's longest-lived poet (1852–1940), saw "The Man with the Hoe" in the museum in San Francisco. The year was 1899; the times vibrated with the ideas of Henry George, Tolstoy, and the agrarian socialists. Markham, child of a more fortunate hemisphere, had scarcely experienced the age-old misery that was implicit in Millet's painting. But the hoe struck a chord in the poet's heart. He wrote down the verses which he modestly called *Illustration of a Picture*. Within a few years they became the most famous verses of America, reprinted in hundreds of thousands of copies. They deserve reprinting once more:

> Bowed by the weight of centuries he leans
> Upon his hoe and gazes on the ground,
> The emptiness of ages in his face,
> And on his back the burden of the world.

Who made him dead to rapture and despair,
A thing that grieves not and that never hopes,
Stolid and stunned, a brother to the ox?
Who loosened and let down this brutal jaw?
Whose was the hand that slanted back this brow?
Whose breath blew out the light within this brain?

Is this the Thing the Lord God made and gave
To have dominion over sea and land;
To trace the stars and search the heavens for power;
To feel the passion of Eternity?
Is this the Dream He dreamed who shaped the suns
And marked their ways upon the ancient deep?
Down all the caverns of Hell to their last gulf
There is no shape more terrible than this—
More tongued with cries against the world's blind greed—
More filled with signs and portents for the soul—
More packed with danger to the universe.

What gulfs between him and the seraphim!
Slave of the wheel of labor, what to him
Are Plato and the swing of Pleiades?
What the long reaches of the peaks of song,
The rift of dawn, the reddening of the rose?
Through this dread shape the suffering ages look;
Time's tragedy is in that aching stoop;
Through this dread shape humanity betrayed,
Plundered, profaned and disinherited,
Cries protest to the Judges of the World,
A protest that is also prophecy.

O masters, lords and rulers in all lands,
Is this the handiwork you give to God,
This monstrous thing distorted and soul-quenched?
How will you ever straighten up this shape;
Touch it again with immortality;
Give back the upward looking and the light;
Rebuild in it the music and the dream;
Make right the immemorial infamies,
Perfidious wrongs, immedicable woes?

O masters, lords and rulers in all lands,
How will the Future reckon with this Man?
How answer his brute question in that hour
When whirlwinds of rebellion shake all shores?
How will it be with kingdoms and with kings—
With those who shaped him to the thing he is—
When this dumb Terror shall rise to judge the world,
After the silence of the centuries?

THE FIGHT OVER THE LORD'S SUPPER

Not things confuse men, but opinions of things.

EPICTETUS

§ 74

THE CLASSES that cut down their brothers, the peasants, did not profit by their victory. All of them were debtors of the man who made their bread, but they so turned it that the peasant seemed to be in their debt. They could not be touched by the words of the Talmud: "If you have taken of a man his plow or his pillow for debt, return his plow in the morning and his pillow at night." Instead they killed those they had robbed; in consequence, they themselves were soon hungrier than before.

Princes, towns, and barons for centuries were forced to feel the effects of their victory over "Adam the Plowman"—famine greater than ever. The Church suffered in particular. The Church had betrayed the plowman and cheated him of his bread, which Christ had entrusted to it; it had handed the tiller of the soil over to the mighty ones of the world. Now bread itself, holy bread, took spiritual vengeance. The peasants, to be sure, had turned away from the Church because the Church no longer seemed to them the Church of Christ. However, the peasants were powerless. But now the very servants of the Church arose to dispute with her about the "nature and purpose of the Eucharist." What should have wrought harmony became a symbol of disharmony. Over the doctrine of bread the Church split into two and then into four new churches.

Armed with staff and ring, Pope Innocence III had proclaimed the Lateran Edict, which was absolute. All doctrines were declared false which denied transubstantiation. Christ was present in the holy bread as soon as the priest consecrated it. Those who believed would win salvation; those who doubted would burn in hell.

The consequences of this imposed doctrine were at first very favorable to the Church. The dogma appealed to the mass of the people, for it promoted the belief in miracles. The people, who even while Christ still lived had demanded miracles and had been angry when the miracles were not forthcoming, were satisfied to experience a magical process in the Mass. A God who had been dead for a thousand years was nothing for the masses of the people. But a God who daily was re-created in the form of bread and wine was something: he was a God of miracles, to be wor-

shiped in myriad forms. It was as though the authority of the Pope had
called forth a springtide in all the arts. Music became grand; scarlet and
gold flashed from the brushes of the painters. Everything combined to
lend to the Catholic Mass, the Miracle of the Incarnation, the transformation of Christ into bread, a beauty and dignity it had never before possessed.

But amid all this beauty, amid the sounds of unearthly choirs, to which
the greatest of musicians contributed, amid the gleaming of the mon-
strance, a certain troubled mood made itself felt. In monasteries and
universities the human appetite for truth spoke out. Now that the symbolic interpretation of transubstantiation had been made a deadly sin by
the Pope, it became apparent that a great number of cultivated men
denied the dogma and secretly adhered to the forbidden doctrine.
Bérenger of Tours, for example, taught that the Eucharist was purely
an act of remembrance whose purpose was to influence the soul to find
union with Christ, and he taught it with great courage. Wrathful
against the casualness with which God was daily put to work in a hundred different places ("like a horse drawing a wagon") to perform a
miracle, he did not abate his words. Bérenger refused to call the Pope
pontifex, and dubbed him *pulpifex* (flesh-maker). Rome, he declared,
had become the seat of Satan. The substance of bread and wine remained
bread and wine *after* the priest's consecration, he insisted. He admitted
that a spiritual and noble element had entered into them—the consecration—but no words of men could convert the substance of a wheat bread
into the actual body of Christ.

Only a desperate recantation at the last moment saved Bérenger from
the stake. But later on he wrote a pamphlet recanting the recantation.
Had he not died soon afterward, he would have been burned as his books
were burned. But Bérenger's spirit did not die; it increased throughout
the Middle Ages, in proportion as the times emerged from the cloister of
scholasticism into the more elegant halls of humanism. Toward the end
of the Middle Ages, the end of the fourteenth and the beginning of the
fifteenth centuries, the symbolists grew openly defiant of the realists. The
greatest scholar of that age, Erasmus of Rotterdam (ab. 1466–1536),
believed that bread could have never been the true body of Christ. He
was, to be sure, not so rude as Bérenger of Tours had been—Erasmus'
weapon was wit—but his attitude was the same.

§ 75

Among Erasmus' admirers was a priest of Zurich whose name was Dr.
Leo Juda. He was the grandson of a Jew, and in his boyhood had suffered a good deal because of the name he bore. He had asked and

received permission from the Pope to change his name to Leo Keller. Later, however, he fell out with Rome, and in order that it might not be said he had accepted any of Rome's gifts, he resumed his former name.

Juda was a friend of Huldreich Zwingli, the Swiss reformer, and not only shared Zwingli's views, but contributed to them.

In 1523 two strangers came with a letter to Dr. Juda. It was a printed letter, written in the style of Erasmus, though its author was Erasmus' fellow countryman, Cornelius Hoen. No printer's name appeared upon the little leaflet, and those who distributed it preferred to keep their own names secret. For even to have on one's person such a letter was enough to incur charges of heresy and burning at the stake.

The leaflet dealt with the subject that was of profound moment for the educated men of the times: the true significance of the Last Supper. In its flowing, Erasmean style, Cornelius Hoen's letter put forth the following argument:

The purpose behind the Eucharist was no more than a kind of confirmation. It was a pledge given by Jesus, so that his followers might not waver in their faith. "Just so does a bridegroom give his bride the ring saying: 'Take, I give you myself!'" This was what Jesus had actually meant when he gave the bread to his disciples. There was no need to be disturbed because Christ had actually said, "This bread *is* my body." For if he had chosen instead of *is* (est) the expression *means* (significat), he would have been putting his metaphor lamely. *Est* gave his meaning far more strongly than *significat*. When Christ spoke in metaphors (which he customarily did), he spoke in the indicative, never using the "as if" form. In the metaphoric manner Christ had often characterized himself as a rock, a door, a road, a stone, a grape. Yet it had occurred to no one to assert that Christ was actually incorporate in a door or a stone. Why, then, did the Roman Church wish to enclose the Saviour in a loaf of bread? If Christ had desired "daily impanation," his incarnation in the bread, at the hands of any priest, he would undoubtedly have said so. But he had *not* said so. The words, "This is my body," had never meant that the Saviour wished to transform the bread into himself; he wished merely to, figuratively, give himself in the form of bread, as one gave a buyer possession of a field by handing him a staff or a bit of straw and saying, "There you have the field!" The Lord had desired to say nothing more than: "Take and eat and regard it not small; for that which I give you here, this bread, signifies my body; but my body shall soon be broken like the bread, and it shall be for you!" Thus, with elegance and eloquence, Hoen's letter discussed this difficult and dangerous question.

As Leo Juda read the Dutch humanist's letter, his heart pounded. He rushed to his friend's home and found him still lying abed. Zwingli was reading fairy tales to his children which he intended to have printed soon as a guide for the child's mind to the understanding of God's omniscience.

"Do not even the very rodents," he was reading, "proclaim the wisdom of God? How cleverly the hedgehog rolls with his spines amid the fallen fruit in order to carry it to his burrow. Who has taught the marmots to gather the softest hay and then to serve one another as carts, one lying upon his back, and clasping with his paws the hay that is loaded upon his breast so that his companion may drag him by the tail like any wagon? Have I not myself seen a squirrel crossing a brook by sitting upon a piece of wood and employing his upright tail as a sail?" At this point the reformer interrupted himself to ask, "Leo, what have you there?" When he had read the letter, the two friends embraced. Here, in literary form, was said the thing the two had known for long, but had never yet dared to proclaim from the pulpit. Yet it must be done! The dogma of transubstantiation was false. Christ had never been in the bread! Zwingli exclaimed the words that became his *confessio fidei: "Sisi adsit Jesus Christus, abhorrebimus a coena* [If Jesus is present in the bread, we would shudder to eat of it]." *"Habemus Lutherum,"* Leo replied. This was their great consolation—that they had on their side Luther, the great German adversary of Rome, a man whose like (in Zwingli's words) "has not been for a thousand years."

But in this they were wholly mistaken. To be sure, years before (in his pamphlet, *Babylonian Captivity of the Church*) Luther had attacked the Catholic Mass as a shoddy and man-made artifice; but it now developed that it was principally the "unworthiness of the priests" that had aroused Luther. The transformation of the bread was a miracle; from the course of his own life he was not disinclined to believe in miracles. Luther (and this is the true secret of his personality!) was of severe and monkish character, who carried through his revolt only because the Pope seemed *pagan* to him—a Pope pretended to the role of successor to Peter while living surrounded by luxury, by statues, and tapestries. But otherwise Martin Luther—and Zwingli and Juda did not know this because Luther himself scarcely realized it—was not a symbolist but a realist in the question of the Eucharist. When Luther was later called upon to declare himself, he said that he would not attempt to solve by reason questions that were far removed from reason.

Luther first became conscious of his stand when in his own precincts there appeared Dr. Andreas Karlstadt, a savage, bitterly mocking man who had put off the garments of a priest and wandered about the country as a peasant because he believed the peasant to be "the only just man." He expressed himself with annihilating directness on the subject of the "Eucharist swindle." Just as the revolutionary peasants looked to Luther for political support, Karlstadt thought of himself as continuing Luther's religious uprising. Who in Germany had delivered the first blow against the Papacy? Understandably enough, Luther hated Andreas Karlstadt as an unwelcome ally who was stirring open rebellion in the land. He transferred this hatred to Zwingli and Juda. These men were quite different from Karlstadt; they were subtle, cultivated philologists who spoke almost ironically of the "abuse of the Sacrament." But it was this very Erasmic suaveness that infuriated Luther. It was not easy for him to speak of the matter; it was something that involved the depths of his being. He had but recently presented to the German people his mighty translation of the Bible. Now came these "distorters," these "interpreters" and "explainers" babbling of *significat* when the Scriptures said plainly: *Est! Est! Est!* Intoxicated by his own rage (which he himself felt to be divinely inspired prophecy), Luther began to assert something that was, perhaps, originally foreign to him: the actual embodiment of Jesus in the Eucharist. He made a distinction, to be sure: not the words of the priest, but the "belief of the believer" created this embodiment. Downcast, Zwingli's friends asked two favors of him: that the disputations be written only in Latin, so that the differences in doctrine would not affect the people; and that he do nothing which would profit the Pope. Luther laughed scornfully at both these requests. He was writing for Germans, not for Latin scholars, he replied; and the truth was the truth, whether it profited the devil, the Turk, or the Pope.

For three years the dispute over the holy nature of the bread raged back and forth. With satisfaction the Catholic world looked on while its opponents *quarreled* among themselves. At last a young German prince, Landgrave Philip von Hessen (1509–57), attempted to reconcile the two parties. He invited Luther and Zwingli—the one in Saxony, the other in Zurich—to meet halfway in his castle at Marburg to discuss their differences and publish a pamphlet resolving them. The intention was to hold the conference quietly, but word of the invitation spread and thousands journeyed to Marburg to hear Luther and Zwingli speak.

Luther came in a gloomy mood. This was not the customary melancholy that often seized him, the manic depression that sent him into tears and doubts. It was rather the dejection produced by his clear intelligence: Luther realized that he would never be able to shake Zwingli's position, for the times were going Zwingli's way. Those who stood outside the Church—and that was where both of them now stood—could, indeed, only believe in the symbolical interpretation. How could one stop at the halfway point? Luther realized the difficulty, but looking into his own heart, he saw that he believed, with utter childlike faith, in the miracle of the bread. In God and Christ all things were possible, including a temporary aberration from the laws of nature. Nevertheless, he did not doubt that the age of the *laity* had arrived. He himself had helped to bring it about. And in a layman's religion the Sacramental miracle had no place.

But a short time before Luther had committed the most grievous error of his life. He had turned against the peasants who had revolted in the name of the Gospels. One hundred and thirty thousand peasants had been slaughtered; European history had been set back hundreds of years. Now he was about to commit his second error. Landgrave Philip was a man who hoped to form a great political league embracing all the land from Denmark and France to western Germany as far as Switzerland. This new great power would be opposed to the Emperor and the Pope; it would be cemented by Protestantism. But the prerequisite for its formation was harmony between the Lutherans and the Zwinglians on the question of the Holy Bread. Luther perceived this clearly, but—tragically—he could not compromise. He did believe in the miracle of the Lord's Supper—all he could do now was to defend his view.

Thus he was angry and sullen at the invitation to the disputation. His feelings are mirrored in the attitude of his secretary. This man, born with the peasant name of "Black Earth," which he later exchanged for the more gracious name of Melanchthon, wrote to their patron, the Electoral Prince of Saxony, and pleaded with him to prevent their departing for Marburg. "For no good can come of this religious conference; the doctrine of the opponent is so attractive that it will be difficult to shake it."

When they arrived at the Hessian frontier, Luther waited until Landgrave Philip sent him a safe-conduct. "Indeed, doesn't he trust us?" Philip grumbled. "Zwingli has come from Switzerland without any safe-conduct. He trusts us!"

When both Luther and Zwingli were together in Marburg, the landgrave invited them to a banquet. But the banquet was a total failure; both disputants sat in moody silence, toying with their food.

On Friday, October 1, 1529, the conversations began. The landgrave sat at the table in the middle; to his left were Zwingli and Oecolampadius; to his right Melanchthon and Luther. Before the discussion began, Luther took a piece of chalk from his waistcoat and wrote in enormous letters on the table: THIS IS MY BODY. "I do this," he is reported as saying, "so that if I lack reasons, I can hold to the letter. For the letter, too, is from God!"

His opponents soon ceased to smile at this. Luther knew well that his opponents were "subtle men" whose Christianity was well mingled with aesthetics. But he knew, too, that the people loved filth, loved the ugly stench of powerful things. When Oecolampadius objected that "it is false to think that Christ can be in bread—in so superficial and external a thing," Luther replied rudely: "If it is written, 'This is my body,' then the bread is God's body. And if God said his body were a horseshoe, we would also have to believe it; if he had commanded us to eat rotten apples or manure, we would have to obey. Christ's body is in the bread like a sword in its sheath, like beer in the can. . . ." Thus Luther battered like an angry bull against the more subtle, but also more ethereal, reasons of his adversaries. Though talk of rotten apples and manure might offend Zwingli, Luther, direct and coarse as he was, was speaking for the "man in the gallery."

Zwingli now advanced his chief reason for considering the papal and Lutheran doctrine false. Every Christian knew, he said, that after his resurrection the Saviour had risen into Heaven to sit at God's right hand. Whoever denied this was not a Christian. How, then, could Christ be in a bread, in many breads at the same time, and in many different places?

To this Luther laughed scornfully. To be sure, it was an axiom of physics that a body could not be in two places at the same time. But they were discussing *religion,* not mathematics or natural science or philosophy. And even though it were contrary to all reason that Christ's body should be in Heaven and in the Sacrament at the same time, nevertheless it was *true.* . . . Moreover, he added, what would his esteemed opponents have to say if he reminded them that God did not dwell only in Heaven, since he possessed "ubiquity," the trait of being everywhere at once? If God were everywhere, then his right hand was also everywhere, and Christ, sitting at his right hand, was also everywhere. . . . Therefore, he would also be present in the sacramental bread. . . . The esteemed opponents could see, Luther said maliciously, that he could meet them on their own ground when it came to playing with logic. But in such questions it was better not to apply deceptive logic at all.

They debated for days, but they could not agree. For Luther, with lordly obstinacy, held his ground; his opponents circled around him without winning the smallest concession. On the third day, when the tired landgrave perceived that all the disputing was useless and that the situation was becoming worse, he suggested that the discussion be abandoned. He requested Luther to write down the points in which his evangelical doctrine agreed with that of Zwingli. All knew that it agreed in almost all points, except for the question of the Sacrament and the role of bread and wine. Luther (who was probably relieved to have come out of the conference with a whole skin) did so—in an apparently conciliatory fashion. But after the document had been read, when Zwingli, with tears in his eyes, went up to Luther and held out his hand, saying: "Dear brother! I desire nothing more on earth than to agree with you!"— Luther once more became extremely rude. "It astonishes me that you call me brother!" he replied. "Your spirit is entirely different from ours. If you wish to agree with us, it is a sign that you believe none too firmly in your own doctrine." Thus they parted inwardly unreconciled.

§ 76

"Posterity will laugh at the contentiousness of our century, and will laugh at us for enduring such unrest for the sake of harmony," wrote the

Humanist Capito in Luther's day. Posterity did not laugh; it wept. For this dispute over bread tore the last frail bond among the Protestant churches. The German Evangelical Church and the Swiss Reformed Church broke apart—the more quickly because Calvin, the Geneva reformer, adhered to Zwingli, declaring it impossible "that Christ's physical body can be at the same time in Heaven and in many places on earth." He taught: "Bread and wine are *symbols* of His body and His blood. Christ breathes into the disciple power, He feeds him—but the real flesh and blood of Christ does not enter us." The Anglican High Church and the American churches accepted this doctrine. For Calvin's statement that "no property can be assigned to Christ's body that is *inconsistent with the nature of true humanity*" pleased the English way of thinking. Thus the Thirty-nine Articles ordered drawn up by Queen Elizabeth declared, "Transubstantiation is repugnant to Scripture and the occasion of many superstitions."

While Luther, in incorrigible blindness, rejoiced that the reconciliation had failed ("I am glad to be called obstinate, proud, pig-headed, uncharitable, and what they please"), Zwingli himself never recovered from the hatred of the man whom he so deeply honored. He lived only two years more, and spoke frequently of his profound sorrow at the division between himself and Luther. In 1531 a war began between the Protestant and the Catholic cantons of Switzerland. Zwingli marched as a chaplain with the Protestant army. As he mounted to depart, his horse shied. "He will not return," exclaimed his wife and his friends. At Cappel the small army met an enemy force eight times its size. Fatally shot, Huldreich Zwingli fell among the roots of a pear tree. Marauders of the Catholic forces bent over him in the evening and asked the dying man whether he wished to confess; they would fetch a priest if he did. He replied smilingly that he could not confess: Jesus alone, no man, was his mediator. Thereupon the Catholics beat out his brains, dragged his body away to be quartered, burned, and his ashes mingled with the ashes of swine, "so that they cannot be worshiped." Luther, who quite forgot that the adherents of the Pope would have treated him no differently, had the baseness to write to one of his followers: "We see the judgment of God a second time—first in the case of Thomas Munzer and now of Zwingli. I was a prophet when I said, 'God will not long suffer these mad and furious blasphemies with which they overflow, laughing at our God made bread.' . . ."

In our times, Adolf von Harnack has exclaimed concerning the theologic disputes over the nature of bread: "In all of religious history there is probably no other example of such a transformation, enrichment, perversion, narrowing, and running wild of a simple, sacred institution." One may question whether the Lord's Supper was something simple, for it was always a mystery. . . . How different from the "champing boars of irreconciliation" are the words of a great poet, Novalis:

> Few there are who know
> The secret of love,
> Who feel the insatiable,
> the eternal thirst.
> The Divine meaning
> Of the Lord's Supper
> Is riddle to earthly senses . . .
> Who has guessed the loftiness
> Of the earthly body?
> Who can say
> that he understands the blood?
> Oh, that the universal ocean
> Might incarnadine
> And the stout cliff swell
> Into fragrant flesh! . . .

How lovely this is: the mystical thought that beyond all time the cosmos itself will take the Sacrament! But was it needful that, on the verge of the modern age, servants of the Church and leaders of mankind should whet their daggers on the grindstone of theology to plunge them into one another's hearts? We must never forget the real, physical torments of those times. How could the sixteenth century afford to tear itself to pieces over an abstraction, over a substance that scarcely existed in reality? Barrenness was spreading over the earth; grain was dwindling. Plows rusted in barns and the mill wheels decayed by the streams. Whether bread was actually or only figuratively the body of Christ—was it not necessary to *have* the bread before men damned each other for its sake? . . .

Fate had ordained that a new bringer of bread would arise in the person of a man who knew not what he did. He gave confused Christianity the means to continue its life by opening up inexhaustible new lands to cultivation, and new, hitherto-unknown cereals. This man, the forerunner of the greatest agrarian revolution in all history, was Christopher Columbus.

When Columbus in 1492 tried the back door to Europe and made for the open sea, he did not intend to do more than to fetch for the King of Spain the gold and silver of the Indies. He did not know that among the things he brought home one would live longer than any gold—maize. Nor did those who sailed the sea after Columbus know that the potato of Peru would outlive the treasure of silver they found in the land of the Incas. Just when Europe's defeated peasants were forgetting what plow and oxen looked like, the god of history took pity on them. He sent them seeds of a grain that required no heavy tools for its cultivation.

BOOK FOUR

Bread in the Early Americas

Drop a grain of California gold into the ground and there it will
lie unchanged until the end of time, the clods on which it falls not
more dead and lifeless.

Drop a grain of our gold, of our blessed gold, into the ground and
lo! a mystery. In a few days it softens, it swells, it shoots upwards;
it is a living thing.

EDWARD EVERETT

The wind and the corn talk things over together
And the rain and the corn and the sun and the corn
Talk things over together.
Over the road is the farmhouse,
The siding is white and green blind is slung loose.
It will not be fixed till the corn is husked,
The farmer and his wife talk things over together.

CARL SANDBURG

MAIZE—THE GREAT WAYFARER

§ 77

THEY HAD EXPECTED to find rice, for the eastern part of the world cultivated rice; this had been known for ages. And Columbus and his men
thought they would reach the East. But they found no rice; they found
something they had never seen before. It was a plant larger than any
grain they had ever heard of. It grew not in tufts or panicles, but on huge
ears that were protected from the sun by long leaves.

On November 5, 1492, Columbus mentioned maize for the first time.
He noted in his diary that "it is good-tasting and all the people in this
land live on it." The Spaniards were astonished. The Indians told them
that these plants grew in ninety days. It must be nearly possible to see
it grow. Each single stalk was like a pillar. The tall, heavy stalk was not
hollow like a stalk of wheat or rye, but filled with thick marrow. The
long leaves soon turned yellow and became dry as paper. The milky,
glassy kernels, at first bluish-white and expressionless, were modeled by
the fingers of the sun until they sat fatly side by side on the ear. It was
strange in appearance and strange in smell, and the Spaniards would not
have eaten it had they not seen how passionately the natives devoured it.

And the natives were as grateful to it, and took it as much as a matter of course, as the Europeans did their wheat.

Cornfields were cultivated differently. The Indian women had a far greater part in the cultivation than the European women. For here the plow was unknown, nor was a plow necessary for the cultivation of maize. The men prepared the soil with stout oak poles, which were often tipped with metal. Then the women hoed holes in the ground at regular intervals, carefully placed two kernels of corn in the holes, and closed the holes. Since they needed no plow, they also needed no draft animals. Life was simple and easy. To be sure, they needed fertilizer, and so they gathered bat droppings, which were to be found everywhere in huge quantities; the Indians obtained the droppings merely by rubbing sticks along the walls of the great rocky caves. Human excrement was also used. But their chief fertilizer was the ashes of burned wood; these were strewn over the wheat fields. When the Spaniards arrived in Mexico in 1517, they were amazed to find no patch of open land uncultivated. Their leader, Cortez, wrote home about it. And he had reason to be astonished, for no one went hungry here, while at home the Spanish soil no longer fed the population.

As in Europe, Mexico had the land divided among the nobility, the Crown, the priesthood, and the people. Maps were employed to show the various owners of the land; the crown lands were drawn in purple, the nobles' lands in scarlet, the priests' lands in blue, and the people's in yellow. As in the Mosaic law, moving a boundary stone was considered a capital crime. The nobles' land was tax free, but they had to perform military service. The land of the people was in common ownership, but the government parceled it out among individual families, who were obliged to cultivate it. Land that had lain fallow for three years reverted to the government and was given to others. These agrarian regulations proved eminently practical; famines were unknown in Mexico.

These gentle, round-eyed people who seemed to be gardeners rather than farmers—for the labor of oxen and plow was unknown to them— nevertheless had customs which made the Spaniard's blood run cold.

The Mexican year, unlike the Christian, consisted of eighteen months —or rather periods—of twenty days each. These periods were marked by *human sacrifices* to the gods of fertility, above all to the goddess of the young maize.

A talented Catholic scholar, the Franciscan monk De Sahagun, in 1577 transcribed the ritual of the human sacrifice in the Aztec and Spanish languages, although the King of Spain had worriedly forbidden him to do so. The king felt that the knowledge of these atrocities should not be passed on to posterity. Not only because they were atrocious, but because they were confusing as well, for the Aztec rites contradicted the accepted theory of the unity of basic human feelings: they smoked of blood like an abattoir, and at the same time breathed an innocence like that of flowers in bloom.

From among the prisoners of war an especially handsome youth was selected. Many pages are filled with the description of the defects he must *not* have. "His head must not look like a knapsack, nor be round like a pumpkin, nor pointed like a stake; he must have no wrinkles in his brow, nor must his nostrils be too flat"—in short, he was chosen as carefully as a thoroughbred horse. Then the people were informed that Vitzilopochtl had been found, the "god of the gods." For a full year he was shown the highest reverence. Priests educated him in the temple, teaching him to speak elegantly, to play the flute, to smoke cigars, and receive the fragrance of flowers. Noble youths brought him his food and drink. His hair was permitted to grow down to his shoulders and white cock feathers were woven into it. A wreath of roasted corn ears surrounded his temples, another his waist; turquoise earrings rang as he walked, and tiny golden balls hung on his legs. . . .

When this bejeweled being proceeded through the streets, playing his flute, smoking a cigar, or inhaling perfume from a vial, the people fell to the earth before him. With sighs and tears they kissed the dust of his shoes and murmured submission. Women ran out of their houses, their infants in their arms, and begged the divinity to bless the children.

Twenty days before the sacrifice four girls were brought to him: the "Flower Goddess," the "Young Maize Goddess," the "Mother Who Lives in Water," and the "Goddess of the Living Salt." To these girls he was married. Days of banqueting and dancing in the presence of the king lifted the popular jubilation to a pitch of frenzy. On the last day the youth, accompanied by his women and his pages, was placed in a festive bark and taken across the lake to a hill. This was known as the "hill of departure," because here the god's wives bade him farewell. Now only the pages remained at his side. They led him to the brow of the hill, where stood a small, isolated temple in the shape of a pyramid. As the youth ascended the steps, he broke at every step one of the flutes he had played in the days of his good fortune. As soon as he arrived at the top, he was seized by a group of priests and thrown upon his back on a stone block. One of the priests struck swiftly at him with a stone knife, opened his breast, put his hand into the wound, and tore out his heart. Then he held the sacrifice toward the sun. The corpse of the dead god was not, like the corpses of ordinary sacrifices, cast down the temple steps, but carefully carried down. Then, in the royal courtyard, he was decapitated and the head was placed upon a lance. This was regularly the end of the representative of the highest god in the Mexican Pantheon.

The ritual insured that the year "would not die of old age, but would end at the height of its beauty and youth, in the springtide of its fecundity." It was not done for the sake of death, but so that the following year the earth would open once more. And twelve million brown human beings—every one of whom was polite, flower-loving, and helpful—believed that the continued existence of the cosmos and of the nation could be assured only by the sacrifice of this human god. They bitterly resented the Spanish monks for forbidding it and could not at all understand their reasons. The Aztecs were greatly afraid that the year might *stand still* if the "stand of the maize" was not encouraged by human blood. This encouragement was given not only by the annual sacrifice of the god, but also by monthly sacrifices. In the beginning of the year children, garlanded with flowers, were sacrificed to the maize goddess, Xilotl. In the later months, as was befitting to a year that was growing older, young girls were sacrificed; and at last women old enough to be mothers. All the sacrifices were performed amid lavish festivities; everyone, dressed in his most splendid new clothes, drank palm wine, cast flowers, and danced. There was a note of joyous submission among the victims which can only be explained by the influence of suggestion upon them.

Europe felt horror when these things became known. Could such barbarisms be possible fifteen centuries after Christ? How the old church fathers had raged against the mysteries of Demeter in Eleusis; against the descent of Persephone into Hades, which ceremonies, after all, involved not a drop of blood. All that the cultured Greeks had done in Eleusis, the "passion of the seed corn," had the innocuousness of a miracle play. But here, in the Gulf of Mexico, hecatombs of human beings had fertilized the maize with their blood.

What seemed most shocking to the Christian priests, what they could talk of only in tremulous whispers, was the fact that the Aztecs aped the holiest of rites of the Christian Church, the transformation of Christ into bread and wine. For the Aztecs had an Easter festival in which they ate bread baked of corn meal and human blood. With utmost humility and sorrow, the madmen, on these occasions, asserted that they were eating the body of their god. . . . Europe had only recently heard of similar horrors with the publication, in 1489, of the *Malleus Maleficarum*, the *Witch's Hammer*, a repulsive book which described the forbidden traffic of men with the potentates of hell. Thirty years after this, when Cortez sent Montezuma's temple treasures to Emperor Charles V, the pious Spanish emperor asked: "Where did this Mexican monster obtain so much gold and silver?" He decided, finally, that it must have been the devil's payment for the Aztecs' human sacrifices. This same Spanish nation whose hands were still stained with soot from the pyre of Granada, from the burning of Jews and Moors, came to use the name Vitzilopochtl as a synonym for the devil.

§ 78

Such was the maize the Spaniards found—which the Indians considered a god. But where had the Indians obtained it? Who had introduced them to the cultivation of the grain? For it must have been brought to them. No one had ever seen wild maize. Like wheat in Asia, maize had become domesticated in America. But how we do not know. We would know a great deal more of America if we knew the story of the origin of maize. In 1868 Brinton wrote:

Every botanist knows that a very lengthy course of cultivation is required so to alter the form of a plant that it can no longer be identified with the wild species; and still more protracted must be the artificial propagation for it to lose its power of independent life, and to rely wholly on man to preserve it from extinction. . . . What numberless ages does this suggest? How many centuries elapsed before men thought of cultivating Indian corn? How many more before it had spread over nearly a hundred degrees of latitude and lost all semblance to its original form? Who has the temerity to answer these questions?

They have not yet been answered. All the civilizations which the Spaniards encountered in Central America had grown up upon the foundation of these domesticated, golden-yellow grains, whose use was even at that time spreading farther in the Americas.

For at least two thousand years the natives and their maize lived in the new hemisphere, politically ununited, a vast horde of individual tribes. When the Spaniards arrived, one hundred and fifty dialects were spoken in Mexico alone. Nine hundred years before they came, the Mayas had ruled (around A.D. 600); about the year 1000 the Aztecs appeared. Civilizations changed and reformed; alphabets and literatures became indecipherable; religions gorged themselves on human blood and philosophically died out; astronomical and mathematical knowledge was lost; constant alone were the sun, the rain, and the maize plant. With maize still growing, all the past was potentially present.

Everywhere were the immeasurable yellow fields. But the farther south the Spaniards explored, the milder they found the customs to be. In the early days of many tribes some Abraham had appeared, forbidden the blood sacrifice, and taught that the favor of the earth could be won with vegetable offerings—though, to be sure, mingled with the blood of animals. These people had few animals, no large animals at all. (Horses were so strange to them that many of these brown people committed suicide from fear at seeing the Spaniards ride about on horseback; they believed the whites were four-footed men.) But there were more than enough birds, and so many birds were sacrificed before each sowing. This was logical enough, since the birds were also regarded as thieves. The Spaniards found sculptures showing the maize god struggling with the birds. Other sculptures presented him sleeping while a host of worms crept upon him. These were magic charms, and corresponded to the natives' degree of understanding of nature. For maize had indeed no enemies but birds and worms. When, today, on a higher level, we strew poison bait against harmful birds and insects, we are merely transforming a magical charm into a chemical one.

When the Spaniards came to Peru, they found another civilization based upon the corn ear. The soil was quite infertile—highlands that descended steeply to the coast. It was soil that could be made fertile only by an ingenious irrigation system. The conquerors looked wide-eyed at what these men had done to the rocky cliffs with their primitive tools, for they were literally still living in the Stone Age. They had built reservoirs with a capacity of thirteen billion gallons, arched great aqueducts across valleys which were in no way inferior to the aqueducts of the Romans. The gold and silver they possessed served them as ornaments, not as money. They had dug them out of the earth with stone chisels, and had no suspicion that in other parts of the world men killed each other for them.

All the maize land was divided into three parts. One part belonged to the sun god, Inti; the second part to the Inca; the third to the people. The people were favored; if a village increased in population, land of the sun and the Incas was assigned to the new settlers. Each couple received a *tupu* (about two acres); each son another *tupu*, and each daughter half a *tupu*. The fields were cultivated in the primitive manner of hacking the earth, which prevailed in Europe before the invention of the plow. Sharpened stakes with crosspieces on which the foot bore down were employed. The men took care of the rough breaking of the soil; then women and children entered the field. They broke up the clods and sowed. Fertilizing, too, was well known. In the mountains it was done with llama manure; along the sea coast guano was used, taken from the vast mounds of bird droppings that had accumulated in the nesting places. This material was economically so important that setting traps on the bird islands at nesting time was a capital crime.

All between the ages of twenty-five and sixty years were obligated to do field labor; after fifty a man was tax free. The obligatory labor required no more than two or three months of the year. The Peruvian villages were inhabited by contented peasants living on a poor soil. At the entrance to the village stood the granary, where grain was stored against crop failures; at the other end of the village was the garner for the Inca and the Court. . . . The soil of Egypt had borne far more richly. But it had also borne tyranny.

The Peruvians knew precisely how maize had come to them. After the Deluge the god of the earth fires had created men within the depths of the earth. He created them of glazed clay, breathed life into them, and put ears of corn in the hollow of their right arms. Then he sent them out of a crater in the vicinity of Lake Titicaca: four brothers and four sisters. They began at once to sow the maize.

According to another version, the four brothers and sisters, who intermarried and peopled Peru with their children, came not from the earth but from the water, and were of a different color from their descendants —Mongolian in color, according to the description of the legend. Besides the maize ears they also had many golden utensils and beautifully woven clothes. They taught men to pray to the sun and instructed them that the sun must be king if the human race were to prosper.

Thus the Inca became the "son of the sun." At the beginning of the year, as soon as the Great Bear appeared in the sky, the Inca himself began the sowing of the maize. The fact that the Inca was the sun was expressed in ceremonies not very agreeable to the ruler. He was not permitted to go anywhere afoot, because the sun did not go on foot; instead he must always be carried in a litter. Should one of the litter bearers stumble, endangering the sun, he was at once executed. Had the sun fallen, the year would have stood still and the maize would not have grown. Moreover, the ruler of Peru was not permitted to touch anything twice: no cup, no cloth, no dress, no woman—because the sun also "passes over its creatures without stopping."

Although the god of the "liquid interior of the earth" had created men and maize, the sun god, Inti, became far more important because he reigned over all that was above the earth. By and by the sun god became a trinity: the sun, maize, and gold. His representative on earth was the Inca, to whom the most beautiful girls of the country, the "sun virgins," were given. These girls were cloistered until they had served the god as concubines. His legitimate wife was, for several centuries, Mamaquilla, the "Mother Moon," to whom silver was sacred. The priests of Mamaquilla attempted to win power for themselves over vegetation and the growth of corn because—they asserted—the maize grew more at night than by day. A long conflict was waged between the priests of the two heavenly bodies, but the weaker moon was defeated.

The entire people gathered to attend the "Festival of the Sun at Zenith." The festival square and the temple of the sun were adorned with green twigs, and thousands of rare birds were caged, chattering and screeching, amid the foliage. Gold-bedecked petty princes carried the images of the lesser gods, for the sun god to consecrate. As in Eleusis, plays were performed on a stage. It was forbidden, under penalty of death, to light fires. For the fire god of the earth's interior was now rejected; the sun god was the highest god. All men were required to fast, "in preparation for the heavenly bowl of maize that floated toward them over the mountains, steaming with gold." It was not permitted to touch a woman. Gold and jewels and the finest of llamas were brought into the outer court of the Temple of the Sun. The night before the "Festival of the Sun at Zenith," the baking of the consecrated maize took place. This was undertaken by the "sun virgins." The bread was called *sanku;* it was round as an apple and symbolized the great sphere of the sun. With profound emotion the people ate "the sun at its brightest."

In the first dawn of the Holy Day secret societies whose members were dressed as animals appeared: jaguars and other great cats, and creatures with condor wings that "desired to fly toward the sun." As soon as the first rays of the sun appeared upon the highest mountain peak, millions of human beings broke out in loud cries. They blew conch shells and copper trumpets until the sun looked round-faced down upon the valley. Then all the people kneeled in silence and buried their heads in their hands. Only the Inca was permitted to look at the sun: he rose and held out two cups of maize wine, or *chica,* which was brewed at night. This he held out to the sun for it to drink. Then he poured one chalice into the gutter that ran down to the court of the temple. From the other chalice he himself drank, and then distributed drops of the wine among the golden vessels of his retinue. Thus the sun, which had already been eaten as bread, was imparted to men as wine.

§ 79

Columbus Came Late is the title Gregory Mason gave a book in which he inveighs against the "hemispheric inferiority complex." When Columbus came, maize was already sowed from the southern tip of Chile to the fiftieth degree of northern latitude. Sown everywhere by the hand of man:

"It was the food of the laborers who built the roads and the stone walls of South America, and of the workmen who constructed the lovely limestone palaces and temples of Central America. A surplus of maize gave the necessary leisure for artists to create the beautiful tapestries and pottery of Peru, and for scientists to build up the astonishing knowledge of mathematics which was current in Guatemala and Yucatan when Romans were trying to civilize the barbarians of western Continental Europe and Great Britain. Far more than any other food, maize supported the great population America had before the coming of the white man . . ."

In Europe, the continent of wheat and rye, of oats and barley, none suspected that the new seed would produce an agrarian revolution. Columbus brought maize home only as a botanical curiosity; returning from his first voyage, he showed the Spanish royal couple ears of maize. Though maize was cultivated in Andalusia thirty years later, it was intended only as a cattle feed—for the pride of the native Spaniards forbade their eating such stuff.

It was more than pride. The sense of smell—frequently standing guard over man's nutrition—warned the wheat-eating gentry against the strange oils in the maize kernel. A large fraction of humanity cannot endure the smell of fresh cow's milk, though no one can explain why. Men who ate wheat as a matter of course were revolted by the oils that were released when corn was roasted. People said that Columbus and his men, after months of starving aboard their vessels, no longer knew what bread tasted like; otherwise they would have observed that maize might be useful, but was scarcely pleasing to the taste.

Soon the Spaniards at home began hearing strange tales of their "New Spain" in America. The colonists who had been sent there forgot wheat and ate maize as though they were Indians. Emperor Charles V, who probably gave the matter little thought, nevertheless had the vague feeling that this de-Europeanization was unseemly for a victorious people. It was, after all, more Christian to eat wheat, "the historic Eucharist bread of the Lord." He therefore ordered the state treasury to pay bounties to the settlers who planted wheat. Bounties as high as three hundred ducats were paid. Strangely enough, this helped little; Garcilaso de la Vega declares that in 1547 there was wheat in Peru, but not enough to bake bread. Today we understand why this was so. Economic pressure was far stronger than gustatory inhibitions. A grain that grew in only three months and that needed neither plows nor oxen for its cultivation inevitably converted the Spaniards to itself—just as later, in North America, the colonizing English necessarily became eaters of maize.

Wheat for the time being remained utterly alien to America, and maize was gathering itself for the leap into the Mediterranean world. It came first in Spanish ships; but then the merchant fleet of the Venetians took it over, and no longer did it serve merely as a cattle feed. The republic of Venice saw that the peoples of the eastern Mediterranean basin, who for centuries had been dying of war and famine, who lived in unimaginable misery, were in need of some new food to mix with their old. Venice therefore established maize plantations upon Crete and sold the crop to all corners of the Mediterranean world. The Venetians sold it even to their worst enemies, the Turks. The Turks took it up with eagerness. Maize, whose ears seemed confirmed Muslemite (they resembled, with their wealth of leaves, a well-wound turban), pleased the eye of the Turk. Maize became the Turk's national grain.

§ 80

The Turks were as poor farmers as the peoples of the Occident. When Mohammed set about creating a third faith upon the basis of the sacred books of the Jews and Christians, he was confronted with the Biblical praises of agriculture. How inconvenient! Could he recommend weary labors of agriculture to his Arabs, who lived on the backs of horses and camels? He avoided mentioning these things altogether. Although the Moslems ate flat breads like other peoples, the Koran mentions no fields of waving golden grain. There is only the brown desert and the green of the oases; storms, sand, and wells; thirst and drinking—these things are in the foreground of the religious landscape of Mohammedanism. Sections of the Koran are entitled "The Wind-Curved Sandhill," or "The Winnowing Winds." Nowhere do we find a stalk of wheat.

The things Mohammed loved:

> By the snorting coursers,
> Striking sparks of fire
> And scouring the raid at dawn,
> Then, with their trail of dust,
> Cleaving, as one, the center of the foe.

Horses, treasures, iron "wherein is mighty power and many uses for mankind"—these were the things to be found in Paradise. Hardly the labor of the farmer. Abu Hurairah, in a commentary to the Koran, told this tale: An Arab once sat at Mohammed's side and asked him about Paradise. Mohammed described to him the joys that there awaited the devout: life in dining tents, the unbelievable beauty of the women. Above all, each man would be permitted to continue the things that he had best loved on earth.

"How would God take it if I should desire to plant grain?" asked the inquisitive Moslem.

Mohammed was astonished. "But God will say: 'Have you not everything you could wish for? What will you cultivate?' "

"Yes, everything is provided, but I personally am fond of cultivating."

"Then," the Prophet hastened to reply, "you will be permitted to cultivate, and you will sow, and quicker than the twinkling of an eye it will grow, become ripe and be reaped, and it will stand in sheaves like mountains."

The story sounds like a jest, but it was meant earnestly. No work was done in Paradise. For those nomads who broke camp to conquer the world at a furious pace, agriculture was something to be despised. The Koran made no mention of it, but Caliph Omar went to the trouble of forbidding it. The ethics of the Arab equestrian, the Arab knight, relegated the tilling of the soil to subject peoples. Upon seeing a plowshare, Abu Umama al Bahali once remarked that he had heard Mohammed say: "Such tools do not enter the house of a Moslem without a base temper also entering. . . ." The Arabs were not interested in tilling; they appeared only to "reap the harvest," and the sickle was highly honored among them—so highly honored that they forged their swords in the shape of a harvest sickle.

Before they knew anything at all about agriculture, the shape of the sickle was familiar to them, for did it not gleam in the night sky? The tribes of that hot climate did their traveling by night; during the day they could not move. And the night was better than the day for battle and sudden attacks. And so the Arabs became "sons of the moon" (*Beni badr*). The moon that "commanded the herd of the stars and pastured them through the night" was the friend of all earthly activities. They saw it more frequently than the sun; therefore they embroidered the moon on their banners—in its most propitious form, the crescent, the sickle shape.

When the victorious Turks took Constantinople, they were astonished to find their own crescent moon among the Byzantines. The half-moon was an ancient, sacred agricultural symbol among the Greeks, for the Greeks knew that grain grew faster at night than by day. When the god of forging, Hephaistos, wished to bring Demeter a present for her work of harvesting, he thoughtfully chose a shape that symbolized the fecund friendship between earth and moon: the sickle.

The Mohammedans now swung this sickle in agricultural toil. They had long been used to it as the proper shape for a Moslem's sword. Now they found it, as a symbol of harvest, upon the coins of the emperor of the Eastern Roman Empire. With these coins from the treasury of Constantinople the Turks bought maize seeds from their enemies, the Venetians. This maize, was it not almost like that plant of Paradise that Mohammed had described to the foolish Arab farmer? It grew "in the twinkling of an eye"; neither oxen nor plow was needed to cultivate it; and though it might not stand "in sheaves like mountains," it did grow much higher than wheat or barley. Above all, it yielded two crops a year. Maize was the salvation of the Moslem, for the nations the Turks had subjugated, like the Persians, which had been great agrarian nations in the days of their independence, were suffering from a technological crisis scarcely less grave than that of the Occident. Their plows barely scratched the surface of the ground; the ancient knowledge of the Orient in fertilizing and irrigation had been destroyed; according to the words of the Prophet, divine glory (*alsakina*) could be found only among the shepherds. For these subject farmers maize meant a great deal. In 1574 a German traveler, Leonhard Rauwolf, found the land of the Euphrates— where Paradise had once been situated—covered with fields of maize.

§ 81

What a traveler, this maize! From its home among the Aztecs and the Incas it crossed the Atlantic with the Spaniards and became almost at once a commodity of trade among the Venetians, soon to cover great stretches of land in the Near East. Then its destiny took a comic twist. In an era when newspapers did not exist,when books dealt only with "intellectual" matters, when practical facts were rarely transmitted by writing, the knowledge of its origins was lost. It was forgotten that maize had come from America. The Italians, who but shortly before had sold maize to the Turks, bought it back from them and called it "Turkish Corn." The Serbs and the Hungarians also, who later became great planters of maize, fancied that the plant was native to Turkey. Around 1540 the humanist Ruellius, writing of the origin of maize, said: "This plant was brought from Persia to France in the time of our fathers." Apparently he was confusing maize with buckwheat.

Other traders, the Portuguese, had brought maize to Java around 1496, and in 1516 to China. It was intended as a "colonial grain" and was destined to compete in vain with the cultivation of rice. Foolishly, all grains strive toward monoculture, although it is one of mankind's greatest pieces of good fortune that almost all soil can bear several grains simultaneously or in rotation. While maize made no great progress in the Far East, it penetrated southeastern Europe to dominate it as one of the most popular foods. However, it was not cultivated upon the Italian mainland until comparatively late. Around 1630 Benedetto Miari in Belluno succeeded in raising especially fine plants; from these, and from other prize plants that were cultivated by the Rumanian prince, Cantacuzene, on the Lower Danube, came the seed for all the maize that was later cultivated in Italy and the Balkans.

By the seventeenth century maize had become permanently established as the food of the common people in southeastern Europe. This new grain, so easy to cultivate, had none of the stubbornness of wheat and proved itself generous in filling the bellies of the poor. So beloved did it become that the people were willing to abandon the bread which was their ancient portion as Christians. Corn meal, they found, was somewhat tough; it resisted ordinary processes of baking. And so they ate it in the form of *polenta,* as a porridge. Moreover, they thought that maize porridge, because it was so filling, was a kind of panacea, uniting in itself the attributes of bread flour, vegetables, and all other foods.

This became a dangerous error. If the people of southeastern Europe had known as much about this plant as had the Indians, they would have been more cautious. The Mexicans, Peruvians, Apaches, and Iroquois never cooked the kernels alone to a porridge, as did the Italians. The Indians roasted the porridge afterward, and very carefully; then they ate it in the form of flat cakes. Moreover, they never ate maize exclusively. On the coast they mixed their maize flour with grated fish and baked pancakes of the mixture. When they had no fish, they mixed maize with squash meal, bean meal, or with the ashes from the stalks of kidney beans. They scarcely ever cooked a dish of maize without the addition of sweet or red peppers; they sweetened it with maple syrup or cooked nuts with it. To their great misfortune, the southern and eastern Europeans knew nothing at all of these secrets of cuisine.

§ 82

.In 1730 a physician named Casal discovered a new disease in the northwest corner of Spain. Certain changes in the skin—inflammation and a roughening of the surface of the skin—were the first symptoms. For this reason the disease was called *pelle agra* (rough skin) or *maldella rosa* (pink skin). The second stage of the disease involved disturbances of the stomach and the intestinal tract. Later the disease affected the spinal cord, producing severe nervous symptoms and even paranoia. Dr. Casal was told by the inhabitants of Asturias that the disease had been known for hundreds of years in the region; no one had paid much attention to it.

Dr. Thierry, a French physician who studied the disease in. 1755, emphasized the discolorations of the skin and wrongly concluded that it was a combination of scurvy and leprosy. Then in 1814 Dr. Guerreschi, an Italian physician, suggested an interesting theory. A certain similarity in the symptoms recalled to his mind the ergot epidemics of the Middle Ages. He advanced the theory that just as the ergot fungus in rye produced ergotism, so closely related molds growing upon maize might produce the pellagra in those who ate infected cereal. The disease was thereupon allowed to shift for itself for several decades, until the increase of pellagra in Italy attracted the attention of a large number of Italian scientists. Dr. Ballardini of Brescia embellished Guerreschi's theory. Maize, he declared, was a plant from a warm, dry climate. Along the Po, in southern Tyrol, on the Danube, and in the Balkans the dampness changed its chemical characteristics: it became poisonous. Pellagra, he insisted, was a chronic maize poisoning. It was a plant suited to a dryer climate of Mexico and the southern United States, but not to damp southern Europe.

Cesare Lombroso investigated the disease in Italy and supported this view. Maize growing in moist soils, he decided, produced a ptomaine, a poison that caused the sickness in the human body. He called this poison pellagrozein. Other scientists discovered other toxins. The small farmer's dwelling in the swamp, the bad water he drank, the malaria from the mosquitoes, and the pellagra from his polenta—all this was too much for the peasant. A popular verse ran:

> *Polenta da fermenton*
> *acqua di fosso*
> *lavora tu, padron*
> *che ia non posso.*

> Porridge out of rotting maize,
> Water from the puddle;
> Master, work yourself,
> For I am no longer able.

Although rotting maize was principally a problem of poor storage facilities, it began to seem that maize was a dangerous thing to grow in Italy. Then began a general flight from its "poisonous effect." In the South of France, too, it was considered not edible for humans. This development went all the more swiftly, since wheat stood ready to take up the position that was abandoned by maize. In the course of years maize fell so utterly by the wayside that Jules Jusserand, once French Ambassador to Washington, declared in reply to an inquiry from American physicians:

Although the production of maize is on an average of about six million quintals a year I can tell you with positivity that an extremely small proportion of that amount is used for human food, almost the whole of it being employed for cattle.

The staff of life of the ancient American civilizations, the food that never failed to appear on the tables of Franklin, Washington, and Lincoln—was this splendid food to become only a feed for cattle? What a tragic decline!

The long injustice that had been done to maize was exposed by Casimir Funk (born 1870 in Warsaw), the famous discoverer of vitamins. The disappearance of the beriberi disease from the Japanese Navy since 1882, when Takaki introduced among the sailors a mixed diet of fruit and vegetables in place of the almost exclusive diet of rice, gave Funk the hint that pellagra, too, might be only a deficiency disease.

At the close of the nineteenth century two Dutch scientists in the East Indies had discovered that the beriberi disease spread to all places where modern machine mills replaced the primitive hand mills of the natives. The seed of the rice grain consists of two layers, an outer and an inner layer. The mills of the natives only incompletely removed the outer layer of the kernel; the modern machine mill removed it completely. The result was a highly polished rice—but a rice that lacked an important nutritional element and the natives showed inexplicable symptoms of disease. At last it was realized that the real nutritive value of the rice was contained precisely in the part that was thrown away. Funk proposed the name *vitamine* for these nitrogenous, crystalline bodies. The United States hailed the discovery and prohibited the polishing of rice in the Philippines. Within a few years the epidemic of beriberi ceased.

Pellagra, too, will cease, for pellagra is a deficiency disease, whose source is not the natural kernel of maize, but the modern mill, which cuts away the precious part of the kernel and makes flour out of the less nourishing part. If we examine a kernel of maize, we find the endosperm and the germ contained within a hard shell. While the kernel as a whole contains only 4.3 per cent fat, the germ alone is 29.6 per cent fat. That is, the germ is the most nutritive part. When it is sifted away, the result is the death of the vitamins. . . .

What a strange, fortuitous course does the history of man pursue. The technological crisis of the Middle Ages made men eat splinters of stone in their flour; the technological progress of our industrial age has produced machines so precise that they grind away the living strength of the flour. . . . The maize was not at all at fault; it was still a friend of man, as Everett had described it:

Drop a grain of California gold into the ground, and there it will lie unchanged until the end of time, the clods on which it falls will not be more dead and lifeless. Drop a grain of our gold, of our blessed gold, into the ground and lo! a mystery. In a few days it softens, it swells, it shoots upwards; it is a living thing. It is yellow itself, but it sends up a delicate spire, which comes peeping, emerald green, through the soil; it expands to a vigorous stalk; revels in the air and sunshine; arrays itself more gloriously than Solomon in its verdant skeins of vegetable floss, displays its dancing tassels, surcharged with fertilizing dust, and at last ripens into two or three magnificent batons, each of which is studded with a hundred grains of gold, every one possessing the same wonderful properties as the parent grain.

THE DAY OF THE POTATO

§ 83

WHEN the Spaniards came to Peru in 1531 they found extensive vegetable gardens in the uplands. These gardens had a plant that was lovingly tended by the natives; it showed white, pink, and pale violet flowers with five-pointed calyces. The plants, which had green, squarish stems, were planted at unusually wide intervals from each other. What was even more odd, the Indians heaped up earth around each plant. "As much of the stem as possible must be married to the earth," they told the Spaniards.

This the Spaniards could not understand, for it was not the stem but the roots that the earth fed—and the roots were already in the ground.

The ripening fruit was a green, fleshy berry. When a Spaniard placed one in his mouth, an Indian rushed toward him wringing his hands in despair. The gardener lay down on the ground, stretched out his arms, and played dead—indicating to the Spaniard that he must spit out the

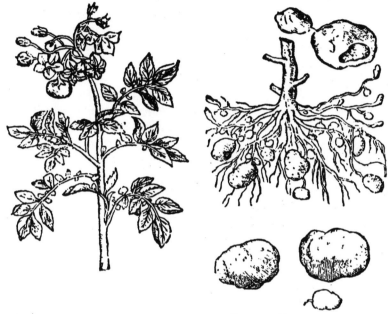

FIRST DRAWING OF THE POTATO PLANT
(A.D. 1580)

berry in his mouth. So the berry was poisonous! The Spaniards knew that these savage peoples poisoned their arrows; they needed poison also to catch fish, for with it they stunned the fish and then caught them with their hands. One might expect these savages would, then, raise poison. But miles and miles of garden devoted solely to the raising of poisonous plants—this was too much. With so much poison these Indians could wipe out the entire vice-kingdom of New Spain. Certainly this was not the purpose of the gardens.

The following day women and children weeded up the plants of the gardens. The white strangers could not believe their eyes. All the bounty of the gardens was gone. But attached to the underground stems of these plants were knobs—enormous ulcerous growths upon the stems. *These* were what the harvesters were seeking. These pale, bluish, swollen stems seemed what was precious to them. All that grew above the ground was burned.

"What is that called?" the Spaniards asked, pointing to the unsightly knobs.

"Pappa," the Indians replied.

"What is it used for?"

The Indians pointed to their mouths. To the Spaniards it seemed fantastic and absurd that a beautiful plant, which was apparently poisonous, was burned, while its ugliest part was kept for food. But later they ate the curious knobs, cut in slices and fried or boiled whole in water. They found the taste rather monotonous, but the food was singularly filling. Perhaps too filling. When one was fond of eating a whole array of fine food, as were these Spanish noblemen, it would be well to be sparing of these tubers—they left room for nothing else.

These "pappas" were *potatoes*. The name sprang from a misunderstanding, for the word potato comes from *batata,* sweet potato. But sweet potatoes are not potatoes at all; they are members of the morning-glory family, and not related to those tubers which the Indians called "pappa." The English name was derived from the mistaken Spanish *batata*. In Italy the name degenerated into *Tartuffoli,* and in Germany to *Kartoffel.* The French preferred to make their own mistakes and called the tuber *pomme de terre,* apple of the ground. The Serbs followed their example in an amusing fashion: after hearing a "damned German" refer to the potato as *Grundbirne,* a pear of the ground, they casually took up the word as *krumpir.*

In 1540, however, the tuber was far from reaching to France and Yugoslavia; it was known only in the uplands of the Andes. And the gardeners of the Andes were artists in the cultivation of it. When the woolly llamas had brought the harvest—baskets loaded with potatoes—to the farmstead, the gardeners sat in the chalky moonlight that cast mournful shadows on the cliffs and, murmuring to themselves, selected the specimens that would serve for the next sowing. For this strange plant was not perpetuated by seed, but from the tubers, and these tubers were selected carefully to reproduce their kind. The goal was a potato that would be wholly useful, with no parts to throw away. Hundreds of years of cultivation and no small knowledge were necessary to raise such a one.

§ 84

The cultivation of the Peruvian potato is to this day as much a matter of artistry as the cultivation of roses in other lands. A. Hyatt Verrill has given an interesting description of the potato markets in Peru:

There are tubers with white, yellow, pink, gray, and lavender "meat"; with skins white, pink, red, yellow, brown, green, purple, orange, black, and spotted and streaked with various hues; potatoes of every conceivable size and shape, some as shiny as a tomato, others as warty as a toad. There are potatoes which are inedible until frozen, potatoes with plants three or four feet in height, and others with low trailing vines. . . . They display every climatic condition of the country—the drenching rains of the tropical belt, the irrigated sandy desert lands, the stony, wind-swept plateaus, and the bleak Andean heights.

When the Spaniards in 1540 saw the Peruvian gardeners "operating" upon the potatoes with sharp stone knives before they replaced them in the ground, they may well have thought of surgeons operating on the heads of children. And indeed the Peruvians themselves believed in a bond between heads and potatoes. They themselves possessed an astonishing surgical knowledge in regard to skull operations. This was extremely important to them, whose weapons were principally clubs and other weapons for striking; for the most frequent type of wound in warfare was concussion of the brain or a broken skull. When the skull is broken the brain is often subject to great pressure; to relieve this, the Peruvian doctor opened a window in the injured skull to permit the fluid to drain out and thus re-establish normal pressure upon the brain. (Such "trepanning" was not discovered by European physicians until considerably later.) The window in the skull healed over by new bone formation. In the graves of the Incas we find many skulls with such windows which successfully healed. No wonder the Peruvians were proud of their surgical skill. The Indians had a naïve and mysterious faith that such acts— changing the character of a human head—had an effect upon the plant world. The potato resembled a human head; and they were convinced that each time a trepanation was successful, a new and beautiful variety of potato arose. There was a magical connection between the two things.

Needless to say, the Spanish conquerors were contemptuous of this superstition. But no matter how strenuous their missionary work in Peru, the primitive religion of magic was never wholly eliminated. The potato was a living thing; since the Indians were stone worshipers, they buried stones shaped like potatoes in the ground, believing these would produce good crops. In 1621 a Jesuit, Father Arriaga, noted the superstition of the "potato mothers." These "axo-mamas," twin potatoes, seemed a promise of fertility. When potatoes were found that had grown together, they were hung on posts at the head of the field so that the other plants should follow their example.

Naturally, the priests stormed against such nonsense—but in vain. To this day twin potatoes are still hung over fields in Bolivia and Peru— though now they are hung upon a *cross*. For the old faith and the new are stronger together than one faith alone!

The *extirpación de la idolatría* was never completed by the Spaniards. In Europe they could succeed in extirpating the faith of the Moors and the Jews, but in the vast territories of America the best they could do was to incorporate the native religions into Christianity. Christianity once more became heathenized. Moreover, remarkably enough, when the Spaniards introduced the potato into Europe, they were introducing the invisible underground roots of the Indian superstitions. All the beliefs of the Indians cropped up in Europe, in places where the Indians themselves had never been heard of. The peasant in northern Sweden, for example, placed the same homeopathic stones in the potato field as a magic invocation of fertility. And in the Baltic provinces it is believed to this day that there is a connection between potatoes and human heads. In these lands, when a family eats their first early potatoes, it is a custom that those sitting at the table should vigorously pull one another's hair. Hair is a symbol of the long roots attached to the tubers, and the significance is that one should smart a little before one's teeth grind up the potato. Similarly, the Greeks were taught to lament for having tormented the seed corn or buried it in the earth. The gods of nature must be appeased before they are killed. For they are always resurrected—woe to man if they were not!

§ 85

How did the potato come to Europe? It is strange that we do not know, for we know so many dates of the political history of mankind—dates of battles and peace treaties. But an event so important that the future life of Ireland, France, and Prussia was based upon it—the date of this we do not know. For thousands of years only political history was considered majestic enough to be remembered. For the past hundred and fifty years it has been recognized that the history of commerce is also important. But to this day few know that the history of mankind is also agrarian history.

Consequently, we have no reports of the stupendous impression that must have been created by the arrival of the first potato ship in a Spanish port. In Spain, above all countries, the poor suffered terribly from hunger. About eighty years before, the last of the Moors had been driven from the peninsula—now the soil of Spain was suffering the consequences. The Saracens in Spain—unlike the Arabs and the Turks of the eastern part of the Mediterranean world—were splendid farmers. Perhaps they were not so by nature; but scholars as well as knights ruled in the Saracen courts. (A ruler like Alhakem, for example, possessed a library of over 600,000 volumes.) The great classics of the Greek and Roman world had been translated into Arabic. And scholarship was transformed into practice. The Arab universities taught according to Columella, Xenophon, Cato, and Terentius Varro what a farm should be and how agriculture could be practiced wisely and profitably. They supplemented the classics by their own knowledge of chemistry. The Arabs came from the desert; consequently they were cognizant of the serious fact that water was the first prerequisite for civilization and cultivation. "At the foot of this fabric of genii," William Prescott writes of Granada, "lay the cultivated *vega,* or plain. The Arabs exhausted on it all their powers of elaborate cultivation. They distributed the waters of Xenil, which flowed through it, into a thousand channels for its more perfect irrigation. A constant succession of fruits and crops was obtained throughout the year. The products of the most opposite latitudes were transplanted there with success. . . ."

When the Christian Spaniards took the land from the Moors, in their ignorance they permitted the irrigation system to decay. Great droughts were the result, and soon the "gardens of the West" looked like the rest of Spain: like the landscape of Don Quixote, where "nothing grows but folly and poverty"; where the grandees possessed lands that were used only for pasturing goats and the towns were too hostile to the peasants to help relieve the technological crisis that had crept upon the farming population.

How eagerly the propertyless peasant in Spain must have welcomed a plant that needed neither plow nor draft animals for its cultivation!

We find the first mention of the potato in Spanish literature in 1553 in the *Chronica del Peru.* The author, Cieca de Leon, mentions it seven times. De Leon was well aware of the role of the potato on the other side of the Atlantic. He knew that the Indians cultivated maize, but considered stored potatoes a better ward against hunger. "The Indians let their potatoes dry in the sun and keep them from one harvest to the next. They have no artificial irrigation; if rain does not come, famine would arise were it not for these potatoes. . . ."

A food that was spoken of in such terms was certainly no delicacy. It was something for the mass of the people, and the Spaniards quickly recognized this. As early as 1573 we find the city hospital of Seville buying large quantities of potatoes as part of its normal food supply. These potatoes were no longer imported; they were grown in the vicinity of Seville. From this it is clear that they were by no means "truffles"—a luxury food would have had no place in a hospital in those days.

From Spain the cultivation of potatoes proceeded hesitantly to Italy, Austria, and the Netherlands. From Switzerland the potato entered France, but here its course was halted, for it ran up against too great psychological obstacles, and did not proceed very far.

Historians long believed that the English had first brought the tuber from America. Today we know that it came to Spain twenty years earlier. But in 1586 Francis Drake brought the potato from an America the Spaniards did not know at all—North America.

In the rivalry between England and Spain, the potato, too, played its part. Queen Elizabeth, and particularly her paladins, envied the Spaniards their ships laden with gold and silver that sailed every month from the lands of the west. The English did not attack Mexico and the southern portion of the hemisphere—they were not strong enough for that— but they took advantage of the vast size of the New World. The North lured them. Were there not gold and treasures here too? Was not all America a land of promise, a land of legendary riches?

Had the English considered the culture of the Indians of the North they might not have deluded themselves. For here was no densely populated Aztec civilization; here were no Peruvian silver mines. In the north there were only endless forests, measureless spaces where hunters and fishermen dwelt. Nevertheless, Gilbert, Raleigh, and Drake went northward. Partly they hoped to establish pirate havens from which to plunder the Spanish fleet; partly they hoped to harvest riches for England from the soil itself. Raleigh died for this dream. Scholar, humanist, and poet, ruthless daredevil and political intriguer, he became involved in the confused political situation after the death of Elizabeth and was executed by the Stuarts. (And the Spaniards rejoiced that the English were beheading their most talented imperialists.)

In 1584 Raleigh had taken possession of a section of coast line which he named Virginia in honor of the Virgin Queen. But the one hundred and eight people he settled there could not maintain themselves. After ten months Francis Drake took the starving settlers away. When these settlers landed in England, they brought with them the potato. Either they had themselves planted it on American soil, or they had taken it from a Spanish ship that was cruising in the vicinity of Virginia. In any case, Raleigh's men were the first Englishmen ever to see and eat a potato. For lack of other gifts, they presented this plant to the London Botanical Garden. The botanist John Gerarde mentions it in 1596. But within a few years Londoners no longer considered potatoes a curiosity. They were something that could be eaten. They increased rapidly, they were easy to cultivate, they were a filling, domesticated plant.

§ 86

One day the groundlings of the Globe Theatre heard the exclamation: "Let the sky rain potatoes." The date was 1596. And Falstaff voiced this cry in *The Merry Wives of Windsor*. We see the lovesick, barrel-bellied Sir John rush upon the stage to keep his rendezvous. He is bursting with cosmic eroticism. In this spring night the elves are at large, and he himself is disguised as a buck. "Let there come a tempest of provocation," he cries. "I will shelter me here." Even though the sky should rain potatoes.

The burghers and artisans of London must have been sufficiently well familiar with the potato. Shakespeare was not the dramatist to make esoteric references to a rarity that grew in greenhouses. Humor in comedy is a matter of instant communication between the speaker and the audience, wherein something well known is shown in a new light or employed in a new fashion.

But the humor of a great poet is never intended solely to produce laughter. When the public laughed, it laughed also at the play upon a Biblical parallel. For what is the significance of the "sky's raining"? In Exodus, Chapter 16, God let manna rain from heaven for the starving children of Israel. "And when the dew that lay was gone up, behold, upon the face of the wilderness there lay a small round thing, as small as the hoar frost on the ground." This was the joke—that Shakespeare was comparing the enormous potato, which was like a stone thrown from a catapult, with the small and delicate manna that the Jews found in the wilderness. According to the Biblical story, manna served the Jews as bread for forty days in the wilderness. Consequently, potatoes were also considered a common *substitute for bread;* since Shakespeare mentioned them in a joking fashion, it would scarcely have applied to some colonial curiosity.

It would seem, then, that the people of London in the time of Elizabeth had stretched their bread by mixing wheat with potato flour. Was this actually necessary? In William Harrison's *Description of England* we read that in times when wheat was scarce, beans, peas, oats, and acorns were baked into the bread. Potato flour is not mentioned—but this book was published in 1577, when the potato was still unknown. It is probable that in the nineties it was already being used for this purpose. After several years of excellent harvests (when wheat was even exported to France), the late summer of 1596 brought famine suddenly to England. Grain had to be imported from abroad, and Theodor Ivanovitch, "King and Grand Duke of All Russia," ordered that grain be sent to England. The distress must have been frightful—at the very time when Shakespeare has his Falstaff speak of potatoes as "manna." In a letter of July 11, 1597, addressed to Lord Robert Cecil, we read:

On Thursday a bowle of rye was sold for 32 shillings in Newcastle, and if, by the good providence of God the Hollanders had not come in with corn on Friday following, what it would have grown into the Lord knoweth, many not having tasted bread in twenty days before, by credible report, and sundry starving and dying in our streets and in the fields for want of bread.

Potato flour must have been eagerly taken up at such a time.

Fifty years later Dr. Thomas Venner, an English physician, remarked in his *Via Recta ad Vitam Longam* that the potato, though somewhat bloating, was of mealy consistency and consequently unusually filling—a fine food for the people. And in 1664 John Forster, in *England's Happi-*

ness Increased by a Plantation of Potatoes, wrote that although the cultivation of potatoes came from the West Indies, all Ireland was already living on potatoes. He called upon English farmers to follow the example of the Irish.

§ 87

The fact that the potato was grown in Ireland and, indeed, was of prime importance to the Irish economy was scarcely a recommendation to the English, for the English hated the Irish as eternal troublemakers whose religious and political differences with England kept them constantly at war with the British. The English also hated the Irish the more for being a poor people. In the rivalry of grains, it is very important whether a nation that recommends its favorite be poor or rich. If a nation's standard of living is low, the food it offers is held to be low. Taste —like fashion—always follows the aristocrats.

In England in the seventeenth century it had become a strong prejudice that the potato was something "for poor people" and especially for cattle. There may, however, be another reason for this. The voyages of discovery of the Spanish, Portuguese, and Dutch had had as their goal not only gold, but spices. The possession of the Dutch East Indies, for example, made the Dutch the greatest spice millionaires in the world. As H. E. Jacob recounts in his book *Coffee:*

These first Europeans to visit the Malay Archipelago stole more than cloves. Their nostrils dilated with covetousness as they inhaled the aromatic odors; and just as the Spaniards had sailed westward to the "isles of gold," so had the Portuguese sailed eastward to the "spice islands." Gold and spices amounted to much the same thing. Pepper could be converted into gold; so could nutmegs, which, in the Moluccas, could be bought for one twentieth the price they commanded elsewhere.

Through the huge imports of spices the palates of the wealthier nations of western Europe had become almost insensitive to milder tastes. As Ezra Parmelee Prentice mentions in his *Hunger and History,* in the seventeenth century a Dr. Thomas Muffett wrote that "melons, pears, apples are insipid and taste of nothing." It is understandable why the Irish— who were poor and could not afford the precious pepper—liked the mild taste of the potato. The charm of the potato was lost upon the overspiced English taste. To impoverished Ireland the potato became the national destiny. For centuries there was very literally a correlation between the number of heads on the Emerald Isle and the number of tubers in the ground. As long as the potato remained faithful to the farmer in his fields and his wife in her kitchen garden, the Irish could continue to live and to hold their own in their "legal civil war" with the English. From the time of Raleigh to the nineteenth century seven generations of Irish cultivated and ate potatoes. But in the nineteenth century the potato betrayed the Irish for the first time—and the result was a disaster that is still remembered all too vividly.

As early as 1822 a poor crop had caused famine in Ireland. A new enemy, potato blight, had suddenly appeared upon the island. It was an inexplicable disease, this blight, like a mildew. Botanists like Chauncey Goodrich suggested that the living force of the potato, which for centuries had been propagated by tubers, not by seed, had been so weakened by the abuse of this non-sexual method of reproduction that the plant could no longer resist diseases. There was a scientific dispute—but at the time of no avail to the farmers. The disease spread; soon it extended beyond the borders of the island. Its poisonous breath touched Belgium, Holland, Germany, and descended the Danube as far as Hungary. But only in Ireland did it transform, within the space of a few days, a rich crop into a heap of rotting plants. No district in Ireland was spared. On July 27, 1846, Father Matthew rode from Cork to Dublin; all along the road he saw potatoes in full bloom. On his return, on August 3, he saw the same landscape covered with decaying vegetation. Wailing and lamenting, the inhabitants sat upon the fences of their rotting gardens. They were Irish and therefore poor. Now they feared they must die—for they had planted nothing else.

England took action at once. The government in London had maize in a quantity worth 100,000 pounds sterling sent to Ireland. But the populace met this gift of Robert Peel's with dull suspicion and defiance. "Shall we eat Peel's brimstone?" Many thought the English wanted to poison them; it had become folk belief that men turned black from eating maize. Finally hunger drove them to eat it.

Instead of immediately planting large acreages in Ireland to oats and rye, the English Government attempted to satisfy only the needs of the moment: vast quantities of maize from abroad were imported. An army of distributors appeared—700,000 it was said. Since Ireland lacked not only enough mills to grind the maize, but actually did not have sufficient cooking vessels, great numbers of brass pots were brought from England aboard steamers and sailing vessels.

All this did not help. Famine made its way, and in the wake of famine came influenza. Within the next five years nearly a million people died—a fifth of the population.

Then there arose, for the first time in Irish history, the mass impulse to flee, the feeling that life was more important than the land. In the first years of the famine thirty thousand people had been forced to give up their small farms. Now the emigration figures soared. In the first ten months of 1847 a quarter of a million stranded Irish landed in Liverpool.

Half of them at once sailed on, back along the road that the potato had followed centuries before: they went to North America. They were sick, broken, poverty-stricken; hundreds of former farmers were crowded into the steerage of transatlantic vessels. Many of them had scarcely been able to raise passage. In the beginning whole families starved during the crossing because at this time shipping lines were not obligated to feed their passengers.

They left the ships and looked around them. These Irish no longer mistrusted only the soil of their homeland; they mistrusted all soils. They did not, like the Germans, for example, go West where there was free land. The Irish who settled in New York, New Jersey, Illinois, Pennsylvania, and other states became cityfolk. They had no money for agricultural tools, and they had no desire to wait. And in farming one must wait. They had to take any work that was offered—and so the great transformation took place. Within a few years the Irishman of America was no longer the European Irishman. Those who did not work on roads and railways became small merchants in the cities. Like potatoes, the Irish took vigorous root—but in the soil of the great cities. By 1850 of the twenty-five million inhabitants of the United States, four million were of Irish descent. And the emigration increased. The disloyalty of a favorite plant had produced famine and despair, and these had driven them from their native land. Their misfortunes were written upon their faces. And the hostility these pale, famine-stricken multitudes encountered among the settled Anglo-Americans strengthened their Irish clannishness. They clung to each other; everywhere there arose Irish quarters that became centers of political power.

The memory of home, of their green isle with its blue sky and straw-roofed peasant huts and the bowl that was their whole supper—this memory never faded. There had been no bread, but the large boiled potatoes sent up fragrant steam into their faces. Those days were past. For a long time the Irish ate the maize bread of Americans (without turning black). But it never had that moist, cool, bitter fragrance that pervaded the air from their potato fields. . . .

Here the Irish may have also remembered that the potato had once yielded them a strong, consoling drink. So, in America the Irish became the most important merchants of alcohol; it was they who ran most of the saloons. These saloons were centers of political activity. In New York, for example, in the world's greatest immigrant city, for thirty years the "Irish potato" held most municipal posts—until 1934, when La Guardia, the Italian, broke the rule of Irish-controlled Tammany Hall.

Thus a distant potato famine thoroughly changed the population and the political face of many of America's cities, and exercised a decisive influence upon contemporary American history. A similar event might still take place at any time. For we should remember that the history of

"The Potato Has Failed"

IRISH FAMINE AND BRITISH RELIEF IN 1847

nations is largely an agrarian history and that man lives truly within the "realm of food."

BETWEEN SQUANTO AND OLIVER EVANS

§ 88

COLUMBUS had set foot upon the coast of America as traveler, diplomat, and scholar. With cunning Fernando Cortez had conquered a great empire, and the Pizarro brothers had accomplished as much with brutality. The English captains under Sir Walter Raleigh in Virginia needed only to imitate the Spaniards; they needed only to believe firmly that London, rather than Madrid, was the center of the world—and new empires might be founded by traditional means. But in what did the real founders of the United States, the Pilgrim Fathers, believe when on December 21, 1620, they landed in Plymouth?

They believed in God.

They had left their native land of England—among so many other countries apparently the best—because they wished to worship in their own way. They had seen that England's separation from Catholicism was no more than a compromise. The Pope indeed was driven out of England, but the altars and ceremonies of Popishness had remained. When James I began his reign by proclaiming that those who did not belong to the official church must leave the country, several hundred people took the king's word more literally than he had meant it. In 1608 these separatists emigrated to Holland, the only country in Europe that offered complete religious toleration.

But they did not remain in Holland. The religious toleration was favorable but not the extreme nationalism. The Dutch were merchants whose activities were controlled by guilds, and only Dutch citizens were permitted to work in the land. Only the textile industries were open to the immigrants—who soon realized that people who had been farmers in England all their lives were meant for more than weaving or tailoring. Even employment in Dutch breweries demanded special qualifications. The artisans in the Netherlands had not been farmers for generations, and apparently they did not have to be; they sold their cloth to the Russians, and their ships returned with grain. In competition with the natives the English farmers were everywhere bested. They could not learn new trades; they had great difficulty learning the Dutch language. After twelve years they were so discouraged that they decided they would rather live in the wilderness than in industrial cities.

Moreover, they heard in their hearts the words of Saint Paul: "Come out from among them, and be ye separate, saith the Lord, and touch not the unclean thing." With trepidation they wrote to London, to the mercantile company that had settled Virginia. They knew that America was broad and that King James did not hope to regulate the religion of such distant subjects. The Virginia Company, eager to have more settlers, agreed to help them. They were granted credits and the *Mayflower* was equipped and set out.

A group of modern boys preparing to set up a summer camp would set about it more practically than did the Pilgrims. Their discovery of America began by their not finding Virginia at all. Instead of landing them in the South, their pilot took them to the North. They were legally only adventurers, "without a patent nor a charter," without any right to the soil nor power to set up a government. With childlike genius they at once set up their own government, which had nothing to do with the Virginia Colony. James Truslow Adams observes that this solution was eminently English; no Spaniard would have dared such a venture. It was soon to become an American trait—for every Anglo-Saxon carries a charter of independence in his pocket.

These devout, adult children landed in the dead of winter. They realized fully that at the beginning they would have to live on fish and game. But when they went on land and looked into one another's faces, it turned out that none of them had ever caught a fish or killed a wild animal. One of them shot a large bird that may have been a turkey; but they thought it was an eagle and would not eat it. They heard animal sounds in the night and took them for lions roaring; since there were no lions in Holland or England, they took it for granted that there would be lions in America. They were absolutely unprepared for the conditions they found and brought nothing but good constitutions, loyalty to one another, good sense, patience, forbearance, and devotion to a high religious ideal. Indeed, they lacked everything but virtue.

The chief cargo of their ship consisted of heavy armor and even cannon —although only one man of them, Miles Standish, knew how to use the cannon. When they went searching amid the thorns and thickets, they clad themselves in their armor, which made them unwieldy and apt to stumble; it was a true act of providence that they encountered no hostile Indians. They had no oxen, no cows, no goats, no pigs—not even a plow. Their only equipment was a few chests of garden tools, and onion, bean, and pea seeds. This seems incomprehensible, for in England they had all been farmers. But clearly they had been taken in by a trick of fate. They had, to be sure, left Holland to escape the industry there; but they had unconsciously become so Dutch that they thought to live by trading. They intended to carry on a fur trade with the Indians, send the furs to England, and receive provisions in return. But for the present England did not even know where they were! And starvation began at once. Roland

G. Usher, one of the many who has told their tale, writes in *The Pilgrims and Their History:*

How is it possible that, in a land fairly alive with game, the waters of which were crowded with fish, the shores of which were strewn with lobsters, clams, eels and oysters, in whose woods and fields grew quantities of edible berries, the Pilgrims literally starved? Perhaps one might say that our amazement results from the fact that they felt themselves to be starving when forced to eat shellfish and game. Some have supposed that the truth lay in their inability to catch the fish or kill the game, and it seems indeed extraordinary that they possessed no nets strong enough to hold cod and the other large fish which abounded, and on the other hand no hooks small enough to catch the fish which teemed in New England waters. They came from a land of fishermen to a land of game and fish, and seem to have been neither prepared nor able to kill the one or catch the other.

Out of this Eden of foods that they did not touch arose suddenly their cry for *bread*. The Pilgrims wanted bread, no more than bread—bread that no one could give them. The Pilgrims were English, but the English were also the heritors of that Mediterranean culture which for thousands of years had lived principally upon bread, heritors of the Egyptians and the Romans. In Europe two thirds of their food had consisted of bread. In Virginia, which had already been settled for decades, the Pilgrims could have had bread. But not here. And they thought they would inevitably die. It was not without pious rage that their leader, William Bradford, quoted to them the words from Exodus in the Sunday sermon: "Man doth not live by bread only, but by every word that proceedeth out of the mouth of the Lord doth man live." But they were as piteously desirous of bread as the Jews in the wilderness. And suddenly it came. Bread, stored up by Providence, came to succor these hungry Christians.

An Indian named Squanto, an extremely intelligent man who had somehow learned the speech of the Pilgrims—perhaps from English fishermen—showed them how to plant maize. Earlier they had by chance come across a great store of maize that had been buried in the ground; an Indian tribe had lived in this vicinity and apparently forgotten the maize when it moved on. Or had the tribe died out of some plague? The somber romance behind this incident remains as hidden and mysterious as the great American forests. The Pilgrims took the gift of God, and Squanto, already an ancient, lived two full years longer—long enough to show them how to grow maize. We may imagine him speaking the words of the maize god Mondamin, as Longfellow later put them:

> ". . . You will conquer and o'ercome me;
> Make a bed for me to lie in,
> Where the rain may fall upon me,
> Where the sun may come and warm me;

Strip these garments, green and yellow,
Strip this nodding plumage from me,
Lay me in the earth, and make it
Soft and loose and light above me.
  "Let no hand disturb my slumber,
Let no weed nor worm molest me,
  Let not Kahgahgee, the raven,
Come to haunt me and molest me,
Only come yourself to watch me,
Till I wake, and start, and quicken,
Till I leap into the sunshine."

This old Indian, Squanto, with his broad face and sharp hunter's eyes, saved them from starvation. The colony had been gravely reduced by death and disease during the winter. For the twenty-one men and their wives who remained, and for six boys, Squanto told them to plant twenty acres of maize. Many were weak from fever, but they intermittently hacked away at the ground. Goodwin reckons that they made some 100,000 holes with spade and trowel. Obeying Squanto's instructions, they placed two small herrings—alewives—in each hole. They must have caught some forty tons of fish and stood guard over them at night with fire and staff so that wild animals would not dig the fish out of the holes. But the fertilized field grew magnificently for the settlers. The threat of hunger was removed forever. Only once more did they fear; two years later a terrible drought threatened to parch the maize fields. In June and July no rain fell. The men gathered in the small meeting room of Fort Hill and prayed incessantly; they prayed seven, eight, nine hours. The following morning it began to rain. From that moment they were convinced that God had blessed their enterprise.

They survived. Miraculously, these people who were wholly unequipped to endure became hard and withstood disease, hunger, Indian wars. At last, after the first seven years, a stream of help poured into their colony: tools, animals, new hands. The seven years had been a test, and splendidly they had stood the test, the words of the Scriptures in their hearts: "Thou in thy mercy hast led forth thy people which thou hast redeemed: thou hast guided them in thy strength unto thy holy habitation."

§ 89

With psalm book, rifle, and maize John Endicott and John Winthrop led the Puritans forward. The English colonies in America grew; fresh contingents of colonists poured across the Atlantic. Around 1640 there were already some 14,000 in Massachusetts, 2,000 in Connecticut, 1,800 in New Hampshire and Maine, 1,500 in Maryland, 8,000 in Virginia.

The entire coast line from Maine to Carolina became English, except for New York, where the Dutch had settled, and along the Delaware River, where there was a Swedish colony. But these were soon engulfed by the Anglo-Saxon stream.

All those who came to America were converted to maize, despite the fact that rye and wheat had been their customary grains. The sowing was ideal woman's work, for it could be done without plowing. In old New England a woman had to be mother, gardener, physician, baker, brewer, cook, washerwoman, and tailor all at once. They praised the grain that needed so little attention. "A hole, four inches deep, four kernels of corn . . ." Dorothy Giles narrates in her *Singing Valleys:*

. . . and the dry earth brought over them with a clamshell hoe. A month later and the ground between the charred stumps would be a-flutter with new green leaves, and crying for the hoe again. Two months more and there would be waving tassels, and there would be new ears full of sweet milk, to boil in the big iron pots and to roast in the embers. And when the moon came up, big and round and golden out of the sea, there would be baskets heaped with ears as golden as the moon, to carry home and hang from the house rafters to dry.

The swift growth of the American settlements bore a direct relation to the swift growth of their maize. "Suppose," reflected a Tennessee preacher in 1900, "our fathers had had to depend on wheat for their bread. It would have taken them a hundred years longer to reach the Rockies. Only think of the pioneer in the woods depending on wheat for bread! Corn will produce four times as much as wheat per acre, and requires only one tenth of the seed to seed it down and only one third of the time from planting till it can be used for food. Wheat must have prepared soil, and be sown in the fall, and watched and guarded for nine months before it is even ready to harvest; whereas a woman can take a 'sang hoe' in April and with a quart of seed plant a patch around a cabin, and in six weeks she and the children can begin to eat roastin' ears; and when it gets too hard for that she can parch it. She needs to gather only what she uses for the day, for it will stand all winter, well protected by its waterproof shuck. Not so with wheat. It must be all gathered at once when ripe, and threshed, cleaned, and garnered. And even then it is hard to get bread out of it without a mill. But a small sack of parched corn with a bit of salt was an ample supply for a ten days' hunt. . . ."

Cultivation was facile, and the ripened grain could be pounded with mortar and pestle, or ground in a simple samp mill. The ease of this process was vital to a folk who had more important chores than the laborious struggle to cultivate the ground. They had to build houses against the weather and palisades against the Indians. By and large the Indians visited them only for the liquor they offered, but sometimes they came on fiercer errands.

The one bond between the alien whites and the suspicious Indians was the common food of maize. The Indians of North America had nothing like the high culture of the *nations* in Mexico and Peru. They were poor tribes without that surplus which is the necessary prerequisite to intellectual production. But what little they did have they owed to maize; when they were asked where they got the maize, they replied reverently that the gods had given it to them. With the gift came instructions as to the planting of it; no one had ever seen maize in wild form. According to the legends of the tribes of the north and east, a female spirit had traveled over the land and left maize and squash in her footprints. Across the land of the Navajos a giant turkey had flown, and from its wings had dropped an ear of blue maize. In the Gulf of Mexico two brothers sitting on a sea cliff were surrounded by the waters of a storm-driven tide. They feared they would starve to death; but two parrots appeared every day and brought them ears of corn. Finally they caught one of the birds; it was at once transformed into a beautiful maiden who showed them how to plant the maize. The legends of the Iroquois Indians told how the Earth Mother, Ataentsik, had borne twin children, the good Ioskeha and the wicked Tawiskara. Tawiskara would not enter the world like the rest of men; he dug a way through his mother's breast, and his unnatural birth killed the mother. From her torn body grew maize, which Ioskeha proclaimed to be sacred. Then Ioskeha made other plants grow out of the body of his dead mother; from her navel grew squash, from her feet cranberries, from her shoulders blueberries, from her head tobacco—which is why tobacco smoke helps to clear the head. Tawiskara was angered by these miracles of his pious brother's. In order to destroy all plant life by drought, he created a monstrous frog which drank up all the water of the earth. But Ioskeha stabbed the frog in the side and the waters poured out again. Then he drove his brother away. And finally Ioskeha created man.

Thus every tribe had a different story of the origin of maize. More important than these myths—to which the whites listened with astonishment—were their recipes. Maize could be eaten all year round without bringing on sickness or any weakness. There were twenty different dishes from it. Huckleberry maize bread was one; another was prepared by crushing the unripe corn to a jelly and cooking it in its own leaves. One of the first governors of the Pilgrim Fathers, Governor Carver, declared that he had never eaten anything that tasted so good. Many tribes maintained that maize must always be planted with beans, for maize and beans had been wedded in ancient marriage; that was why the bean wound itself around the maize stalk. This seemed reasonable to the whites, and succotash became a favorite American dish.

Did none of the new settlers attempt to plant the old grains in the new earth? It was inevitable that they should. When animals and plows were brought from Europe, some tried. But it was in vain. The judgment of God had ruled against the wheat. The soil refused to accept it; it fell victim to a mold, and above all it was eaten by rust—the same rust which the Romans had feared. In New England the rust was transmitted to wheat from the barberry. The colonists did not know this, concluded that wheat itself was to blame, and gave up trying to sow it. Thus on a continent that in the nineteenth century was to become the greatest wheatland of the world not a grain of wheat grew.

Rye, however, they continued to grow. The housewives knew that rye flour reinforced the loose maize flour and made it easier to bake. Both flours, mixed, produced the New England bread that became known as "rye and Injun."

Maize was, besides, extremely useful as a medium of exchange in the new land, especially in fur trading. As early as 1633 the settlers trading with the Indians exchanged maize for a thousand pounds of Canadian beaver pelts. Every bushel of maize was reckoned at six shillings, and a pound of fur was made equivalent to two bushels of maize. At that rate wealth came swiftly, for the furs were sold at tremendous profits to England. To transport these furs to the mother country, ships were necessary. And so shipbuilding became one of the great industries of Boston and the other rising cities of the Eastern coast. One may say that those ships were built from the maize that had been multiplied by fur.

§ 90

The people of the New World were new people, with visages unlike those of their cousins across the sea. Photography had not been invented in the year 1700, but the truth of this is known.

The cause was twofold. First there was the fact that all labored. In a description of Maryland in 1670 we read: "The son of the house works no less than the servant, so that both earn their bread before they eat of it." Second, there was no land famine in the broad lands of America.

When a European peasant's crop failed, it spelled his death sentence. But if an American farmer's soil proved to be infertile, he could move on, clear forests as the Indians did, fertilize the land with wood ashes, and plant maize. To be sure, the land was not a free and no-man's land. It belonged to the king or to the English Company; one hundred acres cost all of two shillings. But if he did not have the money, the authorities preferred to overlook it, for the man with his rifle and ax was after all useful to drive the Indians out of the newly settled country. The American farmer became a kind of "migrating peasant"—something new in the history of mankind; he moved on like a nomadic cattle raiser from poor to better soils. The soil near rivers was always the best. Every river was a Euphrates to the new settlers; moreover, the rivers were lines of communication, trade routes for their produce. Road building was expensive and wagons cost more than boats.

This advance of the farmers into the wilderness became the principal factor in the rapid settlement of the American Continent; and the King of England's ban (in 1763) upon settlement west of the Alleghenies was one of the causes of the American Revolution. The farmer's urge to wander on, searching for better soil and greater harvests, resisted confinement within the mountains. That urge was, at the same time, America's urge to go West; the same urge that had led the settlers to America in the first place. They followed the sun from the Old World—a mystical migration that pervades our entire culture and has no connection with the *Drang nach Süden*—an understandable hunger for warmth.

In the seventeenth and eighteenth centuries money played only a limited part in the American economy. The cities on the flourishing East coast thought in capitalistic terms; but in the greater part of the country money was of less importance than grain, water, axes, and weapons. The priceless commodity was the human hand and arm; this could not be replaced by money.

Life seemed more strenuous and difficult in America than in England, but at the same time it was easier. The great, invisible web of agrarian capitalism and industrial rule was absent here; in England these patterns were ever-present threats of ruin to the farmer.

Life in England had become dreadful indeed for the English yeoman. The medieval principles of the English nobility had been colored over with modern shades, but the situation of the small farmer had not improved. New dangers confronted him. Since England had begun to compete with the Dutch textile industry, the farmer found himself faced with a beast more formidable than the lion. This beast was the sheep; it was far from a harmless creature. Sheep increased incredibly. For their sake fruitful fields were turned into pastureland. It is reckoned that by 1700 the greed of the lords had converted half of the arable land of England and Wales into sheep pastures or dyestuff plantations. The crops of England dwindled steadily and the price of grain rose and rose. To the landowners this did not matter, for one shearing of sheep brought more profit than five harvests of grain had brought. Periodically the desperate people fell upon the hated fences, tore them up and burned them. Then came the soldiers; the mobs scattered, and the armies of grazing sheep moved once more over the grass—a caricature of a peaceful countryside. This was not the age of the lamb that Jesus Christ had meant.

Entire regions became barren. The farmers who had inhabited them were cast into the cities, into the textile industry. They became slaves of the loom. The populations of the cities increased rapidly from year to year, and with this increase came an increased demand for grain. Had the king intervened or had Parliament forbidden the continuance of the "enclosures," the decline of the small farmer class might have been checked. But instead there occurred something that removed the last support from under the feet of the small farmer. This was a kind of "revolution from above"; the birth of scientific thinking and of the "new agriculture."

Those who had converted farm land to pastures, saffron fields, or factories, would not again yield up the land. On the other hand, the demand for agrarian products was increasing constantly. The rich and the wise

HAND MILLING ON THE HEBRIDES

reasoned that in the future, to meet this demand, the soil must be tilled more rationally. Jethro Tull (1674–1741), a lawyer who gave up his profession to become a landowner, invented the first mechanical plow which was combined with a sowing device: a horse drew rows of teeth through the soil; behind these teeth pipes dropped the seed into the furrows. The god-fearing farmers looked askance, but farsighted men saw that it was good. By planting only in the furrows and by planting deeply enough rather than blindly broadcasting the seed, more of the seed was utilized, and the thievish birds were outwitted. This was the beginning of modern agriculture. A contemporary of Jethro Tull, the famous Viscount Townshend (1674–1738), discovered how to prepare seedbeds properly and invented new methods for draining waterlogged lands. He advocated marling—fertilizing fields by spreading marl, an earthy deposit containing lime, clay, and sand, over them—demonstrated that turnips build up light soil and serve as excellent winter stock food, and emphasized the value of clover in replenishing the supply of nitrogen in a field, while at the same time providing an ample store of hay. But his most notable contribution was the evolution of a four-year cycle of crops, making possible the exploitation of all fields each year. His rotation —wheat, turnips, barley, or oats, and clover or beans—maintained fertility to a remarkable degree, called for a minimum of artificial restoration, and dealt the antiquated three- and two-fields systems of cultivation a mortal blow. It cemented the relationship between tillage and stock raising by providing cheap, substantial dry forage.

These ideas were a prelude to the modern preoccupation with agrarian chemistry; they were further developed in the nineteenth century by Sir Humphry Davy and Liebig. Without the Tory Townshend and his disciple, Bakewell (1725–95), England would possibly have experienced a revolution more terrible than the French Revolution. But the reform of agriculture literally created bread for the English townspeople. The irony of it was that this reform acted to oppress those who hitherto had produced bread with inadequate tools. It was the misfortune of the farmer that something which was undertaken for the good of all had, as its first effect, his own doom; the introduction of science into agriculture left no place for the small farmer. By the old methods of plowing and sowing, the exhausted soil of England could no longer have fed the English. Deeper layers had to be plowed and the more thorough sowing was needed, but only the rich and the progressive could do this. The scientists who had conceived the new methods had "thought of humanity, but not of men." The simple farmers were bought out and thrust aside. If they remained on their land, they could not compete, and sank into filth and utter poverty.

Historians of literature sometimes pry into the sources of the "sentimentality" that affected two great and powerful literatures, the English and the German, toward the middle of the eighteenth century—causing the tears of *Weltschmerz* to stream in rivers. One of the causes is certainly the economic tragedy experienced by the two countries; the poets saw the vanishing of happiness and hope from the farm lands of their countries, even though they themselves did not know this was what they were observing. Such was the case of George Crabbe (1754–1832), who in sadness and contempt found everything in the villages repulsive and unworthy of human dignity. The farmer was a "creature no more enliven'd than a clod" and the country scene a "vile prospect." And Oliver Goldsmith in *The Deserted Village* gave gloomy warning in the well-known lines:

> Ill fares the land, to hastening ills a prey,
> Where wealth accumulates, and men decay!
> Princes and lords may flourish, or may fade;
> A breath can make them, as a breath has made;
> But a bold peasantry, their country's pride
> When once destroyed, can never be supplied.

How secure America felt herself to be against such conditions. To drive a plowman from his land and cast him into the city seemed to a man like Benjamin Franklin the pinnacle of social evils. Referring to the situation in which wool had placed the English farmer, he wrote in 1760:

No man who can have a piece of land of his own, sufficient by his labor to subsist his family in plenty, is poor enough to be a manufacturer, and work for a master. Hence while there is land enough in America for our people, there can never be manufacturers to any amount or value.

Nine years later he expressed, more acidly, his dislike of those who wished to take away the people's fields:

There seem to be but three ways for a nation to acquire wealth. The first is by war, as the Romans did, in plundering their conquered neighbors. This is robbery. The second by commerce, which is generally cheating. The third by agriculture, the only honest way, wherein man receives a real increase of the seed thrown into the ground, in a kind of continual miracle, wrought by the hand of God in his favor.

Acute though Franklin was, he was here no prophet of the path America was later to take. But Franklin's stiff-necked contempt was a good indication of what Europe was worth in America's eyes at that time. Europe was sinking lower and lower. When the emigrant ships with their English, Scotch, and Irish passengers docked in New York and Boston, the air resounded with sighs of relief and joy. In her economic felicity, America's contempt for Europe was so thoroughgoing that she rejected not only the evil of the Old World, but the good as well. The American was indifferent to the new scientific agriculture. The land was broad, the soil was virgin; he himself was an explorer, not an inventor. What did he care about technical progress? He was lured by the broad spaces, not the deeper layers of the earth; vast, bright spans of undiscovered life lay before him—there was no need to go to tortuous lengths to improve the old. In 1799, when Thomas Jefferson, President and student of agriculture, offered an improvement of the farmer's plow, the farmer did not understand. What was wrong with the plow? As late as Dickens' time the Anglo-Frenchwoman, Harriet Martineau, wrote that the vastness of the land, the expansion into the distance, the appetite for new soil "seems to be the aim of all action and the cure for every social evil."

§ 91

It was part and parcel of the civilization of the New World that, as in Europe, there were rich and poor. But one feature seemed to be lacking —hunger. For to create hunger, the *Fames Europaeica*, a thousand years of bad rule and exhaustion of the soil were necessary. This history was absent from the New World. In a land where every wage laborer had a small house and garden of his own, poverty did not necessarily signify hunger.

But this applied only to times of peace. How should it be when these people were put to the great test of war? Scarcely any community was ever so ill prepared for such an adventure as the America of those bold Republicans who in 1773 threw the gage before the invincible colossus that was the British Empire. The British Empire was far greater than the ancient Roman Empire. George III of England was Grand Mogul of India; he had diamonds, iron, gold, steel, coal, wool, linen, spices—not alone the riches of the present, but the great unborn wealth of the future belonged to this one man. And America had nothing but her crops and her forests.

For one hundred and fifty years America had had bread every year. Maize at first, then rye—virtually no wheat. There had always been enough bread—but just enough—for the plowman to feed himself and the nearest town. But was this enough for a long and terrible war? In the very first months of the war it became apparent that the lawyers and writers had laid the intellectual ground soundly enough, but the arms of war had been sadly neglected. The rifles were poor; the cannon mysterious machines; the men—magnificent in battle—were contentious and undisciplined in the war of exhaustion that was to last seven years and was to be cursed by so many men. Perhaps it would have been better never to have dumped the king's tea into Boston Harbor, to have paid him the taxes he demanded!

But miraculously this war, which had been instigated by merchants who soon would have preferred to call it off—this Revolutionary War was not lost. It was not lost, thanks to the simple logic of the earth, which continued to produce bread; and to the logic of the farmers, who were the backbone of the war. Everywhere in the world the farmer desires peace and leaves the entanglements of war to the traders and merchants, for victory feeds their trade. But in America it was different. The American farmer might have had little to gain, but he had everything to lose if the war were lost. For then he would once more have become a European farmer; he would have to bear on his shoulders the very system of large landholdings from which he had fled; and he would have become acquainted once more with the famines of Europe in their English or French form. This he did not want. And against this he fought.

The cities on the East coast had lived largely upon fishing. This ceased because the English no longer permitted fishing fleets to sail. Nevertheless, there were no famines. The food supply was so secure that Washington, in 1779, dared to destroy forty large Indian villages, burning 160,-000 bushels of maize. It was a dangerous act and one he would not have ventured had he not reckoned on a good harvest. He was in a position where it was more important to cut off the enemy's provisions than to make sure he had enough for his own men.

The terrible sufferings of the soldiers sprang from the lack of wagons and good roads. There was plenty of grain, but in the winter it was technically impossible to supply the Army with the grain. The military doctor, Thacher, wrote in January 1780 that the snow was now piled four to six feet high and the roads were impassable; they could obtain no supplies. . . . The soldiers were too weak from hunger and cold to discharge their duty. . . . Washington himself praised his army for their fortitude:

We have had the virtue and patience of the army put to the severest trial. Sometimes it has been five or six days together without bread, at other times as many without meat, and once or twice, two or three days without either. . . . At one time the soldiers ate every kind of horse food but hay. Buckwheat, common wheat, rye, and Indian corn comprised the meal which made their bread. As an army, they bore it with the most heroic patience. . . .

This was no famine, for a famine would have forced them to abandon the war; this was merely a transportation crisis. They had no wagon routes, no distribution point; they were too inexperienced in the science of warfare. Men like Christopher Ludwick, the Philadelphia baker, who made efforts to supply the Revolutionary Army with bread, were rare indeed. . . . There were, to be sure, European prescriptions for the provisioning of an army. Frederick the Great had recommended that flour be stored in a fort from which the army was never to advance more than five days' march. The field bakery would be placed three days' march from the fort, and the flour would be transported to this bakery under cavalry guard. Thus the front would be two days' march from the bakery (never farther!). Since the bread remained fresh for nine days, the troops could never go hungry. This was splendidly worked out in the best eighteenth-century style, but unfortunately it applied only to Europe and to the baroque period, when wars were fought like chess games. A colonial revolt such as Washington was leading could not be managed in so orderly a fashion.

Undoubtedly it was the enemy who waged war "on a sounder economic basis." Consequently, life in New York was a good deal easier than the life in Washington's army. Wherever the English administration was established, finical order existed:

Bakers were also closely supervised because it was necessary that the army and the civilians secure good bread at a reasonable price. With that idea in mind, the British commandant renewed the prewar custom of making a bread assize, which allowed the baker a fair profit. In January 1777, when the first assize was made, a loaf of bread weighing three and a quarter pounds was to sell for fourteen pence. Nor could the baker safely give short weight or bad bread, for he had to put his initials on the loaves.

Among the American rebels the storehouses were empty. More astonishing than the lack of food was the lack of shoes in the land that was so rich in cattle herds and had sufficient skins to tan. But the tanning industry had no roots in America at the time.

That there was no real shortage of food is proved by the fact that in 1779 the Congress requested the states to send flour and maize to the Army. This idea was abandoned and instead of the food money was sent—because transportation from states distant from the front would have increased the cost of flour and corn, and it was more practical for it to be bought in the vicinity of the front lines. Normally, it would have been no problem for a nation of one million people—90 per cent farmers —to maintain so small an army with ease. But the situation was complex. Worse than the transportation crisis and the consequent shortage of goods was the device resorted to by the enemy. This was the inflation engineered by London. By 1780 the gold value of American money had dropped 4,000 per cent. In spite of ample harvests, prices rose. A letter of Mrs. John Adams to her husband mentions that a bushel of maize cost twenty-five dollars, a bushel of rye thirty. These precipitate price rises disturbed the amicable relationships between town and country. Like everyone who had something to sell, the farmers were accused of usurious practices. Even George Washington rebuked them. In letters to Warren and John P. Custis he announced strong measures:

If persons will not comply with a reasonable tariff, but still refuse to furnish such necessary articles, the great law of self-preservation must authorize us to compel them.

But since the inflation had also caused the farmer's expenses to rise, it is questionable whether the producers of bread were really deriving profit from the situation. On the contrary, toward the end of the war the small farmer began to be restive—an indication that all was not well with him.

Peace was needed badly when it came in 1783. American arms, the stubbornness of democratic farmers, and the assistance of France, the ancient foe of the English, had helped the colonies to win their freedom. Now came the new and troublesome problems of peace. The lands of the English Crown, the vast landholdings of the Tories in America, were parceled out. The war veterans were given land. As always, those excluded felt that they had been wronged. An economic depression followed the war. The farmers could not sell their products nor pay the taxes and interest that had accumulated during the war. A retired army officer, John Shay, gathered together discontented farmers and instigated a conspiracy. In 1787 the revolt was suppressed, but all the participants were pardoned. It had been merely a touch of fever in a convalescent nation; a little postwar anarchy, but no serious upheaval in a land where, marvelous to relate, everyone had bread in plenty.

§ 92

This plenty came almost exclusively from the earth. This was what Franklin had desired. But the people began to consider. An ideological conflict that bit deep into the life of the country was the dispute between Secretary of the Treasury Alexander Hamilton and Secretary of State Thomas Jefferson. Hamilton, who perceived that America had almost lost her war of independence because she was not industrialized, wanted America to "get rich quick." He wanted her to become a super-Europe, a land of banks and shipping magnates. Jefferson held that money could not be eaten; he wished to base the welfare of the state upon the farmer. Seldom could the two exist peacefully side by side. For in young nations (and America was but in her earliest youth) there are hostility and suspicion between capital and land. Each considers itself the only pillar of society. . . .

There was a time in the early history of America when industry and land united to symbolize power and the entire future of America. This was when Oliver Evans built his mill in Philadelphia. A seven-story, steam-driven mill! In Europe, the land of technicians and inventors, no such structure existed.

It was an English invention (America had not yet discovered her inventive genius). For one hundred and fifty years to come the world was to be harnessed to the device of the inventor, James Watt. Steam! The idea of forcing the raging might of compressed steam into a piston and using the expansion of the gas to outdo the puny labors of water and wind had seemed absurd. In 1641, when a Frenchman, Salomon de Caus, asserted that this force could be employed, he was placed in a madhouse. The English did not lock up James Watt, but when he built his steam mill on the Thames, the London millers screamed vengeance and the mill was burned to the ground almost at once. It was rebuilt. Watt's two steam engines, generating forty horsepower, set twenty pairs of millstones in motion. Each pair was capable of grinding ten bushels of wheat an hour. The competitors in the vicinity saw ruin before them, and for a second time the "Albion Mills" were destroyed by fire (in 1791). Whether the fire was the result of accident or incendiarism is not known; at any rate, the fire-fighting apparatus could not be brought close to the blaze because the area around the building was so crowded with secretly rejoicing people. The profits of the old-fashioned millers returned to normal, and the principle of the steam-driven mill seemed forgotten. But only for a time. In America Oliver Evans (1755–1819) revived it. Evans possessed a creative, technical mind; he was a forerunner by three generations of the age of Edison.

Creative technical minds were rare in America. But space there was, and venturesomeness. America dismissed many of the things of worth

CORN POUNDING IN COLONIAL DAYS

that Europe had, because Americans thought they could do without them. But other things were adapted and were improved with the rapidity of tropical growth. Things that elsewhere took 1,500 years took but 150 years in America. Often the diverse ages proceeded along side by side. In 1620, for example, they crushed maize in the primitive and picturesque Indian mortar, made of a hollowed block of wood or a stump of a tree which had been cut off about three feet from the ground. The pestle was a heavy block of wood shaped like the inside of the mortar and fitted with a handle attached to one side. The block was fastened to the top of a young and slender tree, a growing sapling, which was bent over and thus provided a kind of spring which pulled the pestle up after it was pounded down on the corn. This was called a sweep-and-mortar mill.

Such a mill could be heard from far away. When a ship from abroad groped its way in the mists outside of Long Island, unable to find the dock, it had only to steer toward the place from which the "pounding of the samp mortar" sounded. Nevertheless, in 1621 Governor Sir George Yeardley of Virginia erected the first Dutch windmill. The Indians were horrified by it. Its long arms and great teeth "which bit the corn in pieces" seemed to be moved by the Evil Spirit. In this the Indians were reacting no differently than had the Europeans of the Middle Ages. There was, however, a significant difference: in America the miller's tariff amounted to only one sixth of the grain brought to the mill. Consequently, there was no such phenomenon as hatred of the miller.

The first Roman-type water mill was built a few years later, in 1631, in the town of Dorchester. The primitive mortar, the Roman water wheel, and the medieval windmill—all were employed concurrently until Oliver Evans made his great leap into the future. Whereas Watt had really done no more than to substitute a new power source in the mill, the American revolutionized the interior structure by applying the power source not only to the grinding, but to all the other operations. All the processes that formerly cost the miller great physical exertion were now done by the machinery. Evans invented the elevator, an endless band with cups attached to the outside of it; a conveyor for grain, consisting of two helicoidal surfaces on a revolving shaft; and a conveyor for meal consisting of a shaft with a series of small wooden blades set spirally and at an angle. He also invented the "hopper boy," a mechanical servant. This was a horizontally revolving arm that first spread the warm meal as it came from the millstones and then collected it to the center, where it fell through spouts to the bolts on the floor below. The drill was an endless band with rakes or blades for moving the meal horizontally, and the descender made all the flour flow down of its own weight, without the application of power. Now the miller could sit down and watch his mill grind and his pipes spew the ground flour into ships waiting alongside.

In 1791 the Liverpool *Advertiser* printed the following article of American news:

Mr. Oliver Evans, an ingenious American, has invented a model of a flour mill upon a curious construction which, without the assistance of manual labour, first conveys the grain deposited to be ground to the upper floor, where it is cleaned. Thence it descends to the hopper, and after being ground in the usual way, the flour is conveyed to the upper floor, where, by a simple and ingenious contrivance, it is spread, cooled, and gradually made to pass to the bolting hopper. The whole contrivance does the greatest honour to the inventor, and is likely to be of some pecuniary advantage to him, as he has obtained from Congress an exclusive right to the profits of the invention for fourteen years. A number of mills have been already constructed upon this plan, which are found to answer perfectly in practice. To make inanimate nature thus yield to the power of man's inventive faculties what otherwise manual labor would be obliged to effect, must be of the greatest advantage to a young country where hands are wanted.

This was only eight years after the conclusion of peace, but the Liverpool *Advertiser* had judged America correctly. This invention was not merely a relief to the millers. The epoch-making significance of Oliver Evans was his perception, fifty years before any other American, of one of the basic problems of a hemisphere poor in manpower—labor-saving machinery.

Only five generations earlier Squanto had taught his Pilgrim friends how to use the mortar and pestle; now there arose a seven-story steam mill. A bewildering apparatus guided a stream of grain to the grindstones. An invisible giant within the vast building performed all the labors of Samson, whom the Philistines had made to grind their grain; it was stronger than the brooks of the Romans, than the ox-driven mills of Pompeii, or the windmills of Holland.

No such machine existed in Europe. But perhaps there was no seven-story mill in the Old World because there was not so much grain to be ground. Let us see what was happening at the same time in France, who had but lately lent invaluable aid to America. What manner of bread did the French eat? Who had bread to eat in France?

BOOK FIVE

Bread in the Nineteenth Century

La terre n'est pas labourée,
Et le blé devrait, abondant,
Jaunir la zône tempérée,
Et du pôle au tropique ardent.
Déchirons le sein de la terre,
Et, pour ce combat tout d'amour,
Changeons les armes de la guerre
En des instruments de labour.

On n'arrête pas le murmure
Du peuple, quand il dit: J'ai faim;
Car c'est le cri de la nature:
Il faut du pain!
PIERRE DUPONT: MUSE POPULAIRE (1850)

CAN SCIENCE PREVENT A REVOLUTION?

§ 93

"CLOSE to the year 1750," Voltaire wrote, "the nation, satiated with novels and plays, turned its attention to grain. . . ."

It was late. Was it too late?

By 1750 Renaissance and baroque were long past. The memory of the righteous king, Henry IV, who wished to give every Frenchman his "chicken in the pot," had faded. He had been succeeded by a Pharaoh, Louis XIV. In 1689, a full century before the French Revolution, La Bruyère bitterly described the condition to which the taxes and wars of Louis's radiant court had brought France:

Certain savage-looking beings, male and female, are seen in the country, black, livid, and sunburnt, and belonging to the soil which they dig and grub with invincible stubbornness. They seem capable of articulation, and, when they stand erect, they display human lineaments. They are, in fact, men. They retire at night to their dens where they live on black bread, water, and roots. They spare other human beings the trouble of sowing, plowing, and harvesting, and thus should not be in want of the bread they have planted.

The ant societies which Darwin studied were undoubtedly better organized, for they ate the grain they harvested. The French peasantry at

238

the height of Louis Quatorze's glory were seen in the neighborhood of Blois eating nettles and carrion. Women and children were found lying dead by the roadsides, their mouths stuffed with inedible weeds. Madmen crouched over graves in cemeteries, sucking and gnawing at bones. In 1683, in the vicinity of Angers, there were many peasants who made their bread of ferns. Those who habitually ate it died. In 1698 various governors reported that France was beginning to die of starvation; famine swept over it unchecked. Around 1715, according to Taine, a third of the population—six million persons—had died. Such was the opening of the eighteenth century, France's greatest century and one of the greatest in the world's history!

"The first king in Europe," Saint Simon wrote of Louis XV, "is great simply by being a king over beggars of all conditions, and by turning his kingdom into a vast hospital of dying people from whom their all is taken without a murmur on their part." For they were beggars only because their all was taken from them. "Before men turned to eating grass like sheep and died like so many flies" (as the Bishop of Chartres reported), they tried to hide the rest of their grain, or to pawn their Sunday clothes or the pillows, if they had any. It did not help. The tax collectors, preceded by the village locksmith, forced their way in through locked doors and seized the peasants' tables and chairs, linen and tools. These peasants became streams of beggars, armies of uprooted vagabonds who infested France from north to south. Letrosne wrote in 1779:

The vagabonds about the country are a terrible pest; they are like an enemy's force which, distributed over the territory, obtains a living as it please, levying veritable tolls. . . . They are constantly roving about the country, examining the approaches to every house, and informing themselves about their inmates and of their habits. Woe to those supposed to have money. . . . What numbers of highway robberies and what burglaries! What numbers of travelers assassinated, and houses and doors broken into! What assassinations of curates, farmers, and widows, first tormented until they reveal the hiding place of their money and afterwards killed!

A huge police force that cost a fortune to maintain was set against the criminals. Once, in a single day, 50,000 were arrested. The prisons were not large enough; the hospitals also were filled with them. This was a sensible measure, for many of them were insane from starvation and had committed their crimes in delirium. At still greater cost, the king built a number of strong reformatories. Those who could provide warrants that they would be supported or be able to support themselves in the future were released. Most of them, of course, could not. The stronger among these unfortunates were placed in forced labor on galleys; the greater part of them, human wrecks, wallowed for years amid the straw the government vouchsafed them. To maintain such a poor creature on bread, water, and two ounces of salted lard cost the state only five sous a day. When we read in the account books that the king expended annually a full million francs on this "care" for the poor, we can imagine that the people were crammed like sardines into the "reformatories."

Yet the greater part of these people had once been productive, if not prosperous, peasants. The writers, economists, and lawyers who witnessed these conditions began to ask themselves and others whether it would not have been wiser to have helped these people before they came to these straits. Saint Simon is wrong when he says they endured the injustices "without a murmur." A quarter of a millennium after the discovery of America it was no longer possible for medieval conditions to exist as a matter of course. People had changed; they had begun to reflect—especially in the city of Paris, where the most alert minds in the world lived. Here, as Voltaire recalls, society suddenly ceased to live for love and the theater. People began to think hard about grain—and particularly about its *lack*.

§ 94

The thoughts concerning grain of which Voltaire had spoken were the product of the philosopher Quesnay (1694–1774). His followers called themselves the "physiocrats." With their master they believed that "physics ruled all," that nature and men's relationship to it was the sole decisive factor in society. *"L'industrie ne multiplie pas les richesses, les agriculteurs seuls forme la classe productive; tous les citoyens occupés a d'autres traveaux que ceux de l'agriculture forment, au contraire, la classe sterile* [industry does not increase wealth; the farmers alone form the productive class. All citizens engaged in occupations other than agriculture constitute the sterile class]." This was a classic thought. Demeter and Triptolemos seemed to have returned to these Frenchmen. Solon had advanced almost the same arguments to his Athenians; and in America Benjamin Franklin, an enthusiastic student of Quesnay, proclaimed these ideas.

Quesnay demanded that the lot of the poorest farmers—who were by far the majority—be alleviated by the granting of credits so long as they remained farmers. He considered the existence of famine to spring from the fact that these numberless poor possessed neither animals nor plows—because their beasts had long since been slaughtered and their plows had fallen to pieces. This laboring class literally labored with their hands. Inevitably, the result was reduced yields. . . . But Quesnay's *philosophie rurale* irritated other philosophers; many were offended by his analysis that industry served luxury alone, not the nation. Voltaire and Grimm attacked Quesnay. It is curious that Voltaire should do this, for had he not congratulated the nation for beginning to think seriously about grain? But in this respect Voltaire was very French. He recognized the necessity for agriculture, but he found it boring. Craftsmanship and industry were variegated and alive to him; in them he saw the spirit of the nation actively at work. Like most writers, Voltaire quite unconsciously preferred the city laborer (as a potential reader of books) to the country "lout." It was of fateful moment to France that Napoleon later had the same preference and was, for a thousand reasons, pro-industrialist.

Consequently, many mocked at Quesnay. On the other hand, the romantic enthusiasm with which he spoke of rustic matters piqued the taste of society. Rousseau contributed to this with his lyric notes on bucolic life in the *New Héloïse* (1761). Interest in nature was stimulated; the rich, who had owned land but never visited it because they were afraid to encounter puddles and misery, became adherents of the pastoral life. It became fashionable to belong to the *Société d'agriculture,* which had been founded by Minister Bertin and was subsidized by the government. Several model farms were established; swamps were drained and roads improved. This was not altogether mere play. Nevertheless, grain prices continued to rise; since 1705 they had mounted steadily. Wheat and oats had risen by a fourth in price, barley a half. Any real improvement in the situation was impossible so long as the taxes continued to rob the peasant not of 50, but—with the *taille* and other oppressive measures— of 75 and 80 per cent of his produce. So long as the farmers-general milked the small farmer and prevented him from working his land productively, all the perceptions of the philosophers and economists were worth no more than printer's ink.

But leaflets began to flutter, and the nation began to read them.

§ 95

Coevally with the physiocrats, another group of men set to work to provide France with cheaper bread. These were the natural scientists and the chemists. They, too, reaped no success.

In 1787 the great Lavoisier examined the causes of distress in France. Why was agriculture at a standstill? Why could the land no longer feed its people? After taxes and internal tariffs, he blamed the *banalité des moulins.* As a scientist, rather than a politician, Lavoisier was concerned with the wretched condition of the ancient, crippled French mills.

As we have seen, in the Middle Ages the people had hated the millers "because they adulterated the bread." It was a favorite prejudice that the millers mixed sand or sawdust with the flour. Consequently, the miller was an outcast; he was excluded from the community. The millers may later, under economic pressure, have adulterated the grain, but in the beginning the accusation was unjust, for it was none of his doing that the flour seemed full of sand and sawdust—it was the fault of the mill.

The ancient water mill and the medieval windmill had not been improved since their invention. The first of modern men, Leonardo da Vinci, had drawn plans for their improvement; but in these improvements he was concerned only with increasing the speed and ease of motion; he, too, was not interested in the hygienic aspect, in refinements of the grinding process.

The essence of milling had consisted, since ancient times, in separating the flour from the bran. This was done by breaking up the grain as finely as possible. The actual result was the opposite of what was intended. The rapid, rough grinding did not separate the bran, but pulverized it and distributed it through the flour. After thorough grinding it could no longer be removed by sifting.

In 1760 Malisset in Paris invented a new type of grinding which ground the grain gradually, separating the various end products according to their size and shape. Unlike the older process, the millstones were held at successive intervals of three, then two, then one millimeter apart. At the first rotation the coarser parts of the grain were removed (not ground up with the flour); the medium-sized particles were removed at the second rotation; and only the final, close grinding produced the actual flour. This was a significant innovation, yet it was not adopted; 95 per cent of the mills in France continued to grind flour inadequately. A quarter of a century later Lavoisier saw this fact as a grave danger sign.

It was not Lavoisier, however, but another prominent scientist who came to the conclusion that the state of the mills was of primary import for the welfare of the nation. In his *Expériences et reflexions sur le blé et les farines*, Parmentier, the army apothecary (1736–1812), wrote:

My own experience of many years and above all the things I have seen in wartime have convinced me that in the plan of this world the husks and woody parts of plants were *not* intended to form part of our food. And especially these materials, insofar as they occur in grains, were not meant to be included in our bread. The bran, a woody parenchyma, the husk of the grain, is not nutritious precisely because it contains no meal. The art of the miller should consist in removing this husk from the grain—but without pulverizing it so that it can no longer be sifted out. Close grinding is therefore harmful. I was nearly certain that I could prove the truth of this. I undertook a number of experiments, and since in my opinion I could count on his being greatly interested, I patriotically dedicated the results to Marshal du Muy.

Marshal du Muy was the French War Minister. We may wonder at the author's not addressing himself to the Minister of Agriculture; but Antoine Auguste Parmentier was first and foremost a soldier. He had "seen much in times of war" and knew that peace differed in degree, not in principle, from life in wartime, that peace was a continuation of war. In wartime he had seen starving soldiers eating the bark of trees. In peacetime the entire nation, because of impractical and unscientific milling, ate the husk of the grain instead of the flour. And people imagined that because the bran made the flour heavier, it was the more nourishing. In reality it was eaten and excreted without being digested. This bran bread only deceived the stomach; it left a man as hungry as before.

§ 96

Parmentier, the earliest of modern nutritionists, asserted and proved that the health of nations depended upon the quality of the flour. In other directions he performed significant patriotic services to his country. He attempted a practical and immediate solution of the food problem by recommending the potato as a supplementary food.

No small courage was needed to make such a recommendation. Not alone because the potato was virtually unknown in France—Diderot's Encyclopedia, which mirrors the knowledge of the age, mentioned the potato as "an Egyptian fruit whose cultivation may possibly have some value in the colonies"—but because in the popular mind the potato had been degraded to something unmentionable. In 1700, when potatoes were imported to France from eastern Switzerland, they were looked upon as poisonous.

This charge of poison has cropped up again and again in the long rivalry of grains. A land that was sown with barley, wheat, oats, or rye, would vigorously fend off all competition. Since the earth had first begun to be cultivated, each grain had striven for unconditional monoculture. The Irish potato eaters believed, as we have seen, that eating maize would turn one black. And wheatlands like seventeenth-century France, or rye lands like Germany, believed the potato caused leprosy! It was said that this terror of the Middle Ages broke out anew wherever men ate potatoes.

It was quite understandable that the potato tuber should be considered poisonous. Botanists, like the great Clusius of Vienna, contributed to this superstition when they determined that the potato was a solanaceous plant, and the leaves of the solanaceous plants were indeed poisonous, or at any rate narcotic. (Other members of this family are the nightshade, tomato, capsicum, bittersweet, tobacco, and petunia.) But the solanin content was present only in the green parts of the plants. The tuber was the part that was not poisonous.

Parmentier had encountered the potato in East Germany, not France. In the Seven Years' War, when France fought on the side of Austria against Frederick the Great, Parmentier had been taken prisoner. For years he languished in Prussian camps and learned to appreciate the potato as an emergency food; indeed, for months he lived on nothing else. From his guards he learned that King Frederick the Great had *forced* the people to cultivate the potato. The people had balked at it because in the days of the king's grandfather the potato had brought leprosy into the land, so they said. The skeptical peasants dug up the tubers and threw them to their pigs. Or they burned them. For a time the king had virtually to post a soldier on guard before every plant. This lasted for years. One day, however, the king sat himself upon a balcony in Breslau and publicly ate cooked potatoes. The stubborn Prussians began to wonder; and soon afterward they changed their minds about the tuber, for the potato won them the Seven Years' War. Although the Austrians and Russians had set up a blockade against the import of grain, the Prussian lands where the potato had been planted suffered no hunger.

Parmentier pointed out that no one in Prussia had died from eating potatoes. He recommended the potato to the French not only because it was a filling food, but primarily because it did not require so much farm apparatus (animal power and plows). Quesnay had petitioned for funds to procure such apparatus, but they had not been forthcoming. The improvement of the mills was also an expensive matter and would require an army of mechanics. The potato made this unnecessary; potatoes involved no more cost than the sacks of potatoes for seed.

Parmentier's propaganda at last commanded some attention. The Besançon Academy, alarmed by the ever-increasing distress, offered a prize for suggestions of a food that could at once replace grain *in case of famine!* Parmentier won this prize. King Louis XVI sent for him and graciously granted him fifty acres of land for an experimental planting. This was little enough, and it turned out to be only a game which had as its chief outcome that the king and the court sported potato blossoms in their buttonholes. Afterward, potatoes were frequently served at the court table—but this had not been Parmentier's aim. Nevertheless, Louis had a vague idea of what the scientist hoped to accomplish. At a second audience the king declared: "France will not forget that you found food for the poor." For Parmentier hoped to use the potato not as a vegetable, but as a source of bread flour.

After involved negotiations he secured from the Ministry permission to open an "Academy of Baking" in the Rue de la Grande Truanderie. "If there are schools for veterinaries who study the feeding of horses, why should there not be schools for bakers, to whom the health of the nation is entrusted?" Parmentier had written in one of his memorials. The school concerned itself with *"Nouvelles combinaisons de substances farineuses dont il serait possible dans ces temps de famine de faire du pain* [New combinations of farinaceous substances out of which bread might

be made in these times of famine]." At last this was to be done scientifically; there would be no more of the perilous ruses for stretching of
scarce flour that had been practiced in the Middle Ages. *"Seul le savant,
le microscope en main, peut apercevoir la cause de ces maux* [Only the
scientist, microscope in hand, can perceive the cause of these evils]."

On June 8, 1780, the school for bakers was opened. The chemist Cadet
de Vaux and Parmentier were the directors. In the presence of the
scientists of France, and of America's Ambassador to France, Benjamin
Franklin, various experimental breads were baked and potato flour as
the ideal substitute for grain was introduced. "Potato flour," Parmentier
exclaimed, "has not the sharpness of oats or the dryness of maize." Franklin listened attentively, standing among the French with unpowdered
hair and his democratic beaver hat. He knew the troubles of this country,
but for his own part he did not care very much for the potato. In Boston,
his native city, masters had to include a clause in the articles of apprenticeship agreeing that they would not feed their apprentices potatoes.
Franklin was an eater of maize, and sentimental enough to want to convert the French to maize. The last essay he wrote in Europe was his
"Observations on Maize or Indian Corn," which he sent to Director
Cadet de Vaux. In this essay he recounted everything he had learned
since childhood about green corn, roasted, boiled, or dried, hasty pudding,
hoecake, corn syrup, corn liquor, and corn fodder. Franklin did not succeed in converting the French; he had to return to America to enjoy these
things again.

While within the nation—slowly, slowly—unrest fermented like a sour
dough, the bakers' school went on with its experiments. Parmentier demonstrated an eight-year-old biscuit that was still edible; and a master baker
named Cole received a silver medal for rediscovering the secret process
by which the ancient Peruvian Indians had preserved potatoes by freezing. Poor innocent and candid bakers' school! Two years earlier an immediate program of compulsory planting of potatoes in all France's
provinces might have staved off the Revolution. But opponents were
already active, like the writer Le Grand d'Aussy, who disapproved of
potato flour as a food for the better classes: "Its doughy taste, its unat-
tractiveness, its harmful effects—like all unfermented starch it dilates the
stomach and is difficult to digest—make it unsuitable for a well-managed
household. Only a crude taste and a leathern stomach will become accustomed to the potato." This was a direct insult to the lower classes, for
whom the potato was intended. The reaction of these classes was remarkable indeed, for they considered Grand d'Aussy to have the right slant
and were annoyed with Parmentier. Today, to be sure, the people of
Paris plant potatoes every year around Parmentier's grave in the Père-
Lachaise; but in his lifetime they would have none of it. When his epoch-
making book, *Traité sur la culture et les usages de pomme de terre,* was

published in 1789, it was already too late. The storm broke. Who cared now about the potato?

BREAD: ACTOR IN THE FRENCH REVOLUTION

§ 97

IN THE MONTHS before the storming of the Bastille the people of Paris commenced once more to greet each other with the forbidden greeting of the Jacquerie: *"Le pain se lève . . ."* What bread? There was none. There was only the vision of bread. The hand of destiny was once more at work, kneading, opening the great oven. . . .

The people as such is an amorphous dough. Every popular leader knows that "yeast" is needed before this dough will rise. This yeast is composed of ideas—preferably of only a single idea: a fact or a rumor that gains the ear of the multitude and breeds revolt in the most sluggish minds.

This fact, this rumor, existed. No one knew whence it had sprung, but most Frenchmen believed that the lack of grain was due to a conspiracy. This traditional hunger was now something unnatural; some people must have made up their minds to exterminate the French nation! What did the Court, the rich, the aristocracy, care about the continued existence of so many human beings who merely wanted to eat?

There is no doubt that the grain speculators were making a great deal of money at the time (as they had in the ages of the Pharaohs and of Augustus). The unique factor was the mass delusion that the purpose of their speculation was to "exterminate the French nation." Advocates and journalists spread the whisper among the excitable, famine-weakened masses that for more than seventy years a secret society had existed, a band of traders who had concluded a *pacte de famine* with the government. This pact was an agreement to create artificial famine. That was why there was no grain! It was said that Louis XV had already earned ten millions pounds as a result of this murderous conspiracy. The society was alleged to be buying cheaply all the grain in France, secretly exporting it, buying it again from abroad, and importing it back into France at tenfold the original price. A network of agents was said to have overrun the provinces. All buyers had been bribed by this cartel.

The fact was that all export of grain from France had been prohibited for the past hundred years. Consequently, it could not have been simple to sell in secret vast quantities of grain abroad—certainly impossible to export the entire crop. But the rumormongers had a solution to this apparent inconsistency. "The king himself is in the business! His Grain

Administration gathers all the grain in warehouses and sends it to the border under military guard." No one had any idea how this was technically possible. It was also admitted that the present King Louis could hardly be capable of such chicanery. Nevertheless, the "usurious sale abroad" seemed to bear the stamp of royal approval. Although the heads of this fabulous grain plot were thought to have changed frequently in the course of the past half century, the fact remained that Ministers, the farmers-general, and the Court were always implicated.

No one knew how this tale had been started, but everyone believed it as soon as names and figures were given. It was said, for example, that on August 28, 1765, four men gathered in Paris to discuss once more their technique of starving an entire generation. These men were the Inspector of the French Forests, Le Ray de Chaumont; the Inspector of the Royal Domains, Rousseau; the Chief of the Military Hospitals, Perruchot; and the inventor and mill owner, Malisset. These four men were said to have sent all grain abroad—with the approval of the king; this grain was stored in vast granaries on the English islands of Jersey and Guernsey, whence it would be imported anew into France, burdened with frightful tariffs. There may have been some truth in this, for in September 1765 the price of bread had tripled. But was it all true? Where had the ships been obtained to take all this grain to the granaries on the Channel Islands? Three years afterward the police located the man who was responsible for the story—a certain Prévost de Beaumont, a petty official who had seen certain account books that registered the profits. He was immediately sent to the Bastille, where he spent twenty years. Had there been a trial he might have produced his proofs, or revealed what part of the story was true. But a trial was not necessary; a *lettre de cachet* was sufficient to cause a man to vanish from the midst of Paris —to vanish for twenty years. The people considered this before they spoke of the *pacte de famine* in the streets and squares. But they whispered about it all the more. Malisset, to whom the world owed significant improvements in the technique of milling, was shunned like a leper and branded as a terrible scoundrel and enemy of the people. For 30,000 pounds a year he was said to have sold France. When he died (having lost his mind), he said over and over in his last hours that the grindstones must be placed three millimeters, two millimeters, and even closer together to produce healthful flour. He died in the delusion that he was being strangled—and he did not die rich. He owed the government 115,000 pounds silver. What had happened to his "profits"?

On July 14, 1789, the people, enraged by the "grain plot," rose up. They stormed the Bastille where honorable men and "muckrakers" of the kidney of Prévost de Beaumont were imprisoned. Some historians relate that they not only assailed the Bastille with axes and muskets, but that many were dressed as for a dance and carried ears of grain. This is scarcely credible. Where would the Parisians have obtained grain? But it is significant that the storming of the Bastille, the demolishing of the hated fortress, should have appeared to contemporaries as a kind of harvest festival; an agrarian procession in honor of Ceres. The world was returning to the classic spirit! Tyrannicide, National Assembly, Convention—though the *Demos* of Paris had never heard of Hellas, life costumed itself in Graeco-Roman vestments.

<h2 style="text-align:center">§ 98</h2>

How noble the world became once more. It was as though only the Bastille stood in the way of true chivalry. Gentle breezes of conciliation wafted across Paris. The Estates held out their hands to one another; on August 4, 1789, at the suggestion of the Vicomte de Noailles and the Duc de Châtelet, the nobility voluntarily renounced its rights.

For a thousand years the masses had battered futilely against a closed door—and suddenly it opened of itself. That night in the National Assembly, the night of August 4–5, 1789, had something of the unreality of a dream. The windows of the candlelit hall admitted the hot, fragrant air of midsummer. Revolt was said to be raging in the provinces. But not here. Here was no fighting, here no flashing of pikes. The aristocrats surrendered voluntarily what fifty generations of their underlings had fought for. Freedom was offered on a golden platter. The various sokes and merchets vanished; the peasant was no longer bound to his soil; the heriot went up in smoke. The nobles surrendered their hunting privileges and the clergy their tithes. "We have only one desire: that you establish your freedom as quickly as possible!" the Duke of Mortemart stated to his amazed adversaries. It was a fairy-tale scene—handshaking, cheers, and waving of hats. Enthusiasm and the rights of man! The trampled dead of the Jacquerie, the pyramids of peasant skulls, the blood bath of 1525 on the other side of the Rhine—all were forgotten that night. It was all done, as Madame de Staël wonderfully remarked, in a *"disposition généreuse, disposition si bien française et alors par le besoin d'être applaudi* [in a mood of generosity, in a mood typically French, and from the desire for applause]." And indeed the galleries applauded through the night.

But had it all really been forgotten? While the nobles were making their grand gestures, the peasants were burning the châteaux. The marching peasants cared little for the kiss of peace that their deputies in the National Assembly were exchanging with the landowners. There was still no bread.

"Il se n'agit pas de ça, coquins [That is not the question, you scoundrels]!" cried an infuriated woman during one of the endless debates in

the Assembly Hall. And the gallery roared in chorus, *"Nous voulons du pain!"*

The Bastille had been stormed—but the people of Paris did not yet have their bread. They had found poor devils in the Bastille, prisoners like Prévost de Beaumont, but not a spoonful of grain. In fact, in the days after the storming of the Bastille there was an unusual shortage of flour. The people could not feed on the glory of the Revolution. Why did a four-pound bread still cost 12½ sous and a white bread 14½? The government provided subsidies so that the bakers would lower their price. But this did not increase the supply of bread. The angry populace lost precious hours waiting in front of the bakeries. To be sure, Parmentier's potato bread was much cheaper. But who was interested in Parmentier and his bakers' college? That was old-fashioned nonsense. Parmentier's experiments—it was unjustly said—were conducted only so that the rich could cram something into the mouths of the poor. Let him eat his potatoes himself. "We want bread!" the people shouted before the doors of the bakers' school. And on January 14, 1790, Cadet de Vaux and Parmentier timidly asked for armed guards "to protect their ovens." The people identified the bakers' school with the *ancien régime*.

§ 99

August 1789 saw a disaster so terrible that Heaven seemed to be conspiring with the speculators and profiteers. A drought had come upon France worse than any the nation remembered. The streams dried up. The result was that the mills could not run. There were windmills only in the provinces of northern France. In central and southern France all milling was done in water mills. Now the little grain there was could not be ground! The Minister of Agriculture at once ordered the erection of horse-driven mills. But this took time. In September the supply of bread in Paris dwindled away again, and the price rose shamelessly. The seething masses became convinced that the Court still had grain. In Versailles the king and queen, the priests, the nobles with their silver-buckled shoes, even the deputies of the people, the members of the National Assembly (who, the people began to believe, were betraying them)—they had bread. On to Versailles!

In the early morning of October 5, 1789, Paris spewed her torrents of human beings out into the misty roads. They marched with pikes and scythes, barefoot and in rags. Surrounding a core of men marched the women and children. Here was something new: the Revolution wore skirts. Inspired by their own cries, the women poured toward Versailles —fifty thousand, a hundred thousand. Paris seemed denuded of people. The monarchy would be crushed this day.

The masses were obsessed by hallucinations.

"Did you see the bread wagons?"

"Yes, bread wagons on the horizon!"

When they arrived in Versailles, they were weary from their long tramp; their bodies were covered with dust and their eyes inflamed. There was the park—but not the park that their fathers and grandfathers had told them of. Then it was not true—no leaping fountains shimmering like rainbows and twittering like exotic birds. Weeks before King Louis XVI had turned off the water in the park—it was needed to run the mill. Because the water no longer plashed in the fountains, the villages around Versailles had bread—though there was not enough for Paris. All at once it occurred to the marchers that perhaps the king himself had not much bread, though he had gold and jewels enough. The women's cries for bread died down. They took the king and queen in their midst and forced them to return to Paris; but no one offered them harm.

When they returned, there was general disappointment. Paris had thought it would now begin to rain bread. When the calash, surrounded by women, reached the suburbs late that evening and the people recognized by the glow of torches the fat face of the king within, they cried, "There comes the baker!" and "They're bringing the baker's wife!" These had been the nicknames of the king and queen since the story of the *pacte de famine* had circulated.

But baker though he may have been called, Louis XVI could not conjure up bread. How little he could have done so at this time was revealed thirty years later in a book of Madame de Staël's. In her *Considérations* she remarks that on October 5 Louis could have escaped to the provinces under guard of the Versailles troops "if at the moment he had had enough flour to feed a single regiment." But the king had no flour. The revolutionary guards who escorted the king's coach back to Paris were shown in contemporary copper engravings bearing loaves of bread on the points of their bayonets. But this was due to the starved imagination of the engravers. The soldiers and women returned to Paris without bread.

Fourteen hungry days passed. Robberies occurred in the suburbs; a number of rich dwellings were broken into. "Watch out for the bakers" became the watchword. "The bakers have hidden flour. They want to wait until we can pay more."

On October 20, 1789, Baker Denis François was trying to calm a woman who was making a scene in his shop. The shop was situated near Notre Dame de Paris, in the vicinity of the archiepiscopal palace which was the scene of the meetings of the National Assembly since it had left Versailles—because the Parisians wanted to have it where they could watch it. The woman went on shouting, unappeased. Denis François had just finished baking six sets of bread and was beginning the next. The woman screamed that she had received none the day before, nor the day before that. The baker invited her into the baking room; let her see for herself that he had no concealed bread. She went in, passed through the bakery into the room where the old baker lived, and saw three four-pound breads on the table. The apprentices had made these for themselves. The woman took one bread, escaped shouting to the street, and incited the people with cries of, "He has hidden flour." The crowd broke in, smashed the house, and administered a beating to the old man. In a clothes closet they found six dozen small, fresh rolls; the unhappy baker had baked these for the parliamentary deputies. What? Seventy-two rolls for the representatives of the people, while the people themselves went hungry? . . . The baker was dragged out, to cries of "Hang the traitor!" Police and soldiers of the parliamentary guard intervened and arrested the baker to save his life. But the mob tore the prisoner away from them, took him to the Place de Grève, and hanged him.

Both the National Assembly and the administrators knew that whether the nation were kingdom or republic, the people would hang all authorities who did not solve the bread problem. But the bread problem could not be solved. The National Assembly set aside 400,000 pounds for agricultural aid, but this still did not solve the problem. For everything was decaying in France: roads, means of transportation, plows, animals, the minds of the people. And on the frontiers of the country the speculators lurked and made prices mount.

Where was the bread? The flow of grain dwindled to a trickle, as it had when the despots reigned, and the bakers' ovens remained empty. Even before the war with Europe broke out, all France had fallen prey to the "siege psychology." Grain had to be procured—but how? Trade was unpopular; it was, indeed, considered a betrayal of the people, a crime against the new spirit of the nation. For the nation ought to live by agriculture. (But where were the farmers?) Traders must be speculators, therefore cheats. The Revolution threatened them with death, but the Revolution needed them, and the men of the people knew nothing of trade. At great cost the city of Paris bought grain abroad. At one time —*mirabile dictu*—32,000 sacks of grain were accumulated in the *École militaire*. But in good times Paris had been accustomed to consume 650,000 sacks of *flour* a year. For centuries the Parisians had been monomaniac eaters of bread. They would not touch macaroni, that Italian invention which was so economical and so filling. They did not like the smell of maize flour, and oats were feed for horses. All they wanted was wheat bread, and there was not enough bread.

Then the Revolutionary authorities informed them that soon there would be still less, for in 1792 the war with all Europe broke out. All supplies of bread were directed to provisioning the French Army. The soldiers must have enough to eat, the gallant soldiers who were defending the Revolution against the dreadful plot of the royalists. But even the soldiers did not have enough bread, for in the following year the government learned that its own generals, the traitors around Dumouriez, had transported the grain of the Northern Army into the enemy lines. Here was a crisis indeed. It would mean the end of the Republic. The heads of king, queen, and aristocrats could be cut off, but could avarice and self-interest be cut out of the hearts of the citizens? What monsters there were among the people; such individuals as those who on August 7, 1793, spirited away 7,500 pounds of bread out of starving Paris because they hoped to obtain higher prices in the provinces, where the prices had not yet been fixed. Once again the *pacte de famine* was rearing its ugly head. Was it for this that the people had had four years of revolution?

All the guilty men were executed. But their followers were legion. Let the cities starve for weeks—but the army must have food. The Convention decreed death for anyone who held up a grain wagon or changed its destination. From the remotest provinces grain was scraped together, loaded into carts, and hurried to the front. Robbers and plunderers were shot; a powerful corps of grain police guarded the transportation to the army.

In October 1793 Paris once more received flour. Only a short time before Danton had thundered that the "united nation must have a single bread price." The Commune of Paris decreed that from then on only a single type of bread could be baked in the city—the *pain d'égalité*. The flour sieves of millers and bakers were confiscated, for they were a symbol of fine breads. All, poor and rich, would have bread of equally poor quality. Indigestible bran for all. In their pride, the people's representatives did not realize this, or did not care to realize it. . . .

On December 2, 1793, the bread card was introduced; and eighteen months later the Commune decided upon free distribution of bread: one and a half pounds daily to workers and the heads of families, one pound *to all others*. But before long all there was of bread were the cards. In 1794 the harvest was pitiably small, and in 1795 a dreadful inflation bloated the body of France. "A sack of wheat weighing three quintals is now worth nine thousand francs," Mallet-Dupan reported in July 1795. And in the summer, in some provinces of France, the price of a single bread rose to eighty and one hundred sous. Men killed one another for bread.

Bread became a fata morgana. The less there was of it, the more often the mirage and the shadow of it appeared in the laws of the Convention. "Every Frenchman," Saint-Just declared, "between the ages of twenty-five and fifty years must be obligated to do farm work." And the men of the Terror, in the year of crop failures and hunger, organized a harvest

festival of thanksgiving. Robespierre, in a blue dress coat, with stiff, abstracted features, strode slowly through the streets of Paris behind a team
of oxen that were "dedicated to the goddess of agriculture." He carried
a bouquet of wheat ears and poppies; but the bouquet was considered
obviously an artificial one.

For it was scarcely believable that real ears of wheat still existed. There
was no trace of bread save in the ardent desire for it in the hearts of
men. It was necessary; it created tumult and riot. From one such riot
emerged the miracle of human character—and the resulting drama was
one of the most livid of the Revolution.

Hordes of frantic, savage women, crying for bread, shouting curses
and threats, once more besieged the Convention. A few hundreds of
these "priestesses of hunger" detached themselves from the mob of thousands and began to ascend the steps. They wanted to enter the meeting
room. In the vestibule they encountered the chairman of the session, the
lawyer Boissy d'Anglas. He was well known—an aristocrat who had devoted himself to the people's cause. But he also held a high office in the
Grain Ministry and was therefore especially hated. The raging women
fell upon him, tore at him, kicked and struck him. He succeeded in freeing himself and made his way into the meeting hall, locking the door
behind him. As his addresses indicated, he was a disciple of the Stoics;
the incident did not trouble him.

Just after his escape another door opened and Deputy Féraud, attracted by the noise, came out into the vestibule. "What do you want,
women?" he thundered. *"Respectez la loi!"* In a moment hundreds of
women who were too hungry to respect the law threw themselves upon
him, smothering him with their fists and their dresses. They kicked the
dying man to death. Then they dragged him into the cellar and cut off
his head with a kitchen knife. Behind its doors, the Convention had no
notion of what was going on.

Boissy d'Anglas ascended to the chairman's seat. He opened the session
and was arranging his notes when, to his amazement, he saw Deputy
Féraud, pale and with lifeless eyes, looking in through the courtyard window. He looked closer, and realized that Féraud's head was stuck upon
a pike and the blood was still trickling slowly downward. With incredible
composure, Chairman Boissy d'Anglas raised his right hand in greeting,
saluted the head of the murdered man, and calmly went on with the
meeting. Thus he forestalled a panic among the members of the Convention and prevented the deputies from fleeing—for had a door been
opened, the dangerous mob of women would have poured into the hall.
Precious minutes were saved, for soon a regiment of soldiers arrived and
drove away the rebellious women. They were only housewives and cooks
who wanted to hear no more of the war, but they possessed a great and
terrible power because they were wives and mothers.

Boissy d'Anglas saved Paris from a bread revolt which, in the midst of the war, might have meant the end of the Revolution. This scene occurred at the climax of the struggle. The tremendous exertions of the united nation began to drive the enemy from the borders. The Austrians were beaten. From Holland and Switzerland came signs that the people of these lands were preparing to help the revolutionists. True, France saw no bread until peace came. The Revolution had not been able to produce it, and the war made it impossible to distribute it. It was not until the period of the Directory, from 1796 on, that the soldiers were furloughed; they returned to the fields which now no longer belonged to landowners but to themselves and their families, and they began to till these fields.

Such was the role of bread in the French Revolution. Bread was a great actor; it was dressed in tricolors and enthroned on the stage by all the successive radical parties. It played out scenes of pathos, blood, and tragedy, and had a somewhat comic denouement. For at the end of the Revolution wheat forced all other grains to emigrate from France. This was done in the name of *égalité*. In his book on the rivalry of grains Jasny writes:

Earlier, white wheat bread was the bread of the rich; the Revolution made it the bread of everybody. Moving east, wheat bread expelled rye bread from Belgium also. Almost all the rye grown in the Netherlands is used as feed. A further step, and western Germany was invaded. Coming from the south, wheat entirely conquered Switzerland and occupied a stronghold in southern Germany.

Alongside the battles of men, which fertilized the fields with hecatombs of dead, continued the rivalry of the grains. The conquered or neutral nations worshipfully took over the victor's grain. In 1792, when Goethe participated in the "Campaign in France" on the side of the Prussian troops, he correctly observed that the border between Germany and France was a rye-wheat frontier. The difference amused him; but yesterday he had found in the town "black bread and white girls"—while on the following day, on the French side (that is, on old Roman soil), "the girls are dark, but the bread is white."

Ten years afterward Goethe would have found different fields in western Germany. For in the times of Napoleon, the modern Roman Emperor, only wheat was cultivated.

BREAD IN NAPOLEON'S DEFEAT

Bread is an army's greatest ally: the soldier marches no farther
than his stomach.

RUSSIAN PROVERB

§ 100

THE FIVE YEARS of peace between 1800 and 1805 at last permitted the
French people to return to their fields, and all believed that it would be
forever. France had won the war and would win the peace by cultivating
her gardens. Moreover, the Empire had plenty of money to buy what it
needed. If the crops of France were insufficient, there was always the
inexhaustible sea of grain in Russia. Ukrainian grain traveled up the
Danube through Austria to Strasbourg to feed the French. Or North
Russian grain was shipped from Danzig to Le Havre.

Where had France obtained the money for such transactions? It came
not only from the treasures that the armies of the Republic had seized
in Holland, on the Rhine, in Austria and Venice, but from a new source
of national wealth—industry.

All his life Napoleon believed in the power of industry as fervently as
he did not believe in agriculture. There is no doubt that he was informed
about the theories of the physiocrats concerning land and wealth, but he
took no stock in them. The people had to have bread, voilà; but over and
beyond that the emperor found the soil highly boring. The gods he worshiped were named activité and vitesse. The soil, to be sure, was active,
but it worked too slowly and had too little esprit. Esprit dwelt in machines, which the emperor admired without restraint. He extended an
open purse to inventors, to those who could improve the basic industrial
processes. As early in his reign as 1801 he instituted an industrial exhibition in Paris and supervised every detail with his own eyes. In the new
century, he felt, war and peace would depend entirely upon industry.
What poor idiots Robespierre and the other members of the Convention
had been! In their hopeless love for agriculture (hopeless because they
still had no bread) they marched in parades behind symbolic oxcarts.
How absurd! Bread ought to be grown quietly, or, if it were not grown,
to be bought abroad; trade treaties would see to it that it was obtained
cheaply and placed punctually on the market.

Agriculture did not interest Napoleon. When war flared up anew, he
was concerned with only one problem outside of military questions: how
to replace English industrial products by French products. The problem

of finding substitutes in war industries as well as in food became a passion with him. There must be substitutes for the cloth, spices, and dyes that English ships had formerly brought from India. "Our world is continually changing," he exclaimed before the Paris Chamber of Commerce in 1806:

In former days, if we desired to be rich, we had to own colonies, to establish ourselves in India and the Antilles, in Central America, in San Domingo. These times are over and done with. Today we must become manufacturers, must be able to provide for ourselves what we used to get from elsewhere. We must, let me insist, provide our own indigo, rice, and sugar. Manufacturing industry is at least as valuable as commerce used to be. While I am trying to gain the command of the seas, the industries of France will be developed or will be created.

Here the contrast Napoleon makes is that between industry and commerce. Of another contrast—between agriculture and industry—he says nothing, for he had forgotten it. Simple conceptions were of little interest to him. The emperor put millions of francs into the chemical industry, into the metallurgic and textile industries. Here he could see real profit. His mathematical, technical mind could envisage his money increasing in the chemist's retort; he could see the threads speeding across the loom; and the sum total amounted to an economic weapon against his implacable English foes.

The earth, to be sure, was permitted to play its part in industry, for the emperor one day decided upon a new measure against England: cotton would grow in France! Here the aid of the soil was, alas, imperative; and besides, dyestuffs were needed, and only the soil could grow dye plants. The emperor began to be interested in gardens. Why should the French apothecaries rely on Indian medicinal herbs? They must be raised in France! This growing interest in cultivation led the emperor to old Parmentier, who was still bemoaning his lost potato farms. Napoleon pricked up his ears. Here was an inventive man. He showed favor to Parmentier—as he showed favor to all inventors—and placed him in a high civil position, empowering him to sow potatoes all over France. None dared to laugh at Parmentier now—and indeed the monomania of the old army apothecary was to save the lives of millions.

The emperor was a man of wide interests, especially where complexities were in play. A device that was double-edged instantly appealed to him. Thus it was suggested that he would do well to plant nut trees on all the roads of France. He did so, and thereby established three things: shade for travelers, a supply of nuts, and, most important of all, the best and hardest wood for the stocks of French infantry rifles.

Matters of extreme simplicity, however, did not endear themselves to the emperor. As his carriage passed swiftly over the shaded highways of

France, he might easily have seen that all was not well with the bordering
fields. For years the peasants had worn uniform and fought heroically as
grenadiers in Spain, Prussia, and Austria. Did the emperor think that
grain was as available as air? Slowly shortages began to appear once
more. And when Alexander I., the Russian Emperor, lined up with
Napoleon's enemies, the dream of cheap grain for France faded. And
Napoleon's star faded likewise. There is a heavy, impotent feeling in the
words that Napoleon sent to his Minister shortly before the army set out
for Russia:

*"Je veux que le peuple ait du pain, qu'il en ait beaucoup, du bon
et du bon marché. . . . Lorsque je serai loin de France, n'oubliez pas,
Monsieur le Ministre, que le premier soin du pouvoir doit être d'assurer
constamment la tranquilité publique et que les subsistances sont le prin-
cipale mobile de cette tranquilité* [I desire the people to have bread, sufficient bread and good, cheap bread. . . . While I am away from France
do not forget, Mr. Minister, that the first care of the government must
be to assure public tranquillity, and food is the chief means of securing
this tranquillity]."

But what could the poor Minister do? The farmers had been con-
scripted; the last harvest had been very poor; and eastern Europe was
closed to the French. The emperor's words sound disconsolate; the tone
is almost that of a last testament. Did he know, as he wrote, how empty
were the granaries of France? While Napoleon's vast army rolled through
Poland to Russia, famine knocked on the door back home.

§ 101

The French budget for the year 1812 showed that the textile industry
provided 45.7 per cent of the national income—almost one half. Agrarian
production accounted for only 13.7 per cent—no more than about a
seventh. The net value of all agricultural products was, in round numbers, some 1,400 millions of francs; the income from mines was nearly
twice this sum. And we must realize that agricultural produce included
everything that grew from the soil or had some connection with it, such
as wine, vegetables, tobacco, cattle, hides—not merely grain.

It is obvious that Napoleonic France was no agrarian country. France
was far from having attained autarchy. Rather, we may say that France
lived upon the rest of Europe—even such poorly cultivated countries as
Germany and Italy contributed grain to France.

All the grain France could assemble followed the army eastward.
Wagon train after wagon train wound down the roads that led to Russia. There was wheat and rye for the soldiers, and mountains of oats for
the horses. The soldier's bread was all-important; before the mouths of

the cannon spat fire at dawn, the bakers' ovens had glowed through the night. Napoleon went into battle not only with ample munitions, but with more-than-ample provisions; the *sappeurs blancs*—the flour engineers— of the field bakeries were as much responsible for his victories as the bullet molders and the shell makers.

Napoleon distrusted all quartermasters. In his youth he had found that the quartermasters stole bread. And the knowledge he had gained as a lieutenant, he applied when he became emperor. Henri Beyle (Stendhal) recounts that Napoleon was fanatically suspicious of all men who delivered or administered grain or flour. Stendhal says he would have liked nothing better than to keep personal watch over all the storehouses and ovens, to see that nothing was stolen.

Soldiers' bread was good, and the French soldiers' bread was better than that of any other army. It did not smell sour, like the Prussians', nor was it prepared with questionable condiments, like the Austrians', to cover up the stale taste of flour that had been too long in storage. Moreover, it was remarkably white; firm and porous inside and with a thin, elastic crust. Not in vain had Malisset taught the French to grind their flour three times. Gone were the times when Parmentier, with powdered pigtail and three-cornered army hat, had written his memorials and complained that the French soldier was eating bran rather than bread. Now that soldier ate better bread than any other: two parts wheat, one part rye, from which 20 per cent of the bran content had been extracted. The soldiers' bread would indeed have been a bread for gourmets had not the hasty baking made for too large a content of water. But the water content of the Russian soldier's bread was even greater; every Russian soldier had for daily ration a bread that weighed three and a half pounds—enough to make any ordinary man ill. That bread had the color and taste of pig iron.

Even in the field the French proved themselves born bakers. And in addition to their excellent bread, the French had biscuits, the twice-baked *panes biscocti* or hardtack, a French invention of the Middle Ages which had supported many a sailor's life.

The Neapolitan auxiliary cavalry, on the other hand, ate macaroni; King Murat had seen to that. It was a strange sight to see the cavalrymen before battle, sitting upon their horses and dangling the hot strings of dough into their open mouths.

As early as 1807—five years before the defeat—the emperor had sighed, "If I have bread, it will be child's play to defeat Russia." He saw the problem clearly. But when the time came to strike, he made a strange mistake. He moved so fast that cavalry and wagon train were separated. "Some army corps never saw their bread wagons again," wrote Baron von Richthofen. But this was only the more minor mistake. Napoleon had taken a great mass of provisions and it lasted until late fall. But if the emperor had thought that each empty wagon would be filled of itself in the broad grainfields of Russia, he was sadly mistaken. During their retreat in September and October the Russians took with them every ripe ear of grain. The land through which the French marched resem-

ENGLISH ARMY BAKERY (1852)

bled a desert. And when Moscow was burned and the emperor ordered the strategic retreat to Poland, there began the greatest bread disaster in the history of warfare.

It was not so much the cold as the lack of bread that caused the dissolution of the army. At first the soldiers ate horseflesh and drank the hot blood. This was wisest, for since the oats were gone, the horses could not, in any case, have lived long. But it took not two weeks but three months before the French Army made its way through snow, ice, and polar nights to inhabited regions. The emperor had returned swiftly and unharmed by sled; but the hundreds of thousands who were without horses, wagons, blankets, or furs (among them many men from southern Italy who had never seen snow), froze on the terrible road. Now ahead, now behind them, Cossacks rose up, struck with their long lances, and were gone before the French could shoot.

Corporal Bourgogne, in his memoirs of the great retreat, described it as a bread disaster. When he had gone without bread for the fiftieth day, he thought he would go mad. Somewhere he and his comrades found whisky, but Bourgogne could not drink it because his throat was frozen shut. A few days later they found bread in a hut; they dropped their rifles into the snow and fell upon the food with the savagery of wild animals. Several of his comrades choked to death over too large bites. Fortunately for Bourgogne, his lips were so frostbitten that he could scarcely open his mouth. . . . When they reached Poland, the odor of fresh, warm bread made the French soldiers frantic. With their swords they scraped flour, or what they thought was flour, from the cracks in the floors of rooms. They gave the shocked inhabitants five francs for a piece of bread, and killed one another for the morsel. An entire French company fought over three baked potatoes no larger than walnuts.

Stunned with horror, the population of Prussia gazed at the hollow-eyed men who returned; unable to speak, the soldiers made mute gestures toward their mouths. Polish peasant women had provided the ragged French with skirts and women's hats. Wretched specters, terrible and ridiculous at once, the defeated men plodded on. As Gustav Freytag recounts in his *Scenes of Germany's Past,* the Prussian people considered the soldiers' fate a punishment upon their horrid bread sins. The people said that "their hunger cannot be stilled nor can the cold be driven from their bodies."

When they were brought into a warm room, they thrust their way close to the hot stove as though they wished to creep into it. In vain the housewives tried to keep them away from the dangerous heat. Greedily they consumed the dry bread. Some refused to stop eating—and died from it. Until after the Battle of Leipzig the belief persisted that they had been cursed by Heaven with eternal hunger. Even at that battle prisoners roasted pieces of dead horses, although this was not necessary, for they were given regular food. The burghers maintained that this insane hunger was inflicted by God. Once, it was said, the soldiers had thrown fine sheaves of wheat on their campfires and had hollowed out good breads, despoiled them and rolled them on the ground. For this they were now condemned to find no human food that would sate their hunger.

Thus ended an empire that had depended more upon fame and conquest than upon the gifts of its own soil. When Napoleon returned, he found a famine-stricken France. He recalled that Benjamin Thompson, a scientist who had developed the theory of food calories, had devised a poor-man's soup of bread fragments, vegetables, and bones. Napoleon ordered that two million plates of this soup should be distributed daily

in France to the poor. This was done for five months (until the harvest
of 1813). For this purpose he spent twenty million francs. When the
English learned of it, they knew that the end was near. "The French
now swallow dirt and bones." The English themselves had bread. It
became apparent that he who had bread had victory.

§ 102

What had Napoleon actually accomplished by way of promoting bread
among the Europeans? He had reduced the number of French bread
eaters by two million dead and those of his allies and enemies by another
six million. Moreover, he had fertilized the fields of the Continent with
corpses. . . . That is the most a history of bread can say for him. How
far more significant was an invention made nine years after his death
by several unknown men: the invention of the roller mill.

One night in the year 1830, in Zurich, Switzerland, a man who was
interested in the construction of mills stood before a mirror. He was holding a candle in his hand and studying with pained concern the image of
his mouth. He was an educated man, and the remark of the Greek Posi-
donius had occurred to him: "The first miller used his teeth for millstones. Man naturally derived the idea of grinding grain from the action
of the teeth in chewing food." The engineer laughed heartily as he recalled this mot.

The following day, when he went to see his dentist, he remarked that
the mouth was an ingenious machine. The dentist sighed and said darkly,
"I don't find it too ingenious. In particular the institution of the teeth is
practically worthless. In a few thousand years man will probably have no
teeth left. The material they are made of is not strong enough. Even today
the teeth have to be buttressed and supplemented by metal."

"Why is that?" the engineer asked with more than scientific interest.

"Bread is responsible," the dentist replied. "Since men began eating
the fruit of grains, their teeth have been getting steadily worse. It began
with the Egyptians. . . ."

The engineer was left steeped in thought. It had suddenly occurred to
him that for thousands of years the problems of milling had remained
unaltered. All millers complained about their millstones. They were too
soft, they had to be changed too often. For a long time the millers had
searched for a miracle stone that would be harder than all other stones;
and for a time the French thought they had found it in the flint quarries
of La Ferté-sous-Jouarre. But the tough wheat ruined even those stones
after a few years. Could not some substitute be made, as the dentist had
suggested? God had thought of no better device than the faulty teeth, but
that was no reason for any bright engineer to draw back. . . . The whole

difficulty with the mill and the mouth lay in the fact that they were made to *break up*, to crumble the food. This failed with grains; grains remained hard and in the end broke up both millstones and teeth. The mill, the engineer reflected, ought to have its teeth extracted. But suppose that the grain were *crushed* instead of crumbled? Compressed until it swelled and burst? That ought to be possible with iron rollers, the engineer mused; rollers that turned in counter-motion hundreds of times a minute. Naturally, they would have to be motivated by steam power, like the mills of Watt and Evans. The engineer devoted some time to drawings of these rollers.

But money was necessary to build such a machine. It happened at the time that Switzerland had money. Switzerland had emerged from Napoleon's wars very well; since 1800 no enemies had crossed the borders of the Republic. The Swiss cities were almost as much interested in technical innovations as the English. Hence, the engineer succeeded in finding a group of businessmen who advanced several hundred thousand francs (25,000 English pounds) for the construction of a roller mill. Doubtless the backers would not have been so ready with their money had not the engineer added that he used to own three roller mills in Warsaw years before. He told a great many tales about Warsaw—especially how the Russians, because they hated to see Poland prosper, had burned down his mills. Finally he showed the financiers printed plans of the construction of the roller mill and figures that proved how much labor was saved and how much greater was the capacity of the rollers compared to millstones. It was a long way from Zurich to Warsaw, and the Russian censorship made correspondence difficult. No one questioned his story, and the mill was built. It was a fabulous structure, so large that all the grain grown in Switzerland could have been poured into it. There were five stories; rollers were placed on each floor, commencing with "breaks" on the fifth and ending with finishing rollers on the first.

But to the general consternation the mill ran slower than ordinary mills; it produced less flour and, of course, at far greater cost than the old stone mills. There was a fierce scene between the engineer and the backers, who saw their money vanishing; they accused the inventor of never having owned such mills at all. Since he could not answer this charge, he discreetly vanished from the scene. He disappeared so completely that the world has never learned any more about the inventor of the roller mill. All we know is that his name, properly enough, was Mueller (Miller); even his first name is unknown. . . .

The unhappy capitalists called in Jacob Sulzberger, an engineer who was hardly an expert on mills. But he succeeded in making the mill operate. He undertook the complete reconstruction of the roller plant, placing two pairs of iron rollers in one frame, one above the other, and driving each set separately. The rollers were placed on the first floor, and only the lighter machinery went into the upper stories. The mill was tried, and worked splendidly. The financiers made money and sold models of the mill abroad.

The Sulzberger mills became famous. Clearly, they belonged in the plains, where grain grew in great quantities. Mountainous Switzerland was too small to exploit fully such machines. Almost at once Hungary (a land where *vaczi*, wheat, had long been all-important) saw its opportunity. Thanks to the Swiss invention, the milling industry in Hungary became the most important on the Continent and Hungarian flour became an extremely desirable article of export.

For thousands of years men had been crazy about white flour. Archestratus, who in the fourth century B.C. wrote a book about cooking, relates that on the island of Lesbos the flour was so white that the Greek gods sent Hermes to buy some for them. Very white flour is flour that has been only too thoroughly ground and sifted, and it is well known today that it is not nourishing. But it pleases the eye and flatters the sense of aristocracy. Because of this, Hungary's largest miller, Count Stephen Széchenyi (1791–1860), conquered the world market. Thanks to its white flour, Hungary also ruled neighboring Austria for a long time: that is, the smaller, agrarian half of the Habsburg Dual Monarchy dominated the larger. And Vienna was the first great customer for the white Hungarian flour, which was so much finer ground and sifted than the French or English flour. Vienna became Europe's leading city for bakery products; the "imperial roll" was as famous as the music of Johann Strauss.

At the Vienna World's Fair of 1873 Americans tasted these products of the Viennese baker's art for the first time. They inquired about the flour. This was the beginning of the end for the triumphant leadership of Hungarian mills. The plains of Minnesota were far more extensive than those of Hungary. In 1879 Washburn, the governor of the state, sent for Hungarian engineers, and roller mills were erected all over Minnesota. The tenacious breed of Scandinavian Americans took the matter in hand and began the writing of that chapter which should be entitled, "Flour and Economic Power."

LINCOLN: BREAD WAS GREATER THAN COTTON

§ 103

BREAD SPELLS VICTORY. These words apply even more pointedly to the Civil War than to Napoleon's defeat. Because the North had bread, and because the South could not eat cotton, the Civil War produced a United Nation.

Countless studies have been made of the causes of the war. One of the chief causes, as we know, was that slavery was outmoded. In Europe serfdom had collapsed utterly; in France on that August night of 1789, in Prussia by the October Edict of 1807, which freed the peasantry and abolished all feudal burdens. Austria, Italy, and all the small countries of the Continent followed. Even in Russia the peasant was free; on February 19, 1861, by a stroke of the pen, Czar Alexander II had freed twenty-three million muzhiks.

But in America, which called itself the "land of progress," Roman *latifundia·* and agricultural slavery still persisted. The laborers were Negroes who had been kidnaped in Africa because they worked better than Indians or whites. The struggle of the Abolitionists was less a struggle for the liberation of the Negroes as a race than for the abolition of slavery as an outmoded economic form. It is significant that the movement did not start among the Negroes themselves. There had been, it is true, revolts. In 1789, the year of the French Revolution, the Negro farm workers on the island of San Domingo had revolted. Formerly slaves of the French king, they, too, now wished to be free citizens. Parisian fashion, they transformed a palm tree into a tree of liberty, placed the Phrygian cap upon it, grouped cannon around it, and shot down all the whites in sight. But not because the whites were of another race; rather, because they were plantation owners. Though it took the French long to put down the revolt, this Negro uprising and the new conception of human rights implicit in it remained localized. It is doubtful whether the Negroes of the American mainland—the Negroes of Louisiana, for example—ever heard of the rebellion.

Abolition began among the whites. The states of the North, where no Negro workers were needed, protested against the persistence in the South of an economic form that the rest of the world had abandoned fifty years before. To be sure, no one went so far as to assert that slavery was wholly impractical. And for years after the war the South complained of the loss of its cheap labor.

Some historians maintain that the war was between two equally strong but differing economic systems: the system of the free industrial laborers against the system of enslaved plantation workers. Other historians postulate that the war was inevitable because every nation that extends over many degrees of latitude must one day decide whether it is to be ruled from the north or the south. France decided this when the brain center of the country became Paris rather than Marseilles or Bordeaux. Similarly, Germany made this decision when she chose Berlin for her capital; and Russia when Moscow and Leningrad became the nerve centers of the Empire. These historians refer to a "law of latitudes" which prohibits the establishment of the vital cities too far south. This anthropologic and geographic process, this question of whether the North or the South was to rule, had to be decided in the United States as it had been decided in the rest of the world.

When the states of Mississippi, Florida, Alabama, Texas, the Carolinas, and Virginia sought to solve this question by freeing themselves of the "unendurable patronage of the North," and when the North refused to let them secede, the issue of it all was apparently still in the hands of Fortune. But today we know that the issue was sealed, that the side that possessed bread had victory preordained for it.

§ 104

The South was rich; it was alluring and beautiful; and it had friends all over the world. Even in the Northern states it had friends. Were not the Americans of the South another race, after all? Should one not let them go? Horace Greeley, editor of the New York *Tribune,* wrote shortly before the war:

If the cotton states shall decide that they can do better outside of the Union than in it, we insist on letting them go in peace. . . . We hope never to live in a republic whereof one section is pinned to the residue by bayonets.

The people of the South, "fighting for their liberties, their altars, their firesides—8,000,000 people armed in a holy cause," seemed to themselves invincible. How could they be beaten? A comparison of the two wrestlers who were about to engage each other in a struggle to the death seemed to show all the advantages on the side of the South. Two thirds of the total exports of the United States consisted of Southern cotton—one hundred and twenty-five million of a total of one hundred and ninety-seven million dollars in value. True, only 3 per cent of this cotton was fabricated in the South—for the South was not industrial. But this very fact won the South sympathy abroad, for England and France had to have clothes, and the raw cotton from the South kept the factories of Europe going. The plantation owners of the South knew this; they knew how important they were for the world. It did not occur to them how difficult a matter it would be for cotton to see them through the crisis. They imagined that warfare would not interfere with the loading of their cotton on ships and exporting it. But Northern gunboats blockaded the long coast line of the South, sending cotton ships down in flames or taking the cargoes for themselves.

In Atlanta, Charleston, and New Orleans some foresighted men began to realize that cotton—whether sold or not sold—could not be eaten. Wise men had known this early in the war, and issued warnings. "Limit the cultivation of cotton," the Mobile *Advertiser* had urged in January 1862. "Produce wool, wheat, vegetables, and other foods!" And a month later the Savannah *Republican* wrote: "How foolish it is for our planters in Georgia to go on planting cotton. They will starve our army and drive it from the field. Plant corn, plant corn!"

Although the military situation was not at all bad, by the end of 1862 the Southern states were beginning to worry about losing the war. Flour already cost twenty-five dollars a barrel in Richmond. Rice had been planted, but it was difficult to harvest it because enemy gunboats covered the swampy lowlands. Speculators began to practice shameless usury with the small amount of grain that had been cultivated inland (where every field bearing something other than tobacco or cotton was looked upon with greedy eyes), or that had been smuggled in from abroad. The farmers, looking for higher prices, held back their meager crops, so that early in 1863 the Secretary of War advised President Jefferson Davis to confiscate all wheat. Properly cultivated, the South could have fed the world. But now something hitherto unimaginable took place in the South: famine penetrated even to the white landowners. The aristocratic planters began to eat more poorly than their slaves had ever eaten. Grain bins were empty; living conditions fell from month to month, until at last the entire country witnessed scenes of horror like those in a besieged city. Everywhere. stores were plundered; women and children collapsed from hunger in the. open streets. Wheat, corn, and hay had to be requisitioned and taken by force for the Army; disease broke out; transportation broke down; the resistance dissolved. The bearded Confederate soldiers, pale, starving, and unafraid, who fired on Sherman's men, knew that they were defending the richest lands on the Continent. But those lands were now hollow and empty. In September flour cost thirty-five dollars a barrel, in October forty-five dollars, in November seventy dollars, in December one hundred and ten dollars. After that it could not be bought at any price. "How are we to survive this war?" wrote the Savannah *Republican*. "Flour costs one hundred and twenty dollars a barrel and not a bushel of corn or groats can be bought in our city. . . ."

And the North overcame the brave soldiers of the South who were fighting for their ideals under able leaders. Victory fell to Lincoln because no one in the North went hungry; neither in the towns, the country, nor—above all—in the Army. The lessons of the Revolutionary War had been well learned; the soldiers were given the best bread. In the quartermasters' headquarters in Alexandria there were experts on baking acquainted with the works of the French chemists of Napoleon's day, especially those of old Parmentier. The dough was kneaded more carefully; the ingredients were selected with deliberation; and the bread was baked more slowly.

"Those are weapons," a woman said to her grandchild, who was gazing wide-eyed at the dozens of similar wagons and had wondered what they contained. When a driver threw back the canvas the woman and child saw gleaming dark breads weighing many pounds. "Do the cannon eat those?" the child asked dubiously. "No, but the men do," the soldier-baker replied with a grim laugh. He explained that the enemy did not have this kind of ammunition. "Those are Lincoln's cannon balls. My father and my brothers dug them out of the earth and I've baked them in the oven."

Agriculture in the North did not stand still during the war; it grew. The states of Ohio, Illinois, Indiana, Iowa, and Wisconsin almost doubled their production. The Northern leaders knew what this meant and thanked Providence for the bumper crops. Shortly before the final victory the New York *Independent* wrote (September 8, 1864):

> The greatest misfortune that could have struck our people at this time would have been a crop failure. We would never have recovered from it; the preservation of the Union, our existence as a nation, might have been wrecked by it. . . . Whatever the war may hold in store for us, *our granaries are filled!*

§ 105

How was this possible? How could the North increase its grain production when the greater part of the farmers were in uniform, battling against the South?

First of all there were the women—the women who went out into the fields to replace their absent men. Without difficulty the women of the North returned to a way of life which had been natural to them in colonial times. . . . Then there were the immigrants from Europe. The war did not frighten away these immigrants. Emigration from Europe was a necessity. And the alien who did not want to meddle in the affairs of North and South—as none did—could easily keep clear of the war. He needed only to remain in the North—in Illinois, say—and till the soil. The cheapness of land was a great attraction, for the Washington Government was virtually giving land away. The Homestead Law made it possible for settlers to establish farms at almost no cost for the land. While in the South people were starving to death, in the North Lincoln saw to it that two and a half million acres of land were given to immigrants. This meant twenty thousand new farms of about a hundred and sixty acres each, and an increase in the population of nearly one hundred thousand persons.

Above all, the railroads worked for the cause of the victorious North. The Mississippi, which until the war had been the great highway between West and South, was closed by the war. The railroads now brought the products of the West to the East; the South received nothing. Previously, New Orleans had received ten million bushels of grain and flour annually from the Northwest; now New Orleans went hungry because all the grain was sent to the Northeast. Chicago became the great transit point and terminal. The war made Chicago rich and great. During every year of the war the city shipped twenty million bushels of wheat and twenty-five million bushels of corn. And all of it at prices that the poorest could afford. No one in the North was hungry.

The soldiers were so well supplied that they had the luxury of complaining about the monotony of their diet. Dr. C. B. Johnson, writing in 1917 his memoirs of the Civil War, said: "Our food was sometimes monotonous. For breakfast, bacon, bakers' bread, and coffee; for dinner, coffee, bacon, and bread; for supper, bread, coffee, and bacon." The soldier of the South would have given his shirt for such a daily menu.

The Southern planters were to experience still another disappointment. In the second phase of the war they lost all the sympathy they had enjoyed among their French and English friends. This was hard to understand, for were they not fighting to provide the entire world with cotton? They were, but they had not reckoned on a factor that proved politically decisive. In a choice between clothing and food, the more vital need will always win out. The South had only cotton to sell; the North had bread. Europe needed America's bread. Consequently, Europe had to turn its sympathies first hesitantly, then vigorously, to the cause of the North.

"On the one side," N. S. B. Gras summarizes, "were cotton, the Southern slave system, and the cotton-manufacturing interests of England. On the other side were wheat, the free-labor system of the North, and the humanitarian cotton spinners of England, who chose to oppose slavery even at the cost of their daily bread. . . . England needed American wheat even more than American cotton. The cotton kept the factories going, but the wheat kept body and soul together. Accordingly, the English Government had to throw over its preference in favor of the South. It gave up the idea of recognizing the Confederacy, because the wheat of the North was more vital than the cotton of the South. The large crop of the North was a material bribe to England to throw its influence into the scale on behalf of human liberty."

But neither women's labor, the immigration from Europe, nor the attitude of the railroads could have effected so enormous an increase in Northern production. Another factor was necessary, one that both North and South had been wont to neglect. This was the *mechanization of agriculture*. To be sure, the side that planted bread, not cotton, was bound to win the war. But the war could not be won with those who planted bread remaining on their farms instead of taking up arms. What ultimately decided the war and the fate of America for the remainder of the century were labor-saving machines that replaced the farmer who left for the front.

We have already seen that the land was generally excluded from the technical progress of the towns. Inventions were made for industry. The inventors themselves were townsmen. The needs of industrialists and workers determined the things invented. To simplify, facilitate, and rationalize industrial work—this is what the engineer felt to be his mission. He was married to the factory—never to the field. Most engineers knew nothing of agriculture, had never seen an animal drawing the plow or a mower plying his scythe.

Napoleon never happened to reflect that one day it might be in the interest of the state to mechanize agriculture. Lincoln, Stanton, and their men did chance upon the thought. This was both their personal achievement and the heritage of their American blood. They were intellectual descendants of Thomas Jefferson, the Jefferson who said that America would be a free land of the happiest, best, and most modern farmers in the world—or it would not be an independent land at all.

Nevertheless, it was difficult for these makers of America to bring the machine to the land. The farmers did not want it. Accustomed for thousands of years to doing their work quietly in rain and sun, happy that in America they were at last their own masters, the farmers at first shrugged their shoulders. What good could come to them from the city, from engineers? But the farmers were ultimately not asked. When, in the midst of the war, it became necessary to replace the loss of agricultural labor and to save five years of harvests for the nation, the machine appeared of itself.

McCORMICK: THE MACHINE THAT CONQUERS THE FIELDS

> Behind the pigs comes Jonathan with his all-conquering ploughshare,—glory to him too! Oh, if we were not a set of Cant-ridden blockheads, there is no myth of Athene or Herakles equal to this fact;—which I suppose will find its real "Poets" some day or other; when once the Greek, Semitic, and multifarious other cobwebs are swept away a little! Well, we must wait.
>
> CARLYLE TO EMERSON

§ 106

IN APRIL 1836 Edgar Allan Poe published his essay called "Maelzel's Chess Player." This chess player was an automaton that had been invented by a Hungarian baron in the eighteenth century and later acquired by Herr Maelzel. Poe had seen the instrument in America.

The apparatus was the tin figure of a Turk who sat on a maple-wood box and played chess with all comers. Every time the figure made his move, the grinding of machine parts and the humming of gears were heard. Maelzel willingly showed the inside of the apparatus, which contained countless gears and wheels. It seemed obvious that no human being, not even a child, could have concealed himself inside. When he was asked, "Does the automaton act as a pure machine or not?" Maelzel was wont to reply, "I cannot discuss that." For seventy years his fame rested upon this equivocal answer. Some went to see his automaton to discover how far mechanics had progressed; others went with the attitude of the detective, convinced that there was a man hidden in the box. Poe was one of the latter.

Interest in automatons was rife in the eighteenth century. The French encyclopedists had denied the existence of the soul; one of them, La Mettrie in his *L'homme Machine,* claimed to have proved that life was a mechanism. The thorn in the side of all his contemporaries was that they believed this, but were unwilling to admit it. The vacillation between materialism and sentiment produced such playthings as Maelzel's chess player and a whole romantic literature on the life of automatons. If man were only an automaton, perhaps the automaton was only a kind of man. The great German storyteller, E. T. W. Hoffmann, believed that an automaton was capable of developing occult powers. One German critic has called him the first modern man to experience the fear of the machine.

Such toys scarcely fitted into the pattern of the nineteenth century. The Virginian farmer, Robert McCormick, seemed distinctly old-fashioned when he spent the long winter nights alternating between his hobby of astronomy and another hobby: constructing an automaton like Maelzel's chess player, but one that would do useful work. His automaton was to be a man of iron and wood which would bend and straighten up, swing forward and back, employing a scythe to cut and rake grain. All the neighbors laughed at poor McCormick, "touched in the head." What was the sense of it? Why should an able-bodied farmer have an automaton around to take away his work? It would only give him more time for brooding.

This godless automaton failed completely. For fifteen years Robert McCormick tormented himself with his "mechanical reaper," until in 1831 he at last abandoned the project. But McCormick's twenty-two-year-old son was quite another man. He was not a hobbyist, like his father, but a practical engineer. He had been born not in the eighteenth but in the nineteenth century. And he saw no point in imitating a man, in constructing a robot of metal and wood that would either amuse or frighten all who saw it. He was interested solely in building a machine that would solve an economic problem, for it was an economic problem to reap fields of grain without muscular effort, with speed and with fewer hands. The farmers of the neighborhood were wrong not to see that. But if the machine looked like a wagon rather than like an artificial man, perhaps they would understand it. Thus young Cyrus McCormick reasoned—and his reasoning proved correct.

Cyrus McCormick did not know that in 1825 a Scotch clergyman named Patrick Bell had had similar thoughts. Bell had made a "shearing wagon" which, when pulled by horses, laid the sheaves to one side after cutting them. It seemed beautifully simple; one man could do the work of dozens of reapers. How was it possible that for thousands of years no one had ever thought of it? . . .

As a matter of fact, it had been thought of before. The Persians must have had similar machines. For the "sickle wagons" with which Darius cut into Alexander the Great's army could have been nothing but reaping machines which some army engineer had converted into war equipment. And according to Pliny the Gauls also had a kind of harvester: an ox drew a two-wheeled cart through the field, to one side of which a well-sharpened knife was attached. A man walked alongside and knocked the stalks into the knife with a stick; the ears were cut off and fell into the cart; the stalks remained standing as forage for the cattle. . . . This machine was destined to be quickly "forgotten." We do not know why. Perhaps the people did not like caring for the simple machine. Perhaps the cart was too expensive. Or—this is the most likely reason—it offended against certain religious prescriptions that were attached to harvesting. In any case, it was not adopted.

Bell's shearing wagon was also not adopted. When the English reapers saw that they would be robbed of their earnings because a half-grown boy with a team of horses could reap more in a few days than all of them with their sickles and sweat, they smashed the machine and threatened the inventor.

Cyrus McCormick was more fortunate. When he went out with his experimental machine, drawn by four horses, the first trial failed because of the irregularity of the field. Half-mown wheat was left behind. A neighbor who had a level field invited him to try the machine on his land. Here McCormick's reaper harvested six acres in a day—six times as much as a man could do by hand. This fact convinced those who saw it of the value of the reaper—and the successful reaper became the source of America's agricultural prosperity in the nineteenth century.

§ 107

"It is one of the most baffling mysteries of history," says Herbert Casson, "that agriculture—the first industry to be learned—was the last one to be developed. For thousands of years the wise men of the world absolutely ignored the problems of the farm. A farmer remained either a serf or a tenant. He was a stolid drudge—'brother to the ox.' "

It is true that the Egyptians and Jews, the Greeks and the Romans, were vitally interested in bread. But the measures they took to obtain it were chiefly religious and political. If they forgot that engineering was also of great importance, it was not because they "despised" engineering; they made no technical progress for an entirely different reason.

The classic civilizations were part of an epoch which extended through the Middle Ages to the nineteenth century. This was the epoch of "technical slumber." This slumber resulted from the fact that in prehistoric times a few geniuses had already invented everything that seemed worthwhile to man. The man who invented the wagon, about eight thousand years before Christ, has no equal among any scientist of the present—nor of the future. The device of a rotating wheel to conquer space is incommensurable. And the men who invented the forging of iron, the art of weaving, and the potter's wheel, were the greatest of technicians. They were far greater than Edison, who worked only on the basis of pre-existing knowledge.

Compared to primitive times, the classic civilizations invented nothing. They merely took over their heritage. The necessary transition was effected by the religions, which made men willing to accept that inheritance by placing it under the protection of religious law. Religion decreased the distance which in primitive times had prevailed between the people and the inventive genius. Though the religions did not invent the plow, by blessing it they preserved it from the drunken forgetfulness and the destructive tendencies of mankind.

Since religion was thus alert to preserve technology, why did mankind fall into "technical slumber" when under the aegis of the great civilizing religions of the classic world? These religions were by no means hostile to technology. But the entire classic world believed that the time for inventions was *past*. It simply did not believe in "progress." The classic world was sufficient unto itself. Bread was obtained from the soil; the distribution of it was the concern of the government. The heavenly and earthly governments saw to it that men were fed or went hungry; engineers had no place, or a very small place, for there were such inventions as animal-powered and water-powered mills.

Few thinkers of the ancient world would have conceded that the question of bread rendered them unhappy—not even when they themselves felt hunger. Christ in particular fought against any bread pessimism. Although he lived in an age when technical progress was at a standstill, he believed that lack of bread was the last thing by which mankind would be destroyed. Even without sowing and reaping the birds of Heaven and the lilies of the field were nourished by the Heavenly Father. The real crisis in bread did not threaten until the barbarians laid waste to classic civilization and destroyed what tools existed, the plows and the mills. This was disaster indeed. For although religion had been able for thousands of years to protect the technical heritage of mankind, the priests of religion were unable to repair tools once they were destroyed. They blessed plows and mills that no longer existed, and so hopelessly compromised themselves.

The spirit of technical creativeness still slumbered. But when conditions grew worse, when religion began to be hated for its helplessness, men once more attempted technical improvements. And the awakening was not of one, but of all. After thousands of years of slumber, a frenzy of action began. Not once, but nine and ten times, in the most diverse places of the globe, the same instruments were invented; invented not even in the same decade, but in the same year. The technical slumber was over; and just as in past eras men had wondered that human beings had been blind to religious facts, so they now wondered how the realities of technology, so close at hand, could have waited so long to be developed.

§ 108

The reaper, too, was not uniquely invented by Cyrus McCormick. It was invented at the same time by a Yankee named Obed Hussey, who afterward amiably commented that it was astonishing "that it hasn't been made before." The colorful Hussey, an amateur mechanic whose hands possessed extraordinary skill, had been a sailor. His relations with farming were of the vaguest. In fact, he was drawing up plans for a candlepouring machine when a friend's conversation started him on the reaper. The reaper he constructed was a lineal descendant of Patrick Bell's shearing wagon; Hussey's cutting blade consisted of teeth that moved back and forth (like a haircutting machine). This idea had so many advantages that all future mowing and reaping machines were based upon it. . . .

No sooner had Hussey's reaper begun to rattle across the fields than McCormick initiated a suit over patent rights. He made a practice of branding everyone who dared to build a reaper as a common thief.

Who was first and whose was better? Already third and fourth parties were becoming involved. Manufacturers like John M. Manny of Rockford, Illinois, also built reapers. For years McCormick fought patent suits against his opponents. We would not today be interested (for one of them had to win) and the testimony of the experts would be moldering in the archives, had it not been for the fact that some very great men were among the lawyers. Thus one day an attorney named Abraham Lincoln received a check from the Manny firm for five hundred dollars—by far the largest fee he had ever seen. He was requested to defend the firm's right to build reapers. Lincoln was ardently interested in the case, for he himself had come from the land. "It sent his imagination," writes Carl Sandburg, "back to the day when he went to the fields and harvested grain with scythe and cradle, when he had formed calluses on the inside of his hands from holding the scythe handle. Since that time the reaper had come. . . ." Abraham Lincoln prepared to go to Cincinnati, where the litigation was to be decided. When he strolled into the courtroom in his customarily abstracted fashion, his clothes careless and awry, a fat manuscript in his pocket containing everything he had thought

OBED HUSSEY ON HIS REAPER

about machines, culture, and agriculture, he found another lawyer also representing the firm of Manny. The other lawyer was not pleased to see him. "Where did this long-armed baboon come from?" he was heard to say quite distinctly. (Later, in an effort at politeness, he said that he had compared Lincoln not to a baboon but to another animal: "I said that if that giraffe appeared in the case I would throw up my brief and leave.") To Lincoln himself he remarked, "Only one of us can talk." That one was not Lincoln, and the other lost the suit. This well-dressed and equable lawyer, who later became Secretary of War, was Edwin M. Stanton.

At first Hussey's reaper was far more popular than McCormick's. It was drawn from the front, with the cutter set off to one side. Mechanical fingers guided the stalks against the cutting parts, and the teeth cut the grain close to the ground. It fell upon a platform, where it was gathered together by the driver. Hussey's reaper might actually have won the race against McCormick's except for a peculiarity in the character of the inventor. He was like those inventors of the ancient world who imagined that once a thing had been discovered it could no longer be improved.

Hussey dismissed all the experience of the next twenty years and stuck stubbornly to his model. The pliant McCormick learned from mistakes; he and his brothers worked incessantly to improve the machine. In the end he won out because of a tenacity that sprang more from business than engineering talent. In 1847 he founded a factory in Chicago. Four years later he had already built and sold one thousand reapers; ten years later twenty-three thousand. In ten years the business earned him more than a quarter of a million dollars. His profits increased steadily.

"The reaper is for the North what the slave is for the South," Stanton observed at the beginning of the war. "It releases our young men to do battle for the Union, and at the same time keeps up the supply of the nation's bread." Let it not be imagined that Stanton borrowed these words from that speech of Lincoln's which was never delivered. He had never read Lincoln's brief; in a mysterious fashion it vanished into a scrap basket shortly after the courtroom proceedings in Cincinnati. Stanton knew the reaper's value from practice. . . . The President of the United States—that "long-armed baboon"—was calling every third man to the colors, nevertheless the harvests increased. Europe could not believe it. When the Europeans heard that North America was sending to England three times as much wheat as in previous years, they shook their heads and said it must be a stroke of propaganda. It was considered impossible that the North could feed two great armies and at the same time sell Europe wheat enough to feed thirty-five million people. But it was possible.

Even greater things were possible. Small and medium-sized cities suddenly awoke to find themselves great metropolises: Milwaukee, Minneapolis, Kansas City, Cincinnati, Des Moines, Omaha, St. Paul. These and hundreds of others found themselves situated on the shore of a sea of wheat, which was cut down in the fields by mechanical reapers and transported by the railroads to fourteen thousand mills. Twelve years after one of the bloodiest wars in history—in 1876—America was the world's greatest producer of grain.

In 1868 Napoleon III descended from his carriage and pinned the Cross of the Legion of Honor upon McCormick's coat. The scene was a wheat field in the vicinity of Paris. The imperial nephew was shrewder than his revered uncle: he saw that machines, honored and useful in towns and industries, could also be employed upon the land to increase the wealth of nations. When McCormick died, a sheaf of wheat was laid upon his breast—upon the breast of a man whose last thoughts, unfortunately, had been of business statistics. The sheaf looked strange upon him. The dead man lay like a worshiper of Demeter.

Obed Hussey's death was grimmer. McCormick's opponent had long since sold all his patents and would have nothing more to do with reaping machines. Sitting one hot summer day in a train in Baltimore, he heard a little girl crying for water. The child was a pretty, golden-haired girl, and Hussey was innately courteous. He got off the train and brought the girl a glass of water in his brown mechanic's hands. On the way to return the glass, he stumbled and fell under the moving wheels—a victim of the machine age he had helped to introduce. His death bears an uncanny similarity to that of the poet Verhaeren, who also died on a station platform, torn to pieces, like Orpheus, by the machines to which he had often addressed inspired odes.

§ 109

In 1848 James Fenimore Cooper in *The Oak Openings* related how, during the previous year, in southern Michigan, he had seen a machine drawn by from ten to twenty horses which cut the ears from the standing stalk, threshed them, cleaned the grain, and poured it into bags. Untouched by human hands, the grain was prepared for the mill. . . . The novelist stood staring aghast. No wonder. He used to describe an America of Indians, trappers, dense forests, and solitudes. Now all this was passing. Great arsenals of machinery were established, and were changing the face of America. That same year of 1848 Europe was aflame with political revolutions. In France, Prussia, and Austria republicans fought against royalists. The outcome of all the revolutions was minor indeed. But the combined mower-thresher was the father of a vast economic revolution.

The combine Cooper saw had been invented by Hiram Moore. It harvested and bagged the wheat of thirty acres in a single day. At that time the farms in Michigan were still too small for this machine; it did not pay until it was introduced into California, the huge new territory that had been opened to the wheat kings of the West. What would James Fenimore Cooper have said had he seen the gasoline motor that fifty years later was to drive the combine through a seething, hissing sea of wheat stalks? When the horse was gone, the last feeble memory of five thousand years of agriculture was swept away.

Swept away in all departments of agriculture. "As ye sow, so shall ye reap. . . ." Since the end of agriculture, the harvesting, had been mechanized, it was inevitable that the beginning, too, should be mechanized. But it is significant that mechanical plowing and sowing were later developments; they came after the mechanization of reaping. Fructifying and breaking open the earth were more deeply sacred to men. They welcomed the song of the machines, which promised leisure, human dignity, and a freer life. But they felt a certain sadness in throwing over the Biblical parables of plowing and sowing.

As early as 1731 Jethro Tull in his book *Horse-hoeing Husbandry*, had shown that both in gardens and in wide fields seed would be better utilized if it were planted in drills, instead of being broadcast blindly. For this purpose he invented a combination of plow and sowing machine; a horse drew a row of teeth through the ground; behind the teeth tubes dropped seed into the furrow. Some men were frightened; most laughed. What was the use of this machine?

The nineteenth century furnished the answer. In 1842 the Pennock brothers, Pennsylvania farmers, took up Tull's idea and developed the mechanical sower. . . . Modern machines can drill eighteen furrows at one time, drop seed and fertilizer into the soil, and close the furrow again. The rotary plow cuts thirteen inches deep, brings up thin layers of earth, pulverizes them, draws furrows, plants, fertilizers, and covers the drill. . . . Beyond it and above it are only sun, wind, and solitude. Neither plowman nor sower accompanies it. Only an oil drop may indicate that man's indestructible will swept over the field. . . .

Before the plow was run by oil, it was run by steam. In England, the birthplace of steam power, attempts had been made around the middle of the century to combine plow and steam engine. But the steam plow was too heavy; it bogged down in the soil. Then John Fowler had the idea of running the heavy steam engine on the roads that ran along the fields and drawing the plow through the fields by means of a steel cable. When he attempted to sell this invention to America, he learned that America's fields were too big for such a "remote-control" apparatus. But soon afterward Americans invented the four-wheeled tractor plow, which was lighter than the steam engine.

Fabulous America. It is quite understandable that Scotsman Carlyle (when he thanked Ralph Waldo Emerson for a sack of maize that the American had sent across the Atlantic) rather dourly wished that Greek and Semitic mythology might be swept away in favor of Jonathan with his all-conquering plowshare. What, indeed, were Triptolemos and the other missionaries of the plow compared to the Yankees who lived between 1800 and 1900?

These missionaries of the plow had to fight for decades, as Cain had fought his brother Abel. But lo! in America Brother Abel was the aggressor. The Bible never revealed clearly the reason for the first fratricide. But the Talmud told the tale more fully. It described how Abel the herdsman loosed his beasts in Cain's fields and mocked his toiling brother with the words: "Who dresses himself in my skins must permit my beasts to trample his land." Cain, then, acted virtually in self-defense. Certainly he did so in America, where the plowmen fought again the ancient battle with the herdsmen. "Through showers of bullets the plow stepped forward," Editor Nathan C. Meeker wrote in the New York *Herald* in 1870. (A few weeks later an infuriated Sioux Indian shot him. The Indian, probably saw no reason for putting forest and pasture land to the plow.)

Bullets flew back and forth. And not too far from the front were the headquarters where the plow was continually improved. There was, for example, Charles Newbold of Burlington, who invented the cast-iron plow; he showed the New Jersey farmers that his plow would never blunt, no matter how deeply it plowed. And the fate of the Continent depended upon deeper plowing. (For a time farmers defied it and opined that a cast-iron plow would poison the soil and sow weeds.) After cast iron came steel. John Lane, a Chicago blacksmith, in 1833 screwed a strip of elastic saw steel to his wooden plow; the plowshare cut through the black earth of Illinois like butter. . . . Soon every village blacksmith in the States was building similar plows. One of them, an ordinary smith (overnight the whole nation had become a nation of engineers), made the plowshare and moldboard of one piece. His name was John Deere. His plow was so light—or Deere so strong—that he took it on his shoulder and smilingly carried it out to the field. There it worked wonders. The stubborn earth yielded willingly to the force of the steel. The whole hemisphere began to cry for steel. In Pittsburgh the furnaces burned day and night and were still unable to satisfy the demand for plows.

In the year 1850 four and a half hours of labor were needed to produce a bushel of maize; in 1940 this had been cut down to sixteen minutes. How men employed the time they saved from labor is another matter— a question for sociologists and moralists. They might do good with it and create a happier human race; so Walt Whitman called upon them, of himself saying modestly:

> No labor-saving machine
> Nor discovery have I made.

But he loved the roar of machines and the men who invented them.

Is the plow perfected? It never will be. Certainly not until men sink into a second "technical slumber"—brought on by some event we cannot foresee. Until that time comes the plow will continue to be improved. In the laboratories of steel factories, at the drafting boards of inventors, in the agricultural colleges, men of all races are working upon it at this very moment.

LIEBIG: EARTH WAS IN NEED OF A HEALER

And he gave it for his opinion, that whoever could make two ears
of corn, or two blades of grass, to grow upon a spot of ground
where only one grew before, would deserve better of mankind,
and do more essential service to his country, than the whole race
of politicians put together.

GULLIVER'S TRAVELS: JONATHAN SWIFT

§ 110

THE DEVELOPMENT of agricultural machinery had been prophesied by
Apollonius Rhodius (295–230 B.C.), the Director of the Library of Alexandria, in a little fable where Demeter is visited by Hephaestus, the god
of forging and mechanics, who brings to her the iron sickle. Myths are
not idle games, and they have bearing not alone upon the past, but upon
the future. What took place in nineteenth-century America was the continuation of this myth; plowshare and sickle were becoming emanci-
pated; the fields were conquered by technology.

The ancient world had its technical inspirations, but they were the
result of play, not of necessity. Mass need and mass famine did not serve
to put such ideas into execution. But Horace Greeley was expressing the
belief of millions of Americans when he dedicated his book, *What I
Know of Farming,* "to the man of our age who shall make the first
plow propelled by steam or other mechanical power; whereby not less
than ten acres per day shall be thoroughly pulverized to a depth of two
feet, at a cost of not more than two dollars per acre." Greeley and his
fellow Americans had faith that agriculture was a technical and economic problem. And that faith was something new on earth.

Europe took another course. Around the same time that McCormick
was building his reaper, in the thirties of the nineteenth century, Europe
followed the lead of a man by the name of Liebig. His path led down
into the soil; it was an examination of the conditions under which the
seed grew. In America the machine conquered the fields; in Europe
chemistry and soil biology were summoned to placate the soil. The Europeans turned not to Hephaestus, but to Aesculapius, the herb-wise god
of medicine.

§ 111

Around the time of Napoleon's death Paris had been the center of
natural science. There Gay-Lussac taught his theories of gases. At his feet,

in the year 1821, sat a nineteen-year-old German with fine eyes and a quiet face. He was a man cut out to be a philosopher, a disciple of Schelling and German Romanticism. But young Liebig was loth to devote himself to abstract speculation. He admired the sober, practical genius of the French and their habit of measuring everything. It had often before been asserted that numbers were the basis of chemistry, but Paris seemed to be the only place in the world where scientists took this seriously. "Without number everything is without law. Without number chemistry is a mass of unproved and ill-ordered facts," young Liebig wrote. "It began to dawn on me that a causal relationship exists between all chemical phenomena in the mineral and plant worlds. . . ." What was needed was to learn how to measure these relationships.

The young man returned to Germany, where he became a professor, first in Giessen, then in Munich, and was entrusted with a small chemical laboratory where he made measurements and devised experiments. At the age of thirty-five he apparently abandoned his chemistry and betook himself to the country. In reality, he took chemistry along in his pocket, as a doctor takes his physician's kit, and unpacked it in the fields.

Liebig cried out to all the farmers in the world that for thousands of years they had been tilling the soil wrongly. He accused them of having not tilled the soil, but robbed it. Let them listen to him, Liebig; he could tell them how to take capital out of the soil and how, properly, to return it. If they made no such recompense, the interest would soon cease and humanity would die of hunger.

The farmers of Europe were not disposed to take this meekly. What business had a chemist meddling in their affairs? This was farming; let him stick to his retorts.

Liebig was, as a matter of fact, not the first soil chemist. Thirty years before in England Sir Humphry Davy (1778–1829) had given lectures on the connection between chemistry and plant physiology. But his ideas had remained theory. And the Prussian Minister of Agriculture, Albrecht von Thaer (1752–1858), had been the first to classify the different varieties of grain soils. Since Roman times only two kinds of soil had been recognized, "heavy" and "light"; Thaer distinguished eleven varieties which imposed varying conditions upon the plants that were raised in them. Thaer taught that certain soils must be used, certain soils avoided, for different plants.

In the beginning the farmers heard only the insult. Did this man Liebig claim they were robbing the soil? Indeed! What else were the miners doing when they dug gold and silver? Did they replace what they took out? They did not! This was quite true and quite irrelevant, for gold and silver were not food.

Very well, they admitted, Liebig was speaking of plants, and plants were different from gold and silver. What did he propose? That they give back to the earth the strength that the plant took out of it? Had they not been doing that for centuries? Every grown man knew that plants did not feed only on water and air, but on decaying organic matter, on manures. That was why they manured their fields with the droppings of their cattle. Liebig retorted inflexibly that all grown men were mistaken. The plants in the soil did not feed on decaying organic matter, but on inorganic matter which could not decay. Only the fundamental materials were important, whether they reached the roots in the form of animal manures or in any other form. What, then, were these fundamental materials? After countless analyses of soil Liebig proved, in 1840, that there were four chief inorganic materials: nitrogen, potassium, lime, and phosphoric acid. Wherever grain was to grow, these four substances must be present in the soil. And present in a given proportion. Each of these substances was as important as the other; let one be lacking, the others might be there in surplus but plants would not grow. "The production of a field," Liebig taught, "is therefore dependent upon the quantity of that plant food of which the least is present." This was Liebig's "law of the minimum," and the equalization of the relative amounts of plant food was the task of agrarian chemistry.

People began to understand this formulation. If it were true that these four organic materials were essential—phosphoric acid, lime, potassium, and nitrogen—they must admit that the old method of manuring was not enough, for it did not reckon on the proportions between the various plant foods. Plant foods had been replaced haphazard in the soil, because the farmers had no feeling that they were replacing anything. Manuring was "just done." Now they began to understand why richly manured fields sometimes produced miserable crops.

But how were they to find out which plant food a plant lacked?

"Quite simply," Liebig explained with the modesty of genius. "To know what is lacking in a soil the plant that grew in the soil must be burned. Analysis of the mineral parts of the ash, which contains the necessary substances, will show where the deficiency lies. The deficiency can then be met by applying artificial fertilizers."

Working on the basis of these ideas, Liebig made countless ash analyses and devised a number of chemical mixtures which would supply mineral salts in precisely the proportions that were needed by various plants. A plant which needed a great deal of potassium, for example, should receive fertilizers rich in potassium; and similarly for those that needed more lime, phosphoric acid, or nitrogen.

Some farmers hesitated to apply this new science because it seemed too expensive. The scientist proved to them that it was cheaper. For thousands of years the necessity of manuring had forced the farmer to sacrifice a large part of his land for growing feed in order to obtain the necessary cattle manures for the rest of his land. This would be unnecessary if chemical fertilizers were used. Best of all, in the future—if the chemical constituents of the soil that had been used by the plants were *completely* replaced—the year of lying fallow would become superfluous. It would no longer be necessary to rotate crops. Year in, year out, the same plant could be grown in the same field. And the earth would show no signs of exhaustion.

Here was a genuinely European thought. The earth was like a woman in childbirth. It was her tragedy that for sixty centuries every harvest, in proportion to its excellence, had left the soil so much the poorer. Now the doctor came to examine the soil; he examined it and drew up his prescription. After burning a stalk of grain he could determine from the ash the quantity and type of chemical plant food this stalk had taken from the earth. The product of all the stalks gave approximately the total loss. Justus von Liebig's discovery—which seemed no less great for its apparent simplicity—made it possible to recompense the soil in kind and quantity for the material that was taken out. Here was a fundamental revolution in agriculture. The whims of the soil were no longer inescapable destiny. Demeter's vagaries could be controlled.

§ 112

The discovery caused a great stir among the more progressive farmers. The German peasantry, since it had won its freedom, had established firm ties with the culture and the mentality of the towns. Farmers' sons had long been teaching in the agricultural colleges. On every farm Liebig's doctrines caused contention whose comical side has been described by the humorist Fritz Reuter in his low-German dialect:

Great porgress in agriculture was made becuz Porfessor Liebig wrote a notorious book for the country folks that fair teemed with potash and sawpeter and sulphur and gypsum and lime and spirits of ammonia and hydrates and hydropaths [superphosphates], till it were enough to drive a body crazy. But all the farmers who itched to git on in the world and git a finger inter science got aholt of the book and sat down and read and read till their heads were fair to smoke; and when they got togither they argied whether sawpeter is a stimulant or a food—for clover, not folks, of course—and whether manure stinks because of the spirits of ammonia or because it's jest stinkery by nature.

Liebig and his students had started their chemical fertilizer factories very quickly. By 1843 Dawes in England had begun to manufacture superphosphate, one of the chief sources of phosphoric acid, from bones and sulphuric acid. Lime, which Liebig had also called for, was to be found everywhere; potassium was obtained from incinerated seaweed or, in the form of potash, from wood ashes. Nitrogen was obtained from the vast stores of bird droppings which the ancient Peruvians had used to fertilize their maize. But the supply of guano was not unlimited. In 1873 Admiral Moresby had estimated the total supply of Peru at about nine million tons. But Liebig had taught so effectively that Europe could not get enough of it, the fields of the Continent were so hungry for nitrogen, that the guano would give out in twenty years if no other source of nitrogen were found. Another source must be found.

When Liebig died in the seventies, this question had not yet been solved. But thus early Atwater was teaching his students that the greatest reservoir of nitrogen lay in the air; there must be some means of extracting this nitrogen from the air and putting it into the soil. Certain plants, like clover, could do this, could "fix" nitrogen; where clover was planted the soil was not depleted but strengthened. Atwater only suspected this; ten years later it was confirmed by a German scientist Hellriegel. Then, in the first years of the twentieth century, Haber began his experiments with extracting ammonia from the air by the use of catalysts. He eventually succeeded in uniting the nitrogen of the air with the hydrogen of water to form ammonia. Thereafter, in all countries, the Haber-Bosch process was employed to draw nitrogen from the air and make it available for the field.

The great offensive against hunger, generaled by the agrochemists who followed Justus von Liebig, was ably supported by a simultaneous assault of agricultural engineering. Since sowing and reaping could be done by time-saving and labor-saving machinery, huge new areas were opened to tillage. The agrotechnicians, it is true, had no contact with the agrochemists—most of the former were Americans and most of the latter Europeans. Because America had "too much soil" McCormick was inevitably American; and because the soil of Europe had, in the course of centuries, lost most of its vitality, Liebig was inevitably a European. Nevertheless, the fact that they appeared at the same time might have been a piece of great good fortune for the world. The greatest area of tillable land in the world could have been worked to be the best soil in the world. McCormick the plowman and Liebig the physician were predestined to supplement each other's work. But they never heard of each other. And later on, when agrotechnicians and agrochemists became nodding acquaintances, no friendship developed. The old reciprocal hauteur between America and Europe hindered any exchange of knowledge and experience. Hauteur, at any rate, undoubtedly existed on the part of the Americans. Although one American farmer, Edmund Ruffin, wrote a book on lime fertilizer, the American farmers in general paid little attention to Liebig's work, and rested on the laurels of the all-conquering plow. Fertilizing was slow; plowing went faster. In 1935 the grandsons of those farmers found out what came of plowing that went too fast.

§ 113

By the time Liebig died, in 1873, Europe had so wholeheartedly adopted his teachings that it was necessary to begin at the beginning and correct Liebig's overemphases. It is a law of progress that all progress must be one-sided. The very swiftness with which Liebig invaded a realm that had lain untouched for six thousand years made him liable to error.

After men had neglected to restore the vitality of the soil for six thousand years, the orthodox followers of Liebig now began to poison the soil with too many chemicals. In many European soils the results Liebig had calculated could suddenly no longer be achieved. The chemicals did not dissolve; they were not digested by the soil particles, or they made the soil too sour. Was it possible that Liebig had overlooked some factor? One of the significant points in his doctrine had been the concept of the earth as a retort (filled everywhere to different levels) in which the sun's heat produced chemical changes. The manner and degree of these changes ought to be controllable; the equations ought to be as clear and definite as those of a laboratory experiment. Now it developed that the soil was, after all, something else besides a chemical laboratory. Like the germ of the grain, the soil itself was a living thing, a cluster and symbiosis of countless minute creatures. Millions of microorganisms made up the life of the soil. The earth was not merely a vast trough of inorganic substances, as Liebig had held.

Once more French science—Louis Pasteur's newly discovered field of bacteriology—exercised a reforming, moderating influence. Liebig had not known the complex action of humus. What was humus? It was fermenting earth. And what was fermentation? Here we come back to the question that concerned us when we lingered among the bakeries of Egypt. Was fermentation a process of life—or was it only decomposition, destruction, a kind of the old, chemical death?

Since Pasteur's time we have maintained that fermentation is a life process. The wonderful fragrance of earth that we smell when walking across a tilled field is no odor of death. When we examine a piece of fertile soil under the microscope, we see a landscape that is impressive indeed. Everything that Liebig saw is there—the mineral components which almost alone interested him: grains of quartz, minute flakes of mica, bits of clay, olivenite, and lime. Then there are fragments which the practiced eye at once recognizes as non-mineral: a splinter of atomized wood, a fiber of a dead plant, even a few larger remnants of the chitinous armor of some beetle. And there is something else that is more difficult to name: a host of pure grains of earth, pulverized as though ground by the finest of millstones, and reddish-brown in color. Where do these come from, and how were they pulverized? Modern soil biology has found the answer to the mystery: *humus is earth that has passed through the intestines of worms;* and earth that has been eaten and excreted by microbes. Only earth prepared beforehand by animal creatures is fertile and helpful to plant growth.

Darwin was the first to recognize the service of the earthworm to the soil:

Organic matter is the principal food of the earthworm. It may be fresh or decomposed. When it is decomposed, such soil and its organic matter are taken into the digestive tract of the earthworm. There, in the process of obtaining nutriment from it, the earthworm further breaks down the organic matter chemically and mechanically. . . . In this whole process, an enormous total quantity of soil material passes through the digestive system of all the earthworms in the topsoil of an acre of productive land. This modified soil material is ejected as the familiar "worm casts" that may often be seen on the surface of moist, heavy soils, particularly in the morning after rains.

If Darwin was correct in his belief that earthworms bring to the surface the equivalent of one fifth of an inch of soil a year, then once in thirty-five years (Russell pointed out) the earthworm brings seven inches of soil from below and deposits it on the surface.

But even with the earthworm advancing like a drill or a tank, it alone did not do the main work. This was done by many smaller creatures: nematodes such as the Guinea worms, vorticellae, flagellates, amoebae, and those minutest living things which the microscope fails to reveal, that galaxy of bacteriological life whose existence we only suspect. In a small clod of arable soil billions of living creatures are found. Not only do they prepare the soil chemically, through their juices, but they also aerate it mechanically by their movements. Their effect is far greater than that of the American plow; without the incessant motion of these indefatigable organisms our soils would rot. And indeed the soil does die where these organisms are not present. From this point of view, Liebig's "overmedication" of the earth was dangerous. Too much chemistry killed the small living creatures. Instead of chemicals it became necessary to place living colonies of bacteria in the earth. Since the soil was essentially a product of organic life, it was necessary to introduce new life as soon as the soil began to grow weary. Was this any reason to return haphazardly to the old method of manuring? By no means. Following Liebig's example, scientists attempted to determine exactly how many and which kinds of bacteria were wanting in the soil. The doses administered, the types of medicine, may have altered, but Liebig's discovery was fundamental—that the sick earth could be cured scientifically.

In a sense, Liebig resembled Sigmund Freud, who founded a science in which any of his students and students' students could achieve results that surpassed his. Liebig, the physician, had descended into the under-world of the soil. He recognized that the earth was ill from the pangs of incessant childbirth, and he provided Demeter with the offices of the physician.

CHALLENGE TO MALTHUS

§ 114

LIKE THE WORK of all great givers of bread, the labors of Justus von Liebig impinge upon intellectual history. Although the practical remedies he proposed are somewhat outmoded, his philosophy of history still has profound validity. This philosophy of history was published in his *Familiar Letters on Chemistry* (1844). It reveals a breadth of thought, a perspective, that still strikes awe.

According to Liebig, all national disasters are purely agrarian disasters. Human plundering of the soil's fertility is primarily responsible for the decline of great empires. "The predatory cultivation that lays waste to the land always takes the same course, which is governed by historical law. In the first period the farmer plants the same grain year after year upon virgin soil. Second: the crop declines; he moves on to another field. Third: he can find no more new land and cultivates the old land by letting it lie fallow every other year. Crops continue to decline; to improve the yield the farmer uses great quantities of manure, which he obtains by feeding cattle on natural pastures. Fourth: the pastures prove inadequate in the long run, and the peasant must begin to grow feed upon part of the arable field itself. At first he uses the subsoil as he had used the pasture land—tilling without interruption. Then he also introduces a year of fallowing for the forage plants. Fifth: the subsoil is exhausted; the fields will no longer grow vegetables. First pea rot sets in; then clover, turnips, and potatoes die. Sixth: cultivation ceases; the field will no longer support the man."

What is seventh? The seventh stage is murder. After the murder of the soil comes the murder of men. For every disproportion between the supply and demand of food compels the population of a given quarter of the globe to diminish its numbers so that a balance is once more restored. "Those who can no longer find a place at society's board," Liebig wrote, "either become thieves or murderers, or emigrate en masse, or become conquerors. There are no other possibilities but these three. If men are unable to keep their soil permanently fertile, they must drown it in blood. This is historic law. . . ." Liebig argued that it did not matter whether farmers were exempted from the army and not permitted to leave their soil. Peace did not feed the people, nor did war destroy the population of a country. Both conditions exercised merely a temporary influence. What scattered or cemented human society was, in all ages, the soil—the soil and the length of time it remained fertile.

Predatory cultivation of the soil—not replacing the chemical substances that had been taken from it—had destroyed all great empires from the Roman to the Spanish. "The same natural law controls the rise and fall of nations. Robbing lands of the conditions for fertility means their decline; their culture fades simultaneously. Just as the farmer leaves the field that will no longer feed him, so culture and morals shift and change with the condition of the fields. A nation arises and develops in proportion to the fertility of the land. With the exhaustion of the land culture and morals apparently disappear. However, the intellectual properties of the nations do not vanish; it is our consolation that they merely change their dwelling place."

Such was Liebig's philosophy of history, a distillation of his experience in agriculture. He was a modest man. He assumed that in the past six thousand years many men who thought about agriculture had made discoveries which they were not equipped to interpret. He was acquainted with Quesnay and the precursors of his own ideas in the persons of the French agrarian philosophers of the eighteenth century. But since Liebig himself was the first to see the real connections, what he had to offer was in essence utterly novel.

"In my agricultural chemistry," he wrote modestly but with sincere understanding of the worth of his words, "I tried to place a light in a dark room. All the furniture was there. There were also instruments and objects of pleasure; but all these things were not really clear or distinctly visible to the people that inhabited the place. Groping by chance, one found a chair, the other a table, the third a bed, in which they tried to make themselves as comfortable as possible; but the harmony of the whole was concealed from the eyes of most. After some rays of my light were cast upon each object, many cried that the light had not fundamentally changed anything, for one had recognized this, the other that; they had felt, touched, and guessed at the existence of the object. That does not matter. Henceforth the light of agricultural chemistry can never more be snuffed out from this room. That was my aim, and I have attained it."

Liebig's philosophy of history influenced many historians. Without being acquainted with his work, in 1907 the Russian-American Vladimir Simkhovitch, a professor at Columbia University, wrote the essay which has since become famous: "Rome's Fall, Newly Considered"; and Tenney Frank in his *Economic History of Rome* attributed the decline of Italy as an agricultural country not, as Pliny had done, to the *latifundia*, but to the *exhaustio soli* that Liebig had discovered: the exhaustion of

the Italian soil through overintensive cultivation. To Liebig, who was
not a professional historian, the past served only as a warning; he was
interested chiefly in the future. Consequently, it could not fail that his
optimistic doctrines should cross swords with those of Malthus. If Liebig
spoke true, if men could restore to the soil what they had stolen from it,
then Malthus was answered.

§ 115

The economic doctrines of Malthusianism had come close to triumph-
ing. In 1798—nine years after the most optimistic revolution in history—
an English pastor named Thomas Robert Malthus (1766–1834) published the utmost in pessimistic prognoses for mankind. It expressed the
apparently incontrovertible conclusion derived from the history of the
past decades: that the world faced dreadful overpopulation. During the
first half of the eighteenth century the states of Europe had considered
increase in population as their chief source of wealth. But Malthus, in
his *Essay on Population*, grimly indicated how humanity would inevitably starve if, in the future, families had more than two children. For
fields could only be added to one another: that is, the supply of food
could be increased only in arithmetical progression, while men increased
in geometrical progression. The soil, Malthus said (in this he agreed with
Liebig), became poorer after every harvest. Soon part of mankind would
have no place upon the earth. There was only one solution: no more
births than deaths.

This was terrifying, but persuasive. What argument could be offered
against it? The magic of numbers seemed to be on Malthus' side:

Let us call the population of the British island 11 millions; and suppose
the present produce equal to the easy support of such a number. In the first
25 years the population would be 22 millions, and the food being also
doubled, the means of subsistence would be equal to this increase. In the
next 25 years the population would be 44 millions, and the means of subsistence only equal to the support of 33 millions. In the next period the
population would be equal to 88 millions, and the means of subsistence just
equal to the support of half that number. And at the conclusion of the first
century, the population would be 176 millions, and the means of subsistence
only equal to the support of 55 millions, leaving a population of 121 millions
totally unprovided for.

Malthus' disciple, John Stuart Mill (1806–73), the philosopher of
liberalism, put the situation even more inexorably:

A greater number of people cannot, in any given state of civilization, be
collectively so well provided for as a smaller. The niggardliness of nature,

not the injustice of society, is the cause of the penalty attached to over-population. An unjust distribution of wealth does not aggravate the evil, but, at most, causes it to be somewhat earlier felt.

There is a note in Mill's statement of his grudge against agrarian socialism, against men like Henry George, the "American Gracchus," who in 1871 in *Our Land and Land Policy* called for a just distribution of the land as the best weapon against hunger.

Neither Malthus, Mill, nor George knew that Liebig and Pasteur, agrochemistry and soil bacteriology, had meanwhile placed the whole question on a different basis. If the strength of the soil could be renewed and if crops remained stationary instead of decreasing because of soil exhaustion, the increase in population could no longer hold such terrors. Moreover, America was already demonstrating how much new land could be tilled by machinery, without the need for human labor. It was therefore possible to produce a great deal of bread for a great many human beings. The justification for timidity was slight.

According to a reasonably reliable estimate, Christ's time saw a quarter of a billion human beings dwelling upon this earth. And in spite of the plagues of the Middle Ages, which swept away at least a quarter of the earth's inhabitants, this number had risen to half a billion at the beginning of the modern age. Today, in 1944, there are more than two billion. Lack of food has produced tremendous population pressure, and nations that know nothing of Malthus and his two-children system, like over-populated Japan, would like nothing better than to disperse their surplus population over continents that know too much of Malthus—like thinly settled Australia. Yet today it is not necessary for any land to be thinly populated, for with its mechanical and chemical advances, agriculture can actually support two billion and more human beings. Thinly populated lands may live happily for a time, but they cannot defend themselves. Indeed, how will Canada meet the problems of 1970? But still in 1943 its French-written newspapers stormed against any alleviation of immigration laws.

In no country of Europe did the Malthusian theory of population breed so much ill as in France. Zola—undoubtedly without having heard of Liebig—attempted to fight this evil in his novel *Fécondité*. He succeeded in writing a great book which drew a parallel between the inexhaustibility of vegetable seed and human seed. The whole world read the book; but a large part of the world clung to the despondent, pessimistic belief that preferred fewer men and more bread. The better formulation would read: as much bread as possible for many men.

Much bread for many men would be available as soon as the grandchildren of Cyrus McCormick joined hands with the grandchildren of Liebig. Around the middle of the nineteenth century they were still strangers to one another. Agrochemistry and agroengineering, Europe and America, knew nothing of each other's progress. Technology won out, and America was able to build the Empire of Wheat, one of the strangest configurations of power in the history of humanity.

AMERICA'S EMPIRE OF WHEAT

§ 116

WHY an empire of wheat? Was not America rather fitted to become maize dictator of the world?

But Europe needed wheat. The victorious French armies had convinced all nations that a "master race" ate only wheat. Paris became the ruler of taste as Rome had been two thousand years before, and opprobrium was heaped upon every grain but wheat. "Rye is evil-smelling," Galen, the great physician of the Roman Empire, had declared. Now once more rye came under attack.

In the Middle Ages Europeans were very fond of the taste of rye. Some of the East Germans had called themselves *Rugii* (rye-eaters)—undoubtedly to distinguish themselves from the ignoble eaters of oats. In Anglo-Saxon England August was called *Rugern,* the month of the rye harvest. As late as 1700 rye formed 40 per cent of all English breads; around 1800 the percentage had dropped to 5; and in 1930 Jasny wrote: "There are men in England who have never heard the word rye. . . ."

Where rye bread was very firmly established—in large parts of Germany and Russia—it remained. Physicians and farmers insisted that people who for centuries had eaten the dark bread of their fathers, which gave forth a spicy fragrance like the soil itself, could not find the soft white wheat bread filling. They pointed to the physique of the Germans and the rye-eating Russians. The wheat-eaters countered with the claim that rye made those who ate it stupid and dull. Wheat-eaters and rye-eaters spoke of one another as do wine drinkers and beer drinkers. The old hatred among the different grains, which springs from far deeper levels of the collective consciousness than capitalistic market disputes, burst out in fiery polemics. There was once more the familiar accusation of poisoning, hurled by both sides. The rye-eaters said that wheat bread had no more nutritive value than air.

The nations that had become wheat-eaters after 1800 did not agree that wheat was air. Traditional rye countries like Sweden and Denmark were converted. In Scotland wheat bread had long been so rare that only the well to do had it for Sunday dinner. Around 1850 not only the middle class, but the workers as well, ate it habitually. In 1700 Poland exported three times as much rye as wheat; a hundred years later the proportion had been reversed—three times as much wheat as rye was exported.

This metamorphosis in Europe's taste was a signal to America. In the eighteenth century wheat was of no importance to the new nation. In 1777 it was harvested for the first time in Tennessee and Kentucky. George Washington raised wheat on his farms, but this was little more than a personal hobby. In 1780 John Adams' wife, when she wrote of the high prices caused by war scarcities, did not even mention wheat because it was not a food eaten by the people. But in a purely instinctive manner the victory of the French Revolution also governed the future victory of wheat in America. This occurred at a time when America scarcely dreamed of export; when the American farmer raised crops for himself and the nearest town.

§ 117

Europe's decision to provide for its increased population by feeding it on America's grain was not a voluntary decision. But it was also not involuntary. The decision, when it was taken, seemed to represent an accord between freedom and necessity.

The tremendous increase in population after the Napoleonic Wars imposed on European agriculture the task of feeding far more human beings than it had ever fed before. And this was difficult. The new surplus population was not a farming population; it consisted of city dwellers, industrial workers. New land would have been necessary to feed these armies of workers; Liebig's chemical improvement of the soil would not have sufficed. This new land was available; moors, heaths, and marshes could have been put to the plow. But the powerful American plow was still unknown. Therefore, it seemed simpler and cheaper to buy bread from abroad. The bread could be paid for by exporting European industrial goods. Such were the economic factors. There were also intellectual factors.

After the defeat of Napoleon, the political barometer seemed to promise an epoch of hundreds of years of peace. Nationalism had made room for a Europeanism that was not, like the philosophical Europeanism of the eighteenth century, suspended in a "sky of cosmopolitanism." It was based upon the solid ground of world trade. Never before had there been such general faith in Mercury; Mars seemed dead and buried forever. The best and wisest Europeans said: "The gifts of the soil are obviously not equal everywhere. But the earth is a unit. One part of this world, this globe that belongs to all of us, bears grain; the other factories. Let us exchange our products!"

To insist, cynically, that this thought sprang from mere greed for profits and not from a generous, ethical internationalism is to mistake the men of 1850. It is to fail to understand why the English corn tariffs were abolished.

In England the advocates of free trade taught that the wealth of a nation depended upon its trade. They argued that trade was hindered by tariff walls; that the consumer bought goods at much too high prices so long as protective tariffs existed; and, above all, that the people should be allowed to buy bread cheaply. This would be possible if the corn laws were abolished. If it were objected that the tariffs were necessary to support the Navy and the Army, the free traders replied that both would soon no longer be needed. Free trade in England would force all nations to open their ports; this would lead, necessarily, to world peace and disarmament.

The Tories who ruled in England were, of course, in favor of protective tariffs. Their free-trade opponents, who were led by Cobden, insinuated that the large landowners of England had long since ceased to be deserving of the favoritism they enjoyed. Centuries ago they had been given land for great services in war. "Today," the liberals sneered, "the only great accomplishment they have to show is the mass murder of pheasants and snipe." Cóbden and his friends did not realize that the corn tariffs helped not only the lords, but also the English small farmer. If the tariffs protecting home grain were removed, farming would cease to exist; the last remnants of the farming population would vanish; the agricultural workers would stream to the cities and underbid one another for employment.

The conservative party was far from blind to this danger. Nevertheless, the tariffs had to be lifted. Unrest among the laboring class seemed a more unpleasant issue than disaster to the farming population. The cities, those cities that were swelling to vast metropolises, wanted bread, cheap bread, and they wanted it at once. Pessimists warned that if England's cultivated land were further curtailed, a blockade could starve England into complete famine in eighteen days. (The time limit they set was slightly exaggerated, but the German submarine warfare of 1914 and 1939 proved that the Tories were not wrong in principle.) No one heeded the warnings. Many of the more lowly among the lords, among them Disraeli, deserted to the camp of the free traders. To keep the grain tariffs or to abolish them became an ever more pressing question in the House of Commons. The workers banded together in demonstrations. The socialistic Chartists incited to revolt. Brawls broke out in the factories. In the countryside granaries were burned down. Simultaneously with the Scotch-English crop failure of 1845, the great potato blight devastated neighboring Ireland. The English industrial cities were in ferment. The first measure that was adopted—permitting unlimited importation of grain from abroad—was insufficient. The Anti-Corn Law Association carried on perfervid agitation throughout the land, pouring oil on the existing conflagration. The outcry for cheap bread produced scenes that had not been seen in England since the times of the Plague. Inevitably, the government reversed itself and abolished the tariffs on grain.

A torrent of wheat poured from America. But not at once! It took almost two decades before America understood what had happened in England; understood that the island center of a vast empire, which for hundreds of years had ruled America herself, was now utterly dependent upon the mercy and productivity of the United States. In 1846 America did not yet have the tools to sate the hunger of England and of other European countries. The machine had only begun to plow a part of the West; scarcely any wheat grew on the Pacific coast. But this was soon to change.

France joined England, and in increasing measure, as a country eager for America's agrarian products. Since the smart intellectual circles in France believed even more than their fellows in England in a "cosmopolitanism of trade" and in the natural exchange of goods from continent to continent, no one saw any peril in living permanently on crops from abroad. After the fall of Napoleon, to be sure, agrochemistry had shown the French that intelligent handling of French soil could force it to produce five times what it had produced before. The scientists went out into the country, and from 1842 on French production of all kinds of bread grains mounted. But in 1846 began the widespread, mysterious potato blight; moreover, in that year bad weather conditions produced a poor grain harvest, which resulted in grave shortages in 1847. Then came the year of revolution, 1848, when the farmers had other business besides tilling their fields. Wet seasons from 1853 to 1855 reduced yields; then Napoleon III led the best of the peasantry into the Crimean War; then came cholera; then the campaign against Austria in Italy (1859). Lastly, at Napoleon's command, Haussmann, the great construction engineer, began to rebuild Paris, which withdrew a great deal of man power from the land. All the editorial assistance of newspapers and the encouragement of writers could not compensate for the lack of human hands. The sort of atmosphere prevailed which Pierre Dupont, the Bohemian poet and disciple of Béranger, has caught in one of his chansons:

> On n'arrête pas le murmure
> Du peuple quand il dit: J'ai faim,
> Car c'est le cri de la nature:
> Il faut du pain. Il faut du pain.

Agricultural output around 1860 was so bad, as a result of this constellation of misfortunes, that industrial France finally decided to live by American crops.

And Germany? Germany was rye land, cultivating rye alone. Moreover, Russia was very near; whenever more was needed it could be
bought there. More rye, of course. America was planting only wheat.
Such was the situation until Germany caught up with the change in
taste. The increased self-consciousness of the cities helped; the citizens
of Hamburg and Berlin became too fine to eat the dark peasants' bread.
The German industrial worker looked across the border and determined
that he would eat as well as the French or the Belgian worker: he demanded wheat bread, or at least a bread made of equal parts of wheat
and rye. And the German cities were expanding rapidly; already they
were enormous consumers. Commerce and industry brought about the
same change in Germany that had taken place in the rest of Europe;
against the will of the agrarian interests, of the military and of the con-
servatives, the borders were thrown open to the flow of grain.

In 1865 the German protective tariffs were removed. This was the
signal for America to channel her vast river of wheat in the direction
of the European continent.

§ 118

From 1865 on this nutritive gold dust was borne in ship after ship
from the one continent to the other. It was all wheat, of course; the
peoples of Europe would have none of other grains. In order to be exported, however, wheat had to make a pact at home with maize, the
older national grain. Maize was not the same thing to Americans as rye
had been to Europeans. It was not only the "grain of our fathers," en-
deared by a hundred memories to the taste buds; not only the grain of
their mothers, the inheritance of Indian cuisine which Americans received with their land. Maize was also an economic factor of tremendous
importance. It was America's stock feed, the basic fodder of all cattle and
swine, hens, turkeys, ducks, and geese. Out of the maize plant grew the
emporiums of the meat trade. Cincinnati's and Chicago's smoking abat-
toirs could trace their direct descent to the maize plant. The numberless
by-products supplied by the bodies of slaughtered animals—fats and oils,
starches and glues, soaps and candles—were all gifts of the maize. Wheat,
on the other hand, supplied "bread alone." With this in mind it is understandable that in 1861, when twenty-four million bushels of wheat passed
through Chicago's mart, the figure for bushels of maize was higher by
about half a million.

Monoculture in wheat would have been disastrous for America. In
the beginning of its new glory the recently crowned emperor naturally
attempted to thrust back maize. On the boundaries of the two empires
fields of maize land became wheat's domain. But this process soon ceased.

PRUSSIAN ARMY BAKERY (1866)

As long as maize remained in the country and was not destined for export, wheat had no need to fear its competition. We can declare almost to the day when this relationship changed. At the Paris World's Fair of 1900 Charles R. Dodge opened a maize kitchen to show the astonished French all the various foods Americans could prepare from maize. He failed, just as Benjamin Franklin had failed one hundred and twenty years earlier when he recommended maize so highly to Cadet de Vaux. But wheat was offended. And there at once began a struggle for the West European market which ended in the total defeat of maize flour. This struggle was fought in laboratories—not on American soil, but in the laboratories of France and Italy. The struggle between wheat flour and maize flour was disguised as the decade-old conflict between macaroni and polenta. Many physicians, like the famous Lombroso, had participated in this war; accusations of poisoning, bacilli, pellagra, vital statistics, and vitamins had played their part. . . . But we are running ahead of our story. In 1865 the empires of wheat and maize dwelt peaceably side by side. Indeed, the better did maize feed the mainland of America, the more easily and securely could wheat conquer intercontinental trade.

But to augment and to channelize this river of wheat an iron tool was needed, a gigantic webwork of power stretched across the entire country. The railroads formed this webwork.

In 1840 America had no more than twenty-five hundred miles of railroad—an insignificant trackage. This was not much more than ten years after the invention of the locomotive and tracks, and railroads at best contributed to human comfort and shortened traveling time. But they swiftly became economic necessities, and then economic tyrants. Prehistoric draft animals, sooty and belching fire, bellowing for more loads, they moved across the land. A single railroad train speeded along greater quantities of goods than could be transported by caravans of ox-drawn or horse-drawn wagons.

"Build railroads!" became the watchword in America's counting-houses. And it was encouraged by every device. In 1848 a law was passed permitting twenty-five persons to establish a railroad company if each person could subscribe $1,000 for every mile of track to be built. In actual cash only $100 had to be paid in. Since the cost of construction was $35,000 a mile, and since frequently a total of only $2,500 cash was put up, this law permitted debts of several hundred times the actual capital. The banks supplied the necessary credit. They could do so because large amounts of capital were flowing from Europe to America. Since 1848 Europeans lived in constant terror of revolution; they placed their money first in London and then in the New World. Thus Europe herself helped to build the great network of railroads which brought American wheat to the ships that crossed the Atlantic. The workers in Dublin, London, Paris, and Berlin got the cheap bread they had demanded. But something outside their considerations and beyond any prophesying occurred. As the bread price sank, so also did wages in European industry. Discontent seized the people; bread was cheap, but there was no money to pay for it.

Meanwhile, in America, prairies and forests clanged with the sound of the pickax. Armies of workers laid track, girded East and West with iron. The 2,500 miles of 1840 increased by the sixties to more than 37,500 miles, and by the end of the eighties to 156,000 miles. The crops that the farmers had cultivated on a small scale for hundreds of years —for themselves and the nearest town—the railroads transformed overnight into the stuff of international trade. The Government presented the railroads with vast areas of land: territories as large as European kingdoms. As unlimited lords upon this land, the railroads could produce crops against which, despite all his efforts, the small farmer could not compete. Become haughty servants, the companies were deaf to the desires of the Government that had enriched them. They did not give a fig either for individuals or for the commonweal. Greater profits were their sole aim. *Latifundia* were formed in America whose proprietors were all-powerful far beyond the Roman or English great landowners, though they kept neither slaves nor serfs. The army of machines drove out small farming because small farming was unprofitable. Wheat heaped up in mountains; the mountains crashed into railroad cars; the railroad cars spewed their cargo into the holds of great transatlantic freighters. Every city that was washed by the river of wheat became paved with gold. Chicago, a middle-class town, became a city of millionaires.

Chicago was a saga. In 1815, when Napoleon was defeated, it had been a small village that the Indians called "wild onion place." Since 1833 it had called itself a city, but in 1840 it did not have 5,000 inhabitants. On the other hand, it had a larger number of hogs who rubbed their backs against the walls of all the houses and blocked the streets until they were routed. In 1847 McCormick came to the little town. He had seen the crops rotting in the fields of the Northwest because sickles and scythes were too slow and the hands to wield them too scarce. At the edge of the Northwest, in Chicago, he founded his reaper factory and made his mechanical harvester the symbol and coat of arms of the city of Chicago. Five years after McCormick the railroad came—that other great harvester which poured the crops of the Middle West into the granaries of the city. Wheat and maize ran on tracks to the foot of the elevators; there the cars were unloaded and the grain measured. The world market price depended upon the status of grain in Chicago. Chicago's word was law in London, Paris, Berlin, St. Petersburg, and Shanghai. . . . The wild onion place was a thing dead beyond memory. In 1870 Chicago had three hundred thousand inhabitants, and was growing daily and hourly. The hogs were no longer driven off the streets; they were fattened with maize and slaughtered, and the meat was exported.

> Hog butcher for the world,
> Toolmaker, stacker of wheat,
> Player with railroads and the nation's freight handler;
> Stormy, husky, brawling,
> City of the big shoulders.

Upon the broad shoulders of Chicago were founded the millionaires' fortunes, and these swelled to the billions of the railroad kings, meat kings, machinery and wheat kings.

All this followed from the first ear of wheat, the first grain that was sent to the city in the hope that a mill would be found there. In those days the grain had been packed in the bags of the small farmer; later it arrived in millions of bushels in the freight cars of the rich. The rich had become richer, and the poor man poorer. The world order had not changed. The small farmer, who but a few years before had had no trouble earning his living from his modest harvests, peered with hand over eyes at the freight trains that roared past him. Freight rates he could not possibly afford prevented the small farmer from sending his grain to market. Where, indeed, would he send it? World trade, the stock market —in which men like Hutchinson and Joe Leiter won fortunes—were confounded gibberish to him. He sat down wearily upon a stone and realized he was lost. There was nothing he could do but sell his land to the men in power. The wheat that fed whole nations, that enriched America's millionaires, could no longer sustain the small farmer.

§ 119

In his *Octopus* Frank Norris described the struggle of the wheat farmers with the Kraken of the railroads. The two elemental forces, giants in deadly combat, were wheat and the railroad. At last both united, and the farmer was crushed between them.

Frank Norris (1870–1902), born in Chicago, went to Paris in his early youth to study painting. Instead he became a journalist, and when he returned to America he synthesized his two talents into a third. Retaining the painter's gift of observation, he took from journalism the "nose for news" and became America's *romancier*. When he was twenty-nine, Norris wrote the following letter to a friend:

I have an idea of a series of novels buzzing in my head these days. . . . My idea is to write three novels around the one subject of Wheat. First, a story of California (the producer), second, a story of Chicago (the distributor), third, a story of Europe (the consumer), and in each to keep to the idea of this huge Niagara of wheat rolling from West to East. I think a big epic trilogy *could* be made out of such a subject that would be at the same time modern and distinctly American. The idea is so big that it frightens me at times, but I have about made up my mind to have a try at it.

This scheme was, as his biographer remarks, "surpassing anything attempted before in American fiction." Economic factors had been foreshadowed in the novels of the New World only fleetingly and vaguely. Norris planned to give literary form to the force external to human beings that guided their destiny: the natural force of grain. Indifferent, gigantic, resistless, it moved in its appointed grooves. Men, Lilliputians, gnats in the sunshine, buzzed impudently in their tiny battles, were born, lived through their little day, died, and were forgotten; while the wheat grew steadily under the night. Men clambered anxiously about between production, distribution, and consumption of wheat, crawling up and down the stalk like Lincecum's Texan ants. But the writer looked at these ants through the glass of sympathy, of fellow feeling; he understood their struggle and shaped them anew into men.

Back of Norris' *Octopus* there was a true story. Franklin Walker, the biographer, narrates it:

In the early seventies settlers had moved into the waste lands of the Mussel Slough district, lying in the east part of what was then Tulare County; and had in a decade through hard labor, irrigation, and extensive improvement transformed the region into productive farms. The titles to a portion of their property were in dispute, for the Southern Pacific Railroad, which had built a line through the district on a questionable franchise, claimed the odd-numbered sections on either side of their road under a Congressional act of 1868. From the first the settlers had recognized the rights of the railroad, for that corporation in inviting them to open up the district had indicated that the railroad sections would eventually be sold to them at the rate on undeveloped property, an average of $2.50 an acre. After the region had been developed, the railroad regraded their sections and notified the ranchers that the lands were for sale to anyone at $25 to $30 an acre. They offered nothing for the improvements which had made the land valuable. The ranchers fought the corporation bitterly; they formed a Settlers' League of six hundred members, they petitioned Congress, they conducted expensive lawsuits. The railroad, long experienced in political lobbying, defeated them at every turn. The feeling in the region grew intense; the ranchers asserted that the corporation planted insolent agents in their midst, tightened its monopolies on banking and the press, and cut down their profits with arbitrary freight rates. A crisis was reached when, on the eleventh of May, 1880, the federal marshal and three deputies rode into a mass meeting of settlers at Hanford and asked for a conference with the ranch leaders. . . . During the conference a shot was fired, by whom no one knows; in the confusion the deputies shot indiscriminately; during the fight six men were killed instantly and a seventh was mortally wounded.

Such was the actual story. With this story as kernel, Norris constructed a picture of Californian society of the eighties. The farmer leader Magnus Derrick and farmers of Swedish, English, and German blood obeyed Horace Greeley's call, "Go West, young man, and grow up with the country." With ax and spade they had gone into the wilderness. But thirty years later the profiteers arrived, the railroad men. Among them was a certain president of a trust who told a writer that his part in the trust's victory was of the smallest; the railroad, like wheat, was an elemental thing with an eternal tendency to grow. . . . There was the newspaperman, Genslinger, who also stood on the side of the railroad: "When will you people realize that you can't buck against the railroad? It's like me going out in a paper boat and shooting peas at a battleship." And there were the numerous men between the camps, all of whom became involved in the great struggle: anarchists, deserters, bribed men, and stupid men; the discharged railroad engineer who struck up a friendship with the farmers and became a robber and killer; San Francisco Society with its esthetes and rich men, its social committees and charitable ladies; the grain ships embarking for India. And there was the matchless figure of the railroad agent Behrman, one of the assistant leaders in the struggle. Here was the real winner, whom the guns of the enemy could not touch; who even escaped the bomb that was thrown into his country home:

He was a placid, fat man, with a stiff straw hat and linen vest, who never lost his temper, who smiled affably upon his enemies, giving them good advice, commiserating with them in one defeat after another, never ruffled, never excited, sure of his power, conscious that back of him was the Machine, the colossal force, the inexhaustible coffers of a mighty organization, vomiting millions to the League's thousands. The League was clamorous, ubiquitous, its object known to every urchin on the streets, but the Trust was silent, its ways inscrutable, the public saw only results. It worked on in the dark—calm, disciplined, irresistible.

But this monster of calm and cold calculation was also doomed. In one of the finest scenes in American literature, the unconquerable Behrman meets death while inspecting a ship in port which is to take wheat to Asia. He stumbles and falls into the hold of the ship, into which the grain elevator is spewing a cataract of wheat.

"God," he said, "this isn't going to do at all." He uttered a great shout. "Hello, on deck there, somebody! For God's sake."

The steady, metallic roar of the pouring wheat drowned out his voice. He could scarcely hear himself above the rush of the cataract. Besides this, he found it impossible to stay under the hatch. The flying grains of wheat, spattering as they fell, stung his face like wind-driven particles of ice. It was a veritable torture; his hands smarted with it. Once he was all but blinded. Furthermore, the succeeding waves of wheat, rolling from the mound under the chute, beat him back, swirling and dashing against his legs and knees, mounting swiftly higher, carrying him off his feet. . . .

He retreated to a far corner of the hold and sat down with his back against the iron hull of the ship and tried to collect his thoughts, to calm himself. Surely there must be some way of escape; surely he was not to die like this, die in this dreadful substance that was neither solid nor fluid. What was he to do? How make himself heard?

But even as he thought about this, the cone under the chute broke again and sent a great layer of grain rippling and tumbling toward him. It reached him where he sat and buried his hand and one foot.

He sprang up trembling and made for another corner. "By God," he cried, "by God, I must think of something pretty quick!"

Once more the level of the wheat rose and the grains began piling deeper about him. Once more he retreated. Once more he crawled staggering to the foot of the cataract, screaming till his ears sang and his eyeballs strained in their sockets, and once more the relentless tide drove him back.

Then began that terrible dance of death; the man dodging, doubling, squirming, hunted from one corner to another, the wheat slowly, inexorably flowing, rising, spreading to every angle, to every nook and cranny. It reached his middle. Furious and with bleeding hands and broken nails, he dug his way out to fall backward, all but exhausted, gasping for breath in the dust-thickened air. Roused again by the slow advance of the tide, he leaped up and stumbled away, blinded with the agony in his eyes, only to crash against the metal hull of the vessel. . . .

Reason fled. Deafened with the roar of the grain, blinded and made dumb with its chaff, he threw himself forward with clutching fingers, rolling upon his back, and lay there, moving feebly, the head rolling from side to side. The Wheat, leaping continuously from the chute, poured around him. It filled the pockets of the coat, it crept up the sleeves and trouser legs, it covered the great, protuberant stomach, it ran at last in rivulets into the distended, gasping mouth. It covered the face. . . .

No sound, but the rushing of the Wheat that continued to plunge incessantly from the iron chute in a prolonged roar, persistent, steady, inevitable.

This scene has the logic of the myth. This is a death such as the Roman General Crassus died when the Parthians who had captured him poured molten gold down his throat in order to sate his avarice.

The interlocutor and narrator of the novel is the writer Presley. In this character Norris portrays himself—mingled, however, with certain traits of Edwin Markham, whom he had met in San Francisco. In 1899 Markham had published *The Man with the Hoe* in the San Francisco *Examiner*. It may have been this poem which inspired the plan of *The Octopus. The Octopus* at once made its author the "American Zola." Norris had learned a great deal from Zola, whom he worshiped; his repetitions and cumulative language are essentially French and contrast strongly with Anglo-Saxon sobriety. And as Frank Norris was never to be seen without one of those yellow, poorly bound volumes, read to tatters, which bore the titles *Germinal* or *La Terre,* so the bright young men of America were never seen without *The Octopus.* A new literature had come into being. And Norris' repute increased when the second part was published, *The Pit.*

In *The Pit* the visible wheat of the Californian fields is no longer the hero, but the invisible wheat, wheat as a plaything in the game of the stock market; wheat whose presence and availability for delivery at a given date were subjects for vast wagers. The Pit was the battlefield where the bears and the bulls fought for supremacy; it was "as dangerous as a powder mine." The great gambler of the novel, Curtis Jadwin, seems like some son of Saccard in Zola's *L'Argent*—but he springs directly from American life. The story is really that of Joseph Leiter; with the journalist's instinct, Norris tells it as though it were still "hot." This stock-market king, Leiter, had bought up almost the entire crop of a poor year—1896. He was able to set the market price where he pleased, and extracted $1.50 a bushel. And he went on buying; he sent an army of purchasers into the Northwest, chartered miles of cars and a whole fleet of vessels. Had he been able to hold the price at the level he had determined, his purchases would have made him the richest man in the country. But suddenly, as though by magic, wheat from everywhere appeared on the world market: wheat that had grown outside the United States; wheat that Joseph Leiter had not bought.

Canada opened her granaries; Argentina filled ships; a flood of "wild" wheat challenged the artificially bolstered price of the wheat that Joseph Leiter had monopolized. Leiter, "a man with amazing audacity, with unlimited self-confidence," did not see the signs or refused to see them; he held on, raised the price, and continued to buy, although other men in the exchange sensed the coming fall. Leiter's chief opponent was Philip Armour, the grain-elevator manufacturer, whose interests required cheap wheat and wheat in abundance. In the middle of the winter Armour brought six million bushels of wheat to Chicago. It came from the Canadian border; Armour had had the thick ice of Lake Michigan broken open with steel plows in order to bring the grain into the city and throw it into the battle of the stock market. . . . Leiter now did something insane: instead of abandoning the fight he bought up Armour's entire shipment, thereby automatically increasing the price once more. He planned to sell *all* of America's wheat at usurious prices to Europe.

America could eat Indian corn, as she had done in the old days; it didn't matter what America ate. But the foolish Europeans with their mania for wheat bread would make him, Joe Leiter, the richest man in the world. Then the one thing he had not expected happened. War broke out between Spain and the United States. Europe, superstitiously timid before the reputed power of the Spanish fleet, afraid of complications

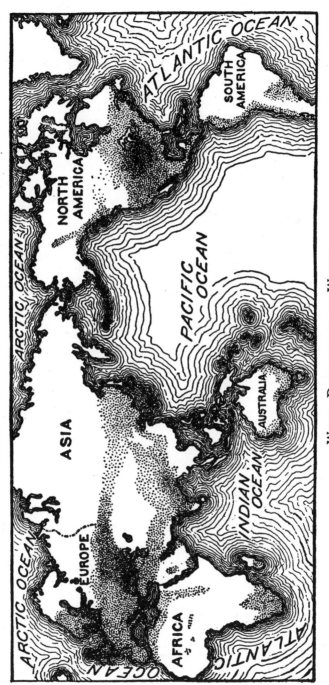

World Distribution of Wheat

and confiscations on the high seas, canceled the import order for American wheat. Before Leiter could sell it, the fifty million bushels he had bought smothered him. He was ruined; the gambler had lost his round against the fecundity of Mother Nature. She had not worried where and to whom he would sell. What were markets and prices to Nature? As Norris puts it in his novel when he condemns Curtis Jadwin, the fictional image of Leiter:

He had his human grasp upon Creation, and the very earth herself, the great mother, feeling the touch of the cobweb that the human insect had spun, had stirred at last in her sleep and sent her omnipotence moving through the grooves of the world, to find and crush the disturber of her appointed courses.

Norris still owed the world the third part of his epic of wheat, *The Wolf*. This was to be the most important part of all. The Wolf was the symbol of famine raging through Europe and Asia. In all parts of the world much had been written about wheat; but Norris wanted to be the first to link up the international experiences of the grain. He would show, as part of the epic of America, the exuberant producer, the epic of the suffering consumer. But where? In what land should he show famine at work? Norris and his young wife decided upon a trip around the world, taking a small, slow steamer, to find some spot where the people were dramatically hungry. And a spot "where famine would be relieved by the timely appearance from across the sea of three huge American schooners—wheat ships—loaded to their capacity with the great crop that, in spite of the quarrels of the farmers and the railroads, and in spite of the manipulations on the stock market, was *to fulfill its destiny as the nourisher of nations*."

But just out of port Norris fell ill. It was a suppurating inflammation of the appendix; Norris could not take it seriously. What could a bit of rotting tissue no larger than a dragonfly do to him, a man of thirty-two, who had just begun to make money out of his books—a man with such vast plans? He was gently amazed when he died of it, when the bit of rotting tissue tore him away from this earth which he had loved, whose regenerating powers he had sung so often.

§ 120

The Empire of Wheat stretched to Europe on its Atlantic wing, to Asia on the Pacific side. It seemed that the exportable wheat of the United States would conquer the entire world, for it was unlimited in quantity and in means of transportation. But when it reached eastern Asia, it began to run into difficulties.

Throughout the Far East *rice* had ruled for thousands of years. For rice and food the Chinese language employs the same general term. The annual world harvest of rice is 440,000,000,000 pounds; the greater part of it is raised in the Far East. Rice and not bread is eaten in the monsoon lands where men live out their lives in marshes and tropical heat. Rice prospers in temperatures in which no bread grain can survive. Climate and soil mold men, shape their customs, their views, and the metaphysics of their ethics. The sense of taste is perhaps only one of the outermost blossoms on the tree of human existence, but it, too, is difficult to change. A middle-class Japanese unaccustomed to bread will react to the finest variety of wheat as a Roman would have reacted to rye; he will find it unpleasantly sour. The white man finds the sourness of bread its vital aspect; the first bite sets his salivary glands working. To Orientals, on the other hand, the bland, silken taste of the rice grain has its own character- istic and beloved qualities.

Good rice may be as rich in protein as good wheat. Yet there is no cor- respondence between the nations that practice a monoculture of rice and those who eat bread. Eaters of bread who are suddenly shifted to a diet of rice begin to show signs of debility. . . . After the capture of Manila in 1942, a high neutral official pointed out to the Japanese that they must feed their American prisoners better. The Japanese replied indignantly that the prisoners received the same ration as Japanese soldiers. Why was that not sufficient? But men whose basic food, besides meat and coffee, had been bread for hundreds of years simply cannot suddenly enter the other food triangle of rice, fish, and tea.

Different physiology, different manners. Paul Ehrenreich, the ethnolo- gist, observed religious rice culture without blood sacrifices in Malacca. Even among the remotest and smallest tribes, pure and innocent verbal conjuring was employed against apes, elephants, and birds; no animals were killed or the soil sprinkled with blood. Unlike the Aztec maize festi- val, at the Malays' thanksgiving festival for rice, no more was done than to strew cooked grains of rice into the children's hair. Simple memory was invoked to assure the continuity of rice cultivation among the chil- dren of the Malays. . . . Radhakamal Mukerdschi, Indian professor in Lucknow, in comparing wheat and rice, called the grain of the West the "grain of capitalism"; its inhuman and acquisitive tendency favored the establishment of large estates both in Rome and America, he said. Rice, on the other hand, he called the "friend of the small farmer," for its cul- tivation is limited to gardens, terraces, and swamps. . . . It is, however, a mistake to blame wheat for its far-reaching social effects; in the hands of the large-scale trader rice also becomes an accumulator of capital.

The distaste for wheat among the Asiatics of the Southeast was, then, quite pronounced. In many parts of Asia there were, in addition to re- ligious and gustatory reasons for rejecting wheat, domestic reasons as well, for wheat straw is not so lasting as rice straw. In a culture where roofs, aprons, hats, mats, sandals, and every sort of basket are prepared in the home, the more adaptable material is naturally preferred—in this case rice straw rather than wheat straw.

The experts of the Empire of Wheat had to reckon on these conditions when, in the seventies of the last century, they began feeling out the Asiatic markets. Fortunately for export, these conditions applied only to the moist and hot Southeast; not to the northerly Japanese islands or the northern mainland of China. In these more moderate climates wheat was known. In North China crop rotation was also known; the same fields were sown to winter wheat and summer rice, alternating with watermelons and soybeans. Here the exporters began. Californian grain was sent to North China, where the tongues of the people already knew the taste of wheat.

From January 1, 1867 on, when the first ship, the *Colorado,* embarked from San Francisco, the route to Shanghai was covered with majestic clouds of steam. Untroubled by the conflict in the countinghouses of San Francisco between the steamship lines and the railroad kings, the grain sailed to East Asia. It was said that every grain of wheat belonged to the Big Four—Marc Hopkins, Charles Crocker, Leland Stanford, and, the strongest among the four, Collis P. Huntington. It was proverbially said that of every three raindrops falling in California, Huntington owned two. It had not been easy for him to acquire his immense wealth against all the competitors, small farmers and large. Now he hoped to make up by high prices what all the struggles had cost him. But when the Chinese mildly explained that they could go back to eating rice, the price of the wheat dropped precipitately.

Bread, however, is a magician. Many of the Chinese of the port towns, seeing the belching smokestacks, the sailors, the careless life on board, became Americanized. The wanderlust seized them. With the steamers that returned from the Far East to San Francisco many bland, smiling men came to America—laundry workers and longshoremen, restaurateurs and day laborers; many, too, opium salesmen. Grayish-yellow, industrious faces—all of them somehow kinsmen. They were happy to live in broad, beautiful, hygienic San Francisco. In death, however, they did not want to remain there; they wanted to repose only in the earth of China. When they died, the undertakers cleansed the body carefully; bones and skulls were dipped in brandy and packed into boxes for the journey. These Chinese coffins, carefully addressed to their native towns, sailed with every shipment of wheat that crossed the Pacific to feed the living Chinese. . . . The peoples met upon the highway of grain; men and grain migrated together. Thus there arose between the Empire of Wheat and the North Chinese provinces a permanent grain trade, though it never took excessive or exaggerated forms.

But the nations had become acquainted.

BOOK SIX

Bread in Our Time

Agriculture is the first of all arts. Without it there would exist
neither merchants nor poets nor philosophers.

FREDERICK THE GREAT

Good farming; clear thinking; right living.

HENRY A. WALLACE

HOW BREAD HELPED WIN WORLD WAR I

§ 121

How WAS IT that in their trading the Americans scarcely ever had hostile
encounters with the Russians? Siberia was much the closer to China. That
the Russian Empire should be outdone in the competition for grain export seemed indeed astonishing.

Until 1850 Russia was the sole supplier of all Europe. And even in
1900 she could, had she desired, have had the greatest area of wheat
plantings in the world. Nevertheless, in that record year America exported 216,000,000 bushels of wheat—almost three times as much as the
Russian Empire. For Russia was convinced that from climatic reasons,
as well as reasons of national taste, she must plant more rye than wheat.
Moreover, there was no vast network of railroads, which alone could
make possible the export of wheat on a grand scale.

In 1903, during the Russo-Japanese War, the Russian General Staff
on its way to the front had to make a long halt; all the high officers with
their St. George's crosses and their embroidered collars waited on a siding
until a trainload of American reapers passed. . . . The world was
amused because the anecdote seemed to point up the superiority of agriculture over war. The point was quite different: it illustrated that Russia
was a land of single-track railroads and that her agricultural products
therefore needed a long time to reach the ports of the world. The quantities intended for export were, it is true, not small. The statistics show that
in the warm year of 1911 Russia exported 150,000,000 bushels of grain.
But the greater part of this grain could be shipped only over short routes
to Odessa and Riga, two ports that could be quickly reached from inland.
In Vladivostok the granaries remained empty—for the Siberian Railroad
was not able to undertake large-scale transportation. Northeast Asia
would have gone hungry had it not been for the American ships that year
after year sailed from the Golden Gate with laden holds.

Because of their lack of transport the Russians therefore abandoned the Eastern markets and offered their surplus to Europe, where, of course, they also encountered the Americans. In the course of this trading the Russians should have remarked Germany's increased demand for grain. Why did their German neighbor need such immense quantities of *barley?* The Russians did not question the purpose; between 1909 and 1914 they happily sold half of their annual barley crop to Germany. Did the Germans intend to increase their consumption of beer? In 1913 the Germans bought 227,000,000 poods (one pood equals about thirty-six pounds) of Russian barley, in addition to enormous quantities of oats.

It was not greater beer consumption that the Germans planned. And in the first week of August 1914, when a host of cavalry squadrons mounted on sturdy, well-fed horses trotted across the Russian border, the Russians realized what the purpose had been.

§ 122

The war Germany planned was to last a single year. It might even last a year and a half. In Germany only short wars were known. The wars of the nineteenth century against Denmark, Austria, and France had all lasted less than a year. . . . Even if the English blockade should eliminate the import of American grain, Germany would not starve. Bread for men and beasts was stored up—native grain and purchased grain. But when the war did not come up to expectations, when the initial German victories did not decide the World War, it became apparent that "those who do not sow enough might as well not sow at all." To all outward appearances the Germans were waging a successful war of movement. But internally—before she herself realized it—Germany resembled a besieged fortress.

The Germans had entered the World War upon the crest of an excellent harvest. Four and a half hundredweight of bread grains per capita —that was ample to feed the people. The English harvest seemed much worse. Nevertheless, Germany was soon starving because the Germans exhausted their hog and cow feed and had to feed their bread grains to the cattle. The farmers were more concerned about their hogs than about feeding the cities. By 1915, when government confiscation of grain stores was instituted, it was already too late; the greater part of the crop had been put into the butchers' profits. When the English blockade commenced cutting off American wheat, Germany swiftly entered a bread crisis.

The great conquests of land made by the German armies in 1915 concealed this condition for a time. For the lands that were conquered were arable eastern lands, and the swift German advance did not lay waste to the land as it did in France, where the battles were lengthier and more destructive. Agriculture followed in the train of the German soldiers to Poland and Russia and took possession of broad areas to supply the German stomach. For a time this seemed to work; but in 1916 and 1917 it developed that the Germans could supply the brains, but not the hands to exploit these lands. The subject peoples had no intention of speeding for the Kaiser the tempo at which they had worked for the Czar. Since most of the peasants were serving in the Russian Army, labor was lacking. At this time neither German nor Russian agriculture was mechanized. The labor of war prisoners was insufficient. And, above all, the transportation system very soon gave out.

The German railroads, although they had the advantage of "internal communications" and could shift their rolling stock more easily than the enemy, decayed when for four years there was less and less material available to make repairs. Since troop trains took precedence, the bread that grew in the East could not be brought to the West in time. Even during the great battles in France in 1916 the Germans were already going hungry. Marx, a Prussian general, narrates that his men "were happy to enter the terrible battle of Verdun because they had heard that there the soldiers did not receive the customary meager provisions, but 'major battle provisions.' Death was less terrible than the eternal lack of bread. . . ." And in April 1918 the van of the German Army suddenly halted in the midst of an attack in South Belgium. An officer explains the incident:

To our amazement the advance halted, though no British defense was holding up the assaulting soldiers. What had happened? Amid the rich stores of provisions in the trenches the enemy had abandoned, German discipline dissolved. Commands were no longer obeyed. These soldiers, starved for years, could not endure the sight of the provisions. They fell upon them. In the midst of battle they opened with their bayonets the bread sacks of the English, the American tin cans, and ate until they were choking. Deaf to all pleas, deaf to all threats, they stopped fighting and ate like animals. . . . No, like men—like the wretched men they were. All they wanted was to fill their bellies once more, even if they must die immediately afterward. These German soldiers had lain for weeks in the rain; without grumbling they had then advanced, hollow-eyed, against the overpowering web of machine guns, mines, and shells that the enemy threw around them. The Allied hail of steel had not stopped them—but now they remained lying where they were when they saw the loaves of white bread and the tins of corned beef. . . .

The Germans' hunger was not appeased by the assurances of nutrition laboratories that for thousands of years they had eaten too much and all the wrong foods. Bread need not be made of rye, wheat, or other cereals; its basic components could be replaced by substitutes without harm.

As we have seen, in all times of famine men have attempted to deceive their stomachs. The starving people of the Middle Ages baked whatever came to hand into their bread. But never before had anyone claimed that quicksand grass was as good or better than oats and that "scientifically treated" straw could replace the protein in grain. Such excesses were left to our age, the "scientific age." Since men possess biology and chemistry, they can lie more plausibly. Justus von Liebig in 1840 was astonished at how ingeniously the bakers of London adulterated their flour; in order to make it appear whiter they employed a chemical that had been unknown in earlier times.

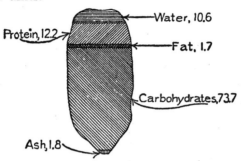

Protein, 12.2
Water, 10.6
Fat, 1.7
Carbohydrates, 73.7
Ash, 1.8

THE CONTENTS OF A GRAIN OF WHEAT

German nutritional scientists could not help seeing the wretchedness into which the German people were sinking more and more deeply from 1916 on, but the scientists lied out of patriotism. Two thousand calories a day were all an adult body needed, they preached, and sixty grams of protein. That was little enough to obtain. Whipped up by the will to victory, they hunted in the streets, the woods, and the fields for substitutes. Hans Friedenthal seriously recommended bread made of straw; Graebner suggested bread of rushes. Jacobi, pharmacologist at the University of Tübingen, wanted to bake bread of Icelandic moss; and Professor Kobert of Rostock, who was accounted an authority, experimented with animal's blood as an ersatz for bread. Harry Snyder, the well-known milling and wheat expert, says of this tragedy:

Numerous were the attempts to treat chemically sawdust and wood pulp so as to make them available as human food. It was hoped that by chemical treatment cellulose could be converted into a digestible carbohydrate. A pound of sawdust when burned in the calorimeter produces as many calories as a pound of wheat flour. But the pound of sawdust refuses to digest, or to yield calories in the human or animal body. It takes more than inert calories to make a food; the calories must be digestible and available, and derived from certain foodstuffs.

But could not one of the most important foodstuffs in grain, the protein, be produced? There seemed to be synthetic and biochemical methods. It was well known, for example, that yeast could manufacture protein by combining nitrogenous salts with carbohydrates. The German scientists hoped to apply this fact to the solution of the food problem. The free nitrogen of the air would be chemically fixed or combined by electrical processes, and then this synthetic nitrogen compound would be fed to yeast to produce protein. A chemist named Delbrück claimed he had discovered a method whereby, out of a hundred pounds of sugar, he could manufacture a food containing 50 per cent protein; and Hayduck, a professor of agriculture, predicted splendid results from "feeding this protein product to pigs, cows, et cetera." The "et cetera" probably meant the German people.

According to the inventors, this food was three times as rich in protein as beef and cost only three cents a pound. Magic! But Harry Snyder commented on this magical food: "This yeast-made protein was a clumsy scientific camouflage, doubtless given out with the idea of making the chemists of other countries believe the German imperial chemists had solved the food problem." Yeast in reality never contains more than 12 per cent protein, and no plant is known that can yield 50 per cent. . . .

The chemical formula that German nutritional science concocted was false. Moreover, it was criminal. For had the common people known that this formula was false, they would not have fought on. They might have laid down their arms two years sooner, for the war was already lost in 1916; humanity might have been spared torrents of blood. And Germany would have been spared the grave biologic enfeeblement that produced the postwar hysteria and the need for overcompensation—psychic states that made for Hitler and World War II.

§ 123

The World War caused an unparalleled situation for the bread producers and consumers the world over. Hitherto all wars had been fought between countries, never between continents. The Seven Years' War, which we know as the French and Indian War, had been a kind of world war; France and England had fought each other upon several continents. But this was happenstance. Both the theaters of war, Europe and America, were independent of each other's bread. . . . August 4, 1914, on the other hand, ushered in for the first time a "global war."

True, the United States was neutral. But since the Empire of Wheat had to deal with both parties, America soon felt the cumulative effect of the gigantic European struggle. More than 70,000,000 men in Europe had been called from productive labor and were devoting their energies either to fighting or to the production of implements of destruction. Women and children were making an effort to replace these men in the production of foodstuffs and other needed products, but they were unable to maintain the full normal supply. Their travail was hampered for lack of draft animals and transportation facilities, as well as by the deficiency in the regular supply of fertilizers.

This falling off in European production meant a larger demand for supplies from abroad. Never before had America's crops been so important to Europe as they were now. But the warring powers had no intention of permitting their enemies to enjoy the benefits of American production. The British did not permit wheat to flow across the free seas to Germany and Austria. And the Germans, whose submarines later took to torpedoing neutral shipping without warning, likewise hoped to force the British and French to abandon the war because of starvation on the home front. In the beginning America considered the attitude of both the Allies and the Germans equally barbarous. War was traditionally an affair of the military, not of the civil population. Now the European enemies were swinging below the belt with blockade and counterblockade. But the follow-through struck American export trade. No one in America could comprehend this injustice. It was felt unanimously and unambiguously in America that Europe must eat and that America must sell her surplus wheat to the hungry Europeans.

Since the ordinary routes by which grain had formerly traveled to the warring nations were now endangered, new routes must be found. Skillfully, America opened new subsidiary routes for her export trade: to neutral Holland and Spain and to Italy, which was neutral for a time. . . . But there was another gap through which American wheat was pumped into starving Europe. This was one of America's boldest strokes: the *aid to Belgium*. When Americans read in the first weeks of the war how Belgium had been overrun, despite her urgent desire to remain neutral, the news produced a dual sentiment: anti-German feeling and the determination not to let the Belgian people starve. A publicity campaign extorted enormous sums. The smallest farmer in Missouri contributed his mite as gladly as the financier in his Wall Street office. The distribution activities were headed by the Belgian banker, Emile Francqui, and by Herbert Clark Hoover.

Hoover was an energetic man, a mining engineer who had devoted himself chiefly to organizing mining enterprises in China and Australia. He was considered a good organizer. But as soon as he began American aid to occupied Belgium, objections were raised in London. The British claimed that he was a dilettante in agrarian matters, and that the Germans were tricking him. Why was there famine in Belgium anyhow? Until the war Belgium had supported herself handily by her own production. The large quantities of grain imported at Antwerp had been an optical illusion: Antwerp was merely a port of entry for France and Germany. Belgium did not need America's grain. Over 60 per cent of her land was cultivated intensively. Normally she produced 2,280,000,000 pounds of bread. Since more than 800,000 of the 7,350,000 Belgians had fled or were prisoners of war, a family of six in Belgium could have from four to six pounds of bread every day. This was no starvation diet, London objected. Why was Hoover permitting himself to be hoodwinked? Perhaps because Hoover knew the Germans. He may have realized from the first that the German Empire, fighting as it was for its existence, would have no regard for the Hague laws, which provided that a conqueror must feed the occupied country. On the contrary. The Germans would begin to plunder Belgium mercilessly as soon as it became necessary to fill the German stomach. The Americans recognized this sooner than the British.

Moreover, America was neutral; she had a right to overlook the tactics of the German administration which permitted her to feed Belgium but cold-bloodedly requisitioned for Germany all the food that grew in Belgium. America was upon the horns of a tragic dilemma. Without the American wheat that came to the Germans by these roundabout routes, the Germans might actually have been forced to quit the war in the late fall of 1916 (before the conquest of Rumania, with its stores of wheat, gave them a new lease on life). America's entrance into the war in 1917 was, among other things, payment for her "humanitarian mistakes"—for her having tried, as long as it was possible, to supply both belligerents with the staff of life.

But the moment America took sides, the moment the Empire of Wheat joined hands with the Allies, the outcome of World War I was decided. It was in the perilous spring of 1917 that America's declaration of war was made—that same perilous spring in which the Russian Empire began to reel, to totter out of the ring and abandon the fight against the German enemy. The breach thus made was filled not only with bayonets, but with sacks of wheat. "Victory through wheat"—this was the program President Wilson placed in the hands of Herbert Hoover. Hoover was given power such as had been possessed by no other American for one hundred and fifty years. Hoover's first public reaction was urgently to request that he be called Food Administrator, not Food Czar. He knew his countrymen.

Had Frank Norris lived to see what now took place, he would have been astonished beyond words. Foreign trade in grain was *nationalized;* that is, it was controlled by a "Corporation of Grain Trade" established by the Government. Maximum grain prices within the country were decreed, and all speculation upon the wheat market was prohibited. This represented a degree of government interference that Washington or Lincoln would never have dreamed of attempting; it was interference with the freedom of the trader. In normal times, to be sure, properly controlled speculation may have played its natural part in the orderly marketing of wheat, furnishing a market in which millers and grain dealers could hedge their sales or purchases to reduce their hazards and increase their margins of profit. But due to the increased demand caused by the war, speculation in any form would have become a menace both to producers and consumers. It was necessary, therefore, for the Food Administration to take all possible steps to eliminate such speculation.

The theoretical grain needs of the Allies, according to Frank M. Surface, were nearly 600,000,000 bushels at the time of America's entry into the war. None of this could be obtained from Russia or Rumania. Russia's crop had been eliminated by the armies of Kaiser Wilhelm, and Rumania's was also in the hands of the Germans. The Germans proclaimed loudly that America was in no position to help her Allies, for German U-boats were sinking a huge tonnage of shipping every month.

The situation was perilous, and becoming more perilous every day. To supply the world's prime foodstuff under these conditions was not child's play. It required men of vision and experience. A few false steps in the control of wheat during the winter and spring of 1917–18 might even have resulted in the loss of the Allied cause.

As early as 1916 the anxious, famine-bitten neutral countries of Europe —and the Allied nations as well—had begged American wheat dealers for their wheat at any price. The disastrous lack of shipping space contributed to the rise in price. Without government control through the Food Administration prices would have skyrocketed. If the price of export wheat had not been checked, the price within America would also have risen; speculation and widespread hunger would have been the result. Without government regulation of wheat, the war could not have been waged successfully.

Julius Barnes, Hoover's aide, declared in 1917 that "all private speculation has been stopped. . . . The Allies will be supplied with every bushel of surplus wheat that can be made available to them. . . . American mills will be assured of a steady normal supply of grain to grind; and neutral buying will be under our absolute control." The successful execution of this program, the supplying of the Allied and neutral nations (including the governments-in-exile, the Serbs, Poles, and Czechoslovaks)—this is a part of the unwritten "Grain History of the World War," which must someday be set down to supplement the military history. Napoleon had said, "An army marches on its stomach." The armies were marching in Europe, but their bread came from America; it was difficult indeed to supply them with the wherewithal to march. Nevertheless, it was done. History will someday record that victory "hung by a stalk of wheat." Italy, wounded in her vitals by the rout at Caporetto (October 1917), would have backed out of the war had not Hoover's wheat held her to the Entente. After the war, when the national monopoly on grain was abolished, Food Administrator Hoover received a gift rich in associations. Attolico, Italian Minister of Food Supply, sent him a copy of an old Roman coin in the Museum of Naples. It showed an image of the grain goddess, the Annona, surrounded by symbols of ships and ears of wheat. Attolico's point was well taken: the American Empire of Wheat had replaced the Roman Empire; and her gifts had saved the motherland of Latin civilization.

RUSSIA'S BREAD—1917

§ 124

KAISER WILHELM II had hoped to save himself with the bread of the Ukraine. But when the grain of Russia remained uncut and the ovens of Germany empty, the Kaiser's country collapsed. The man who was overlord of the Ukrainian bread likewise no longer ruled.

All his life Nicholas II, the last Czar, had suspected that if he wished to remain emperor he must be an emperor of the peasants. Amid the rising hostility of bourgeoisie and proletariat, liberals and socialists, for his regime, the peasants alone seemed not to be his foes. They supplied the main human material for his armies. Patient, dull, trained to obedience by their Orthodox priests, they had for centuries been treated in unchristian fashion but nevertheless remained inwardly convinced that they were the only Christian class. In 1861 Alexander II had "liberated" them. Serfdom was abandoned; but poor methods of tillage, misery, and lack of machinery remained. The articles that came from the city—student agitation and factories—the peasants looked upon with suspicion. When young men came to the village to explain to the peasants that they had not yet been liberated, although they owned their own land; to show them that they were still muzhiks who, as taxpayers and soldiers, maintained the bureaucracy and the Court—the peasants grumbled at the interlopers, the *Narodniki,* or bound them and turned them over to the authorities. The Czar counted upon the blind loyalty and simplicity of such men.

This last of the Romanoffs was a very weak man. In his childhood he had heard the lovely nursery rhyme:

> Where the queen has gone,
> There the rye is thick,
> Where the moon has passed by,
> There laugh the oats.
> Grow, grow,
> Rye and oats—
> Flourish richly
> Father and son.

In his soul faith in the peasants had remained as faith in creatures that were a part of nature. He would lean upon them. Therefore he did something that his father and grandfather had never done: he donned the peasant blouse. We know that clothes influence the mental attitudes of men. The Czar took his masquerade very seriously; he considered himself a peasant with no time for tilling the soil because, unfortunately, he had to govern the state.

The Czar had never in his life spoken to a real peasant. He did not know that the deputations that approached him at agricultural exhibitions were in part carefully selected, in part gentlemen dressed up as peasants. He knew only that the peasants did not hate him. But the reason for this was not at all that they loved him. These peasants, with their patriarchal beards and their faces like the bark of trees, who were the recipients of the Czar's romantic affection, were incapable of so strong a feeling as love for the Czar.

Immeasurable wretchedness weighed upon the Russian village—a wretchedness that could not be changed merely by redistribution of property. The peasant, it was true, owned a patch of land; or, rather, all the peasants of a village owned the patch. The village community, the *mir,* administered the common land under a system of village communism. But since the mir possessed neither money nor animals to cultivate the land, these things had to be borrowed from the noble lord. Since the peasant could never pay back any money, within a few years after the abolition of serfdom a situation existed that was economically, if not legally, the equivalent of serfdom. The services that the peasant or his cattle could not perform, he imposed upon his wife. We know from Gorki, Nekrasov, and many other writers that nowhere was the position of woman so bad as in peasant Russia.

The eternal hunger of western Europe between the ninth and the fourteenth centuries was still a commonplace in Russia in 1900. American commissions wondered how the people could live. "An Englishman," Novikov writes in his description of the Russian village, "would die if he ate for only a week the food of a Russian peasant." Water soup with sour cabbage leaves tinged with milk; millet porridge or buckwheat groats; then sour black bread, a few potatoes, pickles in summer and fall—this was his diet. Curiously enough, Novikov objects that all this food was too sour; but perhaps the Russian people would have died of scurvy with the sourness absent.

This starving empire of peasants possessed provinces with the best soil in the world, the black earth provinces, which produced wheat and rye in great abundance—but only for export. It was only the lack of ports and railroads that prevented more from being exported.

Since the Czar realized that America owed all her greatness to the railroads, he had dreamed of completing the Siberian railroad. Through

Siberia, hitherto worthless to him, through the forests, moors, and tundras, the arteries of trade would run, and back along them would pump gold to the heart of the empire. Riches were within his grasp, if only grain could be transported swiftly from the European provinces for sale in eastern Asia. But the railroad must reach the Pacific. From 1893 on work on the railroad progressed at a furious rate. Russian peasants who had fled from hunger in Europe to become hunters and woodcutters in Siberia were astonished to receive letters of pardon from their government. They were liberally promised gifts of land and money if they would cultivate inhospitable Siberia sufficiently to feed the railroad workers. No more ambitious projects were conceived; it seemed beyond the bounds of possibility that Siberia itself might someday become a land of grain. The Russian Government was thinking merely of slight cultivation, which would be sufficient to speed work on the railroad. Once the railroad was completed, Russia would be rich—America's example proved this. How grain was to be raised in wholly virgin lands, without experts to help drain swamps, without the slightest knowledge of soil-improvement methods, and above all without any agricultural tools or machinery—this was the secret and the tragicomedy of the Czarist regime.

When the railroad at last reached the Far East, it encountered not customers for Russian products, but the hatred of the aroused Japanese. Expansion to the Pacific brought reward not in gold, but in blood, and produced the military defeat of 1904.

The peasants did not take part in the vengeful revolution of 1905, although they had suffered most in the Czar's last war. It was a revolution of workers and middle class. The peasantry and the Church continued to be apparently the only refuge for a Czar forever threatened by infernal machines and concealed revolvers. Both classes had to be strengthened. The Church received rich donations. And for the first time plans to reform the condition of the peasantry were given serious consideration. Prime Minister Stolypin (1862–1911) convinced the Czar that only a well-to-do peasantry could prevent a renewed outbreak of revolution. As in western Europe the peasant, who was fundamentally a conservative, must be given an interest in a moderate capitalism and must be permitted to enrich himself. Had the peasants been other than naturally conservative, they would inevitably have participated vigorously in the recent revolution of intellectuals and workers. But even they had participated to some extent; to prevent further defections they must be freed from the grip of the large landowners. A national peasants' bank would advance money to the peasants, for otherwise they would never gain their independence. Moreover, in order to weaken the landowners, the state must buy land and present it to the farmers. Not, however, to the village mir, for Stolypin was convinced that the mir was the second foe of progress. Village communism made it possible "for the inefficient peasant to eat as much as the diligent peasant." The land would be given to the "dependable, modern peasant who will enrich himself and the region."

In 1906, over the resistance of the powerful princely circles, this reform was introduced. For five years the produce of Russian agriculture increased in quantity. The newspapers were already beginning to hail Stolypin as a "Russian Solon." Then, on September 14, 1911, he was shot under the eyes of his ruler in the municipal theater at Kiev. The Social Revolutionaries, who had another score to settle with Stolypin—he had opposed Parliament and supported autocratic rule—had sentenced him to death.

The ruler in the peasant blouse had often considered that Stolypin's doings could not have the blessing of God. The peasants seemed to him devout children. To make adults of them might inspire them with unrest. The peasants, Nicholas thought, were eternal as the earth; they produced out of themselves a mystical force which overcame all evils—in particular the evil of revolution. What more did a peasant need if he believed in God and the Czar?

And then the Czar's destiny guided to him the man who demonstrated what he himself knew only as an obscure premonition: that the peasant was unhappy only if he were robbed of his innocence; if reforms were imposed upon him. The peasant was the "earth's monk"; his service was its own reward.

Russian society had long been ripe for a charlatan extraordinary. In Dostoevski's great novel, *The Brothers Karamazov,* the hero is fascinated by Schiller's verses on Eleusis. Dmitri Karamazov, this rude, intelligent, passion-rent man, celebrates the prodigies of agriculture. Sobbing, he quotes Schiller's words:

> Would he purge his soul from vileness
> And attain to light and worth,
> He must turn and cling forever
> To his ancient Mother Earth.

But he suddenly interrupts his recitation—for he is an army officer and a city man—and asks soberly: "But the difficulty is, how am I to cling forever to Mother Earth? Am I to become a peasant or a shepherd?" He cannot do either.

Into this society, this leading class in Russia, stepped the great swindler, the Cagliostro who pretended to cling to Mother Earth.

Grigoryi Rasputin was the man who played both parts to perfection: that of peasant and that of monk. In reality he was neither, but a great hypnotist impelled by a boundless lust for power and pleasure. This "Russian priest of Demeter" who had risen from obscure poverty brought into the state sessions and the St. Petersburg salons a breath of perfumed manure and the mystic significance of the ecclesiastical Slavic word *chljebu*—bread and soil. Bearded, pale, possessed of an animal-like vitality, he seemed one of the ancient gods of the field. Demanding fertility of the earth and of the women he encountered, this character, overcharged with erotic appetites, compelled the opposition to acknowledge the power of his peasant blouse and his peasant boots. Before long the liberals at the court fell silent. Hosts believed in Rasputin's magical power with God, in his ability to intercede for Russia. He could make fields more fruitful and stop the hemorrhagic flow of blood of the Czar's child—as almost two thousand years before Christ had stanched a woman's bleeding. And yet it was all theater. Frigid amid the hot tumult around him, the false peasant played his last scene in 1917, when, in the midst of the World War, he was shot by a group of courtiers who felt shamed before their Western allies.

Rasputin was gone. His prophecy that the Czar would not long survive him was fulfilled. Within a few months the other "false peasant" was dethroned and a year afterward killed. The waves of the Russian Revolution rolled over their memory. This was no revolution of peasants, but one of workers. It did not become a peasants' revolution until the workers, struggling with their retreating enemies, on November 7, 1917, issued the decree that made the soil the property of the people. The peasants were called upon to form village soviets everywhere and to confiscate the estates of Church and Crown, of large landowners and nobility, and to take over all means of production. The decree was prepared so hurriedly that it was not even copied on the typewriter. From the tribune of the Congress of Soviets Lenin read the sole copy in its rough form from the penciled notes. Suchanov and Trotsky report that it "was copied so poorly that Lenin stumbled in reading, could not make it out, and finally stopped. Someone from the crowd came to his assistance. Lenin gladly made room on the platform and handed the man the illegible paper."

This was an ill omen. The Bolsheviks, who within a few weeks had won over the army and the city populace, had had no time to feel the pulse of the peasantry. Had they done so, they would have seen that the peasants were but wavering allies. It was the salvation of the Revolution that the peasant decree was unclear. All confiscated property, the decree read, was to be a part of the people's wealth. But to whom did the people's wealth belong? Did it belong to all, or to the state? And, above all, who administered it?

This was a question in which was latent bloody civil war. But for the present it slumbered in the background. On that November 7 the peasant was handed something of which his fathers and older brothers had scarcely ever thought; and this won him to the Revolution. A large part of the peasantry did not realize what it was even now. State socialism in the villages? But a few months earlier Lenin had written significantly:

"The peasants want to retain their small enterprises. Let them. On that account no reasonable socialist will quarrel with the impoverished peasants." But in the same article he added: "Once the land has been confiscated . . . then, after political power has passed to the proletariat, practice will dictate the rest." What that practice would be like the peasants had no idea when they descended upon the lords' estates in the next few weeks of November and, with fire and pillage, instituted a vast carnival. Wherever they did not burn castles to the ground, they plundered so thoroughly that they even carried away doors and windows. Implicit in this was the instinctive desire "that the foe may never again establish himself." For the peasants naïvely believed that their foes—as in the Middle Ages—had walls behind which they dwelt. They did not know that agrarian capitalism had become an invisible thing, hidden on papers in the vaults of banks. They soon realized that the townspeople—who could read and write!—still did not wish them well, for often, when they returned from a gay plundering expedition, battalions of armed workers with soldiers' caps would appear and take away the beautiful tapestries, the porcelain, and the wines—remarking that all these things belonged not to them, but to the state.

§ 125

Before November 1917 the peasants had not dared to dream that they would dispose of so many old enemies and acquire so many new ones. What had happened to Holy Russia? In Tolstoy's immortal novel, *Resurrection*, that compendium of all knowledge of the Russian peasant's character, we find Prince Nekhludoff, intoxicated by English ideas, going to his estates to give up his property. He wishes to put an end to a state of affairs he considers dishonorable. That is, he will rent his property to his tenants at so low a price that it will be the equivalent of a gift.

When Nekhludoff approached the assembled peasants and saw the blond, curly, bald and gray heads bared, the Prince at first felt so embarrassed that for a long time he could say nothing. The rain continued to trickle down, clinging to the peasants' beards and their rude coats. The peasants looked stolidly at the master, waiting to hear what he would say. But he was too confused to speak. The embarrassing silence was broken by the steward, a fat, overfed German who considered himself an authority on the Russian peasant's soul because he spoke Russian correctly.

"The master wants to do you a favor; he wants to give you the land."

The peasants looked at one another in perplexity.

"As he has said, I have called you together because I want to divide all the land among you," Nekhludoff at last began diffidently.

The peasants were silent. They looked at him without understanding and without belief.

A few slow-thinking, prudent peasants ask the prince what he means by "divide." The matter itself seems all right to them, but . . . The prince explains that prices and dates of payment will be established. After the outline has been settled, suspicion arises from the peasants' hearts and befogs their minds. What's that? He intends to help *them?* Why? It can't be anything good if it's a gift. "Nekhludoff," Tolstoy writes, "had expected his proposal to be accepted with great rejoicing. But there was no trace of any joy among the assembled peasants." The peasants at once began to quarrel whether the entire community (the mir) or a few individuals should take over the new land; some were for the mir, others wanted to exclude the bad farmers and poor payers from the privilege of renting. As Tolstoy says, "The peasants were not satisfied, and Nekhludoff departed unsatisfied." The ancient crime, the crime of thousands of years, cannot be atoned for by such an act—this is Tolstoy's thought, which he leaves to the reader. It cannot be repaired by an act in which the peasants have only halfheartedly participated.

But a generation later, when the "carnival of vengeance" began, the peasants took action themselves. The blood of the bad landowners flowed with the good; into the laps of these peasants whom Tolstoy described as having rejected a gift with the "irony of the weak" there suddenly fell the tremendous heritage of the Russian land and of Russian bread. The November decree empowered them to socialize the land. They began at once by cutting down the forests and carrying the wood to their kitchen stoves, for the war with the Germans was still going on and Russia had no coal. Moreover, they wanted to till the land, to sow it and live by the harvest. Then they learned that the cities' concept of socialism differed from their own. The city workers did not plant grain, but they wanted to eat it. "Well, let them buy," the peasants thought genially. But the workers had no money because the industries were at a standstill. "What do we care?" the peasants thought. "We do not need industry; our sheep hides and bast shoes we can make ourselves." If the peasants had been left to their own devices, the cities would have starved. The Marxist theoreticians had foreseen this. Karl Marx had never been a friend of an economy in which the peasants were permitted to govern themselves.

"Equal distribution of the land," Rosa Luxemburg wrote, "has nothing in common with socialism." But give dominion to the city workers who needed bread and could not pay for it, and the peasants who had previously worked for the Czar and the nobles would now have to work unrequited to maintain the cityfolk. . . . Where did a peaceful solution lie? The Revolution was imperiled! One thing alone was sure: the Czar and the nobles would not return because they had been deprived of the basis of their power—possession of the land. But all things else were in flux.

Lenin had ventured to cross the hammer with the sickle in the insignia of the new Russian state. But scarcely half a year after the adoption of this emblem, on August 4, 1918, it became evident that the symbol expressed not co-operation but cross-purposes. A classless society had not been realized in so short a time. There were still workers and peasants whose interests were more than ever opposed. The workers might shout at the tops of their lungs that it was the hammer which had given political freedom to the sickle. Without the smashing blows of the hammer the peasant would not possess all the land he now owned. And in way of gratitude he was permitting the cities to starve. August passed into September, and still the harvest did not arrive in the city. The workers went out to the land. "Bread or death!" was their watchword. Once more villages and barns blazed. The demobilized peasants had taken their rifles back home; they defended every sack of grain. This people of a hundred and eighty million heard the spattering of bullets in thousands of isolated guerrilla fights. During those same weeks that the American Army in western Europe advanced, "behind every bayonet five sacks of good Canadian wheat," in the East the hunger war between the red front and the green front began, a war of blood and fire, sabotage and the withholding of food.

It was the age-old war between town and country; but never before had it been fought so fiercely. As in 1798, when the rural cantons of Switzerland had spilled their seed into rivers and smashed their plows rather than feed the Revolutionary Army of the French, so now did the Russian peasant. In many districts he chose rather to eat his last ox than to continue to till the soil and supply the cities. Scornfully he proved to the commissars that he did not have the means to till his fields. A nihilistic joy in suicide overcame the peasant; death was good if his wicked neighbor died with him.

The Russian peasant was doomed to lose the individual battles of this war because the city workers, hungry as they were, were better armed and better organized than he. But after three years of warfare Lenin realized that the new state could not maintain itself upon a wasted countryside. The peasants were accorded a surprising political and economic concession: on March 21, 1921, the state surrendered its monopoly of food. The peasant was required to deliver only a tax in produce to the state; whatever remained after payment of this tax he could sell freely.

Under this stimulus, agrarian production rose again; hunger vanished from country and city. New struggles and new defeats ensued under Lenin's successor, Stalin, who determined to transform Russia from an agrarian country to an industrial country—if possible into the greatest industrial country in the world. This effort injected a new prideful consciousness into the masses of city workers and removed some of the self-consciousness of the rural masses.

In 1928 the Communists decreed the end of private ownership of the land. The peasants were compelled to join collective farms. We must realize what this meant. The ancient longing of the peasants for their own small plot of ground was trodden into dust. Now Mother Russia herself owned this small plot. But also (it was said) each poor muzhik owned all the vast Russian earth. . . . In 1938 there were 243,000 publicly operated collective farms. These embraced farms formerly held by 39,000,000 individual farmers.

"Whatever," wrote *Life* in 1943, "the cost of farm collectivization in terms of human life and individual liberty, the historic fact is that it worked. By forming large farm units, the collective made possible use of farm machinery which doubled agricultural output between 1913 and 1937. In doing this, it released millions of workers for industry, bringing the U.S.S.R.'s farm population down from 77 per cent of the country's total." Thus an agrarian population shifted to the industrialized cities on a scale hitherto unknown in the history of man.

How did the Russian peasant feel about it? In 1930 I asked A. W. Lunacharsky, the great Russian educator, this question. He stared reflectively at the floor, then replied: "We could not consider personal happiness. It had to be done."

A high price had been paid; but the peasant was happy in another way. The true interests of hammer and sickle were by no means irreconcilable. On the contrary, since industrialization means mechanization, the land was also mechanized. According to the Greek saga, when Hephaestus, the god of forging, wished to make a present to Demeter, he employed the hammer to produce the sickle. The town artisans of the Middle Ages, in their haughtiness and indolence, had refused to come to the rescue of the plow. This time the "labor comrades of the city" came to the rescue of the laborers on the land. The Soviet State gave machines to its collective farmers. By 1932 almost 200,000 tractor plows were biting into the ancient Russian earth. In the driver's seat sat the reconciled peasant, laughing cheerfully, because overnight he had become a mechanic. . . . There was a new element in his laugh—it was not the stubborn, abashed smile of Tolstoy's peasants who had been given a gift. It was a laugh that seemed acquired from those lands beyond the great Pacific. From America came the first plows and the first men to operate them—before Russia's proud city of Stalingrad learned to build them herself.

HOW BOTANISTS CHANGED THE MAP

§ 126

THE PROBLEM of want in Russia had never been solely within the realm of mechanization, of rotary plows and railroads. For above all Russia's

problem was her *climate*. For thousands of years Russians planted rye
fields only in places where the seed did not freeze to death in the soil, and
wheat, of course, only in the black earth provinces of the Ukraine and the
Crimea, where fingers of the Mediterranean climate reached out to ca-
ress the land. As a child of Egypt's soil, wheat needed the Mediterranean
climate. . . . In 1896, when Prince Hilkoff, Russian Minister of Transportation, was asked at a meeting in St. Petersburg about the possibilities
of planting in Siberia, he shrugged and said: "Siberia never has produced
and never will produce wheat and rye enough to feed the Siberian population."

If the Russians seriously wished to increase their arable land, railroads
and mechanical plows were insufficient—the climate would have to be
improved. And that was manifestly impossible. Canada, too, soon faced
the same problem, for Canada is a land so cold that only a fourth of its
area seemed open to agriculture. That anything at all grew in the country
was, so to speak, a fortunate accident, an exceptional circumstance which
the expert on wheat, Sir William Crookes, described as follows in 1897:

In winter the ground freezes to a considerable depth. Wheat is sown in the
spring, generally in April, when the frozen ground has been thawed to a
depth of three inches. Under the hot sun of the short summer the grain
sprouts with surprising rapidity, partly because the roots are supplied with
water from the thawing depths. The summer is too short to thaw the ground
thoroughly, and gateposts or other dead wood extracted in autumn are
found still frozen at their lower ends.

Such favorable conditions of natural irrigation were not present every
year. Canada seemed to have no real future as a wheatland. According
to Crookes, the Dominion would not be able to plant more than 6,000,000
acres to wheat in the next twelve years.

Then how could Canada venture to enter into competition with the
Eden-like plains of California? Canada dared nevertheless. In 1901 the
three wheat provinces of Alberta, Saskatchewan, and Manitoba had not
quite 7,000,000 acres under cultivation; twenty years later this had increased to some 75,000,000 acres, and the Dominion was producing record crops of 250,000,000 bushels of wheat. Such mountains of wheat
were moving toward Winnipeg that once, in 1910, the railroads broke
down under their weight and the wheat remained lying beside the tracks
until it rotted. Such intensive cultivation in a land that for ample reason
had never been a wheatland must be due to something more than the
"all-conquering plow" which the Canadian trapper had bought from
Uncle Sam. An unknown factor had contributed. Was it climate?

No, man had not changed the climate. Climate is destiny. Were you
born between the Tropics of Cancer and Capricorn, on the Equator, or
above the Arctic Circle? The earth has five major climates; they dictate

your thoughts and behavior, your food and your customs, your country's population, politics, economy, and the position of the capital city. Everything depends upon climate. If your capital cities offend against the climatic optimum, if they are situated too far north or south, you must dethrone them. Madrid has long since yielded up its mastery to Barcelona, because it has no proper "labor climate," and Milan is more important than Rome. It is climate, indeed, that is all-conquering; from its decisions there is no appeal.

For six thousand years climate had relegated wheat to the subtropical or temperate zones. Farther north it froze; farther toward the Equator it burned. This was the law. But if this law was something eternal, why was wheat grown in Canada after 1900 and a few decades later in Siberia? Why did it not freeze?

A new type of man had appeared upon the scene, who would not let it freeze. It was a type that had not existed a hundred years before—a type that presented itself when it was needed. This type was somewhat similar to the men who were formerly called "botanists." Most of them were quiet, bespectacled men who devoted themselves to the impractical pursuit of classifying their favorite plants. . . . Now, overnight, this type acquired enormous practical importance. The Empire of Wheat, which had enriched the engineers and impoverished many small farmers, that empire that had created railroad kings, plow barons, and lords of the stock market, also created the grain experimenter, the breeder of wheat, who combined botany, mathematics, and the laws of heredity with astonishing results.

§ 127

In the eighteenth century the Prussian Academy of Sciences in Berlin had posed the question: "Do Crosses Exist in the Plant World?" It was a perfectly foolish question, since every gardener knew that crosses existed. For it was precisely the eighteenth century that was amused by the rococo sight of crossed varieties of fruits and colorful ornamental shrubs. . . . But none of the thousands who tittered and pointed knew that the hybridizations were not the product of chaos, but of strictest laws.

The man who found these laws was Gregor Mendel (1828-84), a priest in Brünn, the capital of Moravia, a descendant of long-settled German peasants. When, in the middle of the last century, German, Austrian, and Czech immigrants flooded into America's farmlands to battle stoically against droughts, locusts, blizzards, cyclones, loneliness, and the tumbleweed, these pioneers did not know that in the land they had left the priestly son of a poor peasant was making experiments in the heredity of plants and discoveries that would make some of their grandchildren rich.

Was it chance that a priest discovered Mendel's law? In primitive times the priests, since they were exempt from the life of toil, were the great observers of all growth. They had helped and advised the women, who alone cultivated the gardens. They had explained to the forgetful women the cycles of the seasons, the good and bad days for sowing, the role of sun and rain; they had given them the good seed, which bore plentifully, and had destroyed the bad. Where had they obtained the good seed? That was a secret of theirs which they anxiously guarded, for they were not only improvers of seed but dealers in seed.

The priest who in 1860 began to alter the seed of plants was not a dealer but a man who worked solely to please God and serve science. One clear, frosty February evening this priest went to a small meeting in the *Realgymnasium* of Brünn. There, every two weeks, a social-scientific club held meetings. Gregor Mendel was a member; he came as an amateur botanist to address the meeting on certain crossings of plants he had for years been making in the garden of his monastery. The lecture dealt exclusively with the pea plant (*pisum*) and the relationships produced when it was hybridized. This was not too interesting to the members. The gymnasium professors and apothecaries had no idea that they were attending the birth of the new science of heredity.

The lecture was not only dull; for a botanical subject its terms were most eccentric. The discourse consisted, for the most part, of figures. Mendel had undertaken hundreds upon hundreds of experiments with peas; now he drowned his audience in a stream of figures. He counted the stamens, pistils, flower petals, and the sepals of the calyx; he divided and multiplied. Yet his results seemed to be no more than peas and more peas. The professors of mathematics wondered what business statistics and calculations of probability had in botany. The botanists wondered even more. Two weeks before another lecturer had spoken of Darwin; his lecture on the "variations of species" had evoked great applause. What bold realms of the mind Darwin had opened up. Here was the fantastic sportiveness of nature, adaptation to the struggle for existence; life, as in Ovid, metamorphosed itself eternally to escape death. . . . The audience did not realize that Mendel—no less great than Darwin—was speaking of the *constancy* of species; of the indestructible hereditary character of all life. All living things bear their inheritance.

Mendel's experiments began with the happy perception that it was pointless to undertake crossings of distantly related plants, which differed from one another in a thousand characteristics. Such crossings would produce a confusion he could not govern; there would be apparent lack of law. Therefore Mendel experimented with parent plants so closely related that they differed in only a single characteristic—red- and white-flowered peas. The first generation resulted in pink flowers; by inbreeding he got, in the second generation, one quarter red, one quarter white, and one half pink-flowered plants. Simple multiplication yielded the proportions for all possible combinations. Soon Mendel found that among some pairs that he crossed one characteristic was transmitted more powerfully —was "dominant," as he called it; it suppressed the other, the "recessive" trait. But then—and this was wholly new—with persistent breeding of the children and grandchildren of the first pair, the suppressed traits emerged again according to the strict numerical law.

Thus there was, as Mendel's successor, Sir Francis Galton, proved in 1897, a "law of heredity." The contribution of the parents to the inherited characteristics of the children consists of one half, of the four grandparents one fourth, of the eight great-grandparents one eighth, so that the contribution of all the ancestors to the inherited traits of an individual can be expressed by the progression $\frac{1}{2}$ plus $\frac{1}{4}$ plus $\frac{1}{8}$ plus $(\frac{1}{2})^n$. This all sounded dreadfully mathematical, but it was potentially of enormous practical value. If nothing in hereditary was chance, the inheritance could be so influenced by crossings as to produce the types that were needed and desired.

No one understood this practical importance of Mendel's doctrines. His little treatise in which he laid the foundation for the planter's future fortune and the world's new abundance of bread gathered dust in the libraries. No university invited him to join its faculty, no academy made him a corresponding member. His only triumph was that his brothers in the order made him abbot of their monastery—which had remarkable consequences for this quiet man. His own behavior proved perfectly the Mendelian principle that no hereditary trait is lost, no matter in how many centuries. Soon after a visit to Rome in which he had interviewed the Pope, Mendel, ordinarily a modest, accommodating person, became involved in a dispute with the secular government: he refused to pay the monastery taxes to Austria. Age-old traits in his heredity had emerged: the peasant stubbornness of his forefathers and his priestly unwillingness to bow to secular authority. At this time a portrait was painted of him, the modest little abbot, with the bishop's crook and the Pope's tiara near him. He had mistaken his century, as the failure of his action proved (for the monastery was finally compelled to pay its taxes), but he had remained true to his heredity.

§ 128

Not until 1900 was Mendel's priceless lore recognized. But when Nilsson-Ehle found Mendel's law confirmed in the hybridization of wheat plants, the world began to erect memorials in word and stone to the modest Father. For all at once every layman realized the economic importance of his discovery. For climatic reasons wheat had never flourished in Nilsson-Ehle's native Sweden. People had tried to cultivate a variety that bore a rich head of grain; it froze in the winter soil. They had then planted a winter-hardy wheat; it survived, but the number of grains on the ear was small. By returning to Mendel's experiments, as Nilsson-Ehle had done, the two varieties could be crossed, conjuring a fruitful ear upon a winter-hardy stalk. Now Sweden no longer needed to import foreign wheat. Like some fur-bearing animal the wheat seed could live through the winter. The botanist had won the struggle against the disfavor of climate.

Until Mendel's time men had considered "good soil" when planting grains, but they had never considered good seed. It had to be healthy seed, of course, capable of germinating. But for the rest—how could one *see into the seed?* How could one know whether one grain, which was exactly like another, would produce a particularly fruitful ear while its neighbor remained sterile? One stalk was hardy, the other fell on its side and died. Was this not chance?

Chance, indeed, had often been kind. Farmers who kept their eyes open occasionally saw things which they passed on to their children's children. Fortunate accidents happened to men like the Scotch farmer Fife, who in 1842 received some red wheat from Russia and planted it in the spring. Since Fife had not known that this wheat was winter wheat, it all died before maturing. Only a single stalk survived, the tribal father of later hard grains. . . . Here we see the hand of chance at work. For such creative chances the agricultural world had prayed for six thousand years; and the world had piously ascribed these chances to Isis, Demeter, and Christ. But chance it remained, whether a seed multiplied a thousandfold or withered before the reaping.

"Take two heads of wheat," writes Luther Burbank, the Californian "plant wizard." "Would you say they are all exactly alike? Look more closely. This one has more kernels, this one fewer. Here the kernels are ill-formed or, perhaps, empty of meat. Some plants are tall, some shorter, some dwarfed." How is this—or, rather, how *was* it that for thousands of years every stalk of wheat in a wheat field might chance to bear grain and might chance to bear nothing? It was because before Mendel it was not known that desired characteristics could be developed by the union of botany and mathematics in the children, grandchildren, and great-grandchildren of a seed. Perhaps the Persian farmers of whom Herodotus told that their fields bore "six hundredfold" knew something of heredity; but if so their knowledge was lost when the Greeks conquered the Orient. No Greek or Roman experimented with propagating grains to produce new varieties.

This could be done only after Mendel had shown the way. Once it could be done, the triumph of the Empire of Wheat was secured. Fertility, lushness, and multitudinous seeds are characteristics of southerly plants. Hardness, hardiness, and poverty of seed exist in the north. Until the turn of the century scarcely any wheat could be grown in Canada or

Siberia. Not because of the soil; the soil was good. But the plant died; for ten thousand years its seeds were not accustomed to terribly cold winters and hot summers. But now the Canadian, Charles Saunders, invented, by crossings, his Marquis Wheat—a miraculous descendant of strong races, hard as a Northern plant, winter-hardy, rich in grains as a Southern plant, ripening in three months. Now the provinces of Saskatchewan, Alberta, and Manitoba became, all at once, waving fields of wheat. Like a dart of yellow flame the grain shot from the Atlantic to the Pacific. Canada, but a short time before the dominion of woodcutters, fur

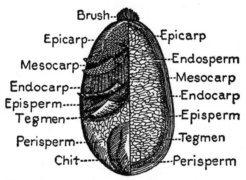

THE SEGMENTS OF THE WHEAT KERNEL

trappers, and fishermen, changed her face within a few years—because in Brünn the small, obstinate priest Gregor Mendel had clung to his assertion that desirable characteristics in plants could be transmitted.

Other men found other seeds that were resistant to disease, to rust, microbes, and insects. Around 1770 the farmers in New England were forced to abandon their last wheat plantings because the barberry bush grew too near their fields. The farmers vaguely suspected the cause. But it proved impossible to exterminate all the barberry bushes; in the end it was the new science that conquered wheat rust. These "hunger fighters" who went between the microscope and the field, the garden and the laboratory, are named Charles Saunders, William Saunders, Angus Mackay, Marc Carleton, George H. Shull, and William Beal. Not the least of them is Henry A. Wallace, Vice-President of the United States, who, out of endless experiments, did for maize what others had done for wheat: produced "bigger yields on smaller fields." For more important than the size of the field is the number of grains on the ear.

§ 129

"It has been the fate of men who by their dreams and brains have fought hunger for mankind to die nameless and unknown." These words of Paul de Kruif apply only to the ancient propagators of grain, not to those of today. Every laboratory sends its findings to the newspapers; few there are today who must die unknown. Trofim Lysenko, for example, the creator of "Arctic grain," is already being compared by his contemporaries with the conquistadors who long ago won Siberia for the Cross and the Czar. He has opened up broad, frozen steppes to the cultivation of wheat.

For a long time the greatest wheat authority of Russia was Vavilov, the president of the All-Union Institute for Plant Cultivation in Leningrad. As we will remember, this geographer of plant life had discovered the cradle of wheat. Basing his work on the principle that a plant must have originated where the greatest number of varieties are to be found, he undertook extensive expeditions, with a large staff of assistants, to Africa and Asia. Vavilov assumed that the primitive agriculturists of the Stone Age, when they were compelled to move on because of exhaustion of the soil, had taken their grain with them. The farther they went from their original home, the more varieties would be abandoned, since they did not prosper in the new environment. Vavilov, after patiently counting, sifting, observing in two continents, gradually began to define a territory in which the number of wheat varieties was highest. This territory was the tableland of Abyssinia. Therefore, Vavilov concluded that this was the place where, once upon a time, the first wheat had sprung from wild grass—by chance or by the hand of man.

This discovery won international fame for the scientist; the Nobel prize seemed in the offing for him. Then, from his own country, a storm of opposition fell upon his head. The opposition was not directed at his geographical work, for no one doubted its value, but at Vavilov as a patient and orthodox Mendelian who in his laboratory had made 25,000 experiments with crossed wheat. Vavilov had promised his government that someday he would supply a wheat that could be planted in the hot Turkmenian steppe and the cold Siberian tundra. These varieties of wheat had already been created, but there was not yet sufficient seed available. Give him a few years and there would be ample grain to plant. This was reasonable enough; even when there are two thoroughbred horses, they cannot beget children, grandchildren, and great-grandchildren in a single season.

But the request for patience struck Lysenko, president of the Soviet Russian Academy for Agricultural Science, as somewhat laughable. "Possibly botany has time. We do not! It seems to me we have made a revolution here in Russia. This whole Mendelian science need not be so insolent about its racial traits and indestructible characteristics. It seems to me we are Marxists. A Marxist cannot believe that it takes generations to change a living thing. According to Darwin and Marx, it's the environment that changes life. New conditions, new forms. We've experienced these with men—now let us see whether plants are more reactionary than men!"

Vavilov heard of the jibe from some of Lysenko's students who were also members of his own staff. He returned the challenge: "If biological changes can be made only by our environment, perhaps Lysenko will take any haphazard seed to the Siberian tundra and *heat* the entire plain so that the seed will not freeze. I'm afraid he'll have difficulty finding sufficient wood to burn."

But Vavilov was mistaken in Lysenko; the latter was far more than a "politician." Lysenko's parents had been farmers. As a farmer's son he had early observed that two environmental factors determine when a plant will begin to flower: the length of the day and the temperature. He now thought it might be worth while varying both these factors.

Two Americans, Garner and Allard, had earlier discovered that there are "short-day plants" and "long-day plants." Tropical plants are short-day plants, because the light always falls upon the plants for twelve hours every day. Polar plants, however, are long-day plants, because in the polar regions daylight lasts for months. If a polar plant is given light for too short a time, it does not bloom. And vice versa, if a tropical plant is exposed to daylight longer than twelve hours, it also remains sterile.

If this were correct—and it was—then sunray lamps, hotbeds, and cold frames could be employed to advantage. Lysenko found that seeds which germinated at low temperatures grew swiftly. The reverse was true of plants which germinated at high temperatures. This was confirmed by the fact that every farmer knew: if winter wheat is sown late and yet germinates before it is too cold, it will grow normally in the spring. But if, because of drought, the germination does not begin until the spring, it will not grow swiftly enough to bear fruit. Lysenko determined to use only seed that had previously been subjected to special light and temperature treatment. In its dormant state he would prepare the seed for all the hardships it was later to endure.

Lysenko's great experiment succeeded. Seeds that by laboratory methods were inured to the climatic factors of their future home took root in the Far North and gave bread to millions of human beings. Previously Russia's most important grain lands had lain in the west, near the German and Polish borders. It was important for the Russians to know that even if their western lands were overrun by the enemy, they would not have to starve. The frozen North yielded bread.

§ 130

But the method does not matter. Whether we follow Mendel and cross the best strains of wheat, or whether we employ Lysenko's discovery and treat the wheat seed so that it is hardy in any environment, the fact remains that climate, the ancient foe, has been conquered. The glory of the botanists outshone the fame of the engineers and agrochemists.

In little more than a generation botanists, engineers, and chemists changed the grain map of the world. Of this vast revolution the cultivation of Canada or Siberia is but a chapter.

In the more temperate parts of India a large crop of export wheat is produced annually, although the average Indian still lives on rice. What

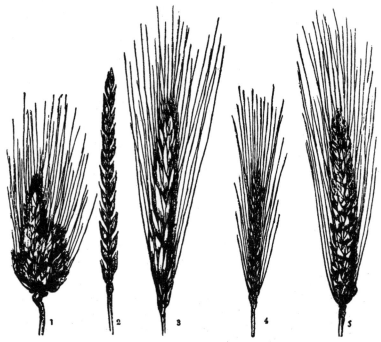

DIFFERENT KINDS OF WHEAT
1) Emmer 2) Spelter 3) Polish 4) Single-grained
5) Common bearded

was formerly inconceivable is now established: a strain of wheat has been found that will withstand the tropical sun. And Australia, that great island in the South Seas, for eons completely isolated from other lands so that it is characterized by forms of plant life found on no other continent —Australia is a desert, a land of drought. What could such country contribute to its own food and the food of the world? Moreover, it was so sparsely populated. It is a continent almost as large in area as the United States, but contains only one eighteenth of the population. But precisely because this was so, the Australians early recognized that they must compensate for their lack of manual labor by machines. One of the earliest mower-threshers employed in Australia did not come from America: it was a native invention. And today the Australians are, perhaps, the most American-minded people on the globe. More than 60 per cent of the arable land produces wheat, and would produce more if the people could "make rain." Even so, science and diligence have wrung moisture from the soil of this driest of lands, and Australia lives by its exports of wheat. Forty per cent of the wheat that sails from Sydney and Melbourne goes to England, and more than 30 per cent to *Egypt*. Thus the youngest wheatland gives of its surplus to the oldest.

Argentina. Who would have thought of turning to this country when bread was needed in the world? Not until 1890 did the first, diffident export of wheat begin. But shortly before World War I 20,000,000 acres of wheat were already under cultivation. The provinces west of Buenos Aires were apparently the most fertile; but slowly cultivation was extended to the south—and here it expanded with bewildering speed. On the broad plain from the Atlantic to the Andes wheat prospered exceedingly; an acre yielded forty bushels. But, in contrast to Australia, Argentina was still cultivating wheat primarily for home consumption; for its wheat, because of the sandy soil, was peculiarly hard and suitable less for bread than for *pasta*. But wait. Did not Italy need macaroni? This Argentina could supply in ample quantities, and did.

In *The Pit* Frank Norris portrayed a man who tried to corner all the wheat in the world from Chicago. Today this would no longer be possible. Although the United States' supremacy in wheat has by no means been wiped out by the progress of science, it is no longer possible for any one country to be the exclusive great producer of wheat. With climate as a fundamental factor eliminated, the nature of world economy prevented any one portion of the globe from remaining the only realm of wheat. What empire there is exists chiefly in relation to other grains; but it is established in no one place and there are no emperors. Since 1910 none of the wheat millionaires in the United States have become billionaires. The great wheat magnates who crushed the small farmer within the framework of a *laissez-faire* economy, and the stock-market speculator who wiped out his rivals in the market—all these figures suffered from the effects of the free competition they so piously worshiped. Today the production of wheat is too widespread, too universal for any handful of men to control it. Not a month passes without a wheat harvest somewhere in the world. In January the wheat ripens in Australia, New Zealand, and Argentina. In February and March in India, Brazil, and Uruguay. In April there is North African, Mexican, and Persian wheat. In May it ripens in southern Spain, China, Florida, and Texas. In June in California, Italy, Southern France, and Japan. July brings the wheat crops of the Ukraine and Central Russia, as well as of the Northern states of the Union, and the entire Canadian harvest. In August, England, Sweden, Norway, and Germany reap; in September Scotland, in October large parts of Russia, in November Peru and South Africa, and in December Abyssinia. It is true that only a few of these countries are producers for the world market. Nevertheless, this calendar of wheat makes it amply clear that no single country can control supply and price as the United States did between 1870 and 1910. The nations of the world have, for the most part, resurrected their protective tariffs to help their native agriculture. Since, after 1914, no nation believed in world peace, no nation could allow itself to rely fondly on an uninterrupted supply of bread from abroad. Engineering, soil chemistry, and botany would have succeeded to show them how to produce enough to cover their own needs, if not —tragedy!—the German onrush in World War II had early smashed these efforts.

FARMERS' SALVATION

§ 131

THE BEGINNING of the summer offensive of 1918, which decided the outcome of World War I, occurred at the same time as the harvest of Canadian winter wheat. The twenty-year-old Americans ("the bread-fed man is the well-fed man") who, bayonet in hand, stormed out of the woods of Château-Thierry were the sons of farmers. Their fathers had doubted that the American earth would continue to feed their sons, for their earth seemed to be providing only for the trusts and the octopuses. But the self-balancing faculty that seems to dwell in grain had finally helped the farmers and made them again what they had once been—the backbone of the nation.

The Government had helped them little. Respect for the spirit of enterprise is a trait of Americans; and any check upon this spirit would contradict the letter of the Constitution. Trade was trade. Rugged American individualism forbade imposing restrictions upon traders for the sake of agriculture. Thomas Jefferson and Benjamin Franklin would undoubtedly have had opposite preferences; but the United States had become a land of merchants, the kind of land Hamilton desired. The railroads had helped to establish the greatness and world power of the country. Should the Government, for the sake of the farmers, try to run after the locomotives and bind the powerful railroads? Probably the rope would break. . . .

Nevertheless, toward the end of the eighties President Cleveland began the struggle. Maximum freight rates were established in Washington, but they remained paper rates. The court declared them unconstitutional, and the weight of public opinion backed this decision in favor of free enterprise. Cleveland, the foe of the railroads, was in the end forced to send soldiers to help Pullman, the railroad king, fight a strike. The socialist leader, Debs, who had called upon his supporters to boycott the Pullman line, was arrested.

No one helped the small farmer. He was surrounded by enemies;

among them the railroad was only one. The small farmer was compelled to realize that hand labor could not compete with the machines of the great land magnates. He therefore mortgaged his land to buy machinery. In order to meet payments, he had to use his machines to the utmost to produce the biggest possible crops. On the other hand, the larger the surpluses grew, the higher the mountain of grain towered, the lower the prices dropped. In the midst of this flood of golden wheat the farmers earned less and less. New grain markets were established—to rescue the price of wheat, it was said. But the farmers saw that instead of holding the price, the market value was now being influenced by speculation. The speculators wagered upon the size of the future harvest. This was beyond the understanding of the farmers.

Since the beginnings of the world, had not the justest minds determined that bread, like air and water, must not serve to profit individuals? In the eighties, under the pressure of the great upswing in wheat production, men and parties throughout the world began demanding nationalization of the grain trade. In September 1887, Jean Jaurès rose in the French Chamber of Deputies and moved "that the state shall have the sole right to import foreign grains and flours. It will sell them at a fixed price to be determined by law every year." A month later this socialistic motion was repeated almost word for word by an ultraconservative in the Prussian House of Lords, Minister of Agriculture Count Kanitz. For the entire world trembled before the practices of the grain traders. But liberal America upheld them. It would not be American to stab courageous enterprise in the back. A government monopoly of the grain trade did not appear in America until World War I, and it was at once abolished after the war. To most Americans government monopoly of grain resembled conditions under Pharaoh or Le Roi Soleil. For how to know who the government would be tomorrow?

The farmers were assured that the stock market did serve a purpose. It established scientific standards for the products, estimated the quantities of grain, and provided in advance for export. But all the farmers could see was that a ring of traders had come to an agreement, so that none outbid the other for the farmers' produce; while the speculators continued to make the market prices extremely unsteady. The old foe, the railroad, whipped its freight rates higher, and, when it could, transported only the grain that belonged to the masters of the railroads. When the farmers turned to the banks for credit, they learned that it was forbidden by law to lend money on farm mortgages. Then usurers came to the farm, giving money and at once deducting a fourth for interest. With their new money the farmers intended to buy machines, which were being improved beyond recognition every ten years. But the machines were far too expensive. The farming class seemed done for. All economic factors seemed to have conspired against them. In their desperation the farmers thought of uniting. They did not congregate with a few hundreds of their fellows, armed with petitions or revolvers, to suffer a new defeat like that of Mussel Slough. This time hundreds of thousands became conscious of their power, for these hundreds of thousands were both producers and consumers. The farmers' victory sprang from a wholly modern idea, that of the economic co-operative.

The "grange" was of instant effectiveness. The grange was an economic form which in the Middle Ages had made even the smallest unit independent, self-containing. The small medieval farm had produced everything for itself and had not been dragged into a world economy by traders and speculators, with resultant depreciation of its products and increase in the cost of living. To the American farmers of the last third of the past century the word "grange" was, of course, only metaphoric; but it was a very good metaphor. Wherever a grange began to organize common purchase and sale of machines and grain, the lot of its members improved. The single granges soon united by districts and finally by states. Every district appointed agents who sold the products of the district as advantageously as possible and forced manufacturers to sell cheaply to the group. Iowa led all other states in grange organization. By 1872 5,000,000 bushels of grain were sent by the grange, without benefit of middlemen, to Chicago; and the members of the grange had already saved $400,000 by buying machinery in large lots. With alternating fortunes, granges sprang up in other states. Purchasing houses, machine factories, and even banks were founded everywhere by the granges. Some met failure, but many others triumphed. In spite of many setbacks the co-operative idea survived; it could no longer be smothered. By 1900 there were 1,000, by 1920 more than 11,000 co-operatives. Only a part of these, of course—though the most important part—were devoted to grain.

Not only the farmers, but the Government as well, began to recognize the value of agrarian co-operation. Some time before Theodore Roosevelt, President of the middle classes, vociferously remarked that he would eat a trust for breakfast every day. And public opinion was swerving markedly to the side of the farmers. The farmers' organizations were based on free agreement, not power—and for this reason they were strong. What could be more American? Without any spilling of blood men had escaped from the clutches of modern economics—as the Pilgrim Fathers had escaped from Old England. In 1914, when the anti-trust law was passed—and the big investors, not without some logic, claimed that the farm ring had long been a kind of trust—the co-operatives were excluded from the limitations imposed by the law upon the trusts. The profits which accrued to the traffic in grain during and after the war were not earned by the trusts alone. Everyone had his rightful due, including the farmers.

Today the influence of the breadmaking class on America's legislation can hardly be overrated. Although the independent farmer—unlike his cousin in Europe—has not a political party of his own in Congress to vote amiable laws, he exerts an enormous influence on both the Democratic and Republican parties—an influence far greater, perhaps, than an official "Party of the Bread" would have granted him. In any case the founders of the National Grange, William Saunders and O. H. Kelley, the men of the "old hard days," would rub their eyes if they could see the political and economical achievements of their grandchildren.

It is needless to say that in the economic struggles and victories of the American farmer a spiritual factor has also always been present. In most farm organizations the open Bible is a feature at every gathering. Indeed, where could a book be found containing so much information about agrarian matters, from the drawing of furrows to the destroying of locusts? People of Minnesota do not forget that, in 1877, Governor Washburn ordered the reading of the 91st Psalm from the pulpits—a mighty prayer against "the pestilence that walked in the darkness and the destruction that wasteth at noonday," and that the locusts' plague then ceased. But with some amazement one learns from a book of Wesley McCune that the "National Grange of the Patrons of Husbandry" soon started an Eleusinian hierarchy of officers: with a Master, Overseer, Lecturer, Stewart, Chaplain, Treasurer, Secretary, Gate Keeper, and Lady Assistant Stewart, as well as three women ritualistic officials acting as Ceres (grain), Pomona (fruit), and Flora (flower). In addition, the inner sanctum of agrarian masonry, the Assembly of Demeter, is presided over by a High Priest, Archon, and Annalist. This *"Eleusis in America"* is by no means merely a costume society. It shows rather that the American farmer is willing to maintain the same connection with the old agrarian religions, because, as Louis I. Taber, national master from 1923 to 1941, stated, "they were founded on eternal truth." And, as in the times of Isis, secrecy is also required by the agrarian masonry; but a few secrets have leaked out. We know that each granger is provided with a knife "to remind him never to break a twig or a flower, but always to cut it smoothly so as not to injure the plant." It is a happy land where secret societies can provide their members with knives and stay within the law. In Germany, Hungary, and Rumania, without doubt, such a thing would be considered as "a murderous threat to the political order. . . ."

§ 132

Today every law that favors the farming class has the overwhelming moral support of the whole population. This is remarkable indeed, for the larger part of the public is nonagrarian. The economic friction between town and country, the contradiction between consumer and producer, is no less present in America than it has been anywhere else since the days of Athens and Rome. Nevertheless, the sympathies of the city dwellers are all with the farmers.

The cornerstone of the American farm program is the idea of *parity*. "Parity price," runs an official explanation, "means a price for the farmer's product which will give it an exchange value for things the farmer needs to buy, equivalent to that in a specified base period. The base period mostly used as 'par' has been the five prewar years, 1909–14." Those years were chosen because they represented a high point in agriculture. Using another way of saying it means that if a farmer got a hundred dollars for one hundred bushels of wheat, for example, in 1909–14, and could buy a new stove and a new suit with that hundred dollars, then his returns today should enable him to buy the same goods for one hundred bushels of wheat. It would be very understandable now, if the cobbler or the laundryman would raise the question, "How about *my* stove and *my* suit?" But he will scarcely do it. A kind of chivalry seems to forbid it. For things concerning peasants and farmland—although they are matters of politics also—are largely a matter of sentiment. And this is an entirely new thing, and a very considerable one.

Yes, the fondness of agriculture among American city-dwellers is somewhat an amazing trait, just because there is no joint political root. Contrarily, townspeople have to realize that sometimes they are hailing their own disadvantage because bread, milk, or eggs follow a policy not always friendly to the customer. But that doesn't matter. The average American reads in his paper a speech of a representative of the "Farm Bloc"—it may be a Democrat or a Republican—and he enjoys it. He listens when an agrarian, such as Senator La Follette, coins such well-formed phrases as this: "The problem of farm labor is as old as civilization and as fresh as this morning's newspaper," and deliberately he forgets it is not his own business. We have to stress this: the broad-mindedness of the town majority against the minority on the land is a very wonderful thing and an American one. Do we remember what, only a few hundred years ago, European townspeople used to think of the average farmer? It was the general feeling as the German poet Sebastian Brant expressed:

> The clown's purse bursts full of money;
> They put the wine and wheat away
> And all things else, nor sell will they;
> They hold it long to price it higher
> Till thunder and lightning, heavenly fire
> Consumes the barn and corn entire.

Nobody, today, would think in such terms. And why? What neither religious nor economical enlightenment could achieve, a new great power did: *literature*.

This is the work of literature! The power of modern literature is almost comparable to the power that religion formerly exercised. As religion was formerly, so literature is today spiritually sovereign. It may seem for a while to be held in line by politics or economics, but then it suddenly recollects that it is free and launches a backhand blow at the prevailing economic system. Since, in a democratic nation, thought is really free, the power of literature is unlimited. Literature sways the idealist and the snob, the sentimentalist and the mere curiosity seeker. It compels a large part of the nation to consume plays and novels which apparently do not concern it. More than that, they are works that question the very social foundations of the reader. When a man with a bankbook goes to see Erskine Caldwell's *Tobacco Road,* he is acting as much against his own interests as the French nobleman of the eighteenth century who enthusiastically attended Beaumarchais' *Figaro.*

This is the power of literature. It effected vast changes in the American mind between 1910 and 1940. We do not feel that there is only one generation between those dates. If we thumb through the books of America we find that the "gilded age" is little esteemed. No one hails the robber barons, the "men like Caesars who founded the happiness of their fellow citizens." The captain of industry may still rule in politics and in reality, but in the intellectual life of the nation he is *sine arte et littera;* no work of art studies this type and finds admirable qualities in it.

America's leading novels are agrarian and devoted to the little man. In Pearl Buck's prose poems flood, drought, pestilence, and revolution stand between the patient farmer and his good earth; but he vanquishes them all. In Europe, too, the need had long been felt for good agrarian novels; but they appeared only slowly and timidly. The reason for this lay in the European background, its history and the psychology of its inhabitants. . . . It may be said that all the agrarian novels since the French Revolution derive from two great Swiss who represent the sentimental and the realistic trends: Jean Jacques Rousseau (1712–88) and Jeremias Gotthelf (1797–1854). Rousseau wrote in French, Gotthelf in German. They were pillars for further building; but because of her very landscape Switzerland could never provide the impulse for further agrarian novels of any stature. Switzerland is a land of dairy cattle. She might have produced the "epic of milk" but never the epic of grain. The poets of the grain epic sprang up not in the land of mountainous pastures, but in the fertile flatlands. In France and Germany during the nineteenth century the shadow of industry dimmed the sunlight the agrarian novel needed to prosper. In Norway, too, Knut Hamsun would have been considered a great poet, if he had praised the true national wealth of mines, timber, and fish. Instead, he wrote the *Growth of the Soil,* an agrarian novel few of his compatriots read. It was in the East, in the vast fields of Poland and Russia, that the agrarian novel came into its own. Here, be-

sides the work of Tolstoy, there appeared the four-volume novel of the
Pole Wladyslaw S. Reymont, *Chlopi* (*The Man of the Soil*). Out of the
East came the great epic poems of the timeless peasant.

Timelessness and the vastness of the land produced agrarian writers in
America as well. Here, where the cities were more urban than any other
cities in the world, the land still remained rustic. Men lived in many ages
at once; and side by side with the apex of industrialization there were
places, perhaps four days' journey distant, where a struggle between
farmers and herdsmen, the ranchers, was taking place—a struggle which
in Europe had been played out two thousand years ago.

The award of the Nobel prize to Pearl Buck (1938), whose novels of
China are also novels of the universal earth over which the plowman
passes, helped the trend of American novels toward agrarianism. These
novels celebrate the "industrious small farmer." Those voyagers who are
used to the pitches and swells of literature know that this, too, is a fashion
which may give way to another after only a few years. But it is nevertheless phenomenal that suddenly millions of people who never in their lives
heard of Liebig or Viscount Townshend should know all about soil
exhaustion, crop rotation, winter wheat, and harmful insects from the
reading of their favorite novels. Thus the seed has sprouted that Frank
Norris and Edwin Markham sowed in 1899. To be sure, *The Octopus*
too seldom leaves its place on the shelves of public libraries. But Norris'
disciples are read—those who went out to the land with him and wrote
of the problems of farms and bread: the Caldwells, Faulkners, and Stein-
becks. There is a good reason for this. These men are closer to the American soil than Frank Norris. Pathfinder though he was, his writing was
too French. Words and ideas formed within him with classical facility.
As in Zola or at a trial in court, the evidence was presented; Norris'
farmers, friends and foes both, all speak like lawyers.

The Joad family, on the other hand, the hero of Steinbeck's *Grapes of
Wrath,* is scarcely capable of speech; and Jeeter Lester's family in
Tobacco Road express themselves in brute stammerings and inarticulate
gestures. It is the opposite pole; forty years ago the farmers in novels
spoke as though they had just read Henry George. The present fashion
(and it is a fashion) is again reminiscent of the period when "the peasant
had no tongue," when he could not complain to the German emperor
for lack of speech. Now the writers complain for him. And they do it by
saying nothing themselves, by letting the circumstances speak. "You'll
lose it if you talk about it," Hemingway once said; and Ford Madox
Ford's aesthetics reduced it to the thesis: "The object of the novelist is to
keep the reader entirely oblivious of the fact that the author exists—even
of the fact that he is reading a book."

But writers are more than faithful amassers of fact. Steinbeck's opponents accuse him of not portraying the environment and the circum-

stances as they really are. Such conditions as he describes could not exist in Oklahoma or California, they cry. Like Harriet Beecher Stowe in *Uncle Tom's Cabin,* his method is one of exaggeration, Steinbeck's foes hotly maintain. . . . But whether he has or has not portrayed reality, there is a degree of spiritual truth which makes it of no importance whether a thing could "really happen" that way. In this sense the American novels are agrarian realism and their countless derivatives on the stage and in the cinema justly enjoy their popularity. It does not matter that their realism is perhaps not as realistic as author and readers believe. The *ethics* are what matter.

§ 133

All these books deal with courageous, ordinary people. Whether they are fortunate or unfortunate—to understand America it is necessary to know what the courageous, ordinary man means to America. America needs models. And the face of the ordinary small farmer who, pipe clenched between his teeth, looks out of the film, his hand on the gear-shift of the jalopy that rattles into the nearest town where he does his shopping: the figure of the contented countryman, a man full of humanity and decency—such pictures are beloved by the people. The large landowners who in the past shaped culture in Europe remained anonymous in America. They were not seen. The wheat magnates in the West never developed into a kind of landed nobility, as the tobacco and cotton planters of the South had done two hundred years earlier. Perhaps this was chiefly because the wheat magnates, in their pursuit of fortune through the West, did not become settled anywhere. Large profits in wheat depended upon too many factors; the land magnate was aware that he could stay long in no one place. His vast, ruthlessly exploited farm soon became exhausted, and after a few years he moved on. (It was the old mode of the herdsman, five thousand years old, although now it was not cattle that migrated but seed and tractors.) Consequently, no culture arose in those regions, no aristocratic culture; for it did not occur to the rich man to build himself a castle as a social center, with servants, musicians, and rustic scholars. There arose no such courts as dotted Hungary in the seventeenth and eighteenth centuries—courts that could give shelter to a Haydn. The rich man did not consume on the land the money the land brought him; he spent his profits in the metropolises or on the French Riviera, as the owners of the Roman *latifundia* had done.

The footprints of migrating wheat capitalism left their stamp of ugliness—deserted cabins, sagging village churches, and broken-down schoolhouses. But the grange, the spirit of the small farmer, maintained the land; sitting by their stoves in winter, the small farmers read the books the rich did not read. They sent their children to the schools, and the land was reanimated by their presence. There were crises, to be sure, severe crises. The 1929 setback to the entire economy, an aftereffect of the war, imperiled the very existence of the farming class. The false prosperity collapsed; overproduction, crises in distribution, bank crises followed in rapid succession. But, for the most part, individuals emerged from the bread-producing class who helped. McNary, for example, introduced a bill in 1927 providing subsidies to maintain the falling prices of agricultural produce. And the man who is now Vice-President of the United States, Henry A. Wallace, proposed that the Government rent land and keep it out of production, so that the decline of farm production would correspond to the industrial decline. Wallace's measure supported prices and gave a breathing spell to the farmers. By the early thirties America could well say of herself that she had understood Demeter's warning— that ancient warning repeated so often throughout six thousand years of agriculture. Whether pronounced by Solon, Moses, Quesnay, or Liebig, the different voices united in the one idea: only a free and prosperous farming class permits a nation to live freely and prosperously. And a free and prosperous farming class means, in the final analysis, the small farmer who works his land alone, with the help of his wife, his children, and his machines. His is no frenzied desire for riches; he wants his simple, his comfortable living. And 40,000,000 human beings depend upon him and his kind. It is of his work that Joaquin Miller wrote:

> Who harvests what his hand hath sown,
> Does more for God, for man, his own—
> Dares more than all mad heroes dare.

DEMETER WARNS HER PEOPLE AGAIN

§ 134

FRIENDSHIP with the earth is requisite. The whole history of agriculture teaches that there must be this friendship between man and the soil, if the soil is to bear for man. Mastery alone will not do it. Indeed, the natural disasters of 1934 revealed that in America the relationship between man and the soil had been far too much like the false relationship between master and servant. And the earth rebelled.

We are told that the Athenian artisans carried two gods in their insignia: Athene, the goddess of wisdom, and Hephaestus, the god of the forge. When wisdom and technology are wedded, Plato declares, industry and commonweal are generated.

But what if technology can no longer live at peace with wisdom? What if it overplays its part? The legend recounts that the god of the forge commenced to molest the virgin goddess Athene. He pursued her out of the city, chased her around the walls and into the fields, and tried to rape her. The sooty, limping god was strong; he clutched the goddess from behind, but she tore free and kicked her heel mightily into his loins. He stumbled into a furrow, his manhood was ejaculated, and the earth bore of him Erichthonios.

Clearly, then, the kindly god of the forge, the inventor of so many ingenious objects, could also run wild. Two thousand years later the American novelist, John Steinbeck, in his *Grapes of Wrath,* saw that Hephaestus, the engineer, was raping the earth. Although Steinbeck knew that no bread could be made without plowing—deep plowing!—he saw in plowing an act of violence:

The man sitting in the iron seat did not look like a man; gloved, goggled, rubber dust mask over nose and mouth, he was a part of the monster, a robot in the seat. The thunder of the cylinders sounded through the country, became one with the air and the earth, so that earth and air muttered in sympathetic vibration. . . . The man could admire the tractor—its machined surfaces, its surge of power, the roar of its detonating cylinders; but it was not his tractor. Behind the tractor rolled the shining disks, cutting the earth with blades—not plowing but surgery, pushing the cut earth to the right where the second row of disks cut it and pushed it to the left; slicing blades shining, polished by the cut earth. And pulled behind the disks, the harrows combing with iron teeth so that the little clods broke up and the earth lay smooth. Behind the harrows, the long seeders—twelve curved iron penes erected in the foundry, orgasms set by gears, raping methodically, raping without passion. The driver sat in his iron seat and he was proud of the straight lines he did not will, proud of the tractor he did not own or love, proud of the power he could not control. And when that crop grew, and was harvested, no man had crumbled a hot clod in his fingers and let the earth sift past his fingertips. No man had touched the seed, or lusted for the growth. Men ate what they had not raised, had no connection with the bread. The land bore under iron, and under iron gradually died; for it was not loved or hated, it had no prayers or curses.

The earth had borne willingly for the small plows drawn by oxen. But now, when Demeter felt upon her back the six-ton burden of machines, she grew resentful. And she began to revolt against the machine.

Ships steering toward Virginia about the middle of March 1934 beheld a strange sight. In spite of the bright sunshine a black veil was drawn over the coast of America, as though billions of tons of coal had been atomized and blown miles high into the air. This black substance blew at great speed from north to south. As the ships approached closer to the shore, the dust heaped upon their decks. It was the earth of America which had risen into the air and whirled across the land. What disaster had visited the Happy Continent?

It was a natural disaster which, in its economic consequences, was greater than that of Pompeii had been. But this time it was not the violence of underground forces which had spewed death upon guiltless men; guilty men had themselves created this disaster. For fifty years they had been warned that pulverizing the earth too finely and too deeply, pulverizing such as was done by the new, gigantic plows, would rob the soil of its fatty content. But the farmers were unheeding and eager only for what the earth would bear. And now something came that swept away their soil. It was the wind, the ancient terror. The wind took the pulverized earth and carried it hundreds of miles away.

According to statistics, the storm of 1934 was no more violent than storms in other years. It was a good equinoctial storm that lasted for days—no more. But in the years before there had been droughts. The atomized soil, naturally dry enough, had lost almost all of its weight for lack of moisture. The storm swooped under it, and the American farmers saw their Demeter, veiled in black, ascending into the sky.

Here was tragedy indeed. In three centuries of tenacious struggle the Americans had wrested this soil from the forests and the prairies. Squanto and the Pilgrim Fathers, Oliver Evans, Washington, Thomas Jefferson, and Lincoln, had devoted their solicitude to this soil; for the sake of the soil men had pushed to the West, had crossed mountains and cut down forests; farmers had fought the railroads; Pittsburgh had manufactured steel plows; chemistry had been mobilized to fight insects and diseases.

In the year 40 B.C., as Varro tells us, the Spaniards implored Octavius —who was later to be the first Roman emperor—to send soldiers to help them fight the plague of wild rabbits; but before the soldiers came the Spanish grain was eaten. In America it never came to this pass. Government and funds, universities and endowments, were all there. A sanitary cordon surrounded the fields; through it no Hessian fly, no corn-ear worm could pass unscathed. On every insect larva a doctoral thesis was written. It was not the famine-ridden Germans or the other Europeans, who were traditionally known as thorough, who most merited this reputation. As scientific agriculturists the Americans had outstripped the world. Had all this been in vain? For the soil itself was refusing to serve.

The cloud of dust that hung over the continent settled into the cities, penetrated into men's respiratory organs. The lungs were affected; infants and old people died first. In stalls and on pastures the cattle became terrified; they broke out of barns and through fences and died in the uninhabited portions of the country. Everywhere the dust penetrated, smothering and burying the new-sown seed. A few months later came prehistoric cloudbursts that led to a new great disaster. What soil the storm had left was eroded by water. Paul B. Sears, agricultural expert in Oklahoma, pointed out that dust storms and floods had the same source: predatory cultivation of the soil. In time of drought the pulverized soil flew off. When it rained, the sponginess was lacking which would retain the moisture in the humus. Instead, the rain flowed off, taking the humus with it. There was no sense in building dams to stop the water once it had become a host of raging streams. Rather, every drop of rain as it fell must be made to serve the vegetation. Only the spongy, dark, doughy topsoil of all good earth could so utilize the rain. Now that was gone. Sandstorms and floods, Sears warned, were only omens of the powers that were gathering to assail men. It was still time to employ agricultural methods similar to those of Europe: to tend the earth instead of exploiting it.

What did Sears mean by European methods? Annual rotation of crops, which had been recommended by English scientists in the eighteenth century, was taught in all American agricultural colleges. But the farmers, big and small, did not practice it. Not only the ruthless plowing but the permanent monoculture of one single variety of grain dried out the soil and furthered erosion. Even before 1934 Missourian agriculturists had calculated that where wheat, corn, and clover were sown alternately, in the European fashion, an average of only three tons of earth were lost annually from flood. But where wheat alone was cultivated, erosion carried off ten tons of earth, and where only maize was cultivated, twenty tons. The statisticians reckoned that with proper rotation of crops the good earth of Missouri would continue to bear crops for three hundred and seventy-five years; but if wheat alone were cultivated, it would bear for only one hundred years, and maize alone would cut this down to fifty years.

In the eighteenth century, when Arthur Young and the other soil reformers recommended crop rotation, they had done so with the purpose of increasing fertility. They did not know that crop rotation husbanded the *physical* as well as the chemical characteristics of the soil. It was crop rotation that prevented the soil from breaking up. In Missouri, Hans Jenny, an agricultural expert from Switzerland, determined that the humus and nitrogen content of the soil had fallen by 35 per cent. It had become worthless for agriculture by the time the wind began to carry it away. And what happened in Missouri happened elsewhere. A third of the cultivated land of the United States was on the way to becoming useless.

Another authority, I. N. Darling, saw the situation even more pessimistically. He declared that if America continued to exploit her soil as she had done, she would face hunger in the next thirty-five years. By 1960 the curve of increasing population would cross the descending curve of tillable land, and every American would have no more than two and a half acres of land for his food. This would be an approach to Chinese conditions. For more than a hundred years, Darling warned, Americans had been working toward the ruination of their soil by too intensive cultivation.

§ 135

The dust storms were still raging, the floods were still sweeping off the topsoil, the experts were still lamenting, when a man with turned-up collar stepped out of the Department of Agriculture in Washington and called a halt to all the sound and fury. This man was the Secretary of Agriculture, Henry A. Wallace, the son of a farmer-minister. His was a family who, concerned with growing and marketing—the things of this world—also had due regard for the loftier, Christian aspects of their work.

By this time Henry Wallace was no longer of the same temper as the young man who, in the twenties, had launched the slogan "bigger yields on smaller fields"—the man as Paul de Kruif had described him to the world. This minister's son, a practical farmer and a competent horticulturist, had since realized that the soil had been sinned against. It had been made to labor like an overworked manservant, and had been granted no Sabbath. Wallace and his circle had long favored *limiting* agriculture in America; they had forced through a law which, in increasing units, caused land to be withdrawn from production. Years before Wallace had seen that it no longer paid for the farmer to extract the last bushel of grain from the depleted soil. The law of diminishing returns was already beginning to make itself felt; the costs of production would have to be reduced by returning to less intensive measures. In 1934 the Department of Agriculture declared that in the current year it would convert over 4,000,000 acres of tillage lands to meadows. This was no longer merely a measure to fight overproduction and prop up prices; Wallace understood the danger and was ministering to the fundamental physical facts.

Farmers who wished to convert some of their fields to mowings and pastures were promised government aid.

Why were the wheatlands being turned back to meadowlands? Meadow grass *binds* the earth. Storms cannot carry away the soil of mowings and toss it as a killing sand upon neighboring fields. Previously, the exclusion of large sections of land from cultivation had been a purely economic necessity; now reasons of soil conservation dictated the agricultural program. Grass roots and the roots of trees—forests, above all, were needed—would hold the earth fast and protect it against wind and water. Every field of grain was to be couched in a protecting girdle of grass and forest. Where had this been seen before? It was the planting of European landscapes in America.

Variegated landscape arouses a great sense of pleasure in men. Amid lakes, forests, and hills the fields of grain wave; watercourses and roads dwindle into the distance; marshes glisten darkly. . . . Why is this so and why is it beautiful? Every painter would reply, "That is the way it must be because that is the way it is." Perhaps the painter suspects that for thousands of years a "beautiful landscape" has always been a well-proportioned vista of biologically correct factors. To be sure, Demeter could establish fields of grain only at the cost of older types: forests, lakes, and plains. But one must not be permitted to overwhelm and expel the other.

We read in the diaries of Leonardo da Vinci that the earth is a living creature, the rocks its bones, the plants its hair, the water its blood. Nor is this poetic exaggeration, but the purest realism. The earth *is* a living creature; common fluids course through its body. Every part of it has joined hands in the dance with all the other parts. Everything that grows upon the earth is united by the earth itself and by the air, underground and aboveground, by climate and the soil water. Everything combats or comforts everything else. By the mysterious decree which the artistic mind calls "harmony"—we would do better to speak of "balance"—one thing cannot exist without the other.

No one type of landscape, not excluding the grainfield, must be permitted to dominate the husbandry of the earth. It matters little whether a forest is cut down so that Pompey's warships can pursue pirates or whether it is cut down so that New York can read more newspapers in 1940. Under all circumstances, cutting down too much forest is a crime against the husbandry of nature, because forests produce the air we need to live. From the cells of myriad leaves the air draws its moisture, and only if there is moisture can the earth bear fruit. Men know this. But how many things do they not know! There is, for example, the function of marshes. "The marsh breeds only malaria. Away with this relic!" But, reflects Ehrenfried Pfeiffer, the Swiss agronomist, in *Bio-Dynamic Farming and Gardening,* the marsh supplied moisture for the air of the entire surrounding plain. Perhaps this marsh alone made possible the formation of dew in periods of drought. What does it avail to follow the ideal of the technological age and convert the marsh into a few acres of arable land? What is gained and what is lost? These must be weighed.

Everything has a biologic importance for the life of the whole. As each thing has its time, so has each thing its place, and must not be wrenched therefrom. There it stands well. Let the prairie grass stand and do not turn it under with the plow. This was the lesson of the great dust storms and the great floods. Demeter, we remember, is not only the goddess of grain, but of all growing things. She guards her own and warns the nations.

§ 136

There were new arts that Americans had to learn; but Americans enjoy learning. At first the city man felt, with astonishment, the actual taste of the black dust on his tongue. Then he learned the cause and wished to eliminate it. The Government dispensed the information of the cause in the schools. Soon the youngest children knew that the Mississippi annually carried 300,000,000 tons of fruitful soil forever out of sight to the ocean. The fight against erosion became a national cause. Millions of people had lost all their possessions, but a vigorous will and an unconquerable optimism offered defiance to disaster. A governmental department for soil conservation was established. There was ample knowledge, ample money—could not a new, improved technology repair the mistakes of the old?

It seems to be an American gift to make frank confession of errors when the determination to avoid them in the future is already formed. Thus Roosevelt, in his historic speech of June 3, 1937, was able to speak of the danger as something of the past when he told Congress: "Nature has given recurrent and poignant warnings through dust storms, floods, and droughts that we must act while there is yet time, if we would preserve for ourselves and our posterity the natural sources of a virile national life.

"Experience has taught us that the prudent husbandry of our national estate requires farsighted management. Floods, droughts, and dust storms are in a very real sense manifestations of Nature's refusal to tolerate continued abuse of her bounties. . . ."

And he was, indeed, speaking of something that was past. Already woods and hedges grew where they had never been. Terraces were molded to regulate the flow of water. Men sowed grass seed; the green carpet spread across the plains—the great conqueror of whom Carl Sandburg has written, "I am the grass; I cover all." An army, millions of minds and hands, had set out to settle the earth anew in its ancient beds.

BREAD, HEALTH, BUSINESS, AND THE SOUL OF MAN

> Bread hath understanding.
> ITALIAN PROVERB

§ 137

THE MACHINE committed violations against nature not only in the realm of agriculture, but in the realm of nutrition as well. Scientists became aware that the modern mill was doing no good to the health of the people.

What could be wrong with the mill? Certainly, amidst all his tools, man had encountered no better friend than his power-driven mill, and he had many reasons to endorse the marvelous verses of Emile Verhaeren:

> *Chaque meule est dard et couteau*
> *Contre ce qui tord, use ou casse.*
> *Contre les poings du gel et les griffes de l'eau,*
> *Et les grands vents trouant l'espace.*

> Every mill is a spear and a knife
> Against all what is trying to break us.
> Against the fists of the cold, against water's grasp,
> And the terrible winds lacerating the heavens.

But in spite of this indisputable truth man's mill also crushed things which should not have been crushed.

It is astonishing with what rapidity scientific opinions spread in America. It is something like the lightning course of superstitions through medieval Europe. No sooner does some knowing one proclaim, "We are eating badly," or "The food we eat is all wrong" (as for example, Kallet and Schlink did in 1930 in *100,000,000 Guinea Pigs*) than millions take alarm. The tremendous capital invested in the food industry creates huge profits (and thereby fresh capital) every day; but it also gives cause for suspicion that grows daily. Millions of consumers have become so many millions of suspicious guardians of their food. Modern man (and this is something wholly new) not only wants his meals to fill him, but to make him healthier.

For this reason Americans, shortly after World War I, began to think hard about their bread. What kind of bread were they eating? It was a bread that Parmentier had considered the ultimate desideratum: bread without bran. According to Parmentier, the absence of such bread was a cause of serious social misery. Men were eating bran instead of bread and all they ate made them no less hungry. There was no escaping the bran, because there were no machines to remove it from the flour. (Lavoisier had spoken of the *banalité des moulins*.)

But in 1830 Müller and Sulzberger, as we have seen, invented the modern mill. Instead of stones they fitted together seven sets of porcelain and chilled-steel rollers. The first set of rollers were fairly wide apart, and their action cracked the kernel, separating the germ and the oil, which were thus removed from the flour. Other rollers then scaled off the middlings, which were set aside and used for patent flour. Finally, closer-set rollers broke up the starchy part of the kernel into white flour. With the removal of the wheat germ, which spoiled quickly, and the bran, which absorbed moisture, the flour obtained better keeping qualities. This milling apparatus, called the Swiss or the Hungarian mill, revolutionized milling in Minneapolis in the eighties of the last century. The Washburn and Pillsbury companies swamped the United States with white flour. . . .

Hitherto, only soft wheats had been millable; it had not been practicable to grind the winter wheats of the North because they were too hard and wore away the millstones. But now this was possible. The great milling companies promoted railroad construction eastward, to their consumers, and westward, to the wheat region. Then, from 1903 onward, there began a steady movement of all the millers toward Buffalo. The lure was Niagara; the millers would employ its vast torrents as the Philistines had employed Samson—to turn the mill.

Man had made progress. In 1875 Charles B. Gaskill had linked the first flour mill to the hydraulic system created by Horace H. Day to harness the energies of Niagara. Five million horses with white manes tossing in an electric dance could grind all the wheat in America. In Pompeii every mill had been dragged around by two small horses. Man had made progress!

Quantity there was. But what about quality? The mills were still tending toward the great centers of power when, around 1920, the first voices began to cry, "But you have killed the wheat berry!" When flour had been milled between two stones, all the elements of the kernel—bran, starch, and germ—had been ground up together. But the high-milling process removed bran and germ. How could such bread be nutritious, inasmuch as bran contains minerals and the germ is a source of the vital vitamin B_1? Hundreds of physicians began to ask these questions.

True, bread was rich in calories. Despite all the technical developments in the production and milling of wheat, the energy value of bread had remained virtually unchanged: twelve hundred calories per pound and seventy-five calories per ounce. And bread was cheap; in no food could seventy-five calories be obtained more cheaply than in an ounce of bread. Modern science has stressed and proved what was well known to Moses, Christ, Solon, Plato: that bread satisfies hunger and is a source of strength far beyond any other kind of food. Nevertheless, about 1920 the per-capita consumption of bread in the United States declined by at least one fifth. Americans had begun to eat vegetables, fruits, juices, and other foodstuffs richer in vitamins. This trend was helped by the propaganda against refined, high-milled flour.

Many food-conscious Americans now began to eat whole-wheat bread. A powerful advertising campaign taught them that only whole-wheat bread was equal to the "stone-ground flour" of their grandparents; it was estimated that their grandparents' flour had contained some 60 per cent of the thiamin in the wheat. But shortly afterward white bread began to reconquer its old position. Though the millers had taken the wrong turning, the bakers corrected their course. It was, in fact, not too easy to persuade them, and it took the Federal Food Commission three big volumes to give them the right push. But afterward, with the help of chemists, they restored the lost thiamin to the dough. Henry Clapp Sherman, professor at Columbia University, has determined all the ways to compensate for the loss of nutrients in the mills: by adding dried skim milk and vitamin-rich yeast; by including the wheat germ in the flour or returning it to the dough; and by introducing vitamins and mineral salts in the baking. Such methods are now employed to restore nutrients to the 15,000,000,000 loaves baked annually in the United States. The *Bakers' Weekly* has summarized the result: in October 1941, 30 per cent of bakers' white bread was enriched; in June 1942, 55 per cent; in January 1943, 75 per cent; and at last enrichment of all white bread was made compulsory by the Government as an important wartime health measure. (Whole-wheat, naturally, did not need to be enriched.) The order defined enriched bread as bread made from enriched flour or bread in which "equivalent ingredients have been added to plain flour during the mixing of the dough."

In 1941 a revolutionary milling technique was developed from experiments undertaken by the Continental Baking Company. The Earle process (which removes only the outermost hull of the wheat and takes the bitterness out of whole wheat) was improved to a point where 75 per cent of the vitamins was retained in the white flour. This discovery struck a blow at brown whole-wheat flour, and also at the vitamin interests, which were very strong. The battle still rages. The commercial and scientific rivalry between whole-wheat and enriched white bread is not yet settled. But the consumer profits; both sides exert themselves for his sake. The consumer has always profited since 1673, when the University of Paris opened the "yeast question" by investigating whether *pain mollet* was more nutritious than the hard country bread. Competition compelled the bakers to better baking. In the Paris of the periwig era the battle was of epigram and verse; in America the two camps of advertising put out snares for the soul of the consumer.

§ 138

The history of bread must dub the period between the two world wars as the "hygienic decade." The term smacks of irony. For if, a year after Roosevelt's speech on the future of American agriculture, Hitler was to invade all Europe and beset it with artificial hunger, of what use were all the newly discovered methods for preserving the best things in bread? But, as Liebig had once remarked, wars are but incidents. Progress moves past them, around them. What was accomplished by way of hygienic bread could not again be lost.

One would think that cleanliness of bread had been a matter of concern since it was invented. But this was by no means the case. In 1886 Émile Verhaeren in *Les Flamandes*, his first book of verse, gave a realist's account of the way bread was baked in Belgium.

> Les servantes faisaient le pain pour les dimanches,
> Avec le meilleur lait, avec le meilleur grain,
> Le front courbé, le coude en pointe hors des manches,
> Le sueur les mouillant et coulant au pétrin.
>
> Leurs mains, leurs doigts, leur corps entier fumait de hâte.
> Leur gorge remuait dans les corsages pleins.
> Leurs poings enfarinés pataugeaient dans la pâte
> Et la moulaient en ronds comme le chair des seins.
>
> Une chaleur montait: les braises étaient rouges.
> Et deux par deux, du bout d'une planche, les gouges
> Sous les dômes des fours engouffraient les pain mous.
>
> Mais les flammes soudainement, s'ouvrant passage,
> Comme une meute énorme et chaude de chiens roux,
> Sautaient en rigissant leur mordre le visage.

> The serving maids were preparing the bread for Sunday.
> They took the best of milk and the best of flour.
> Their brows were knit, their elbows thrust through the sleeves;
> The sweat soaked their sleeves and dripped into the trough.
>
> Haste fumed from their hands and from their waists.
> Their throats throbbed within the tight bodices.
> Their flour-whitened fists pummeled the dough
> And molded it to roundness like a woman's breasts.
>
> Fierce heat arose; the coals glowed red.
> Two by two, upon a board, the soft loaves
> Were swallowed by the domed ovens.
>
> But the flames, suddenly, clearing their way,
> Hot, red and vast, like some horde of hounds
> Leapt furiously forth and bit at their faces.

Hygiene was by no means associated with bread. Verhaeren's girls baked their bread as, thousands of years before, Greek serving girls had baked theirs. (The terra-cottas in the Louvre show this.) The Bible has it that the sweat of the brow is a God-sent accessory to all human labor. But sweat would seem a good ingredient in the preparation of dough also.

Human sweat contains sodium chloride in various concentrations. Further-more, it contains urea, uric acid, and lactic, formic, butyric, and caprylic acids. For thousands of years these substances were present in the bakery—and the bread did not taste bad at all.

But around 1920 bread was no longer baked as it had been in the days of Verhaeren's young manhood. The machine had entered the bakery and supplanted the human hand. In one of his stories, *Bread,* Joseph Hergesheimer describes what an American bakery was like toward the end of World War I:

The following morning August Turnbull drove to the Turnbull Bakery. The bakery was a consequential rectangle of brick, with the office across the front and a court resounding with the shattering din of ponderous delivery trucks. All the vehicles, August saw, bore a new temporary label advertising still another war bread; there was, too, a subsidiary patriotic declaration: "Win the War with Wheat." He was, as always, fascinated by the mammoth trays of bread, the enormous flood of substance produced as a result of his energy and ability. Each loaf was shut in a sanitary paper envelope; the popular superstition, *sanitation,* had contributed as much as anything to his marked success. He liked to picture himself as a great force, a granary on which the city depended for life; it pleased him to think of thousands of people, men, women, and children, waiting for his loaves or perhaps suffer-ing through the inability to buy them.

The satire is directed against the hero, an unpleasant fellow. The "pop-ular superstition, sanitation," however, is no subject for sarcasm. In 1913, when the Factory Investigation Commission undertook a thorough in-spection of New York bakeries, the results of lack of hygiene became amply clear. Almost 2,400 of the bakeries were located in cellars, because rents were cheaper. A committee of six doctors, headed by Dr. C. M. Price, examined 800 of the bakers employed in those cellars. Four hun-dred and fifty-three proved to be ill. Thirty-two per cent suffered from tuberculosis, rheumatism, anemia, and venereal diseases; 26 per cent had chronic catarrhs; 12 per cent optical diseases; and 7 per cent had "baker's itch," the eczema that was well known even in the Middle Ages as an occupational disease of bakers. Such conditions demanded reform, but it was not in the nature of the sweatshop to practice hygiene. Only large-scale business could take the necessary steps.

Naturally, it was not sanitation that was the motive for the establish-ment of large-scale bakeries; it was the logic of economics. It is an eco-nomic law that 20,000 small enterprises cannot conduct the industry of coal mining; small business could not satisfy the world's vast demand for coal. A similar law became operative in breadmaking. Here, how-ever, the law was less absolute. For thousands of years baking had been a craft. In villages and small towns even today a few good bakers who know how to organize their work can very well provide the necessary bread. But in cities of millions like New York, London, and Leningrad, the private bakery has been driven out by the bread factory. Bread is no longer supplied by individual artisans, but by manufacturers whose fleets of trucks deliver the loaves to sales shops every morning.

The bread consumption of a modern metropolis is huge. In 1924 the 106 bakeries of the Continental Baking Corporation used over 3,000,000 barrels of flour, 60,000,000 pounds of sugar, 10,000,000 pounds of eggs, 25,000,000 pounds of milk, 11,000,000 pounds of salt, 1,750,000 pounds of shortening, and 9,000,000 pounds of yeast. Consumption on a large scale produced a difficulty that had been unknown to the old artisan baker: excessive losses from stale bread. Bread is one of the most perishable of foodstuffs, not only in a physical sense, but in a commercial sense as well. The consumer invariably chooses fresh bread in preference to old bread. It is impossible for the manufacturer to estimate how many loaves will be bought on any given day. In 1923 Stancliffe Davis and Wilfred Eldred investigated stale bread losses for the Food Research Institute of Stanford University. Both found that the factories averaged losses from 6 to 10 per cent of production. Exceptional cases ran much higher—as high as 25 per cent. The situation was complicated because the large manufacturers did not have any fixed contract with the grocers; unsold breads were returnable. Consequently, fearful quantities of oldish but wholesome bread were fed to the bakers' ovens to bake new loaves! In November 1917 the United States Food Administration estimated that the loss from the return of stale bread to the bakeries amounted to "upwards of 600,000 barrels of flour a year." The dollar value of the losses ran into millions. In World War II one of the first acts of the Government was to forbid stale bread returns. Bread has to be consumed, fresh or not; any other practice is an economic and ethical sin.

To our children or grandchildren, stale bread may be unknown. They will not understand the medieval legend of the "miser of Mainz," who was taken off by the devil because he had kept a sack of bread until it was stale, having refused to give it away to the poor while it was still fresh. . . . For staleness is a chemical problem that someday will certainly be overcome. Formerly chemists believed that the loss of moisture was the chief cause of the development of staleness; but the experiments of Ostwald (1919) seem to indicate that a variation in starch content is the main factor in the process. Chemists can generally "redress a process" if they can determine the steps by which the end result was produced. Ostwald found that a gelatinized starch paste would return to its state of freshness under the influence of heat. This was a vital discovery, but the bread industry was not interested in pursuing the investigation. Like other industries, the bread industry desired a quick turnover; it had no interest in making bread a kind of preserve. But war's exigencies may lead to improvements that the profit motive neglects. In Napoleon's time (1810) the Swiss, Nicholas Appert, appeared to show the world how to preserve fruits by cooking them and sealing them in airtight containers. Today there seems little doubt that the man will come who will show the world's armies how to be independent of their burdensome field bakeries.

The soldier wants good bread. And in this World War II, in jungles and in deserts, under the most unfavorable atmospheric conditions, good bread is baked for him. But is it necessary to contend with such difficulties? Could not the bread be baked beforehand under better conditions?

It cannot yet be done. But even this is not certain. In November 1942 stories were published of German prisoners taken by the British Eighth Army at El Alamein who had with them "fresh bread that was baked months before in Munich. . . ." Perhaps this story is untrue; but it foreshadows the probable course of the future.

§ 139

The first man in America to recognize that bread was a product adapted to mass production was W. B. Ward. Ward was the actual founder of the American bread industry; he was the "Napoleon of baking." Starting in 1849 with a small plant in New York City, by 1912 the Ward family was managing a $30,000,000 combination of Eastern and Midwestern bakeries. In 1924 Ward formed the Continental Baking Corporation, which subsequently bought up other baking companies— taking over no less than twenty in the first six months of the corporation's existence. Ward then raised capital amounting to $2,000,000,000 to amalgamate the General Baking Corporation with Continental into a super-corporation, a mammoth firm which would control the entire bread industry. Ward professed altruism; he wished to control the "marrow of mortals" "to the end that the American people may have and enjoy wholesome food at fair prices, and that every child may enjoy the right to be born well, to reach school age well, and to grow to maturity physically and mentally fit for American citizenship." But at this point the Government intervened. It seemed clear that this new bread corporation would be a trust calculated to smother all competition—and this was illegal under the anti-trust laws.

When Ward died in 1929 he had not succeeded in his far-reaching plans. But he had succeeded in giving a thorough fright to the large millers. For if any group of capitalists should succeed in uniting the entire baking industry under unified management, the milling industry would be forced to sell its flour at the price the bakers dictated. As a preventive measure, the milling companies began to buy their way into the baking industry. In 1931 the Gold Dust Corporation and the Standard Milling

Company did something unprecedented for almost two thousand years: they fused their financial interests with those of the baking trade. Since the days of the Roman Empire miller and baker had been separated. Now they attempted once more to unite.

Ward's program illustrates the interesting fact that in modern America (and in the rest of the world) the chief trick of advertising is the insistence on "health." To call this pure hypocrisy is rash indeed. Purity is a by-product, but a very important one, of modern industrial development. By promoting health, industry "makes atonement," as it were, for its very existence. In the bread industry the slogan "untouched by human hands" became the be-all and the end-all. It meant the exclusion of countless potential employees from the industry—but the slogan was not bad in itself.

The idea of producing bread which would never be touched by a human (i.e., germ-carrying) hand, "from mill to mouth," has been carried very far indeed, for the entire baking process is mechanical. The first mechanical dough-kneader was demonstrated by the famous Arago to the French Academy in 1850. It was a rather small drum which seemed to be thumped by goblins. Today the dough-kneader is a machine whose mighty steel arms move with dazzling swiftness through the dough, mixing and aerating it. And the machine does not sweat! Like agriculture, baking today has its iron servants—sifters, mixers, kneaders, and what not that were unknown to earlier times.

While the baker was still an artisan, the process of baking was a capricious one. Since the machine has entered the bakery, the loaf has become a product of the strictest determinism. Its making differs greatly from the procedure used by the old artisan or the individual housewife. The ingredients are weighed accurately beforehand and assembled ready for use beside the mixing machine. These ingredients are turned into the mixer in proper sequence; the batch is mixed until the resulting dough has acquired just the proper consistency and exactly the correct temperature; it is then poured into great troughs and brought to a warm room for the raising process before being sent down the chute to the scaling and dividing machines. From the dividers the accurately scaled pieces of dough pass through the overhead proofer, then to the molder, which forms the round balls into loaves and automatically drops them into pans; the panned loaves then glide to the proofing box, which gives them another chance to rise; and finally the pans are pushed into the great ovens, which are maintained at accurate temperatures of about 450° F to 500° F. When the loaves are baked, they are drawn from the oven and emptied into racks to cool before being wrapped and delivered to the salesman.

§ 140

The baker's oven has become an automaton!

Uneasily we approach the monster—made in Cincinnati. We see a huge, smooth wall covered with dials and gauges that only the engineer can read. Everywhere switches and levers gleam, intimidating the laity. There is a "minute minder," a "thermostat," a "tray indicator," a "hood exhauster switch." . . . Can this be an oven? Is this the house in which goddesses such as Fornax and Ishtar dwelt? It is—but it is also an automaton.

It has come to an end, then, the fervor and ferment that has inspired men since earliest times, the mystical marriage and transformation of matter, the mystery of the creation of bread? No, it has not ended at all; it survives in folklore, in dreams, and, above all, in those places that have not yet been reached by the urban machine: in the villages of eastern Europe.

In the bread factories of America many Polish workers are employed to whom bread may be no more than any other article of manufacture. But these workers are the sons of emigrants and the cousins of peasants who remained at home, and to their fathers and cousins the bread is still something entirely different. In their homeland {in peacetime, of course) molds and rising troughs are handed down from father to son and grandson, for these old instruments are steeped in the ways of bread and one knows how the dough will behave in them. When, in a Polish village, a new trough is needed because the old one has cracked, the cooper is urged to be quick about his work, for the cooper's diligence will be transferred to the dough; the dough, in its turn, will be "diligent" and will rise quickly and well. Every baking trough is considered a living creature; each has its peculiarities. One loves warmth, the other cold; some demand quiet; others are not disturbed by noise. No family will lend away its trough; for on returning the trough will have taken on the smells and the habits of other people. When it is filled with dough, it is handled with extreme care; it is covered with sheep hides or placed under the feather bed. For this is a living thing; the growing bread demands tender care, like a child that must not be permitted to take cold.

The age of the machine is a stage in the economic and social history of man—but it is a stage that has not extinguished previous stages. Examined more closely, civilization is but a deceptive show; mankind lives in all ages at once and repeats continually the experience of all ages. The writer, Fueloep-Miller, tells this story of his childhood in Rumania:

One night I dreamt that a great loaf of bread stood on the breakfast table. Mother was just about to cut the bread when she was called away. As soon as she was gone, the crust of the loaf burst open and Ida, the baker's wife, rose from the soft, white bread. Nothing remained of the bread; the inside became Ida's body, the crust became her hair. Her warm fragrance filled the entire room; it was so strong that the new nurse at once fell from her chair in a faint. Then Ida said to me, "I've done this just to let you know that it is I who come to you every morning in the loaf of bread. But you must not tell anyone." Thereupon her body once more became the soft inside of the bread, her hair was transformed back into crust which enclosed the whiteness. When Mother entered, the uncut loaf of bread lay on the table as before. The dream memory of Ida arising out of the bread remained so vivid within me that whenever Mother cut the bread, I saw Ida clearly before me. And when I ate the bread, I thought secretly, "It is Ida I am eating."

The magical erotic power of bread, exemplified in this dream of a modern child, was well known to most earlier peoples. For the arched oven was the symbol of the mother's womb. The oven could be jealous; among the inhabitants of the Marquesas Islands a man who had been baking with the banana flour customary with this folk was not permitted to touch his wife that same night. . . . The "return to the womb"— using the oven to hide men from their enemies—is an element in many a legend and fairy tale. After the Seven Years' War a Silesian woman boasted she had hidden the Prussian King Frederick the Great in her baking oven from the pursuing Austrians; and in order to foil their search she had put two earthen pots with excrements in front and behind this hiding place. . . . If Freud had known something about the folklore of bread he would have used its many wish-covering and wish-expressing symbols for his theory. It may also be called a particular hint that the great Swiss anthropologist of the nineteenth century who developed the theory of matriarchy—the theory of woman's supremacy in earlier human social organization—bore the name *Bachofen* (baking oven). Thus, as happens not infrequently, a symbolic name coincided with the choice of a lifework.

Though it is made mechanically, bread seems to have lost none of its manifold powers. In 1452, a year of bountiful harvests, two Swiss noble-men riding in a wheat field found a sleeping child which was so heavy that their combined efforts did not suffice to lift it. When they called some peasants to help them, the child vanished magically, but the entire region was redolent with the odor of bread. This fable reappeared in eastern Europe in 1940; in the war-torn countries of Europe it became a wishful myth. No one had brought such a story to these lands; the people had con-ceived it anew. Bread hath understanding, say the Italians. It has more; it is a diviner and hunter possessed of supernatural powers. American soldiers who stayed in England in 1942 learned to their amazement that many Englishmen soberly believed that bread could locate drowned men. If some quicksilver (symbol of unrest) were baked into bread (symbol of rest) and the loaf cast upon the water, the drowned man would be drawn to it and so come to light. The superstitious Britishers offered in their defense the fact that on September 18, 1885, before some ten thousand people, the experiment had been made in Stamford (Lincolnshire) and had succeeded. Now war and the numberless sinkings of ships had resurrected this old belief—which is perhaps derived from a frequently misunderstood passage in the Bible (Ecclesiastes, XI): "Cast thy bread upon the waters: for thou shalt find it after many days."

And just as the magic of bread is not dead, so also have the religions, great compendiums of popular beliefs and traditions that they are, lost none of their faith in the sacred force of bread. In 1942, when the American soldiers landed in Morocco, they were informed by an instruction booklet prepared for them by the Army that they must never cut bread in the sight of Mohammedans. The Mohammedans originally did not consider bread a living creature meriting special respect. But religions *grow.* In a world in which Christianity ascribed such great importance to bread, Islam was eventually moved to modify its indifference. The Americans learned to break their bread instead of slicing it, in order not to offend. And a few months later those same Americans saw the Jews in Tunis offering shewbreads to Jehovah. The cakes, molded in squares, were piled one above the other and hollow golden tubes conducted air between them. By this device the shewbreads were aerated (a custom unknown to Jews elsewhere) so that nothing moldy would be offered to their God. Two thousand years before Josephus Flavius had described this custom as prevailing among the Jews. . . .

All the customs attached to bread have remained living. All over the world they are to be found. More significant than ever before is the great bread hymn of Saint Thomas Aquinas which was sung in 1943 in the Cathedral of Saint Peter in Rome, before Pope Pius XII:

> *Ecce panis angelorum!*
> *Factus cibus viatorum,*
> *Vere panis filiorum!*

> Lo! The Angel's food is given
> To the pilgrim who hath striven,
> See the children's Bread from Heaven!

"Sumunt boni, sumunt mali," says Thomas Aquinas. The good take it, the wicked take it. The Eucharist blesses all. The priest teaches the Catholic child never to take the wafer in his teeth, but to swallow it whole; one may swallow God, he explains to the child, but not bite Him. *Sumunt boni, sumunt mali!* Many deny that eating the Sacrament can be helpful to unbelievers. Others believe differently. Some decades ago the poet,

Guillaume Apollinaire, wrote a discussion of the question of a church mouse that had eaten a piece of the holy wafer; would it thereby win to a higher life? It was not intended as a jest. During the scholastic age this question was often treated by French writers.

The Christian sects no longer quarrel over the conception of bread. But each maintains its opinion. According to Rulon S. Howells, there are at present more than ten Christian churches in America which have variant interpretations of bread as the body of Christ—ranging from extreme realism to extreme symbolism. All these churches flourish and give their worshipers *their* bread. But they also give it unquestioningly to their neighbors if need be. On the battlefields of the United Nations, when the priest gives consolation to the dying, it is love and not dogma that rules.

§ 141

Thus we live in many ages at once, contemporaries of many periods, and bread is as important as ever. Superficially its importance is restricted to the purely material realm; but this is merely appearance. In the spectacle of commercial life those with eyes to see can detect manifestations of other than materialistic forces. Indeed, materialistic forces are frequently warriors in broader spiritual battles. Such intermixture is typical of our twentieth century.

In 1899 in America a controversy over baking powder broke out. Baking powder was a harmless invention of Liebig's to provide German housewives and bakers with a means to raise bread more quickly. Nor was it anything new in American history when two competing firms—the American Baking Powder Association and the Royal Baking Powder Company—tried to outlaw each other. What was new were the public repercussions. Within a year the battle, which had begun by each company's stigmatizing the other's product as poisonous, turned into a national war; all over the country frenzied partisans debated whether an aluminic sulphate known as alum had a deleterious effect on health. Famous men, such as Harvey W. Wiley (1844–1930), leading American chemist and archfoe of food adulteration, entered the controversy. The alum quarrel merited greater headlines than the Russo-Japanese War. Lobbyists besieged Congress. Trials lasting years followed; all the apparatus of bribery, of corruption of senators and representatives, so familiar in the American politics of the day, was hauled out. Lobbyists were indicted, made attempts at suicide, turned state's evidence, or fled. Later the statements, opinions, indictments, and so on were accumulated by Abraham Morrison in two volumes of two thousand pages.

The struggle was waged by competing firms—but it was waged in the name of bread; for the purity of bread and the purity of public life. This was the time when Theodore Roosevelt "threw his sausage out of the window after reading in a novel by Upton Sinclair what this sausage probably contained." The Government began to enforce the Pure Food

THE BAKING-POWDER TRUST EXPLODES

Act, and millers were given prison sentences for bleaching flour with acids.

Perhaps this was "materialistic"—but at stake essentially was the healthfulness of bread. And in that same year of 1899, in the eastern part of the world, the old battle of spiritual bread was resumed upon the soil of Holy Russia. Transubstantiation had been attacked by Zwingli, by the street crowds of the French Revolution, but nowhere had it been so scorned as in Tolstoy's novel *Resurrection*.

Tolstoy was too great an artist to condemn; he described.

> The service began. . . . The priest, having dressed himself up in a strange and very inconvenient garb of gold cloth, cut and arranged little bits of bread on a saucer and then put most of them into a cup of wine, repeating at the same time different names and prayers. Meanwhile the deacon first read Slavonic prayers, difficult to understand in themselves and rendered still more incomprehensible by being read very fast. . . .

> The essence of the service consisted in the supposition that the bits of bread cut up by the priest and put into the wine, when manipulated and prayed over in a certain way, turned into the flesh and blood of God. These manipulations consisted in the priest, hampered by the gold cloth sack he had on, regularly lifting and holding up his arms and then sinking to his knees and kissing the table and all that was on it; but chiefly in his taking a cloth by two of its corners and waving it rhythmically and softly over the silver saucer and the golden cup. It was supposed that at this point the bread and wine turned into flesh and blood; therefore this part of the service was performed with the utmost solemnity. . . .

> . . . No one present seemed conscious that all that was going on here was the greatest blasphemy, and a mockery of that same Christ in whose name it was being done. . . . The priest himself did not believe that the bread turned into flesh. . . . No one could believe this, but he believed that one ought to believe it. What strengthened him most in this faith was the fact that, by fulfilling its demands, he had for the last eighteen years been able to draw an income which enabled him to support his family.

For this mockery of the Sacrament Tolstoy was expelled from the Eastern Orthodox Church in 1901. Very material forces stood behind this expulsion; for an attack upon the orthodox Mass was an attack upon Czarism, upon the throne, upon civil security. The materialistic motives were accompanied by spiritual ones. The highest church dignitary in Russia, Konstantin Pobyedonostsev, High Procurator of the Holy Synod, conferred Tolstoy's soul, if not his body, to the flames. To the historian, the efficacy or inefficacy of such pronouncements is immaterial; for us the question is: did Tolstoy accomplish what he sought to accomplish? There is little doubt that he did not reach the larger part of the Russian faithful. And certainly he did not touch Roman Catholicism. Pope Leo XIII (1878–1903), a distinguished politician, thinker, and psychologist, declared, "The bread of the Eucharist will be the dominating factor of the twentieth century." Forty years have passed since he made this statement. He was not entirely wrong. In World War II the Catholic Church —and with it the transformation of bread, the central point of its liturgy —is playing a mightier part than ever before.

HITLER'S "PACTE DE FAMINE"

That which the palmerworm hath left hath the locust eaten; and
that which the locust hath left hath the cankerworm eaten; and that
which the cankerworm hath left hath the caterpillar eaten.

JOEL I, 4.

§ 142

WHICH COURSE does the bread take in World War II? Does it use the
same track as in World War I? Or are there early deviations?

Immediately upon the outbreak of World War II, the Minister of
Agriculture in Berlin began propagandizing rye. This propaganda campaign had been carefully prepared. Prominent posters cast aspersions
upon wheat without actually mentioning it. "Eat rye bread. Color is not
nourishment. Rye bread makes cheeks red." The German Government
did not know how long this world war would last. But it knew from the
experience of the last world war that home-grown wheat would not suffice, and that American wheat would no longer arrive from overseas.
Therefore, the people were prepared for dark bread.

No special pains must be taken when the product to be advertised is
something good. Against rye it might be said that wheat contained more
proteins, but the taste for wheat was young in Germany and could easily
be uprooted. The French and the British might hold with Pliny that "rye
is deficient in value and good only for satisfying hunger; its ear is rich
in grain, but its flour is unattractive because of the dark color. . . ." But
rye tasted better to the Germans. In 1936 the German mills (some
28,000) had processed about 9 million tons of grain: 4.8 million tons
of rye, and 4.2 million tons of wheat. Thus there were about 300 pounds
of grain per capita. When the war began, the proportions of wheat to rye
changed materially—but not the total consumption of flour.

The German bread law of May 3, 1935, had admitted rather shame-
facedly that 10 per cent of the bread flour must consist of potato flour.
Germany was the home of rye—but the rye had to be stretched. In 1935
the Ministry of Agriculture seemed well aware of the plans of the War
Ministry.

The potato is a wonderful vegetable, but it is not a cereal. The history
of the past four hundred years has amply indicated that whenever it is
introduced into bread, the tendency is for its proportion to grow. It does
not remain at 10 per cent—and in consequence the water and starch
content of the bread goes up.

But Germany, as she entered the war, held the largest stores of potatoes in her history. In 1937 the Germans had harvested almost 53,000,000 tons of potatoes—about a fifth of the world harvest. As the Germans well knew, the tuber would yield almost everything but fats and protein. The potato had long been their best friend, materially, at any rate; although after the failure of the Revolution of 1848 the philosopher Feuerbach had exclaimed angrily, "Potato blood can make no revolutions." Presumably he meant that the low-protein diet of the German masses was a source of their weakness. It is a rather questionable theory; the potato-fed Irish have always had plenty of revolutions.

Since the days when Frederick the Great had eaten potatoes in public to convince the Prussians that they were not poisonous, the potato had become dear to the heart of the Germans. The Nazi Minister of Agriculture, Darré, considered it a fine stroke of propaganda when, in the first days of the war, he spread the rumor that "English planes have dropped larvae of the Colorado potato beetle." This alleged attack upon German potato culture aroused the German peasants more than many an atrocity story. The "English potato crime" was credited; the German peasant was convinced that he had to do with an utterly ruthless enemy.

§ 143

The German peasants had taken Hitler's word that he would be a "peasants' chancellor." Their gullibility does little honor to their shrewdness. Had they listened more closely they would have heard the same megaphone that promised to help the "little man on the land" trumpeting similar promises to the "little man in the city"—that is, promising the seller of food high prices and the buyer low prices. It seemed obvious that this was a double negative, but the peasants did not notice the contradiction; nor did they hear that the same Nazi propagandist who promised them the breaking up of the large estates also assured the *Junkers* of armed protection against agrarian uprisings. Never before had all the classes of a nation been so thoroughly betrayed. The peasant was no more stupid than any other class; but he was no more intelligent. Hitler succeeded in beguiling him from his traditional suspiciousness.

For the German Republic one of the most important questions had been the opening up of new arable land. Had this question been solved in time, Hitler might never have come to power. The Republic's ineffective and faltering action gave Hitler the pretext for crying: "The longing of the settlers has been betrayed." The "settlers" were those who hoped to be settled on new land. When the master betrayer came to power, he betrayed these betrayed settlers once more.

In imperial Germany the food-producing class had scarcely been held in esteem. This was the fault less of the big cities, where the people knew nothing of the peasants, than of the German small towns, whose inhabitants knew too much of the peasant. The ideal of German life was embodied in the small town. There, where the keeper of the beer cellar was the leading light, who threw his rooms open to the gentry of the town; where the pettiest postal clerk was as one made in the image of the Kaiser because he wore a uniform—here, in the small town, the peasant was thoroughly despised. The townspeople scowled upon this sweaty man with high boots who reeked with manure when he came to town to shop.

World War I changed this fundamentally. Possibly it was the contact with real peasant nations, with the Russians and the Serbs, that made countless German townspeople homesick for the land. Amid the roar of an artillery barrage they dreamed that a piece of their own land would be the best antitoxin to militarism and pan-Germanism.

Indeed, in the course of the terrible war the Germans encountered strange peoples. There were the Bulgarians, for example. The Berlin General Staff was distinctly surprised when, in the spring of 1918, it heard that the Bulgarian common soldiers were prophesying that they would go home on the fifteenth of September of that year. Hindenburg, who reports this fact, blamed the rumor on Allied propaganda. Imperial Berlin did not know that for thousands of years in southeastern Europe September 15 had marked the beginning of the "Eleusinian weeks," when the seed corn returned to the earth—the beginning of the winter sowing. Promptly on September 15 the Bulgarian peasants threw off their uniforms, left the Salonika front, and returned home to cultivate their fields.

By 1919 growing and baking their own bread had become the dream of many Germans. In November 1918, when Hindenburg led the beaten army back home, he spoke to it:

Comrades, the preparations for large-scale settlement are in progress; execution will soon begin. The returning soldiers will be the first to receive this expression of their Fatherland's gratitude. . . . Hundreds of thousands of places shall be made on land bought cheaply with cheap, public money— for farmers, gardeners, and artisans. . . . The great work has already begun. It will take some years to complete it. Have patience for but a short time. Help your wounded Fatherland over the most difficult period; save it once more through German discipline and German sense of order. Thus you will be assuring your own future and your own happiness.

This proclamation was the opening stroke in the new German Republic's agrarian program. In August 1919 the Reich Settlement Act, written by Professor Max Sering, set aside one third of the property incorporated in large German estates for resettlement.

Perhaps one must have lived in Germany during the early twenties to understand how faithful and deep-rooted was the people's longing for this resettlement. Day after day the industrial worker as well as the intellectual worker (carrying a book of Hamsun in his pocket) asked Destiny for a piece of land. . . . Never had the great cities looked uglier than in those days, squirming with political troubles, food troubles, and coal famine. Lincoln Eyre, the correspondent of the New York *Times,* mistook the situation when he wrote: "There is virtually no movement toward the land in Germany." Yes, there was; only the deception "to see settlement postponed until St. Nevermore's day" finally changed Germany's mind. For no German statesman, neither of the left nor of the right, as the Catholic Chancellor Bruening, could wrest the land from the great landowners.

For centuries eastern Germany had belonged to 13,000 families. Intricately related, hostile to all who did not belong to their families, they were the actual Prussian state, and at last they became Germany herself. No king could uproot them, no government place limitations upon them. Berlin needed good army officers—and they supplied the best officers. They had also been good managers of their land. Frederick the Great admired the noblemen of these eastern provinces—and cursed them at the same time. "During the last war I had every reason to be dissatisfied with the East Prussian nobility. Its temper was more Russian than Prussian; for the rest, it was capable of all the evil deeds that are ascribed to the Poles," he wrote in 1768. The great-grandsons of these Prussians had learned nothing, forgotten nothing. When *Junker* privileges were threatened in 1920, they stabbed the Republic in the back. They cried "expropriation" and "bolshevism" and prevented the enforcement of the law. The law contained in actuality no hint of expropriation; it intended merely to compel the nobility to *sell* a part of their land. "What for?" growled Hindenburg—himself a large landowner and an officer—when he became President of the Republic. "We large landowners have always taken care of the small farmers in the best possible way."

In 1941, when Wilhelm II, the last German Kaiser, died, he still owned 240,000 acres of land in Germany. The richest landowner after him was the Duke of Pless; then followed Prince Hohenlohe with 120,000 acres, and the princely family of Hohenzollern-Sigmaringen with 112,000 acres. Had the German peasantry had the opportunity to read truthful newspapers, it would have learned that in Masaryk's Czechoslovakia, in King Alexander's Yugoslavia, and in Narutowicz's Poland the division of large estates was successfully carried out after the end of World War I. But the German newspapers, concerned with the *Kulturlosigkeit,* the "cultural barbarism" of the newly founded Slavic states, and with their "oppression" of German minorities, neglected to pass on this important fact. The *Junkers* remained on their large estates. And the German Republic appointed a host of commissions to investigate the agrarian question before any action was taken. By the time the reports were finally ready, the fire of the revolution had been put out. The opportunity was past.

Hitler began to incite along this line. "What," he screamed, "is the Republic doing against the enemies of the small farmer?" Hitler had an acute talent for finding the nations' wounds and rubbing salt into them. As early as 1925, eight years before he seized power, the National Socialists initiated a memorial day for the fearful slaughter the German peasantry had suffered in 1525 at the hands of the towns and princes. The Nazis considered appointing the anniversary of the Battle of Frankenhausen, in which Thomas Münzer fell, as a national day of mourning for the peasantry; but they finally thought better of it. For, historically speaking, Münzer had been a Communist, and such a celebration would have offended the industrialists and landowners whose money Hitler needed. Instead the Nazis persuaded the peasants that their direct foe was the democratic German Republic; it was not democratic, they maintained, but bolshevistic. The peasants must refuse to pay taxes to the Republic. It was the fault of the bureaucrats and the Jews that the peasants were suffering hard times. The clumsy treatment of the peasants by the officials of the Republic, the increasing burden of debt upon farms, and the forced auction sales of many farms, acted as accompaniment to Hitler's pipings. The peasants permitted him to use them for his own purposes.

§ 144

Hitler had no liking for peasants. This was inevitable for him, the son of *petit bourgeois,* who longed to climb the social ladder. To be sure, he knew the value of bread, for often enough he had been in want of it; but he had no scruples against betraying those who produced it.

To his mind, the highly industrialized world around him could be either fascist or communist—there was no third choice. The peasant was not able to rule; nowhere in the world had he succeeded. If some of Hitler's followers thought otherwise for a time, they were severely checked by the sad fate of Stambuliski.

Alexander Stambuliski (1879–1923), the Bulgarian dictator, had tried to rule his native land with the sole support of the peasantry. As an agrarian leader he had objected to King Ferdinand's policy of plunging his country into the Balkan wars; a self-sustaining people, Stambuliski argued, could live at peace with all its neighbors. When, in 1915, the German-born Ferdinand sought to associate Bulgaria with the Central Powers, Stambuliski entered the king's chambers and threatened the monarch with violence. "Ferdinand of Coburg," he shouted, "you are a foreigner in this land and you have a crown to lose!" For this offense he was court-martialed and sentenced to life imprisonment. In September 1918, on the eve of the German defeat, he was liberated and led the peasant soldiers into Sofia, the capital of Bulgaria. King Ferdinand fled. His successor, Boris, had no choice but to give all power to Stambuliski.

Stambuliski was a broad, husky man with a rough-hewn face and piercing eyes and a head crowned by a thatch of black hair. From 1920 to 1923 Stambuliski ruled Bulgaria with an iron plowshare. Four fifths of the people stood behind the agrarian dictatorship; that is to say, all the peasants. But the other fifth, their pockets bulging with Italian bribes, organized a *Putsch,* and on June 9, 1923, overthrew the government. Mussolini backed the revolt because he hated Stambuliski, not so much for his agrarian socialism as for his naïve friendliness with Bulgaria's Yugoslavian neighbor. Mussolini was attempting to isolate and encircle Yugoslavia; for this purpose he desired a Bulgaria of another stamp. Consequently he financed the *coup d'état.* Stambuliski fled to Slavovitsa, his native village, but was trapped by armed Bulgarian fascists and riddled with bullets. His last words were, "Green Internationale of the world, avenge my death!"

But the Green Internationale did not exist.

Hitler, at this time preparing for his Beer Hall Putsch (November 1923), was much impressed by Stambuliski's death. It taught him that "fascism was more powerful than the peasantry," and that one who sought real power would do better not to lean on the peasant's plow.

Nazi literature, however, retained the peasant policy, the "friendliness toward the peasantry," for some time. Long after Hitler had become the Führer of all Germany, he enjoyed discussing academically at Berchtesgaden such questions as, "Were the Germans of the pre-Christian era agrophiles or agrophobes?" He stood godfather to a book that was written for him by Darré, *The Peasantry as the Source of Vitality of the Nordic Race,* which "proved" that Christianity had not been necessary to transform the Germans into farmers. . . . When Hitler saw written in black and white what he dearly wished to believe, he made this drivel a cornerstone of his *Kulturpolitik.* The German peasantry appeared to him a bulwark against Christianity. He sent agitators into the countryside to proselytize for the abolition of the Christian festivals; sowing and harvesting were to be placed once more under the protection of the Teutonic gods. It was an absurd idea, for no such protection ever existed. As we have seen, the old Nordic gods were gods of storm, wind, and clouds— foes of cultivation. The peasants, however, were not taken in by the nonsense; if they were to have any religion at all, they countered, they would abide by the guardianship of Mary and by the Christian holidays. Hitler never forgave them for refusing to co-operate in bringing back the "mythus" of the Northland.

§ 145

When the guilt and folly of all classes in Germany had permitted Nazism to come to power, the half promises to the peasantry were soon forgotten. The former German Republic had committed the mortal sin of paying subsidies to its worst enemies; about 700,000,000 marks yearly were poured into the inefficient estates of the *Junkers* in the years 1926–30 alone. When Kurt von Schleicher, last Chancellor of the German Republic, attempted to explain to the German taxpayers what had become of the "Eastern Aid," Hindenburg was forced to dismiss him. Hitler took his place. At this time the most urgent need of the peasant was machinery to lighten his labor and increase his productivity. After six years of Hitler's rule, Herbert Backe, the new German Minister of Agriculture, had to admit that less than 2 per cent of German farms were equipped with tractors. Hitler had contented himself with opening his bag of tricks and demonstrating some fireworks to the peasants. These were the "Reich Hereditary Farm Act" of September 29, 1933.

This law provided that farms up to 125 hectares (about 309 acres), farms large enough for the maintenance of one family but not large enough to constitute an estate for capitalist exploitation, would be established as "hereditary farms." Such farms could neither be sold nor mortgaged. They would be passed on undivided to the peasant's oldest son. . . . The banning of mortgages was a helpful measure to hundreds of thousands of peasants; it forestalled the possibility of forced auction sales. On the other hand, the peasant could not sell his land even if he wanted to; this law fettered him to the soil—though to his own soil. And the indivisibility of the farm created widespread dissatisfaction, for this patriarchal decree could not be hailed with joy by the younger brothers who were excluded from inheritance; they were left only the choice of leaving the land for the town or becoming landless agricultural laborers. Moreover, the directives for the enforcement of the law contained a significant catch: it was provided that a farmer who practiced poor husbandry could be expropriated from his land. What farmer practices poor husbandry? In a fascist dictatorship an inefficient farmer is not the man who forgets to sow, but a farmer who is not a good party member. Undoubtedly Hitler's hereditary farm act won him a good many yea-sayers, for the nay-sayers did not remain on their "hereditary" farms.

In politics Hitler has never been a dilettante or bungler. His speech of October 1, 1933, ushering in the new law, proved that he recognized the power of the bread-producing class. "The ruination of the German peasant would be the ruination of the German people." A ruined artisan class might conceivably regenerate itself, he went on to say; a middle class reduced to misery might one day recover its affluence; industry reduced to nothing might rehabilitate itself through its own efforts; a town pauperized and depopulated might conceivably raise itself to new prosperity. But the peasant driven from his land disappears forever as a peasant class after it has been allowed to disappear. The peasant not only assures the nation of its daily bread; he is the guarantor of its future and provides a people with force, health, equilibrium, and endurance.

Hitler was surely no dilettante. He was a cold-blooded deceiver who knew very well the economic *valeur* of his victims. The farmers were poorer than ever at the moment when the bread-producing class was hurled into war in 1939. Their labor power had been exploited and they had been given nothing in return. They sweated on their hereditary farms and received low prices for their produce. But the *Junkers* were once more army officers, as they had been under Kaiser Wilhelm. What had become of the breakup and distribution of the great estates and their transformation into small settlements? In 1932, a year before Hitler took power, 9,000 new farms had been established and 250,000 acres of land settled. In 1937, under the rule of the "peasant chancellor," scarcely a third of this was given to land-hungry settlers. At the agricultural conference in Goslar in 1938 Minister of Agriculture Walter Darré felt it necessary to apologize for the poor condition of the German peasants:

The total loss in farm workers during the last ten years can without exaggeration be estimated at 700,000 to 800,000. . . . I am aware how grievously the economic difficulties, the poverty of the workers, and the overburdening of the farmer's wife run counter to the biologic laws of life. Working conditions on the land, and in particular the shortage of female workers on the farms, place such a burden on the German farm woman that it is almost impossible for her to be the mother of a large number of children. . . . This overburdening of the farm woman has produced such a situation that the actual purpose of our farm legislation can hardly be fulfilled. We must call earnest attention to the fact that conditions on the land have begun to develop along lines which may do irreparable damage to the entire body politic. The rehabilitation of the German farming class has not yet been possible; the class has so far been unable to free itself from its capitalistic bondage.

Darré could not, of course, admit that it was military slavery rather than capitalistic bondage that was ruining the German farmers. Germany's insane rearmament was depopulating the countryside and driving the agricultural workers into the towns. But unlike Russia and America, no large-scale system of machinery was making up for the loss of farm hands. From 1935 on the German Führer devoted his every thought to the coming war. Goering recklessly cut down the German forests, partly to sell the wood at good prices, partly to clear land for military highways. More than 1,500,000 acres of good, fertile soil was withdrawn from production for the construction of barracks and the laying out of airdromes and enclosures for military exercises. Martin Gumpert in his *Heil Hunger* has calculated that the land lost to food production for the sake of war preparations exceeds in area the Reich's total area for truck gardening.

And then came September 1, 1939. War! And the Nazis had the impudence to tell the farmers that this was a war to acquire new land for settlement. The German farmer would now be able to take up the Polish peasant's land, for the Poles did not know how to cultivate their land. . . . Now the millennium-old hunger for land in Germany would be satiated at last. The newspapers that purveyed these promises also informed the German middle class in other columns that clothes would be cheaper as soon as the garment center of Łódź, with its huge textile factories, fell into German hands.

And Poland fell in twenty days. The harvest, which had been gathered a few weeks earlier, was unharmed. Half a year later German armed might seized the fruitful lands of Holland, Belgium, and France. The vast wheat stocks that had been accumulating for years in western Europe began at once to pour into Germany. In Denmark the Nazis seized fats, in Norway fish. The alliance with Hungary and Rumania yielded other booty to supplement that of Poland and western Europe. The German High Command proclaimed that the Germans would not again suffer a bread disaster like that of 1917. The world had some ground for believing so. For war feeds war, though it is difficult to say how long.

§ 146

In the period between the two world wars Europe had been inordinately proud of the advances she had made in agriculture. The improvement of a combine, new wheat crosses, or record onion harvests, would scarcely have made the newspapers before 1910. But after 1920 such matters were given considerable space, for Europe was sensitive to her agricultural prowess. During World War I she had been unable to feed herself. She now felt impelled to take steps so that mass hunger such as had been suffered in 1917 could never again overtake her. . . . The budgets of almost all European nations in the postwar years are indicative of how much the Europeans were in earnest about this. Nevertheless, the agricultural expenditures did not come up to military expenditures. How could they? In 1942 the Minister of Agriculture of the Yugoslavian Government-in-exile admitted that there were still 300,000 wooden plows in his native land. One might compare this figure with the number of rifle barrels—articles definitely *not* made of wood.

European autarchy had been very carefully and consideredly established. Its complete collapse in 1940 was, therefore, all the sadder. It was blown up, dynamited. Deliberately the Nazis caused the ruin of the food economy of the nations they had vanquished.

Why were they doing this? Taken in itself, hunger is a phenomenon that seems natural and beyond the control of man, like the cold of the polar regions or the flames of volcanoes. Expressive of this aspect is Laurence Binyon's poem, published in the London *Nation* for December 1918:

> I come among the peoples like a shadow.
> I sit down by each man's side.
>
> None sees me, but they look on one another,
> And know that I am there.
>
> My silence is like the silence of the tide
> That buries the playground of children;
>
> Like the deepening of frost in the slow night,
> When birds are dead in the morning.
>
> Armies trample, invade, destroy,
> With guns roaring from earth and air.
>
> I am more terrible than armies,
> I am more feared than the cannon.
>
> Kings and chancellors give commands;
> I give no command to any;
>
> But I am listened to more than kings
> And more than passionate orators.
>
> I unswear words, and undo deeds.
> Naked things know me.
>
> I am first and last to be felt of the living.
> I am Hunger.

But the Nazis contrived to make this elemental thing a weapon of war, to exploit it as they would exploit gas and shells. Today Hitler is the chief engineer of the European famine. The Nazis kill with hunger; they reckon its effects with ballistic accuracy.

Only those are fed who serve the conquerors. All others must starve— quickly or slowly, according to their physical reserves. This is the true *pacte de famine,* the French nightmare of the eighteenth century, the people's delusion that the Court and the nobles were determined to depopulate France. Then it was nonsense. But today the nonsense makes sense. Even had the French nobles and Court desired something of the sort, the organizational talents of the *ancien régime* would have been insufficient for the task. But the wonderful Nazi machine is accomplish-

ing its end almost noiselessly: the depopulation of Europe through artificial famine.

It is nothing new in history for alliances to be made and broken with
bread; the Roman emperors followed the evil example of the great Augustus. Hindenburg's memoirs relate that in the winter of 1917 Turkey
would have dropped out of the war had the Turkish population not been
appeased at the last moment by wheat from conquered Rumania. It is
preferable to feed friends at the expense of enemies. But what is new in
human history is the diabolic system of confiscation and withholding,
which condemns to starvation not only the enemies of the regime but the
neutrals as well—those who do not co-operate.

Hitler's *pacte de famine* first serves as a war measure. He needs Belgian
industry: 75 per cent of Belgian coal production is sent to Germany, 80
per cent of the textile production, 80 per cent of manufactured leather
articles. What is the simplest device to recruit labor slaves? The lure of
additional bread cards. The quality of the bread is revolting. Belgian
bread is only 50 per cent flour; the other 50 per cent is foreign matter. It
is black and sticky, impossible to cut with a knife, and can be eaten only
in shapeless lumps. But happy the workers who have the opportunity to
eat it. Only workers for Germany receive enough to keep body and soul
together. For the average Belgian the German rationing system of November 1941 provided a daily ration of one quarter of an ounce of mar-
garine, one fifth of an ounce of butter, one and a half ounces of meat
(including 20 per cent bones), seven ounces of bread, one fifth of an
ounce of rice, one twelfth of an ounce of sugar, one fifth of an ounce of
dried vegetables, fifteen ounces of potatoes. This sounds like a joke, a diet
for crickets. But it is the ration for adults. And the magnanimous fifteen
ounces of potatoes were purely theoretical; in the province of Brabant
most of the people were unable to obtain a single potato.

But the *pacte de famine* is not only a war measure. The system of scientific looting that Hitler's armies practice whenever they enter new land
serves purposes beyond the purpose of warfare. It is consciously intended
to alter the population figures of Europe for the benefit of Germany.
Hitler stated bluntly to Rauschning: Depopulation is a science. And as
chief engineer of that science he practices it—somewhat shyly in the west
(because the eye of the British is close) but with monstrous, murderous
lust in the eastern and southeastern parts of Europe.

It is difficult for Americans to realize that scientific crime is a real
thing in the world of politics, for they have seen it only in the movies or
in detective thrillers. But it *is* a real thing. Before Hitler and his accom-
plices commenced scientific starvation they examined the studies of the
League of Nations concerning protective diet and malnutrition produced
by specific deficiencies; they examined the human body's need for cell-
replenishing foods. And then they exploited this medical knowledge as a

weapon to strike down the entire population of the Eastern countries, that they might fill the lands with Germans. In the distribution of food they make fine distinctions. Some of the peoples under the Nazi heel are to be reduced to the status of feeble helots and serfs, like the Poles; others are to vanish entirely from the face of the earth, like the Jews. According to Boris Shub, who investigated these matters for the American Jewish Congress, their infamous science of "racial feeding" dictates that the Germans receive 100 per cent of their needed calories, the Poles in the Government General only 65 per cent, and the Jews 21 per cent. In the distribution of fats (and there is a shortage of fat among all the countries adhering to the New Order) the Germans still receive 77 per cent of their requirements, but the Poles 18 per cent, and the Jews 0.32 per cent. There is no doubt that this is a deliberate and carefully elaborated plan to create three races: a well-fed Master Race, a race of workers too weak to rise, and a race of corpses. In their ruthless logic Hitler's gangsters have not even ignored the possibility of ultimate defeat. Should Germany be destined to fall again on the battlefield, they will leave this world with the comforting consciousness that their system of systematic starvation during the war years will have resulted in a permanent, radical shift in the demographic balance of power in Europe.

In 1941, when the Germans invaded Greece, everything edible was either consumed at once or packed and sent to Germany within five days. The cattle were shot and slaughtered on the spot. No sooner had the Germans arrived in Athens than the bread changed color. Betty Wason, an American woman who watched the entry of the modern Goths into the Holy City of Demeter, wrote: "Bread was the thing the Athenians were most disturbed about. . . . It was not black; it was gray. All the cereals of the country were put together . . . and also a large proportion of sawdust." In the summer of 1942 Georgios Koliakis reported that corpses in Athens were no longer carried to the cemetery in a funeral procession; they were placed on the sidewalk in front of the door. . . . Athens is a fine, modern city, a city where no bombs fell. But it is poisoned from within by the German Command, which has created an artificial starvation that is more savage than bombing.

The refugees from Europe, those who have escaped from Serbia, Holland, France, and Norway, tell of shootings of hostages, of revolts crushed, of bombs placed by the underground to produce the deaths of a few murderers. Sometimes they speak of the long bread lines in the dying French towns. Hour after hour the people move forward a step at a time; then the glass rattles and the door to the store shuts. But they do not speak of the less colorful matters, for these are not seen. No one speaks of the offices, of the atrocities of the typewriters which hammer out starvation decrees and translate them into reality. The refugees cannot find out about these things; they must wait for a victorious Allied army to break

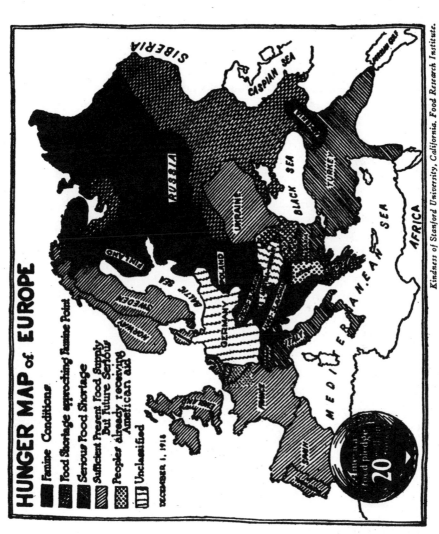

HOOVER'S HUNGER MAP OF EUROPE (December 1918)

open the filing cabinets and for Allied statesmen to bring the guilty to trial.

Meanwhile, Europe is dying. Typhus and starvation in Poland; tuberculosis and rickets in France and Czechoslovakia; a rising incidence of miscarriages in Holland. The Norwegians lack fish; their aged are dying twenty years before their time. Shortening the war by three months can save the lives of hundreds of thousands (for bread would arrive from America). Today it is not as it was in 1918, when a starving Central Europe, a diseased Germany and Austria-Hungary, threatened to infect the Continent. Today the Continent threatens the entire world with the consequences of its dissolution. If this infection is not checked a sick generation (not of Germans, but of Europeans) will wreak vengeance in another twenty years. As Dr. George N. Shuster, president of Hunter College of the City of New York, has written in the New York *Post:*

The real power of the Nazis comes from the generation which was below military age at the time of the last war. These young people suffered from malnutrition to an alarming degree—and from the psychical ills which are just as sure to come from it as the more obvious physical ills. The barbaric savagery of the Nazi movement is rooted in the pathology of the generation. If we had had the Dawes plan in 1918 and thereby prevented inflation in Germany, and if we had allowed food supplies to enter Germany at the time of the armistice, we could have remedied the problems of the younger generation and therefore some of the problems of Germany as a whole.

Substitute the word Europe for Germany and we have a prognostication of the future dangers.

§ 147

Few can speak with more authority of the biologic dangers latent in the present European famine than Herbert Hoover, chief of the American Relief Administration after World War I. Within two weeks after the armistice Hoover set up headquarters in Paris, having brought to Europe some key men from the United States Food Administration and expanding his nuclear group to a skillful staff of 1,500 assistants.

Hoover mapped the European situation as follows. There was a "neutral group" of six nations with a population of 43,000,000 (Denmark, Holland, Norway, Spain, Sweden, and Switzerland) which could furnish their own shipping and funds. The "Allied group" of five nations (Britain, France, Italy, Greece, and Portugal), embracing 132,000,000 people, could, of course, also furnish their own funds and shipping. The "enemy group" comprised the four reduced countries of Austria-Hungary, Bulgaria, Germany, and Turkey, with 102,000,000 people. Finally there was the "liberated group," consisting of thirteen countries of varying sizes (Albania, Armenia, Azerbaijan, Belgium, Estonia, Latvia, Lithuania, Czechoslovakia, Finland, Georgia, Poland, Rumania, and Yugoslavia), with a population of 98,000,000. This was a total of twenty-eight nations, or, roughly, 375,000,000 human beings, not all starving, of course, but hungry and needy in different degrees.

Hoover's offensive against hunger rolled forward imperturbably. It was halted only where civil war rendered the distributors of bread and clothing suspect—and this was the case in Russia. Additionally, there were months when it was impossible to feed the starving Hungarians. Hungary underwent four revolutions while the Americans were trying to provide her with bread. Distributing food is an art, not a hit-and-miss matter. The givers must rely on the native officials—and most of the former officials had been driven from office. Panicky officials would sometimes ask that all the food be delivered at once; their people were starving and they could not believe that America was rich enough to keep her promises consistently. . . .

The problems became increasingly formidable as the helpers moved eastward. The fall of the four erstwhile empires had precipitated complete anarchy in much of Europe. Those who had the means grabbed food from the farmers and either hoarded it or sold it on the black markets. The poor of the helpless cities were for a time in greater distress than they had been before the armistice, when rigid food controls had prevailed. In consequence it was necessary to create new and more competent food administrations in each of the new governments. This was a difficult task for the Americans, for the hungry people of eastern Europe were now being governed by men with small experience in administration, whose minds were intent more upon political and social ideologies than upon the tedious business of government housekeeping.

But Hoover's diplomacy succeeded. He fed Europe in spite of the difficulties with financing and shipping; he turned schoolhouses, public buildings, and private dwellings into kitchens and eating places; he fed 15,000,000 European children, handled over 175,000 tons of donated clothing. The total of American expenditures for charity amounted to about $325,000,000.

Only in one case was Hoover defeated. He made the judicious proposal that the blockade against Germany be raised immediately after the signing of the armistice. Here he was opposed by the iron will of Marshal Foch and the stern refusal of the other Allied military leaders. Hoover realized the enormous cost to life and health that was inevitable if the food blockade were continued; but although he managed to see the blockade lifted from the neutral and liberated countries, his will was vetoed where Germany and her former satellites were concerned. Foch decreed at Compiègne: "The existing blockade conditions set up by the Allied and Associated Powers are to remain unchanged, German merchant ships found at sea remaining liable to capture." This was, to be sure, softened by the declaration: "The Allies and the United States contemplate the provisioning of Germany as shall be found necessary." But this latter clause remained pure paper.

Until the day peace was concluded, June 28, 1919, Germany literally starved. In the military sense Foch may have been right; he feared that a well-fed Germany would not sign a treaty of peace; but in the long run this procrastination poisoned the German people, and the spiritual damage made them easy prey for a new wave of nationalism. Undoubtedly it helped to usher in Hitler. Hoover predicted this. His struggle (backed by Woodrow Wilson) against the Allied military leaders has now been brought to light in papers arranged by Suda L. Bane and Ralph H. Lutz, some eight hundred pages of documentation. These letters, telegrams, and memoranda present a panorama of historic achievements and errors that is most instructive.

§ 148

Hunger means insanity. Everywhere. As the famous Russian-American sociologist Sorokin in his last book shows, "man and society in calamity sever all ties to inherited ethics." In 1922, when the German writer Arthur Holitscher traveled down the Volga River, he encountered cannibalism rife along its famine-stricken shores. With the naïveté of savage creatures the people had eaten their fellows who had died. They themselves lived. But could the memory of their acts of desperation ever fade? . . . In Dresden in 1919 bread riots broke out. A socialist was Minister at the time. The mob broke into the Ministry, dragged the Minister whom they had recently elected to the bridge over the Elbe, thrust him into the water, and shot the drowning man. When a few of the mob were arrested, the madmen explained that they had forgotten Saxony was a republic; they believed they were disposing of the pre-revolutionary Minister of the King of Saxony, General d'Elsa. . . .

At Eastertime, 1919, Hoover in his Paris hotel received a telegram; it was from Poland and stated that pogroms had broken out in connection with the distribution of American wheat. He could scarcely believe it. But it was true; on April 5, 1919, thirty-seven Jews had been executed in Pinsk "after having been rounded up during a meeting at which they were discussing the distribution of Passover flour from America." This was hardly any reason. But the baking of unleavened bread was dangerous in a country demented by starvation and harried by medieval fears for its own soul's safety. . . . Hoover pounded on the table, summoned Ignace Paderewski, then Premier of Poland, rejected his feeble explanation that "those Jews probably were Communists," and demanded that racial and religious riots be put down at once.

Then there was insanity everywhere. But the hunger unleashed in the past four years, a hunger whose end is not yet in sight, is in no way comparable to the hunger of 1918. If Hitler is permitted to continue his diabolic *pacte de famine*, he will imperil not only the subjugated peoples existent today, but Europeans unborn as well. The world will be faced with generations of physical degenerates and potential gangsters.

After this war a starving world must be fed. That has been pledged to the victims by President Roosevelt and Prime Minister Churchill; but it is a greater and more difficult task than it was after World War I. In October 1918, with the armistice in prospect, Hoover was able to lay before President Wilson an inventory of world supplies. It showed a total of about 30,000,000 tons of food. This time such a quantity would not be nearly enough. After World War II some 390,000,000 people will be in need of food. Not only the peoples of Europe will want; China, too, needs relief. There is a proverb to the effect that where rice is cooked no bread is baked; but when the people do not have their rice, they will have to import American wheat. And Russia, too, will need American bread. Though the miracles of the botanists have enabled Russia to produce bread even to the Arctic Circle, though a growing army of specialists have made the frozen tundras flower and produce generous crops (things which astonished Wendell Willkie on his world tour in 1942), Russia will have to rely on American bread until such time as the scorched earth of her western fields can be redeemed.

To plant and harvest crops sufficient to feed such a multitude will be a tremendous task for American agriculture. Every war—and this has been so for six thousand years—is a blow to agriculture. With heavy draft upon farm labor, with equipment scarcer—wearing out more swiftly and not being replaced—with fertilizers being converted into explosives, American bread production is more likely to decrease than to increase in a long war. Only if agriculture is conceived as being on as essential a plane as the munitions industry can a peace be won that will deserve the name of "Bread Peace."

Herbert F. Lehman, head of the newly created United Nations Relief and Rehabilitation Administration, faces the biggest job of social and economic reconstruction in the history of mankind. Before undertaking such a venture, one should recall God's pledge to the people, related by the Prophet Joel: "And I will restore to you the years which the locust and the bruchus and the mildew and the palmerworm have eaten . . . And you shall eat in plenty, and shall be filled." For it is a very great thing to establish freedom from want for the whole world!

The forty-four united and associated governments who sat down on the Food Conference in Atlantic City, November 1943, know that the victims of Nazi and Japanese aggression will need not only bread, clothing, and drugs, but also seed, livestock, raw materials, machinery, tools, implements, and even houses. Even if, as it is hoped, the British Empire and its dominions will contribute a vast amount to this work, the United States will probably be asked to give 1 per cent of one year's national income, more than $1,000,000,000. President Roosevelt wisely stated that war is infinitely more expensive! Nor will this sum be given for charity alone. The United States have an enormous interest in transforming the idle, half-starved peoples of the globe into workers for a common purpose.

Naturally, this cannot be done without full co-operation by both supplying and receiving nations and, above all, by some form of world rationing. It is obvious that the American people also—even long, long after the war!—will not enjoy the same ease in purchasing goods as before the war. Though every politician dares only to speak cautiously about this, America has no other choice. If she provides only for herself, an isolationist country would soon face World War III. A hungry globe might arise against this too-well-fed continent.

"World peace means a peace of bread," Hoover told me in May 1943. "The first word in a war is spoken by the guns—but the last word has always been spoken by bread. . . . And we'll have to feed the world *again!*" And then he added, "It is difficult for Americans to picture widespread hunger or starvation. We have not had such a thing in America. . . ." How true this is. And all the goods of the earth, which for Europe are become dim memories, are still available in America. Everyone enjoys them as a matter of course—far too much as a matter of course. There is a surplus of cereals; every kind of bread is available. The American of Italian descent may choose his beloved egg bread, *di pasquale;* the Franco-American his Parisian white bread, "airy as a summer cloud"; the New York German his hearty rye bread; and Minnesota's Norwegian his crisp, unleavened *knaekke* bread. These people can scarcely understand that in the continent of their grandparents bread no longer exists.

I can realize this only too well, for I have lived it. In the Buchenwald concentration camp we had no real bread at all; what was called bread was a mixture of potato flour, peas, and sawdust. The inside was the color of lead; the crust looked and tasted like iron. The thing sweated water like the brow of a tormented man. . . . Nevertheless, we called it bread, in memoriam of the real bread we had formerly eaten. We loved it and could scarcely wait for it to be distributed among us.

Many died there without ever tasting real bread again. I still live. It seems remarkable to me that I can eat real bread. Bread is holy. And bread is profane. It is most wonderful when all can have it. In the six thousand years that men and bread have lived side by side there have often been moments when each of God's creatures had all they wanted. "And they were filled," the Bible says. No simpler words can be written to describe happiness, satisfaction, gratitude.

Postscript and Bibliography

THE HISTORY OF BREAD is a science whose roots are hidden in many other sciences, stretching from botany to agricultural economy, and from the technology of baking to politics and theology. If an author is really indebted to 4,000 works for facts and thoughts, but the lack of space permits him to mention a tenth of them only, he has to apologize to the nine tenths not mentioned, as herewith I do.

Also I have to express my gratitude for the kindness with which the great libraries of Paris, London, Zurich, Stockholm, and Leningrad made possible my studies. Above all, I am most utterly thankful to the library of the Columbia University and the New York Public Library, who sheltered my research work for the last four years since I was compelled to flee Nazi-dominated Europe.

Without the help of my wife, who succeeded in hiding it, the barbarians would have burned the bulk of the then uncompleted manuscript. I wish to thank her; also I wish to thank my friend Robert Eisler, historian of religion, who, in the dark days of Dachau and Buchenwald, kept awake my hope to finish and to publish this book. For matters of natural sciences Dr. Kurt Rosenwald (New York) was helpful in research.

BREAD OF THE PREHISTORIC MAN

BOAS, Franz: The Mind of Primitive Man, New York, 1924. BRAUNER, L.: Die Pflanze, eine moderne Botanik, Berlin, 1930. BURKITT, Miles Crawford: Prehistory, Cambridge, 1921. CHILDE, Gordon V.: Dawn of European Civilization, New York, 1928. CLELAND, Herdman F.: Our Prehistoric Ancestors, New York, 1928. DAWSON, Christopher H.: The Age of the Gods, London, 1928. EBERT, Max: Reallexikon der Vorgeschichte, Berlin, 1924–32. ENGELBRECHT, Theodor: Die Entstehung des Kultur-Roggens, Leipzig, 1917. FOREL, Auguste: Le monde social des fourmis du globe comparé à celui de l'homme, Genève, 1921–23. FURNAS, C. C. and S. M.: The Story of Man and His Food, New York, 1937. GOETSCH, Ferdinand: Die Staaten der Ameisen, Berlin, 1937. GRANT, James: Chemistry of Bread Making, New York, 1912. HAHN, Eduard: Die Entstehung der Pflugkultur, Berlin, 1909. HEER, Oswald: Die Pflanzen der Pfahlbauten, Zuerich, 1865. HEHN, Victor: Kulturpflanzen und Haustiere, Berlin, 1810. HOERNES, Moritz: Natur-

und Urgeschichte des Menschen, Leipzig, 1909. HROZNY, B.: Sumerisch-Babylonische Mythen, Berlin, 1903. JASNY, Naum: Competition among grains, California, 1940. LESER, Paul: Entstehung und Verbreitung des Pfluges, Leipzig, 1931. McCOOK, Henry S.: Ant Communities, New York, 1909. MOGGRIDGE: Harvesting Ants and Trapdoor Spiders, London, 1873–74. OBERMAYER, Hugo: Der Mensch der Vorzeit, Berlin, 1912. PEAKE, H. J. E.: Early Man, London, 1931. RENARD, S.: Life and Work in Prehistoric Times, New York, 1929. ROMANES, George J.: Animal Intelligence, New York, 1897. SCHIEMANN, Elisabeth: Die Entstehung der Kulturpflanzen, Berlin, 1932. SCHRADER, Otto: Reallexikon der Indogermanischen Altertumskunde, Berlin, 1917–29. SCHWEINFURTH, Georg: Im Herzen von Afrika, Leipzig, 1874. SOROKIN, ZIMMERMAN, GALPIN: Systematic Sources Book in Rural Sociology, Minnesota, 1931. VAVILOW, Nikolaus: Geographical Regularities in the Distribution of Cultivated Plants, Leningrad, 1927. WASMANN, Erich: Comparative Studies in the Psychology of Ants and of Higher Animals, St. Louis, 1905. WHEELER, William M.: Ants, New York, 1910.

BREAD OF THE ANCIENT WORLD

ANTON, S.: Die Mysterien von Eleusis, Naumburg, 1899. BACHOFEN, I. I.: Das Mutterrecht, Basel, 1867. BARTON, George H.: Archeology and the Bible, Philadelphia, 1937. BERTHOLET, Alfred: A History of Hebrew Civilization, London, 1926. BLOCH, Leo: Der Kult und die Mysterien von Eleusis, Hamburg, 1896. BOECKH: Der Staatshaushalt der Athener, Berlin, 1851. BREASTED, James H.: History of Egypt, New York, 1912. BREASTED, James H.: Dawn of Conscience, New York, 1933. BRION, Marcel: La Vie d'Alaric, Paris, 1930. BUECHER, Karl: Arbeit und Rhythmus, Leipzig, 1909. BUSOLT, Georg: Griechische Staatskunde, Muenchen, 1920–26. CREELMAN, H.: An Introduction to the Old Testament, New York, 1917. CUMONT, F.: Les Religions orientales dans le paganisme Romain, Paris, 1929. DARENBERG et SAGLIO: Dictionnaire des Antiquités Grecques et Romaines, Paris, 1873–1912. DIELS, H.: Sibyllinische Blätter, Berlin, 1890. DREWS, Arthur: Das Markus-Evangelium, Jena, 1921. DUNCAN, John G.: The exploration of Egypt and the Old Testament, New York, 1909. EISLER, Robert: Weltenmantel und Himmelszelt, Muenchen, 1910. ERMAN, Adolf: Aegypten und aegyptisches Leben im Altertum, Tuebingen, 1885. FARNELL, Lewis R.: The Cult of the Greek States, Oxford, 1896–1909. FERRERO, Guglielmo: The Greatness and Decline of Rome, New York, 1907–9. FERRERO, Guglielmo: Ancient Rome and Modern America, New York, 1914. FLEMING, James: Personalities of the Old Testament, New York, 1939. FOUCART, Paul: Les mystères d'Eleusis, Paris, 1914. FRANK, Tenney: An Economic Survey of Ancient Rome, Baltimore, 1933–40. FRAZER, J. G.: Taboo and the Perils of the Soul, London, 1922. GINZBERG, Eli: Studies in the Economics of the Bible, New York, 1917. GLOTZ, Gustave: The History of Civilization, New York, 1926. GLOVER, T. R.: The Influence of Christ in the Ancient World, New Haven, 1929. GOLDBERG, Oskar: Die Wirklichkeit der Hebraeer, Berlin, 1925. GRUPPE, Otto: Griechische Mythologie und Religionsgeschichte, Berlin, 1906. HASTINGS, James: Dictionary of the Bible, New York, 1901. JUNG, C. G. and KERENYI: Das göttliche Mädchen, Amsterdam, 1941. KLAUSNER, Joseph: Jesus of Nazareth, New York, 1925. LARSEN, Hjalmar: On Baking in Egypt During the Middle Kingdom, Copenhague, 1936. LEHMANN-HAUPT, Ferdinand: Solon of Athens, Liverpool, 1912. LOUIS, Paul: Ancient Rome at Work, New York, 1927. LOWRIE, R. H.: Primitive Society, New York, 1920. LOEWY, Gustav: Die Technologie und Terminologie der Müller und Bäcker in den rabbinischen quellen, Berlin, 1926. MOMMSEN, Theodor: Römische Geschichte, Berlin, 1865–85. MYLONAS, George, E.: Hymn to Demeter and Her Sanctuary at Eleusis, St. Louis, 1942. NEUBURGER: Die Technik des Altertums, Leipzig, 1919. OVERBECK, Joh.: Pompeji, Leipzig, 1884. PAPINI, Giovanni: Life of Christ, New York, 1923. PAULY-WISSOWA: Real-Encyklopaedie der Klassischen Altertumswissenschaft, Stuttgart, 1894–1939. PHILIOS, Demetrios: Eleusis, Her Mysteries, Ruins and Museum, London, 1906. POEHLMANN, Robert: Geschichte des Sozialismus und der sozialen Frage in der antiken Welt, Muenchen, 1912. ROSTOVTZEFF: Social and Economic History of the Roman Empire, New York, 1926. SCHINDLER, Franz: Aus der Urheimat unserer Getreide-Arten, Wien, 1934. SEECK, Otto: Geschichte des Untergangs der antiken Welt, Berlin, 1895–1920. SIMKHOVITCH, Vladimir G.: Toward a Better Understanding of Jesus, New York, 1921. SPECK, E.: Handelsgeschichte des Altertums, Leipzig, 1906. STEINDORFF, Georg: The Religion of the Ancient Egyptians, New York, 1905. STRAUSS, David Fr.: Das Leben Jesu, Tuebingen, 1835–36. STRUBE, Julius: Studien über den Bilderkreis von Eleusis, Leipzig, 1870. THIERRY, Amédée S.: Récits de l'histoire Romaine au V. Siècle, Paris, 1880. VERINDER, Frederick: My Neighbours' Landmark, London, 1911. WEINEL, H.: Die Gleichnisse Jesu, Leipzig, 1918. WELLHAUSEN, Julius: Prolegomena to the History of Israel, Edinburgh, 1885. ZIEGLER: Die Königsgleichnisse des Midrasch, Breslau, 1903.

BREAD IN THE MIDDLE AGES

ASHLEY, Sir William: Bread of Our Forefathers, Oxford, 1928. BACHTOLD-STAEUBLI, Hans: Handwörterbuch des Deutschen Aberglaubens, Berlin, 1927–38. BARING-GOULD: Life of the Saints, Edinburgh, 1914. BAUMANN, Franz L.: Akten zur Geschichte des deutschen Bauernkrieges, Freiburg, 1877. BAX, Ernest B.: The Peasants' War in Germany, New York, 1899. BELOW, Georg von: Die Ursachen der Rezeption des Römischen Rechts in Deutschland, München, 1905. BENNETT and ELTON: History of Cornmilling, London, 1898–1904. BERNHART, Joseph: The Vatican as a World Power, New York, 1939. BLOCH, Ernst: Thomas Münzer als Theologe der Revolution, München, 1921. BRING, Ragnar: Dualismus hos Luther, Lund, 1929. BROWE, Peter: Die eucharistischen Wunder des Mittelalters, Breslau, 1938. BUEHLER, Johannes: Die Kultur des Mittelalters, Leipzig, 1931. BURCKHARDT, Abel: Das

Geistproblem bei Huldrych Zwingli, Leipzig, 1932. THE CATHOLIC
ENCYCLOPEDIA, New York, 1907–13. CLAASSEN, Walter: Schweizer
Bauernpolitik im Zeitalter Huldrych Zwinglis, Zuerich, 1928. COULTON,
George G.: Chaucer and His England, London, 1921. COULTON, George
G.: The Mediaeval Village, Cambridge, 1925. CRISTIANI, Léon: Luther
et la question sociale, Paris, 1911. CURSCHMANN, Fritz: Hungersnöte
im Mittelalter, Leipzig, 1900. DOPSCH, Alfons: Die Wirtschaftsentwick-
lung der Karolinger-Zeit, Weimar, 1921–22. EHRENBERG: Verhand-
lungen der Königlich Preussischen Akademie der Wissenschaften, Berlin,
1848–49. FORTESCUE, Adrien: The Orthodox Eastern Church, London,
1929. FRAZER, I. G.; Spirits of the Corn and the Wild, London, 1912.
FUSTEL DE COULANGES, Numa D.: Histoire des institutions politiques
de l'ancienne France, Paris, 1930. FUSTEL DE COULANGES, Numa D.:
The Origin of Property in Land, London, 1927. GARNIER, Russel: An-
nals of the British Peasantry, London, 1895. GIBERGUES, Emmanuel:
Entretiens sur l'Eucharistie, Paris, 1919. GILLETT, E. H.: The Life and
Times of John Huss, Philadelphia, 1870. GOOSENS, Werner: Les origines
de l'Eucharistie, Gembloux, 1931. GRIMM, Jakob und Wilhelm: Deutsches
Wörterbuch, Leipzig, 1854–1938. GRIMM, Jakob: Deutsche Rechtsalter-
tümer, Leipzig, 1899. GRUPP, Georg: Kulturgeschichte des Mittelalters,
Paderborn, 1908–25. HARNACK, Adolf von: History of Dogma, Boston,
1898–1903. HERZOG-HAUCK: Realenzyklopaedie für protestantische
Theologie und Kirche, Leipzig, 1896–1913. HEYNE, Moriz: Deutsche
Hausaltertümer, Leipzig, 1900–3. HOLMQUIST, Hjalmar: Luther, Loy-
ola, Calvin i dera reformatoriske genesis, Lund, 1912. HUEGLI, Hilde:
Der deutsche Bauer im Mittelalter, Bern, 1929. HUIZINGA, J.: Eras-
mus, New York, 1924. THE JEWISH ENCYCLOPEDIA, New York,
1900–5. KOEHLER, Walther: Zwingli und Luther, Leipzig, 1924. LA-
CROIX, Paul: Moeurs, usages et costumes au moyen âge, Paris, 1877.
LAMPRECHT, Karl: Deutsche Geschichte, Freiburg, 1904–10. LAVERAN,
A.: L'hygiène de la boulangerie, Paris, 1910. LIPSON, E.: The Economic
History of England, London, 1929–31. LOSERTH, Johann: Huss and
Wyclif, München, 1925. LUCHAIRE, Achille: La société française au
temps de Philippe-Auguste, Paris, 1902. MANN, Horace: The Lives of
the Popes in the Middle Ages, London, 1925–29. MANNHARDT, Wil-
helm: Wald- und Feldkulte, Berlin, 1875–77. MANNHARDT, Wilhelm:
Zeitschrift für Deutsche Mythologie und Sittenkunde, Göttingen, 1853–59.
McGIFFERT, Arthur: A History of Christian Thought, New York, 1932.
MEIER, Albert: Das Bäckerhandwerk im alten Bern, Bern, 1939.
MEITZEN, A.: Siedlung und Agrarwesen der Westgermanen und Ost-
germanen, Berlin, 1895. MEYER, Elard Hugo: Germanische Mythologie,
Berlin, 1891. MOFFET, James: The First Five Centuries of the Church,
Nashville, 1938. MUNCH, Peter Andreas: Norse Mythology, New York,
1926. MURRAY, R. H.: Erasmus and Luther, London, 1920. NIESEL,
Wilhelm: Calvins Lehre vom Abendmahl, München, 1930. ORDNUNG
der Bäcker in Frankfurt am Main, Frankfurt, 1560. PETRUSCHEWSKI,
D. M.: The Rebellion of Wat Tyler, Moskau, 1914. PICKMAN, Edward
M.: The Mind of Latin Christendom, London, 1937. POLLOCK and

MAITLAND: History of English Law, Cambridge, 1898. RESSEL, Gustav: Das Archiv der Bäckergenossenschaft in Wien, Wien, 1913. REUTER-SKIOELD, Edgar: Die Entstehung der Speisesakramente, Stockholm, 1907. SCHAFF, Philipp: The Creeds of Christendom, New York, 1919. SCHNUERER, Gustav: Kirche und Kultur im Mittelalter, Paderborn, 1927–29. SCHULTZ, Alwin: Deutsches Leben im 14 und 15, Jahrhundert, Wien, 1892. SCHWEITZER, Albert: Das Abendmahlsproblem, Berlin, 1901. SMITH, Preserved: A Short History of Christian Theophagy, Chicago, 1922. STOBBE: Die Juden in Deutschland während des Mittelalters, Berlin, 1923. STRACK, Hermann Leberecht: Der Blutaberglaube in der Menschheit, München, 1892. VINOGRADOFF, Paul: The Growth of the English Manor, London, 1905. WHITE, Andrew D.: The History of the Warfare of Science with Theology, New York, 1910. WUERTTEM-BERGS erneuerte Müller-Ordnung, Rösslin, 1701. ZINSSER, Hans: Rats, Lice and History, New York, 1938.

BREAD IN THE EARLY AMERICAS

ADAIR'S History of the American Indians, London, 1775. ADAMS, James Truslow: The Epic of America, Boston, 1931. ADAMS, John: Letters to His Wife, Boston, 1841. ALISON, William P.: Observations on the Famine of 1846–47 in Ireland, Edinburgh, 1847. BASALDUA, Florencio D.: Agricultura; cultivo del maiz, Buenos Aires, 1897. BAYLEY, L. H.: Cyclopedia of American Agriculture, New York, 1912. BELT, Thomas: The Naturalist in Nicaragua, New York, 1928. BIDWELL and FALCONIER: History of Agriculture in the Northern United States 1620–1860, Washington, 1925. BOLLMAN, Lewis: Indian Corn, Washington, 1862. BONA-FOUS, Matthieu: Histoire naturelle, agricole et économique du maïs, Paris, 1836. BRAYLEY, Arthur: Bakers and Baking in Massachusetts, Boston, 1909. BRINTON, Daniel G.: The Myths of the New World, New York, 1868. BRUCE, Ph. A.: Economic History of Virginia in the XVII Century, New York, 1896. BRUYERINUS: De re cibaria, Lyon, 1560. CAMPBELL, James: Ireland; Its History, Past and Present, London, 1847. CARRIER, Lyman: The Beginnings of Agriculture in America, New York, 1923. CLARK, Dora M.: British Opinion and the American Revolution, New Haven, 1930. COLON, Fernando: Le historie della vita e dei fatti di Cristoforo Colombo, Milano, 1936. EARLE, Alice Morse: Home Life in Colonial Days, New York, 1899. EAST, Robert A.: Business Enterprise in the American Revolutionary Era, New York, 1938. ELLET, Elisabeth: Domestic History of the American Revolution, New York, 1850. ERDO-ZAIN, Ernesto Ruiz: Estudio sobre el cultivo del maiz, Mexico, 1914. EVANS, Oliver: The Young Mill-wright and Millers guide, Philadelphia, 1853. FRAZER, J. G.: The scapegoat, London, 1913. GANN and THOMP-SON: The History of the Mayas, New York, 1931. GARCILASO de la VEGA: El Inca. The Royal Commentaries of Peru, London, 1688. GIL-BERT, Arthur W.: The Potato, New York, 1917. GILES, Dorothy: Singing Valleys. The Story of Corn, New York, 1940. HARRIS, Henry: Pellagra, New York, 1919. HODGE, F. W.: Handbook of American Indians.

HOWE, Henry: Memoirs of the Most Emerited American Mechanics, New York, 1840. JEFFERSON, Thomas: Writings, New York, 1892–99. KALM, Peer: Beskrifning om Mais i Norra America, Stockholm, 1751. LEVY, Reuben: An Introduction to the Sociology of Islam, London, 1931–33. MARGOLIOUTH, D. S.: The Early Development of Mohammedanism, London, 1926. MASON, A. E.: The Life of Francis Drake, New York, 1940. MASON, Gregory: Columbus Came Late, London, 1931. O'CONNOR, James: History of Ireland, London, 1925. PARKER, Arthur C.: Iroquois Use of Maize, Albany, 1910. PARRINGTON, Vermont: Main Currents in American Thought, New York, 1927. POINDEXTER, Miles: Peruvian Pharaohs, Boston, 1938. PRENTICE, Ezra Parmelee: Hunger and History, New York, 1939. PRESCOTT, W. H.: Conquest of Mexico, New York, 1847. PRIESTLEY, H. J.: The Mexican Nation, New York, 1923. RAUWOLF, Leonhard: Reis' in die Morgenländer, Augsburg, 1582. SCOTT, S. P.: History of the Moorish Empire in Europe, Philadelphia, 1904. SERRES, Olivier de: Le theatre d'agriculture, Paris, 1600. STEFFEN, Max: Landwirtschaft bei den altamerikanischen Kulturvölkern, Leipzig, 1883. STUART, W.: The Potato, Philadelphia, 1923. TARBOX, J. N.: Sir Walter Raleigh and His Colony in America, Boston, 1884. THACHER, James: Military Journal During the American Revolutionary War, Hartford, 1854. USHER, Roland G.: The Pilgrims, New York, 1918. VERRILL, A. H. and BARRETT, O. W.: Foods America Gave the World, New York, 1937. WALLACE, Henry A., and BRESSMAN, E. A.: Corn and Corn-growing, New York, 1937. WASHINGTON, George: Writings, Washington, 1931–41. WHEATERWAX, Paul: The Story of the Maize Plant, Chicago, 1923.

BREAD IN THE NINETEENTH CENTURY

ARASKRANIANZ, A.: Die französische Getreidehandelspolitik bis zum Jahre 1789, Berlin, 1882. ASHTON, John: The History of Bread, London, 1904. AULARD, Alphonse: Paris sous le premier Empire, Paris, 1912–23. BEARD, Charles and Mary: The Rise of American Civilization, New York, 1930. BOYLE, James: Chicago Wheat Prices for Eighty-one Years, New York, 1922. BRITNELL, G. E.: The Wheat Economy, Toronto, 1939. CASPARY, Adolf: Wirtschaftsstrategie und Kriegführung, Berlin, 1932. CASSON, Herbert N.: Cyrus Hall McCormick, Chicago, 1908. CASSON, Herbert N.: The Romance of the Reaper, Chicago, 1908. CURTLER, W. H. R.: The Enclosure and Redistribution of Our Land, Oxford, 1920. DAVY, Sir Humphrey: Elements of Agricultural Chemistry, London, 1813. DONDLINGER, Peter C.: The Book of Wheat, New York, 1903. FAY, Bernard: L'esprit revolutionnaire en France et aux Etats-Unis à la fin du 18 siècle, Paris, 1925. FAY, Charles R.: The Corn Laws and Social England, Cambridge, 1932. FOURNIER, August: Napoléon I., New York, 1912. FRANCÉ, Raoul: Das Leben im Acker, Stuttgart, o.J. GARLAND, Hamlin: Companions on the Trail, New York, 1931. GEIGER, G. R.: The Theory of the Land Question, New York, 1936. GEORGE, Henry: Progress and Poverty, New York, 1908. GEORGE, Henry: The Land Question,

New York, 1911. GRAS, N. S. B.: A History of Agriculture in Europe and America, New York, 1925. GREENO, Follett: Obed Hussey, Who, of All Inventors, Made Bread Cheap, Rochester, 1912. GRIFFITH, I. T.: Population Problems of the Age of Malthus, Cambridge, 1926. HALLUM, John: Reminiscences of the Civil War, Little Rock, 1903. KAEMPFFERT, Waldemar: Popular History of American Invention, New York, 1924. KOZMIN, Pjotr: Flour Milling (*mukomolje*), London, 1917. LAVISSE, Ernest: Histoire de la France Contemporaine, Paris, 1920–22. LE CLERC: International Trade in Wheat and Wheat Flour, Washington, 1925. LIEBIG, Justus von: Familiar Letters on Chemistry and Its Relation to Commerce, Physiology, and Agriculture, New York, 1843. MALTHUS, Thomas Robert: Observations on the Effects of the Corn Laws, London, 1814. MAURIZIO, Adam: Die Getreidenahrung im Wandel der Zeiten, Zürich, 1916. McCORMICK, Fowler: The Development of Farm Machines, Princeton, 1941. MICHELET, Jules: Histoire de la Révolution Française, Paris, 1898. MILLER, Francis T.: The Photographic History of the Civil War, New York, 1911. PARMENTIER, Augustin A.: Traité sur la culture et les usages des pommes de terre, Paris, 1789. PARMENTIER, Augustin A.: Le parfait boulanger. La fabrication et la commerce du pain, Paris, 1778. PERCIVAL, John: The Wheat Plant, London, 1921. PERLMANN, Louis: Die Bewegung der Weizenpreise und ihre Ursachen, München, 1914. QUAINTANCE, H. W.: The Influence of Farm Machinery on Production and Labor, London, 1904. RIESENBERG, Felix: Golden Gate; the Story of San Francisco Harbor, New York, 1940. ROGERS, George D.: History of Flour Manufacture in Minnesota, St. Paul, 1905. RUSSELL, Edward I.: Soil Conditions and Plant Growth, London, 1921. SANDBURG, Carl: Abraham Lincoln. The Prairie Years, New York, 1926. SANDBURG, Carl: Abraham Lincoln. The War Years, New York, 1930. SCHAFER, Joseph: The Social History of American Agriculture, New York, 1936. SMITH, Rollin E.: Wheat Fields and Markets of the World, St. Louis, 1908. STEPHENS, H. M.: The Principal Speeches of the Statesmen and Orators of the French Revolution, 1789–95, Oxford, 1892. TAINE, Hippolyte: L'ancien régime, Paris, 1891. VALLERY-RADOT, René: La vie de Pasteur, Paris, 1918. VAN DOREN, Carl: Benjamin Franklin, New York, 1939. VOLHARD, Jakob: Justus von Liebig, Leipzig, 1909. WAKSMAN, Salmon A.: Humus, Baltimore, 1938. WAKSMAN, Salmon A.: The Soil and the Microbe, New York, 1931. WALKER, Franklin: Frank Norris, New York, 1932. WHITE, John: A Treatise on the Art of Baking, Edinburgh, 1828.

BREAD IN OUR TIME

AGRANOWSKIJ, Aleksandr: Kommuna, sovkhoz, kombinat, Moskau, 1930. AKERMAN, Ake: Swedish Contributions to the Development of plant breeding, Stockholm, 1938. ALSBERG, C. L.: Combination in the American Bread-baking Industry, Stanford, 1926. ANTSIFEROW, BILIMOVICH, BATSHEV: Russian Agriculture During the War, New Haven, 1930. BANE, Suda L. and LUTZ, Ralph H.: The Blockade of

Germany after the Armistice, Stanford, 1942. BEACH, Joseph Warren: American Fiction 1920–40, New York, 1941. BULLER, Arthur H.: Essays on Wheat, New York, 1919. BURBANK, Luther: Partner of Nature, New York, 1939. CARLETON, Marc Alfred: The Small Grains, New York, 1916. CONFERENCE INTERNATIONALE DU BLÉ: La distribution du froment dans le monde, Rome, 1927. CONTINENTAL BAKING CORPORATION: The Story of Bread, New York, 1925. COX, Joseph F.: Crop Production and Soil Management, New York, 1936. CROOKES, Sir William: The Wheat Problem, Bristol, 1898. DARBISHIRE, A. D.: Breeding and the Mendelian Discovery, London, 1911. DARRÉ, Walter: Das Bauerntum als Lebensquell der Nordischen Rasse, München, 1928. DAVIS, I. ST.: Stale Bread Loss, Stanford, 1923. DE KRUIF, Paul: Hunger Fighters, New York, 1928. DOUGLAS-IRVINE: The Making of Rural Europe, London, 1923. EBENSTEIN, William: The Nazi State, New York, 1943. GERHARD, Albert: Handbook for Bakers, New York, 1925. GUMPERT, Martin: Heil Hunger! Health Under Hitler, New York, 1940. HEVESY, Paul de: World Wheat Planning, London, 1940. HINDUS, Maurice: Mother Russia, New York, 1943. HOLT, John B.: German Agricultural Policy 1918–34, New York, 1936. HOOVER, Herbert and GIBSON, Hugh: The Problems of Lasting Peace, New York, 1943. HOWELLS, Rulon S.: His Many Mansions, a Compilation of Christian Beliefs, New York, 1940. HUBBARD, Leonard E.: The Economics of Soviet Agriculture, London, 1939. ILTIS, Hugo: Gregor Mendel, Berlin, 1924. JACKS, V. and WHITE, R. O.: Vanishing Lands, New York, 1940. JAGO, William: The Technology of Bread-making, London, 1911. KRUEGER and TENIUS: Massenspeisungen, Berlin, 1917. KUHL-MANN, Charles B.: The Development of the Flour-milling Industry in the United States, Boston, 1929. LIBKIND, A.: Agrarnoje perenaselenje (The Agrarian Overpopulation), Moskau, 1931. LICHTENBERGER, André: Le third Reich, New York, 1937. LUDWIG, Emil: Hindenburg, Philadelphia, 1936. MACADAM, I. H.: Collection of Proverbs of All Nations on Bread and Baking, London, 1926. MARTIN, Louis: De Tolstoi à Lénine, Montpellier, 1920. MENASSEYRE, Robert: Politique du blé, Toul, 1934. MOHS, Karl: Mehlchemie, Dresden, 1931. MOLOTOV, Viacheslav: Food for All. The Abolition of the Bread-card System in the Soviet Union, New York, 1934. MORGAN, Thomas Hunt: The Theory of the Gene, New Haven, 1926. MORRISON, Abraham E.: The Baking-powder Controversy, New York, 1904–7. MOTZ, Roger: Belgium Unvanquished, London, 1942. NEUMANN, Max Paul: Brotgetreide und Brot, Berlin, 1929. OLDEN, Rudolf: Hitler, New York, 1936. OSBORNE, Thomas Burr: The Proteins of the Wheat Kernel, Washington, 1907. RATHSACK, Karl H.: Der Speisewert der Kartoffel, Berlin, 1935. SAN-DERSON, E. D.: Insect Pests, New York, 1931. SCHIMPER, A. F. W.: Pflanzengeographie, Jena, 1935. SEARS, Paul: Deserts on the March, Norman, Oklahoma, 1935. SELIKHOV, M.: Russkoje mokomolje (Russian Flourmilling), St. Petersburg, 1912. SERING, Max: Die deutsche Landwirtschaft, Berlin, 1932. SHERMAN, Henry C. and PEARSON, Constance: Modern Bread from the Viewpoint of Nutrition, New York, 1942.

SHUB, Boris and WARHAFTIG, Zygmunt: Starvation over Europe, New York, 1943. SNYDER, Harry: Bread, New York, 1930. SOROKIN, Pitirim A.: Man and Society in Calamity; the Effects of War, Revolution, Famine, Pestilence upon Human Mind, New York, 1942. STAHL, C. J.: Die Geschichte des deutschen Bäckers, Stuttgart, 1911. STOKLASA, Julius: Das Brot der Zukunft, Jena, 1917. SURFACE, Frank M.: The Grain Trade During the World War, New York, 1928. SWANSON, Charles D.: Wheat Flour and Diet, New York, 1928. TIMOSHENKO, Vladimir P.: Agricultural Russia and the Wheat Problem, Stanford, 1932. TROTZKY, Leo: Die russische Revolution, Berlin, 1920. WACHSMANN, Kurt: Das Osthilfe-Gesetz, Berlin, 1932. WALLACE, Henry Agard: Agricultural Prices, Des Moines, 1920. WALLACE, Henry Agard: Statesmanship and Religion, New York, 1934. WALLACE, Henry Agard: The New Administration and Farm Relief, Philadelphia, 1933. WALLACE, Henry Cantwell: The Wheat Situation, Washington, 1923. WHITNEY, Milton: Soil and Civilization, New York, 1925. ZISCHKA, Antoine: Brot für zwei Milliarden Menschen, Leipzig, 1938.

INDEX